T0176968

Software Technology

IEEE PRESS

IEEE computer society

About IEEE Computer Society

IEEE Computer Society is the world's leading computing membership organization and the trusted information and career-development source for a global workforce of technology leaders including: professors, researchers, software engineers, IT professionals, employers, and students. The unmatched source for technology information, inspiration, and collaboration, the IEEE Computer Society is the source that computing professionals trust to provide high-quality, state-of-the-art information on an on-demand basis. The Computer Society provides a wide range of forums for top minds to come together, including technical conferences, publications, and a comprehensive digital library, unique training webinars, professional training, and the TechLeader Training Partner Program to help organizations increase their staff's technical knowledge and expertise, as well as the personalized information tool myComputer. To find out more about the community for technology leaders, visit http://www.computer.org.

IEEE/Wiley Partnership

The IEEE Computer Society and Wiley partnership allows the CS Press authored book program to produce a number of exciting new titles in areas of computer science, computing, and networking with a special focus on software engineering. IEEE Computer Society members continue to receive a 35% discount on these titles when purchased through Wiley or at wiley.com/ieeecs.

To submit questions about the program or send proposals, please contact Mary Hatcher, Editor, Wiley-IEEE Press: Email: mhatcher@wiley.com, Telephone: 201-748-6903, John Wiley & Sons, Inc., 111 River Street, Hoboken, NJ 07030-5774.

Software Technology

10 Years of Innovation in IEEE Computer

Edited by Mike Hinchey

WILEY

This edition first published 2018
© 2018 the IEEE Computer Society, Inc.

The right of Mike Hinchey to be identified as the author of the editorial material in this work has been asserted in accordance with law.

Registered Office
John Wiley & Sons, Inc., 111 River Street, Hoboken, NJ 07030, USA

Editorial Office
111 River Street, Hoboken, NJ 07030, USA

For details of our global editorial offices, customer services, and more information about Wiley products visit us at www.wiley.com.

Wiley also publishes its books in a variety of electronic formats and by print-on-demand. Some content that appears in standard print versions of this book may not be available in other formats.

Limit of Liability/Disclaimer of Warranty

While the publisher and authors have used their best efforts in preparing this work, they make no representations or warranties with respect to the accuracy or completeness of the contents of this work and specifically disclaim all warranties, including without limitation any implied warranties of merchantability or fitness for a particular purpose. No warranty may be created or extended by sales representatives, written sales materials or promotional statements for this work. The fact that an organization, website, or product is referred to in this work as a citation and/or potential source of further information does not mean that the publisher and authors endorse the information or services the organization, website, or product may provide or recommendations it may make. This work is sold with the understanding that the publisher is not engaged in rendering professional services. The advice and strategies contained herein may not be suitable for your situation. You should consult with a specialist where appropriate. Further, readers should be aware that websites listed in this work may have changed or disappeared between when this work was written and when it is read. Neither the publisher nor authors shall be liable for any loss of profit or any other commercial damages, including but not limited to special, incidental, consequential, or other damages.

Library of Congress Cataloging-in-Publication Data
Names: Hinchey, Michael G. (Michael Gerard), 1969- editor.
Title: Software technology : 10 years of innovation in IEEE Computer /
   edited by Mike Hinchey.
Description: First edition. | Hoboken, NJ : IEEE Computer Society, Inc.,
   2018. | Includes bibliographical references and index. |
Identifiers: LCCN 2018024346 (print) | LCCN 2018026690 (ebook) | ISBN
   9781119174226 (Adobe PDF) | ISBN 9781119174233 (ePub) | ISBN
9781119174219 (hardcover)
Subjects: LCSH: Software engineering–History. | IEEE Computer Society–History.
Classification: LCC QA76.758 (ebook) | LCC QA76.758 .S6568 2018 (print) |
DDC 005.1–dc23
LC record available at https://lccn.loc.gov/2018024346

ISBN: 9781119174219

Cover image: © BlackJack3D/Getty Images
Cover design by Wiley

Set in 10/12 pt WarnockPro-Regular by Thomson Digital, Noida, India

Printed in the United States of America

V10003522_081518

Table of Contents

Foreword

Generally, you cannot claim to fully understand software engineering until you have attended at least 1-day-long planning session. Even then, you may not completely grasp how all the pieces work and interact. Software engineering involves a surprisingly large number of topics, ranging from the purely technical to the unquestionably human, from minute details of code and data to large interactions with other systems, from immediate problems to issues that may not appear for years.

However, if you confine yourself to a single planning meeting, you will never see the dynamic nature of the field, how software engineers learn and grow over the lifetime of a project. Like all engineering disciplines, software engineering is a process of self-education. As engineers work on the problems of building new software systems, they learn the limits of their own ideas and begin the search for more effective ways of creating software.

The great value of this book is that it exposes the educational nature of software engineering. Based on a column that appeared in *IEEE Computer* magazine, it shows how both researchers and practitioners were striving to learn the nuances of their field and develop ideas that would improve the nature of software. It deals with issues that were prominent during the past decade but at the same time all of its chapters discuss ideas that have been prominent for the entire history of software and software engineering.

The opening chapter explores the idea of a crisis in software development. Historically, software engineers have pointed to a crisis in the mid-1960s as the start of their field. At that time, all software was custom built. All customers employed had to develop software to support their business. This approach was challenged by the third-generation computers, notably the IBM 360 family, which radically expanded the computer market and created an unfulfilled demand for programmers.

The computing field responded to the crisis of the 1960s in two ways. First, it created a software industry that would sell the same piece of software to multiple customers. Second, it created the field of software engineering in order to create software products that could be run at multiple sites by different companies. Any present crisis in software, according to author Brian Fitzgerald, is driven by forces similar to those that drove the 1960s crisis. However, in the second decade of the twenty-first century, the software market is shaped by a sophisticated group of users or "digital natives." These individuals have born in a technological world and make strong demands on software and on software engineering.

Many of the chapters that follow address the perception that we are unable to produce the amount of software that we need. Cloud computing and Agile development have taken over the position held by the software industry and the original software engineering models in the 1960s. The cloud is an approach that offers computing as a service. More than its 1960s equivalent, time-sharing services, it has the potential of delivering software to a large market and allowing customers to buy exactly the services that they need. However, cloud computing demands new kind of engineering and design, as a single piece of software has to satisfy a large and diverse customer base. So, in this book, we find numerous chapters dealing with the complexity of software and the need to satisfy the needs of sophisticated customers without producing burdensome and inefficient programs. In these chapters, we find that many of the traditional techniques of software engineering need to be adapted to modern computing environments. The tool of software product lines, for example, is a common way of reducing complexity. It allows developers to use a common base of technology while limiting the complexity of each application. At the same time, as the chapter by Hallsteinsen, Hinchey, Park, and Schmid notes, software product lines do not always work in dynamic programming environments where many constraints are not known before runtime. Hence, developers need to recognize that the needs of customers may not be known in advance and that the development team may not always be able to identify those needs that will change.

To create software, either for the cloud or any other environment, software engineers began turning to the ideas of Agile development since 2001, when a group of software engineers drafted the Agile Manifesto to describe a new approach to creating software. The Agile Manifesto drew heavily from the ideas of lean manufacturing, which came to prominence during the 1980s, and from the ideas of Frederick P. Brooks, the original software architect for the IBM 360 operating system. The proponents of agile argue for a close relationship between customer and developer, a short time line for creating new code, a rigorous approach for testing software, and a distinctive minimalism. They claim that software is best produced by small, self-organized teams. The chapters in this book show how thoroughly the ideas of agile have permeated software engineering. The chapter by Margaria and Steffen argues that the core idea of Agile is indeed managerial simplicity.

These chapters are valuable not only from the perspectives of their completeness but rather that they deal with the full scope of cloud-based software or

Agile development as well as the other topics that have gained importance over the past decades. They offer some insight into key topics such as formal methods, model-based software engineering, requirements engineering, adaptive systems, data and knowledge engineering, and critical safety engineering. Above all, these chapters show how experienced software engineers have been thinking about problems, how they have been expanding the methods of the field, and how these software engineers are looking toward the future.

Washington, DC   *David Alan Grier*

Preface

Although not always obvious, software has become a vital part of our life in modern times. Millions of lines of software are used in many diverse areas of our daily lives ranging from agriculture to automotive systems, entertainment, FinTech, and medicine.

Software is also the major source of innovation and advancement in a large number of areas that are currently highly hyped and covered extensively in the media. These include IoT (Internet of Things), Big Data and data science, self-driving cars, AI and machine learning, robotics, and a range of other areas. Software is the enabler in cyber-physical systems, wearable devices, medical devices, smart cities, smart grids, and smart everything.

More and more industries are becoming highly software intensive and software dependent, and this is not restricted to the IT sector. Automotive manufacturers are using software at an unprecedented level. The world's largest bookstore (Amazon) is in fact a software vendor and a major provider of cloud computing services; one of the largest fleets of cars for hire (Uber) is completely dependent on apps to run its business.

Software development is far from being perfect (as covered by a number of chapters in this book), and new technologies and approaches are constantly emerging and evolving to bring new solutions, new techniques, and indeed entirely new business models.

The *Software Technology* column of *IEEE Computer* published bimonthly for 10 years produced 60 columns on a broad range of topics in the software arena. Some of the topics covered were short-lived, or were very much the subjective opinion of the authors. Many others, however, have had a long-term effect, or led to further developments and remained as research topics for the authors.

Structured into six parts, this book brings together a collection of chapters based on enhanced, extended, and updated versions of various columns that appeared over the 10 year period. They cover a diverse range of topics, but of course all have a common theme: software technology.

Part I: The Software Landscape

In Chapter 1 Fitzgerald warns that we are approaching a new impasse in software development: The pervasiveness of software requires significant improvements in productivity, but this is at a time when we face a great shortage of appropriately skilled and trained programmers.

Margaria and Steffen in Chapter 2 argue that an approach based on simplicity – "less is more" – is an effective means of supporting innovation. They point to a number of organizations who have learned this lesson and highlight a number of technologies that may facilitate agility in software organizations.

Claes et al. in Chapter 3 consider component-based reuse in the context of the complex software ecosystems that have emerged in recent years. They analyze issues of interdependencies that affect software developers and present two case studies based on popular open-source software package ecosystems.

Beecham et al. in Chapter 4 question whether practitioners ever really read academic research outputs and whether academics care enough about practical application of their results to warrant a change in the way they disseminate their work.

Part II: Autonomous Software Systems

In Chapter 5, Hinchey and Sterritt describe an approach to developing autonomous software systems based on the concept of apoptosis, whereby software components are programmed to self-destruct unless they are given a reprieve.

In Chapter 6, Vassev and Hinchey address the issue of how to express requirements for adaptive and self-adaptive systems, recognizing that additional issues need to be addressed above and beyond nonadaptive systems. In Chapter 7, these authors further describe an approach to achieving awareness in software systems via knowledge representation in KnowLang.

Part III: Software Development and Evolution

In Chapter 8, Margaria et al. point out that agile approaches to software development mean less documentation and an emphasis on code. However, they highlight that we should focus on the level of models, not on the code.

In Chapter 9, Broy does exactly that, and approaches functional system requirements in a different way.

In Chapter 10, Holzmann gives guidance on developing high-integrity software for critical applications; in Chapter 11, Meyer gives testing tips in software. This chapter originally appeared in *IEEE Computer* and is simply reprinted here.

Updating their original column 5 years on, Meurice et al. in Chapter 12 describe the state of the art in the evolution of open-source Java projects that make use of relational database technology.

Part IV: Software Product Lines and Variability

In Chapter 13, Hallsteinsen et al. introduce the field, which brings the concept of software product lines to dynamic, adaptive, and self-adaptive systems, as a means of handling variability. This chapter is reprinted here exactly as it appeared in the original column. Many more papers on dynamic software product lines have been published since then, including those by Hallsteinsen et al., but this chapter is widely cited in the literature.

In Chapter 14, Capilla et al. again address dynamic software product lines in the context of the challenges, benefits, problems, and solutions offered by dynamic variability.

Part V: Formal Methods

In Chapter 15, Hähnle and Schafer consider the role of formal methods in software product lines; in Chapter 16, Bowen et al. consider the inter-relationship of formal methods, agile development methods, security, and software evolution.

Part VI: Cloud Computing

While technical aspects of cloud computing have been well-addressed, what makes cloud computing relevant and beneficial to an organization has not been well studied. In Chapter 17, Morgan and Conboy report on a field trial in 10 organizations and what influenced their uptake of cloud computing.

In Chapter 18, Hähnle and Johnsen point to the role of formal methods, executable models, and deployment modeling as means of moving deployment decision up the development chain to meet SLAs at lower costs and provide the client with better control of resource usage.

Acknowledgments

First and foremost, I would like to acknowledge Science Foundation Ireland for Grant 13/RC/2094 for the preparation of this book.

I am grateful to David Alan Grier, a regular columnist in *IEEE Computer* and former President of IEEE Computer Society, for writing such a nice introduction to the collection, to all of the authors of the chapters, and all of the authors who contributed to the column over 10 years without whom this book would not have been possible. Many thanks to Mary Hatcher, Victoria Bradshaw, Vishnu Narayanan, and all at Wiley, as well as Abhishek Sarkari at Thomson Digital, for their assistance and support in the preparation of this book.

Doris Carver was the Editor-in-Chief of *IEEE Computer* who invited me to edit the book in the first place. Subsequent Editors-in-Chief – Ron Vetter, Carl Chang, and Sumi Helai – were also very supportive. The editors at IEEE Computer Society Press – Chris Nelson, Bob Werner, Yu-Tzu Tsai, and Carrie Clark – did a great job of taking often scrappy notes and turning them into a polished column. Managing Editors Judi Prow and Carrie Clark were always great to work with. Dozens of people contributed to making the column, and hence this book a success over 10 years. But it would not have been possible without the late Dr. Scott Hamilton, a great editor and a really great friend.

List of Contributors

Sean Baker
Lero – The Irish Software
Research Centre
University of Limerick
Limerick
Ireland

Sarah Beecham
Lero – The Irish Software
Research Centre
University of Limerick
Limerick
Ireland

Jan Bosch
Department of Computer Science
and Engineering
Chalmers University of
Technology
Goteborg
Sweden

Jonathan P. Bowen
School of Engineering
London South Bank University
Borough Road
London
UK

Manfred Broy
Institut für Informatik
Technische Universität München
München
Germany

Rafael Capilla
Department of Informatics
Rey Juan Carlos University
Madrid
Spain

Maëlick Claes
COMPLEXYS Research Institute
University of Mons
Belgium

Anthony Cleve
PReCISE Research Center on
Information Systems Engineering
Faculty of Computer Science
University of Namur
Namur
Belgium

Kieran Conboy
Lero – The Irish Software
Research Centre
NUI Galway
Galway
Ireland

Alexandre Decan
COMPLEXYS Research Institute
Software Engineering Lab
Faculty of Sciences
University of Mons
Mons
Belgium

Brian Fitzgerald
Lero – The Irish Software
Research Centre
University of Limerick
Limerick
Ireland

Mathieu Goeminne
COMPLEXYS Research Institute
Software Engineering Lab
Faculty of Sciences
University of Mons
Mons
Belgium

Reiner Hähnle
Department of Computer Science
Software Engineering
Technische Universität Darmstadt
Darmstadt
Germany

Svein Hallsteinsen
SINTEF ICT
Trondheim
Norway

Mike Hinchey
Lero – The Irish Software
Research Centre
University of Limerick
Limerick
Ireland

Gerard J. Holzmann
JPL Laboratory for Reliable
Software
NASA
Pasadena
CA
USA

Helge Janicke
Software Technology Research
Laboratory
De Montfort University
Leicester
UK

Einar Broch Johnsen
University of Oslo
Norway

Anna-Lena Lamprecht
Department of Computer Science
and Information Systems
University of Limerick
and Lero – The Irish Software
Research Centre
Limerick
Ireland

Tiziana Margaria
Department of Computer Science
and Information Systems
University of Limerick
and Lero – The Irish Software
Research Centre
Limerick
Ireland

Tom Mens
COMPLEXYS Research Institute
Software Engineering Lab
Faculty of Sciences
University of Mons
Mons
Belgium

Loup Meurice
PReCISE Research Center on
Information Systems Engineering
Faculty of Computer Science
University of Namur
Namur
Belgium

Bertrand Meyer
E.T.H. Zürich
Zurich
Switzerland

Lorraine Morgan
Lero – The Irish Software
Research Centre
Maynooth University
Maynooth
Ireland

Csaba Nagy
PReCISE Research Center on
Information Systems Engineering
Faculty of Computer Science
University of Namur
Namur
Belgium

John Noll
Lero – The Irish Software
Research Centre
University of Limerick
Limerick
Ireland

and

University of East London
London
UK

Padraig O'Leary
School of Computer Science
University of Adelaide
Australia

Sooyong Park
Center for Advanced Blockchain
Research
Sogang University
Seoul
Republic of Korea

Ita Richardson
Lero – The Irish Software
Research Centre
University of Limerick
Limerick
Ireland

Ina Schaefer
Institute of Software Engineering
and Vehicle Informatics
Technische Universität
Braunschweig
Braunschweig
Germany

Klaus Schmid
Institute of Computer Science
University of Hildesheim
Hildesheim
Germany

Ian Sommerville
School of Computer Science
University of St Andrews
Scotland
UK

Bernhard Steffen
Fakultät für Informatik
TU Dortmund University
Dortmund
Germany

Roy Sterritt
School of Computing
and Computer Science Research
Institute
Ulster University
County Antrim
Northern Ireland

Emil Vassev
Lero – The Irish Software
Research Centre
University of Limerick
Limerick
Ireland

Martin Ward
Software Technology Research
Laboratory
De Montfort University
Leicester
UK

Hussein Zedan
Department of Computer Science
Applied Science University
Al Eker
Bahrain

Part I

The Software Landscape

1

Software Crisis 2.0

Brian Fitzgerald

Lero – The Irish Software Research Centre, University of Limerick, Limerick, Ireland

1.1 Software Crisis 1.0

> In 1957, the eminent computer scientist, Edsger Dijkstra, sought to record his profession as "Computer Programmer" on his marriage certificate. The Dutch authorities, probably more progressive than most, refused on the grounds that there was no such profession. Ironically, just a decade later, the term "software crisis" had been coined, as delegates at an international conference in 1968 reported a common set of problems, namely that software took too long to develop, cost too much to develop, and the software which was eventually delivered did not meet user expectations.

In the early years of computing during the 1940s, the computer was primarily used for scientific problem solving. A computer was needed principally because of its speed of mathematical capability, useful in areas such as the calculation of missile trajectories, aerodynamics, and seismic data analysis. The users of computers at the time were typically scientific researchers with a strong mathematical or engineering background who developed their own programs to address the particular areas in which they were carrying out research. For example, one of the early computers, ENIAC (Electronic Numerical Integrator and Calculator), which became operational in 1945, by the time it was taken out of service in 1955 "had probably done more arithmetic than had been done by the whole human race prior to 1945" [1].

During the 1950s, the use of computers began to spread beyond that of scientific problem solving to address the area of business data processing [2]. These early data processing applications were concerned with the complete and accurate capture of the organization's business transactions, and with automating routine clerical tasks to make them quicker and more accurate. This trend quickly spread, and by 1960, the business data processing use of computers had overtaken the scientific one [3]. Once underway, the business use of computers accelerated at an extremely rapid rate. The extent of this rapid expansion is evidenced by the fact that in the United States, the number of computer installations increased more than twentyfold between 1960 and 1970 [4].

However, this rapid expansion did not occur without accompanying problems. The nature of business data processing was very different from the computation-intensive nature of scientific applications. Business applications involved high volumes of input and output, but the input and output peripherals at the time were very slow and inefficient. Also, memory capacity was very limited, and this led to the widespread conviction among developers that good programs were efficient programs, rather than clear, well-documented, and easily understood programs [3]. Given these problems, writing programs required much creativity and resourcefulness on the part of the programmer. Indeed, it was recognized that it was a major achievement to get a program to run at all in the early 1960s [5].

Also, there was no formal training for developers. Programming skills could only be learned through experience. Some programmers were drawn from academic and scientific environments and thus had some prior experience. However, many programmers converted from a diverse range of departments. As Friedman [3] describes it

> People were drawn from very many areas of the organization into the DP department, and many regarded it as an 'unlikely' accident that they became involved with computers.

Also, during the 1960s, the computer began to be applied to more complex and less-routinized business areas. Aron [6] identifies a paradox in that as the early programmers improved their skills, there was a corresponding increase in the complexity of the problem areas for which programs had to be written.

Thus, while the term "software" was only introduced in 1958 [7], within 10 years, problems in the development of software led to the coining of the phrase "software crisis" at the NATO Conference in Garmisch [8]. The software crisis referred to the reality that software took longer to develop and cost more than estimated, and did not work very well when eventually delivered.

Over the years, several studies have confirmed these three aspects of the software crisis. For example, in relation to development timescales: Flaatten et al. [9] estimated development time for the average project to be about 18 months – a conservative figure perhaps given that other estimates put the figure at about 3 years [10] or even up to 5 years [11]. Also, an IBM study estimated that 68% of projects overran schedules [12]. In relation to the cost, the

IBM study suggested that development projects were as much as 65% over budget [12], while a Price Waterhouse study in the United Kingdom in 1988 concluded that £500 million was being lost per year through ineffective development. Furthermore, in relation to performance, the IBM study found that 88% of systems had to be radically redesigned following implementation [12]. Similarly, a UK study found that 75% of systems delivered failed to meet users expectations. This has led to the coining of the term "shelfware" to refer to those systems that are delivered but never used.

Notwithstanding the bleak picture painted above, the initial software crisis has largely been resolved, while the Standish Chaos Report continues to report high rates of software project failure – estimated at 68%, for example [13].[1] Although there has been no "silver bullet" advance, using Brooks [16] term, which affords an order of magnitude improvement in software development productivity, a myriad of advances have been made in more incremental ways, and software is now routinely delivered on time, within budget, and meets user requirements well. Software is really the success story of modern life. Everything we do, how we work, travel, communicate, entertain ourselves has been dramatically altered and enhanced by the capabilities provided by software.

1.2 Software Crisis 2.0

However, a new software crisis is now upon us, one that I term "Software Crisis 2.0." Software Crisis 2.0 is fuelled by a number of "push factors" and "pull factors." Push factors include advances in hardware such as that perennially afforded by Moore's law, multiprocessor and parallel computing, big memory servers, IBM's Watson platform, and quantum computing. Also, concepts such as the Internet of Things and Systems of Systems have led to unimaginable amounts of raw data that fuel the field of data analytics. Pull factors include the insatiable appetite of digital native consumers – those who have never known life without computer technology – for new applications to deliver initiatives such as the quantified self, lifelogging, and wearable computing. Also, the increasing role of software is evident in the concept of software-defined * (where * can refer to networking, infrastructure, data center, enterprise). The Software Crisis 2.0 bottleneck arises from the inability to produce the volume of software necessary to leverage the absolutely staggering increase in the volume of data being generated, which in turn allied to the enormous amount of computational power offered by the many hardware devices also available, and both complemented by the appetite of the newly emerged "digital native" consumer and a

---

1 It is worth noting that the Chaos report findings and methodology have been challenged (e.g., [14,15]).

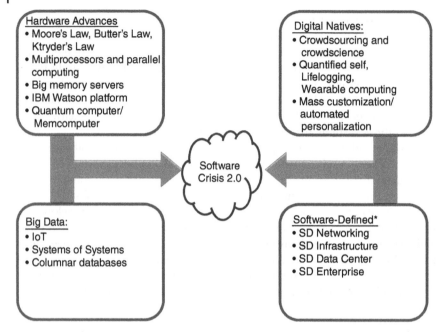

Figure 1.1 Software Crisis 2.0.

world where increasingly software is increasingly the key enabler (see Figure 1.1).

1.2.1 Hardware Advances

There are many eye-catching figures and statistics that illustrate the enormous advances in the evolution of hardware capacity over the past half-century or so. Moore's law, for example, predicted the doubling of hardware capacity roughly every 18 months or so. To illustrate this in a more familiar context, if one had invested just a single dollar in some shares when Moore was declaring his prediction initially in 1964, and if the stock market return on this shares had kept pace accordingly with Moore's prediction, the individual's net worth would now exceed $17 billion – not bad for a $1 investment. On each occasion when hardware appears to be halted due to an insurmountable challenge in the fundamental laws of physics – the impurity of atoms, sculpting light-wavelength limits, heat generation, radiation-induced forgetfulness, for example – new advances have emerged to overcome these problems as we move into the quantum computing area.

Moore's law is paralleled by similar "laws" in relation to storage capacity (Kryder's law) and network capacity (Butter's law) that portray similar exponential performance with decreasing costs. Big memory servers are disrupting the technology landscape with servers now capable of providing terabytes of physical memory. This has led to the observation that disks have become the new magnetic tape, as it is now possible to use physical memory for random access operations and to reserve the traditional random access disk for purely sequential operations.

1.2.1.1 Parallel Processing

In the era of Software Crisis 1.0, the programming paradigm was one based on serial computation. Instructions were executed one at a time on a single processor. Parallel processing allows programs to be decomposed to run on multiple processors simultaneously. Two significant advantages of parallel processing are significantly faster execution times and lower power consumption. Certain types of processing graphics, cryptography, and signal processing, for example, are suited to parallel decomposition.

1.2.1.2 IBM Watson Technology Platform

The IBM Watson platform uses a natural language and machine learning to allow a computer to appreciate context in human language, a task in which computers traditionally perform very poorly. Watson achieved widespread recognition for its ability to beat human experts in the game of Jeopardy. Configuring Watson to achieve this victory was far from trivial as it was underpinned by 200 million pages of content (including the full text of Wikipedia), 2800 processor cores, and 6 million logic rules [17]. Watson has been deployed in a variety of contexts: as a call center operator, hotel concierge, and chef as it has even published its own cookbook. However, IBM believes it has the power to revolutionize human–computer interaction with many applications in domains very beneficial to society, such as medicine where Watson technology is being used to create the ultimate physician's assistant as a cancer specialist. IBM estimate that a person can generate 1 million gigabytes of health-related data across his or her lifetime – roughly the equivalent of 300 million books. These large data problems are ones in which Watson can perform well as Watson can process 500GB (the equivalent of a million books) per second.

1.2.1.3 Quantum Computer and the Memcomputer

Although still primarily theoretical in nature, quantum computing has significant advantages over the traditional digital computer in terms of its vastly superior performance in solving certain problems. Digital computers are so called because they are based on the binary system of two digital states, 0 and 1, which conveniently map to electronic switching states of "off" or "on." Quantum computers, on the other hand, operate on quantum bits or *qubits* in short. Qubits are not restricted to being in a state of 0 or 1; rather they can be either 0 or 1 or through what is termed superposition, they can be both 0 and 1 (and all points in between) at the same time. As mentioned, digital computers typically perform only one instruction at a time, whereas a quantum computer performs many calculations simultaneously, and hence it is inherently delivering parallelism. Estimates suggest that a quantum computer could solve within seconds a problem that might take a digital computer 10,000 years to calculate [18]. Quantum computers are suited to optimization problems, an application of artificial intelligence that IBM Watson is also addressing, albeit still operating within the overall digital computer paradigm. In 2015, Google and NASA announced their collaboration on the D-Wave 2X quantum computer that has over 1000 qubits.[2]

Other alternatives to the traditional digital computer are also being investigated. These include the memcomputer, so called because it seeks to mimic the functioning of the memory cells of the human brain [19]. However, while the D-Wave 2X quantum computer requires an environment 150 times colder than interstellar space, in contrast, the memcomputer operates at room temperature. The fundamental innovation in the memcomputer is that, like the human brain, it stores and processes information in the same physical space, thereby overcoming a central problem in traditional digital computers that of transfer of information between the central processing unit and memory. The traditional computer uses millions of times more power than the brain on such data transfer, which is ultimately extremely wasteful of time and energy as such transfers do not add any essential value.

1.2.2 "Big Data"

While it is extremely difficult to quantify the increases in the volume of electronic data that potentially exists, there is undoubtedly a similar pattern of exponential increases paralleling that of the hardware arena. Eric Schmidt, CEO of Google, suggested in 2005 that the amount of data available electronically comprised 5 million terabytes (that is 5 million billion megabytes), of which only 0.004% was being indexed by Google. He estimated the amount of data as doubling every five years.

Dave Evans, Chief Futurist at Cisco Systems estimated in 2010 that there were about 35 billion devices connected to the Internet, which is more than five times the population of the planet [20]. This figure was estimated to increase to 100 billion devices by 2020. This has given rise to the concept of the "Internet of Things" (IoT) [21] or network of everything. An exemplar project designed for the IoT is the plan by HP as part of the Central Nervous System for the Planet (CeNSE) project to place a trillion "smart dust" sensors all over the planet as a planet-wide sensing network infrastructure. These sensors would detect a wide

---

2 http://www.dwavesys.com/blog/2015/08/announcing-d-wave-2x-quantum-computer

variety of factors, including motion, vibrations, light, temperature, barometric pressure, airflow and humidity, and have obvious applications in transportation, health, energy management, and building automation.

Similar predictions were made, such as that of the World Wireless Research Forum's (WWRF) that there would be 7 trillion devices for the world's 7 billion people by 2017 – which is a thousand devices for every human being – all of which would be intelligently connected to create an individual personal network for all. This suggests that more structure is needed for IoT, in that a "systems of systems" approach is necessary to govern and deliver these networks.

To cope with this proliferation of devices, a migration is underway from the IPv4 protocol that has about four billion unique addresses to the IPv6 protocol that can support 21^{28} addresses – enough to uniquely address every grain of sand on every beach in the world. In this brave new world, the vast majority of communications will be machine-to-machine rather than machine-to-person, thereby generating an enormous amount of electronic information that is available for processing.

Big Data needs has several technological implications. For example, columnar databases that invert the traditional row-oriented relational databases can perform much more efficiently on search tasks as the data becomes the primary key effectively. Columnar databases lend themselves to greater compression and therefore require less space and can achieve faster transfer rates.

Complementing the basic "push" factors of hardware advances and big data availability are a number of "pull" or demand factors that underpin the need for more software. These include the software-hungry "digital natives" and the trend toward software-defined *, where * can represent networking, infrastructure, datacenter, or enterprise, reflecting the fact that software is the primary mechanism mediating the modern world. These pull factors are discussed next.

1.2.3 Digital Natives Lifelogging and the Quantified Self

An interesting distinction has been drawn between "digital immigrants" – those who began using digital technology at some stage during their adult lives, and "digital natives" – those who have been immersed in the world of technology since birth and have as a consequence developed a natural fluency for technology [22]. By the age of 20, digital natives will have spent 20,000 h online [23] and can cope with, and indeed even welcome, an abundance of information [24]. This category of digital native consumer represents a significant "pull" factor in seeking to take advantage of the opportunities afforded by advances in processing power and increased availability of data. The advent of wearable computing fuels big data and has led to initiatives such as lifelogging and the quantified self. With such initiatives individuals can collect data about all aspects of their daily lives – diet, health, recreation, mood states, performance – in some cases recording a terabyte of data per annum [25].

The paradoxical success of the open-source software phenomenon has led to a broader interest in crowd science or citizen science as a collaborative model of problem analysis and solving. Notable areas of success are user-led innovation, cocreation of value, and high-profile crowdsourcing of solutions for solving complex R&D problems in NASA, Eli Lilly, and Du Pont, which provides real testimony to the potential of the digital native.

Mass customization has been succinctly defined as "producing goods and services to meet individual customer's needs with near mass production efficiency" [26]. While not a new concept, it resonates well with catering to the personal needs of the digital native. Also, it is now typically delivered through some form of software-mediated configurability to meet individual customer needs. The concept of automated personalization is linked to the desired benefits of big data.

1.2.4 Software-Defined*

The increasing demand for software already discussed is fuelled by the increasing capability of software to perform tasks that were previously accomplished through hardware. This is evident in phenomena such as software-defined networking [27] or software-defined infrastructure [28], even software-defined datacenters [29], right through to the concept of the software-defined enterprise that has enough intelligence to automate all business processes. This is also evident in the move beyond IoT to Systems of Systems where the sensors and sources of data, such as household appliances, are fully integrated into web-enabled systems capable of utilizing machine-learning techniques to offer real-time data analytics on the morass of acquired raw data, with the ultimate goal of enabling societal benefits for citizens through the provision of useful and precisely customized information – the quantified self, for example.

1.3 Software Crisis 2.0: The Bottleneck

Given these "push" and "pull" factors, it is clear that a massive increase in the volume of software being produced is required to address these emerging initiatives. This creates a Software Crisis 2.0 bottleneck as we illustrate further. There are two dimensions to this crisis. One is the massive increase in the volume of software required to fuel the demand in new domains where software has not been always of primary significance – medicine and healthcare for example – where terabytes of raw data need to be analyzed to provide useful actionable insights. The second dimension, however, is a more challenging one as it requires software development practitioners to acquire fundamentally

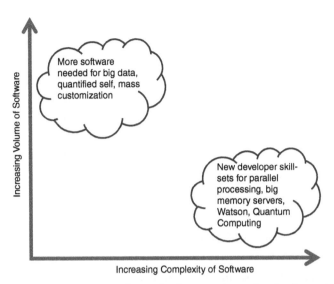

Figure 1.2 Increasing volume of software and complex developer skill sets.

different new skills to take advantage of advances in hardware – parallel processing, big memory servers, and quantum computing, for example – these will all require significant new skills on the part of practitioners (see Figure 1.2).

1.3.1 Significant Increase in Volume of Software Required

"Our organization has become a software company. The problem is that our engineers haven't realized that yet!"

This is how the Vice President for Research of a major semiconductor manufacturing company, traditionally seen as the classic hardware company, characterized the context in which software solutions were replacing hardware in delivering his company's products. This situation is replicated across several business domains as the transformation to software has been taking place for quite some time. The telecommunications industry began the move to *softwareization* in the 1970s with the introduction of computerized switches, and currently, the mobile telephony market is heavily software focused. The automotive industry has very noticeably been moving toward softwareization since the 1960s–today, 80–90% of innovations in the automotive industry are enabled by software [30,31]. This is evidenced in the dramatic increase in the numbers of software engineers being employed in proportion to the numbers employed in traditional engineering roles. Indeed, an extremely striking example of the growing importance of software arises in the automotive industry. In 1978, a printout of the lines of code in the car would have made a paper stack

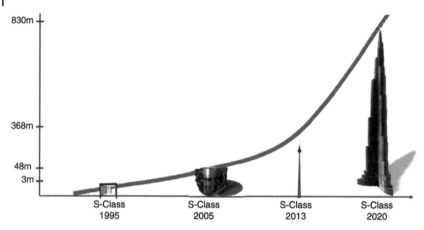

Figure 1.3 Height of software printout in Mercedes S-Class [32].

about 12 cm high. By 1995, this was already a 3-m-high stack, and by 2005, the printout was about 50 m tall. By 2013, the printout had grown to 150 m in height. By 2020, the estimate is that the stack would be a staggering 830 m tall, higher than the Burj Khalifa – the tallest man-made structure in the world [32]. This is illustrated graphically in Figure 1.3.

1.3.2 New Skill Sets Required for Software Developers

This demand for additional software is clearly replicated in several other industry domains. However, the software required for these domains is typically "more of the same" in that no major paradigm change is present that requires developers to possess new skills and techniques. In the overall backdrop to this software bottleneck, however, it is worth bearing in mind that estimates suggest the population of professional software engineers worldwide to comprise no more than 500,000 people [33]. Clearly, there are more software development practitioners in the world, and development resources may even be boosted by a general willingness for additional people to get involved based on a crowd-sourcing model. However, the skills required in this brave new world are not those possessed by the average software developer.

In the area of parallel processing on multicore architectures, for example, a number of fundamental challenges emerge. The traditional programming paradigm is one of runtime task allocation and scheduling, that is, the operating system allocates tasks to processors and takes care of scheduling and load balancing. In a multicore architecture, these decisions can be made at design-time or compile-time and developers need to design program threads accordingly. The analysis, design, and debug phases are significantly more challenging, and also an optimization/tuning phase is necessary. In the analysis phase, for example, new questions arise. For example, not all code might benefit from parallelization. Code which is executed more frequently would be likely to lead to greater benefit, but code may be so simple that no performance benefit may arise through any potential parallelism, or there may not be any parallelizable loops. In the design phase, issues such as method of threading and decomposition need to be addressed. In the debug phase, handling data races and deadlocks and implementing thread synchronization accordingly is the focus. The optimization/tuning phase considers performance issues such as the amount of code parallelism, and whether performance benefits can be achieved as the number of processors increases.

1.3.2.1 From Runtime to Design-Time Switch

This is an interesting issue as much focus in recent times in software engineering has been on runtime adaptation, that is delaying decisions that are normally taken at design time until runtime [34]. This is evident in work on adaptive security and privacy, for example [35]. However, in the case of programming for multicore processors, issues such as the allocation of tasks to processors and load-balancing must be done at design time.

Programming big memory servers is also likely to lead to significant new programming challenges. The concept of garbage collection, for example, could be extremely problematic in a 64 terabyte single RAM space. Likewise, the mechanisms for dealing with a crash, or the notions of transient and persistent memory need to be reconceptualized when programming for a big memory server environment.

Quantum computing is not likely to replace traditional computing in the near future. However, understanding the quantum concepts of superposition and entanglement is far from trivial. At present, only a certain class of problem lends itself to be solved more efficiently by a quantum computer, optimization problems for example. Analyzing and understanding such problems is clearly not the *forte* of the majority of software developers at present. Quantum computing languages have also been created – QCL or quantum computing language [36] and Quipper [37], for example, but the quantum operations in these languages will be completely alien to the traditionally trained developer.

1.4 Conclusion

Given the scarcely comprehensible increases in hardware power and data capacity mentioned already, it is perhaps surprising that there has not been a "silver bullet" to deliver even a modest one order of magnitude improvement in software productivity. Without wishing to deny the enormous advances that have been brought about by software, which has truly revolutionized life and society in the twentieth and twenty-first centuries, it is intriguing to imagine what life would be like if the software area had evolved at the same pace as that of hardware and data. But that has not been the case: Wirth's law [38] effectively summarizes the comparative evolution in the software domain, namely, that software is getting slower more rapidly than the hardware is becoming faster.

References

1 B. Cohen (1988) The computer: a case study of the support by government, especially the military, of a new science and technology. Cited in Pickering, A. Cyborg history and WWII regime.

2 G. Davis and M. Olson (1985) *Management Information Systems: Conceptual Foundations, Structure and Development*, 2nd Edition, McGraw-Hill, New York.

3 A. Friedman (1989) *Computer Systems Development: History, Organisation and Implementation*, John Wiley & Sons, Ltd., Chichester.

4 C. Lecht (1977) *The Waves of Change*, McGraw-Hill, New York.

5 M. Shaw (1990) Prospects for an engineering discipline of software. *IEEE Software* 7, 15–24.

6 J. Aron (1976) Estimating resources for large programming systems. In Naur, P. Randell, B., and Buxton, J. (eds.), *Software Engineering: Concepts and Techniques*, Charter Publishers, New York, 206–217.

7 I. Peterson (2000) Software's Origin. Available at http://www.maa.org/ mathland/mathtrek_7_31_00.html (accessed Oct. 2011).

8 P. Naur, and B. Randell (eds.) (1968) *Software Engineering: A Report on a Conference Sponsored by the NATO Science Committee*. Scientific Affairs Division, NATO, Brussels.

9 P. Flaatten, D. McCubbrey, P. O'Riordan, and K. Burgess (1989) *Foundations of Business Systems*, Dryden Press, Chicago.

10 Anonymous (1988) The software trap: automate—or else, Business Week, 142–154.

11 T. Taylor and T. Standish (1982) Initial thoughts on rapid prototyping techniques. *ACM SIGSOFT Software Engineering Notes*, 7 (5), 160–166.

12 P. Bowen (1994) Rapid Application Development: Concepts and Principles, IBM Document No. 94283UKT0829.

13 Standish Group (2009) The CHAOS Report, The Standish Group, Boston, MA.

14 J. Eveleeens and C. Verhoef (2010) The rise and fall of the Chaos reports. *IEEE Software*, **27**, 30–36.

15 R. Glass (2006) The Standish report: does it really describe a software crisis? *Communications of the ACM*, **49** (8), 15–16.

16 F. Brooks (1987) No silver bullet: essence and accidents of software engineering. *IEEE Computer Magazine April*, 10–19.

17 I. Paul (2010) IBM Watson Wins Jeopardy, Humans Rally Back, PCWorld. Available at http://www.pcworld.com/article/219900/IBM_Watson_Wins_Jeopardy_Humans_Rally_Back.html

18 D. Basulto (2015) Why Google's new quantum computer could launch an artificial intelligence arms race, Financial Review, Available at http://www.afr.com/technology/why-googles-new-quantum-computer-could-launch-an-artificial-intelligence-arms-race-20151228-glvr7s

19 F. Traversa, C. Ramella, F. Bonani, and M. Di Ventra (2015) Memcomputing *NP*-complete problems in polynomial time using polynomial resources and collective states. *Science Advances*, 1 (6). doi: 10.1126/sciadv.1500031.

20 A. Jeffries (2010) A Sensor In Every Chicken: Cisco Bets on the Internet of Things. Available at http://www.readwriteweb.com/archives/cisco_futurist_predicts_internet_of_things_1000_co.php

21 K. Ashton (2009) That 'Internet of Things' Thing. RFID Journal.

22 M. Prensky (2001) Digital natives, digital immigrants. *On Horizon* 9 (5), 1–2.

23 P. M. Valkenburg and J. Peter (2008) Adolescents' identity experiments on the Internet: consequences for social competence and self-concept unity. *Communication Research* 35 (2), 208–231.

24 S. Vodanovich, D. Sundaram, and M. Myers (2010) Digital natives and ubiquitous information systems. *Information Systems Research* 21 (4), 711–723.

25 C. Gurrin, A. Smeaton, and A. Doherty (2014) LifeLogging: Personal Big Data. doi: 10.1561/1500000033.

26 M.M. Tseng and J. Jiao (2001) Mass Customization *Handbook of Industrial Engineering, Technology and Operation Management*, 3rd Edition, John Wiley & Sons, Inc., New York, NY,

27 K. Kirkpatrick (2013) Software-defined networking. *Communications of the ACM*, 56 (9), 16–19.

28 B. Fitzgerald, N. Forsgren, K. Stol, J. Humble, and B. Doody, (2015) Infrastructure is Software Too. Available at http://papers.ssrn.com/sol3/papers.cfm?abstract_id=2681904

29 Dell (2015) Technology Outlook White paper. Available at dell.com/dellresearch.

30 J. Mössinger (2010) Software in automotive systems. *IEEE Software*, 27 (2), 92–94.

31 Swedsoft (2010) A Strategic Research Agenda for the Swedish Software Intensive Industry.

32 J. Schneider (2015) Software-innovations as key driver for a Green, Connected and Autonomous mobility. ARTEMIS-IA/ITEA-Co-Summit.

33 D. Grier (2015) Do We Engineer Software in Software Engineering. Available at https://www.youtube.com/watch?v=PZcUCZhqpus

34 L. Baresi and C. Ghezzi (2010) The disappearing boundary between development-time and runtime. *Future of Software Engineering Research* 2010, 17–22.

35 M. Salehie L. Pasquale, I. Omoronyia, R. Ali, and B. Nuseibeh (2012) Requirements-driven adaptive security: protecting variable assets at runtime. 20th IEEE Requirements Engineering Conference (RE), 2012

36 B. Omer (2014) Quantum Computing Language. Available at http://www.itp .tuwien.ac.at/~oemer/qcl.html

37 P. Selinger (2015) The Quipper Language. Available at http://www.mathstat .dal.ca/~selinger/quipper/

38 N. Wirth (1995) A plea for lean software. *Computer* **28** (2), 64–68.

2

Simplicity as a Driver for Agile Innovation

Tiziana Margaria[1] and Bernhard Steffen[2]

[1]*Department of Computer Science and Information Systems, University of Limerick and Lero – The Irish Software Research Centre, Limerick, Ireland*
[2]*Fakultät für Informatik, TU Dortmund University, Dortmund, Germany*

2.1 Motivation and Background

Exponential organizations [1] are the most radical witnesses of simplicity-based agile innovation, colorfully illustrating what we mean by simplicity and agile innovation. Simplicity is not an absolute notion. Rather it strongly depends on the current circumstances, like the global and local state of the art and infrastructure and the mindset of the addressed audience. Agile innovation is the exploitation of the current circumstances with comparatively little effort. It is characterized more by its sensitivity to new externally provided (infrastructural) potential and (commercial) impact than by the specific technology involved. Reference [1] discusses a number of impressive success stories that typically heralded the end of some traditional business era. When in 2007, Nokia acquired the navigation and roadmap company Navteq for $8.1 billion with its market leading road sensor technology, it aimed at regaining market share as a dominating online traffic information provider. Essentially at the same time, Waze was founded. Its business idea exploits the ubiquitous GPS sensors in smartphones to crowdsource the collection of traffic information. In contrast to Nokia's own dedicated and highly expensive infrastructure, Waze had no infrastructural investments: It was simply built on globally available and steadily growing volunteer resources. A few years later, Nokia was sold to Microsoft for essentially the same price it paid for Navteq while Waze attracted 50 million users and was sold to Google for $1.1 billion. A posteriori, Nokia as an established company was too fixed in its mind set of resource ownership to

Software Technology: 10 Years of Innovation in IEEE Computer, First Edition.
Edited by Mike Hinchey.
© 2018 the IEEE Computer Society, Inc. Published 2018 by John Wiley & Sons, Inc.

recognize and react to the enormous potential of the new global infrastructure[1]. In fact, established companies seem to be particularly weak in innovating their core business [2]. In contrast, exponential organizations like Waze (and Facebook, Whatsapp, Snapchat, and many others) ideally exploit untapped potential and achieve staggering market success with only comparatively little technical effort and risk. In fact, (technologic) simplicity of what remains to be done is an important trait of their success: it allows them to easily fill a market niche of gigantic dimension, thanks to available global communication infrastructure. This illustrates the enormous potential impact of simplicity in the IT domain.

The maturity required to exploit the potential of simplicity has not yet reached the mainstream industrial software development. Rather, looking at today's software system production and use, we can pretty easily compare this industry's life cycle to that experienced by the automobile industry almost a century ago. Attributed to Gottlieb Daimler, this statement characterizes carmakers' expectations at that time: "The market for automobiles will never grow beyond one million cars, for a very simple reason: Who would educate all those chauffeurs?" His skepticism to scale at large scale is understandable: back then, cars were handcrafted, hard to operate, expensive to maintain, costing upfront more than a house. At the time, they were technically amazing – they could speed up to 100 km/h – but with a hefty downside – the mean distance between flat tires stretched to 30 kilometers, thanks to nail damage from horses and carts, the still prevalent mass transportation medium.

Not surprisingly, the number of extra tires constituted a status symbol: two full wheels were normal, with some cars carrying up to eight extra wheels to weather longer trips. But those who could afford a car were neither willing to change tires themselves, nor eager to personally maintain the engine, making well-trained chauffeurs an indispensable commodity in the 1920s.

So it goes with software today. Despite the promises and effort, working with software products still offers a comparable adventure, one that rarely proceeds as expected. Difficulties with deployment and use lead to enormous system, organizational, and personal performance losses, not only at first deployment but even more so when we factor in the inevitable upgrades, migrations, and version changes.

Millions of users suffer when standard software with a large market share evolves. Maybe it undergoes a radical redesign of the graphical user interface (GUI) or offers a new generation of tools not readily compatible with previous versions. Users must then desperately search for previously well-understood

---

1 One could say that Nokia missed the opportunity 'this time', as it stunningly succeeded to transform itself from a rubber boot producing company into a market leading mobile phone company only a decade earlier. We see in particular how quick is the rise and fall in case of reaping or missing innovation.

functionality, spending hours or even days bringing perfectly designed documents to a satisfactory state within this changed technical environment.

This frustrating catch-up phase causes an enormous productivity loss that can force customers to shy away from updates and migrations, sticking instead with old and even outdated or discontinued products or versions. In many situations, customers fear any kind of innovation involving IT because they immediately associate a change with enormous disruptions and long periods of instability. With technology-driven innovations, this fear may be justified due to the new technologies themselves. However, even small and technically simple adaptations to a business process typically require a major IT project, with all its involved risks and costs.

Thus, decision-makers act conservatively, preferring patches to old workhorses and exchanging functionality only when it is absolutely necessary. Even the automobile industry fails when it comes to IT adoption and, particularly, IT agility. Much of a car's control software runs on specific hardware, which limits the software's applicability, especially after the hardware becomes obsolete: the software cannot be ported to new platforms (for fear of unexpected side effects), meaning that manufacturers are more or less stuck with that initial hardware. Considering that cars last about 10 years, and IT platforms between 2 and 3 (or how old are your laptop, tablet, and mobile phone?), it is understandable that customers until recently missed USB chargers, the ability to listen to music from their own mobile device, and stuck instead to outdated CD readers and built-in GPS navigation devices purchased years before at high cost.

Although it takes engineers years to innovate, the product life cycle outlives the electronics and software within by factors. In most industries, an IT lock-in at design time has become a central problem: decisions on which technology to use and long-term deals with the manufacturers are frozen before production starts and often last beyond the facelifts that periodically refresh these products.

In the aerospace industry, this lifetime mismatch is even more evident: it takes decades to plan and design a mission, which leaves the IT used in the field in a typically decades-old state. IT innovation is the fastest we observe, systematically outpacing the life cycle of the products built using it. Inevitably, the products' life spans shorten to those of the IT they embody, as in consumer electronics, but this is unacceptable for expensive products, where it leads to steep depreciation.

Today, we have a similar situation within the IT industry itself: singularly taken, technologies and products are well-designed and innovative, but they are not made for working together and cannot evolve independently. Consequently, we work with systems whose stability is not proven and in which we can thus pose only limited trust. Once a bearable situation is achieved, and a constellation works satisfactorily, we tend to stick to it, bending the business and procedures to fit the working system, then running it until support is discontinued and too often even beyond. In fact, even pure software-based IT can be caught in the platform lock-in trap: The business needs to often outpace the life cycle of the IT platforms that steer a company's organization and production.

2.2 Important Factors

Various factors contributed to our current dismal state of the art. Some are rooted in the business models of major software and hardware vendors who long avoided interoperation for fear that the consequences of customers opting out from their own product lines would be dire. Some of this has been recognized as a brake to market freedom and to innovation, and even the European Community has reacted by cofunding large initiatives that promote platform interoperation in the Internet business space. As an example, the main goal of the European Future Internet PPP[2] is "to advance a shared vision for harmonized European technology platforms and their implementation, as well as the integration and harmonization of the relevant policy, legal, political, and regulatory frameworks."

The frantic pace of technology replacement provides its own chaos: before a certain technology reaches maturity and can repay the enormous investments for its development and production, a newer option attracts attention with novelty and fresh promises. New processors every 6 months, new product updates every 6–12 months basically are self-dictated races that try to boost revenue but destabilize the pyramid of IT and products at whose core they sit.

Decisive change came to the automobile industry not from the isolated improvement of single elements but from a holistic evolution and maturation on many fronts, with the interplay of numerous factors:

- *Better, More Robust Components.* The modern car platform approach builds on comparatively few well-engineered individual components, such as the tires, motor, and the chassis. Custom and bespoke components, once frequent, are now seldom to nonexistent.
- *Better Streets.* Today, we hardly need to worry about flat tires, to the point that even the reserve tire is often just a small unit, for an emergency drive to the next (frequent) service station.
- *Better Driving Comfort.* Cars run smoothly, reliably, and safely, even if maltreated. User orientation has made a huge difference: drivers do not need anymore to be also skilled mechanics.
- *Better Production Processes.* Modern construction supports cars tailored to their customers, even if all are built on platforms. Essentially, no two delivered cars are identical, yet they all are bound to only a few well-developed platforms. Platform and configuration management are here the decisive tools.

---

2 Future Internet Public-Private Partnership, see www.fi-ppp.eu

- *Better Maintenance and Support.* Drivers expect to have and indeed do have access to support worldwide, "anytime everywhere," which can even include home transportation. This encourages the willingness to depart from home and go explore different places.

These modern developments have on one side a straightforward match to the situation in IT, yet they also reveal the weaknesses of today's IT industry:

- *Better, More Robust Components.* Today's IT components are typically too complicated and fragile, and therefore are difficult and risky to integrate in larger contexts. Service orientation seems to be a potentially strong step in the right direction, but it must be combined with a clear policy of quality and enhanced descriptions of what is inside the components and their properties. Should we annotate the code? The interfaces? The services? What information is produced, consumed, and therefore useful to whom? The level of information provided for services is insufficient, even for semantically enhanced services. In particular, still today the description, annotation, and classification must be done largely manually, one of the reasons why nowadays, a decade after the Semantic Web Service Challenge, we still do not have service repositories that are semantically annotated beyond small collections within research projects.
- *Better Connection and Interoperation.* We still lack seamless connection and integration, with numerous mismatches at the protocol, interface, or behavioral level. Big data is hampered by different, incompatible, and historically grown data and processing formats to the point that data cleansing and restructuring takes an exorbitant part of (big) data projects. Projects like CONNECT have shown that in the presence of sufficient information, connection and interoperation are feasible, but in practice the reconciliation of different and independent data sources is still a nightmare. Even when standards exist, as in health care with HL7 (which has gray zones and numerous, incompatible versions) or in IoT, the IEEE has been working on standards for smart transducers since 1993 (IEEE 1451.4 Standard for Smart Transducers), yet sensors today still work largely the way they want, and Information Logistics is a bustling business with a bright future, thriving on incompatibilities. Meanwhile, the intended semantics and accompanying security provide an everlasting concern and a hot research topic.
- *Better User Comfort.* Experts might know various specifically optimized solutions for the myriad cases where one needs to do something different, but normal users find none. Even getting a modern phone to simply make the first call can be rather painful, with many perceived unnecessary extra steps and commands that serve the IT platform, not the user. A declarative approach, where the platform user states a goal and the platform figures out a way, or the best way, to achieve it, is still out of reach. Whether expert

systems, agents, planning, and other forms of AI, simplicity of uncommon tasks for end users is still underserved.

- *Better Production Processes.* Application development and quality assurance should be directly steered by user requirements, controlled via user experience, and continuously subject to modification during development. While production speed and user feedback are part of the agile philosophy, they largely come with a "doing" and prototype-driven approach that often trades the systematic care of the more traditional software design and development processes for a spontaneity that however penalizes the creation of analyzable artifacts (models, documentation, descriptions, and annotations). In the long term, this skimpy information may lead to higher maintenance costs, lower reuse, and altogether to an unnecessarily higher volatility of the code base.

- *Better Maintenance and Support.* Established scenarios and often-used functionality should continue to work over a long lifetime, while support should be immediate and integrated into the normal workflow. A combination of agility with model-driven approaches, as advocated in Ref. [3], is here a viable sweet spot: models can be changed easily, they contain rich information, are analyzable and checkable, and code is generated from them as a throwaway by-product aimed only at machine execution. Support and maintenance foot themselves also in the models, evolving the models as central artifact, and not the code. While this is a revolutionary idea for the software industry, it is the standard practice since about 2 decades in hardware design: nobody today seriously designs complex systems (processors, ASICS, or Systems on a Chip) from scratch and at the level of transistors or gates. Designs are typically based on the composition of complex IP cores for each component, each of which is a high-level description of the functionality and its desired characteristics. It is then combined with other cores to compose the chip's description, in turn synthesized toward the target platform by means of high-level automated synthesis tools, that is, tools capable of automatically generating the transistor level implementation starting from a behavioral description of the target core. Companies like Mentor Graphics, Cadence, and Synopsys produce, maintain, and support the target libraries, while the system designers live completely in the high-level description space.

2.3 The Future

The transition to overcoming these weaknesses will depend on adopting economical principles that favor dimensions of maturity and simplicity over sheer novelty. In our analogy, Formula One car racing is an attractive platform for high-end research, but is unsuited for the needs and requirements of mass driving due to different skill, costs, and traffic conditions. Taking ideas and results from the high-end and specialized laboratory to a product requires diverse and extensive translational research to succeed. Transferred to the IT domain, this kind of research spans several dimensions:

Human–computer interaction has led to GUIs that provide an intuitive user interface, Software development profits, for example, from graphical modeling environments [4–7]. Here, UML, BPMN, Live sequence charts, and similar notations are highly formalized, in the sense discussed by Harel in Ref. [8] of notation having a precise formal definition, but this comes at the price that models drawn in one of these languages "look" pretty much the same, both within and also across application domains. In contrast, in our own research we have created a tool that decouples the "look" of the iconic symbols on the formal model from the formal semantic itself. As shown in Figure 2.1, there is a clear correspondence between activity diagrams and jABC's formal design diagrams. However, users can "facelift" the naked formal diagram (called service logic graph in our terminology) and associate with primitives a symbol they like [9]. It can be an icon for the person or "role" who executes or is responsible for this activity, or any other symbol useful to self-explain it to beholders. Examples of meaningful icon customization are as follows:

- The logo of the tool (e.g., Gnu R, Matlab), or of the service platform used to carry out certain data processing steps in bioinformatics and geoinformatics workflows, as shown in Figure 2.2.
- Photos of the person who carries out an action (the specific nurse in-charge for this procedure in Sao Paulo, as in Ref. [11]), or the role or group, as in Ref. [10], where diagnostic steps of children dyslexia that are carried out by an expert in presence of parents, or parents and child are represented with icons that show those roles (Figure 2.2).

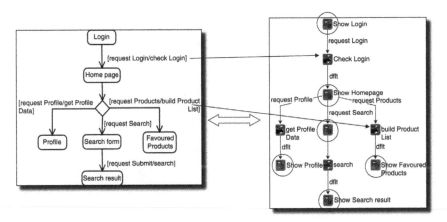

Figure 2.1 Correspondence between UML activity diagrams and SLGs – representation matters.

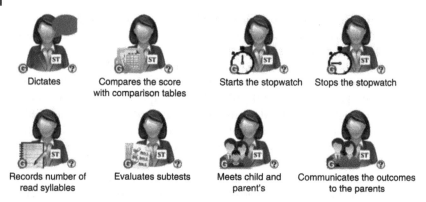

Dictates	Compares the score with comparison tables

Starts the stopwatch	Stops the stopwatch

Records number of read syllables	Evaluates subtests

Meets child and parent's	Communicates the outcomes to the parents

Figure 2.2 Roles and actor groups in the dyslexia diagnosis case study. (Reproduced with permission from Ref. [10], p. 97.)

- The specific device used in that process step (the specific centrifuge, the specific fridge drawer assigned to this project in the Crio-lab, or the runner in the physiotherapy lab [11]).

For example, in Figure 2.3, we see a snapshot of the design and execution of the case study described in Ref. [12], where a large selection of externally created and maintained tools are used in the workflows of the ci:grasp climate information platform (http://www.cigrasp.org) [13]. They are based on scripts in the GNU R language that comprises several tools for spatial analysis. The srtmtools package [14] used for the data analysis provides the methods required

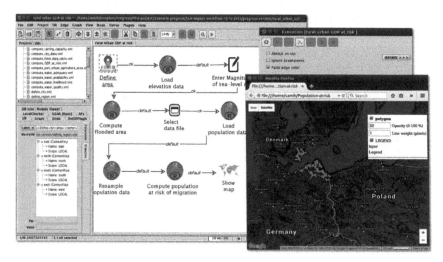

Figure 2.3 Custom icons in jABC–Gnu R and other tools in the live process model of the case study in [12], and execution outcome.

to produce results as presented on ci:grasp. It combines various tools that are based on different packages, such as the raster package tool for data reading, writing, manipulating, analyzing and modeling of gridded spatial data (http://cran.r-project.org/web/packages/raster/), the Gdal tool for data conversion (http://www.gdal.org), and other packages for data visualization such as Png (http://www.rforge.net/png) and plotGoogleMaps [15].

As discussed in Ref. [16], there is an entire dimension of semiotics engineering in HCI that is still untapped by most tools for system specification and design, that can effectively help intuitively "grab" the idea behind an otherwise very formal representation, de facto lowering the access barriers to them, and simplifying the knowledge prerequisites.

Another dimension is the kind of *representations* single facet or multifacet? UML diagrams try to be single facet, concentrating on one concern. To express different concerns, one should use different diagrams, raising the issue of consistency maintenance. However, architectural representations like most AADLs, widespread bioinformatics and scientific workflow tools like Taverna (http://www.taverna.org.uk) and Labview (http://www.ni.com/labview/), and most service-oriented design tools and paradigms like SCA [17], concentrate on just data and its potential connectivity. How does one then understand and represent the control behavior? The Taverna Workbench and other dataflow oriented workflow design systems have recognized that it is difficult, and have created some provisions on top and around their dataflow languages to deal with simple control primitives. Conversely, what is the use of a control flow without "seeing" what happens with the data? This was the dilemma with the original METAFrame environment [18], and its successors ABC, jABC, up and including the jABC4, as discussed in Ref. [19]. An explicit dataflow representation was included for the first time in the WebABC of Ref. [20], then the data modeling became a first class citizen with DyWA [21], reconciling the dychotomy between data and control in an integrative approach in DIME [10,22,23]. Here, the solution is more a tradeoff, based on on/off switchable layers that can be shown or hidden as most opportune, adopting a solution that has been successfully practiced for a long time in architectural CAD.

But there are also technically more involved techniques for simplification: generating parsers or even entire compilers from simple language specifications is a long stated goal [24], with strong implications still today where such techniques become integral part in complex meta modeling environments [25]. Similarly, also complex dataflow analysis algorithms can be generated from short temporal specifications, which can often be specified using simple patterns as shown in Refs [26,27]. This generation principle, which is also inherent in approaches like generative programming, aspect-oriented programming, or meta programming will increasingly influence future software development.

Domain modeling and semantic technologies can establish a user-level understanding of the involved entities. Using ontologies here to express some simple form of semantics is very popular [28] and can be used as a basis for model checking and synthesis [29–31], practically illustrated in Ref. [32]. This approach is particularly scalable when combined with service orientation [33–35]. More general are approaches that generate full domain-specific tools like Metacase [36,37], GME [38,39], and CINCO [5]. This allows one to strongly enhance the productivity for the addressed application domain, as the more constraint the domain-specific language is the better can the development be controlled and more code can be generated as described already.

Cloud computing and other forms of *platform virtualization* provide stable user-level access to functionality. Cloud computing and other forms of platform virtualization provide stable user-level access to functionality. Here, various form are offered, ranging from infrastructure as a service (IaaS) over platform as a service (PaaS) to software as a service (SaaS), as in Ref. [40], or even "everything as a service" (EaaS).

Service orientation and *process technologies* offer easy interactive control at the user process level, where functionality provided by third party can be easily integrated [4,33,41,42]. This may even reach a point where such functionality can be dynamically integrated [43], be it as dynamically discovered service or as functionality that results from synthesis [30,32]. This concept cannot only be applied at the application level, but also at the metalevel, to integrate framework functionality cite [44].

Integrated product line management and quality assurance requires validation and monitoring to guarantee correctness criteria at design, orchestration, and runtime. Integrated product line management and quality assurance requires validation and monitoring to guarantee correctness criteria at design, orchestration, and runtime. Type checking here is the classical example, which has been so successful that it is taken for granted and is not further discussed today [45]. Model checking consistency of compliance rule can be regarded as a straightforward generalization of type checking [7,46]. Today, this is complemented by statistical model checking and runtime verification [47], to the extent that models of the underlying system are learned via testing or monitoring [48,49].

Rule-based control helps developers react flexibly to unforeseen situations and preempt time-consuming error detection via, for example, testing [28]. Model checking [29,50] has turned out to be particularly adequate here, but also the other methods mentioned in the previous item may be applied. Rule-based control, for example, to guarantee certain essential invariants (sometimes called Archimedean Points [51]) is the key to the effectiveness of domain-specific development frameworks.

Security and safety affect not only business-critical applications but also technologies for establishing a high level of fault tolerance, be it at the infrastructural, software, or human level. Here are numerous approaches to apply the aforementioned methods, and in some case, security is directly supported at the hardware level in a way that a potential user does not have to worry about it at all [49,52].

Major application domains, such as business, biology, or medicine, keep the focus on constant awareness of the primary issue – *user requirements*. Business process modeling is a prominent example here, with BPMN (www.bpmn.org/) [53–57] and there is a whole community working on scientific workflows (see the STTT special issue [58] and Refs [59,60]) in order to increase productivity.

The contributions of these individual research areas must be combined holistically to successfully control, adapt, and evolve systems composed of mature components.

2.4 Less Is More: The 80/20 Principle

Achieving a sufficient level of maturity across components, connections, interoperation, and evolution is a complex and highly interdisciplinary task that requires technological knowledge and deep domain modeling expertise. In this setting, standard investigation topics in IT such as complex architectural design and computational complexity are only of secondary and ancillary importance. The key to success is application of the "less is more" principle, using tradeoffs along some identified Pareto optimality criteria, with the goal of treating simple things simply, by a correspondingly simple design reminiscent of Lego blocks: primitive and well-defined blocks combine to reliably create complex solutions.

Developers will argue that there is no universal approach, but several domain-, purpose-, and profile-specific approaches within their scope are possible that capture the vastness of today's programming problems much more simply, reliably, and economically than most people think. This approach trades generality, which must be complex to accommodate diverse and sometimes antagonistic needs, for simplicity.

Companies such as Apple have successfully adopted simplicity as a fundamental design principle – for example, insights that simplify users' lives concern both the handling of their products and their maintenance and robustness. Users adopted these innovations enthusiastically and pay a premium price for this "IT simply works" experience. Similarly, Windows 7 attempts to overcome the tendency to provide cutting-edge and increasingly complicated technology in favor of a more user-driven philosophy. Combining extensive interviews and agile methods in its development accelerated this paradigm shift.

While promising beginnings, these initiatives fall short of making mature technologies that simply work on a widespread reality. We need extensive research and a clear engineering approach tailored to simplicity.

2.5 Simplicity: A Never Ending Challenge

While we are praising the maturity and achievements of car production, this industry is facing a number of severe threats:

- The increasing maturity of electrical cars, like the new TESLA, is an indication that the traditional combustion engine technology may approach the end of its life cycle.
- Autonomous driving moves the competitive edge of car manufacturing more and more into the IT domain, in order to realize reliable fleet coordination, and at the same time re-enforces the delegation principle: the "driver," master, and commander, is freed from the steering activity and largely becomes a passenger too.
- Technologies for autonomous driving will shift from image recognition and radar more in the direction of communicating systems where cars "talk" with each other, and with land posts, traffic signs, and so on, in an augmented and instrumented environment. This shift reminds of the very successful shift from generic image recognition to recognition via RFID in modern logistics.

Disruptive changes of this kind show that maturity is no guarantee for ongoing success. It is very important to sensitively check the developments and to see what is/becomes simple due to large-scale changes of the overall situation: the environment and infrastructure combined with behavioral changes. In the Waze case, this was the ubiquity of smart phones and the acceptance of their users to share information. Perhaps, in near future it will be the availability of "talking" traffic signs or, as important for a large-scale success of electric cars, a dense network of recharging stations. Such changes and their potential need to be closely observed and proactively adopted, if a company does not want to fall dramatically behind newcomers that leverage these large changes.

A proper preparation for the electric revolution in cars production is difficult and cannot be achieved just by trying to stay generically flexible: The architecture of a TESLA car so far foresees one electric engine for each wheel with respect to axis and does not require much of the sophisticated mechanics for transmission in today's four-wheel drive cars. Still, the preparation for autonomous driving seems to be just a perfect application of the simplicity approach: It is mainly concerned with communication, sensors, and control, and it could be handled in a modular fashion using mature components as soon as these exist. Traditional car manufacturing typically builds on specialized hardware with dedicated real-time runtime environments that would make such a change complicated. In contrast, TESLA integrates standard hardware and software, with a clear advantage for agile innovation steps. This is a good example of the pattern discussed in Ref. [2]: big players are often trapped in the area of their unique and formerly very successful competence, and unable to jump on the next level of technology. This is where newcomers like TESLA, free of technological and organizational legacy, can take over; this the better, the more mature the underlying IT infrastructure constructed. Providing this maturity is the goal of simplicity-driven system development.

2.6 IT Specifics

IT has a double role in simplicity-driven innovation support: as support for innovation in third party domains and as a driver of innovation of IT-related systems. In both roles, the potential of a slogan like "IT simply works" offers vast opportunities unrestrained by the physical limitations of classical engineering. In principle, every software component can be exchanged at any time, almost everywhere, without leaving any waste – an ideal situation for truly component-based engineering. Leveraging this potential would economically surpass the impact of producing new products based on leading-edge IT. Studies of product innovation (cite) show that technological leadership corresponds only to a relatively small fraction of market success and new market creation. Most often, technology-driven innovation accompanies risk caused by the new technologies themselves. Innovations rooted in the business purpose, such as the service to the user or customer, have a much higher chance of success because user-level advantages are easier to communicate in the market, especially if detached from technological risks.

2.7 Conclusions

Improved levels of maturity with their imposed simplicity can enable a new culture of innovation on the application side. Once we overcome the fear of change, true agility will guide the application experts, leading to new business models and new markets. History shows that with the availability of reliable cars, totally new forms of transportation and business arose, promoting freedom and trade. For the software industry, maturity could revolutionize the software mass construction and mass customization far beyond our experience in the automotive industry. This is especially likely to happen in cloud environments, whose customers have already embraced the commoditization of hardware and several layers of software. Theoretically, in software we can easily "change wheels while driving" and decompose and reassemble the IT equivalent of the entire car or bring new "passengers" aboard at the speed of light rather than being bound to specific hardware.

These are new dimensions of future development, both concerning markets and technology with implication colorfully laid out in Ref. [1]: We seem no longer to be bound by traditional laws of physics, the mindset of linear growth organizations.

Acknowledgments

This work was supported, in part, by Science Foundation Ireland grant 13/RC/2094 and cofunded under the European Regional Development Fund through the Southern & Eastern Regional Operational Programme to Lero – The Irish Software Research Centre (www.lero.ie).

References

1 S. Ismail, M. Malone, and Y. van Geest (2014) *Exponential Organizations: Why New Organizations are Ten Times Better, Faster, and Cheaper Than Yours (and What to Do About It)*, Diversion Publishing. ISBN 978–1626814233.

2 C. M. Christensen (1997) *The Innovator's Dilemma: When New Technologies Cause Great Firms to Fail*, Harvard Business Review Press, Boston, MA.

3 T. Margaria and B. Steffen (2012) Service-orientation: conquering complexity with XMDD. *Conquering Complexity*, Springer, pp. 217–236,

4 B. Steffen, T. Margaria, R. Nagel, S. Jörges, and C. Kubczak (2007) Model-driven development with the jABC. *Hardware and Software: Verification and Testing*, LNCS 4383, pp. 92–108.

5 S. Naujokat, M. Lybecait, D. Kopetzki, and B. Steffen (2017) CINCO: a simplicity-driven approach to full generation of domain-specific graphical modeling tools. *International Journal on Software Tools for Technology Transfer.* doi: https://doi.org/10.1007/s10009-017-0453-6.

6 T. Margaria and B. Steffen (2004) Lightweight coarse-grained coordination: a scalable system-level approach. *International Journal on Software Tools for Technology Transfer*, **5** (2–3), 107–123.

7 B. Steffen, T. Margaria, V. Braun, and N. Kalt (1997) Hierarchical service definition. *Annual Review of Communication*, **51**, 847–856.

8 D. Harel and B. Rumpe (2000) Modeling Languages: Syntax, Semantics and All That Stuff, Part I: The Basic Stuff. Technical report Weizmann Science Press of Israel. Available at http://www.ncstrl.org:8900/ncstrl/servlet/search?formname=detail\&id=oai%3Ancstrlh%3Aweizmann_il%3Ancstrl.weizmann_il%2F%2FMCS00-16.

9 T. Margaria (2007) Service is in the eyes of the beholder. *Computer*, **40** (11), 33–37.

10 V. Brullo (2016) Modellizzazione di processi per l'individuazione e il trattamento di disturbi specifici dell'apprendimento in bambini in età scolare e prescolare. Master thesis, Politecnico di Torino, Torino (Italy), July.

11 S. Boßelmann, A. Wickert, A.-L. Lamprecht, and T. Margaria (2017) Modeling directly executable processes for healthcare professionals with XMDD. *Service*

and Business Model Innovation in the Healthcare and Hospital Management, Springer.

12 S. Al-Areqi, A.-L. Lamprecht, and T. Margaria (2016) Constraints-driven automatic geospatial service composition: workflows for the analysis of sea-level rise impacts. *Proceedings of the Computational Science and Its Applications: ICCSA 2016*, LNCS, vol. 9788, pp. 134–150.

13 M. Wrobel, A. Bisaro, D. Reusser, and J. Kropp (2013) Novel approaches for web-based access to climate change adaptation information – mediation adaptation platform and ci:grasp-2. In Hřebíček, J., Schimak, G., Kubásek, M., Rizzoli, A. (eds.), *Environmental Software Systems: Fostering Information Sharing*. IFIP Advances in Information and Communication Technology, vol. 413, Springer, Berlin, pp. 489–499. http://dx.doi.org/10.1007/978-3-642-41151-9_45.

14 S. Kriewald (2013) srtmtools:SRTMtools (2013), r package version 2013-00.0.1.

15 M. Kilibarda (2013) Aplot GoogleMaps tutorial.

16 C. Sieckenius de Souza (2005) *The Semiotic Engineering of Human–Computer Interaction*, MIT Press, p. 312.

17 OASIS (2006) Service Component Architecture. Available at http://www.oasis-opencsa.org/book/export/html/21 (accessed March 19, 2018).

18 B. Steffen and T. Margaria (1999) METAFrame in practice: design of intelligent network services. In Olderog, E.-R. and Steffen, B. (eds.), *Correct System Design*, vol. 1710 Lecture Notes in Computer Science, Springer, pp. 390–415.

19 A.-L. Lamprecht, B. Steffen, and T. Margaria (2016) Scientific workflows with the jABC framework: a review after a decade in the field. *International Journal on Software Tools for Technology Transfer*, **18** (6), 1–23. doi: 10.1007/s10009-016-0427-0.

20 M. Merten and B. Steffen (2013) Simplicity driven application development. *Journal of Integrated Design and Process Science (SDPS)*, **17**, 9–23.

21 J. Neubauer, M. Frohme, B. Steffen, and T. Margaria (2014) Prototype-driven development of web applications with DyWA. *Proceedings of the 6th International Symposium on Leveraging Applications of Formal Methods, Verification and Validation, Part I, (ISoLA 2014)*, number 8802 in LNCS, Springer, pp. 56–72.

22 S. Boßelmann, M. Frohme, D. Kopetzki, M. Lybecait, S. Naujokat, J. Neubauer, D. Wirkner, P. Zweihoff, and B. Steffen (2016) DIME: a programming-less modeling environment for web applications. In Margaria T. and Steffen B. (eds.), *Leveraging Applications of Formal Methods, Verification and Validation: Discussion, Dissemination, Applications* – 7th International Symposium, ISoLA 2016, Imperial, Corfu, Greece, October 10–14, 2016, Proceedings, LNCS vol. 9953, Springer, pp. 809–832.

23 G. Airò Farulla, M. Indaco, A. Legay, and T. Margaria (2016) Model driven design of secure properties for vision-based applications: a case study.

Proceedings SAM: International Conference on Security and Management, Las Vegas, July 2016.

24 M. Eysholdt and H. Behrens (2010) Xtext: implement your language faster than the quick and dirty way. OOPSLA'10, pp. 307–309.

25 R.A. Brooker, I.R. MacCallum, D. Morris, and J.S. Rohl, (1963) The compiler-compiler. *Annual Review in Automatic Programming*, **3**, 229–275.

26 B. Steffen (1991) Data flow analysis as model checking. International Symposium on Theoretical Aspects of Computer Software, TACS '91, Sendai, Japan, LNCS N, 526, pp. 346–364,

27 B. Steffen (1993) Generating data flow analysis algorithms from modal specifications. *Science of Computer Programming*, **21** (2), 115–139.

28 S. Jörges, A.-L. Lamprecht, T. Margaria, I. Schaefer, and B. Steffen (2012) A constraint-based variability modeling framework. *International Journal on Software Tools for Technology Transfer*, **14** (5), 511–530.

29 E. M. Clarke, O. Grumberg, and D. A. Peled (1999) *Model Checking*, MIT Press.

30 B. Steffen, T. Margaria, and B. Freitag (1993) Module Configuration by Minimal Model Construction, Fakultät für Mathematik und Informatik, Universität Passau.

31 B. Steffen, T. Margaria, and A. Claßen. (1996) Heterogeneous analysis and verification for distributed systems. *SOFTWARE: Concepts and Tools*, vol. 17, Springer, pp. 13–25.

32 A.-L. Lamprecht, S. Naujokat, T. Margaria, and B. Steffen (2010) Synthesis-based loose programming. Proceeding of the 7th International Conference on the Quality of Information and Communications Technology, pp. 262–267.

33 T. Margaria, B. Steffen, and M. Reitenspiess (2005) Service-oriented design: the roots. *Proceedings of the 3rd International Conference on Service-Oriented Computing (ICSOC 2005)*, LNCS 3826, pp. 450–464.

34 M. N. Huhns and M. P. Singh (2005) Service-oriented computing: key concepts and principles. *IEEE Internet Computing*, **9**, 75–81.

35 J. Lee and G. Kotonya (2010) Combining service-orientation with product line engineering. *IEEE Software*, **27** (3), 35–41.

36 MetaCase (2015) http://www.metacase.com/ (accessed July 08, 2015).

37 S. Kelly and J.P. Tolvanen (2008) *Domain-Specific Modeling: Enabling Full Code Generation*, Wiley-IEEE Computer Society Press, Hoboken, NJ.

38 A. Ledeczi, M. Maroti, A. Bakay, G. Karsai, J. Garrett, C. Thomasson, G. Nordstrom, J. Sprinkle, and P. Volgyesi (2001) The generic modeling environment. Workshop on Intelligent Signal Processing (WISP 2001), 2001.

39 A. Lédeczi, M. Maróti, and P. Völgyesi (2003) The Generic Modeling Environment. Technical report, Institute for Software Integrated Systems, Vanderbilt University, Nashville, TN. Available at http://www.isis.vanderbilt.edu/sites/default/files/GMEReport.pdf

40 M. Bajohr and T. Margaria (2006) MaTRICS: a service-based management tool for remote intelligent configuration of systems. *Innovations in Systems and Software Engineering*, **2** (2), 99–111,

41 D. Messerschmitt and C. Szyperski (2003) *Software Ecosystem: Understanding an Indispensable Technology and Industry*, MIT Press.

42 T. Margaria and B. Steffen (2012) Service-Orientation: Conquering Complexity with XMDD. *Conquering Complexity*, Springer, London, pp. 217–236.

43 J. Neubauer (2014) Higher-order process engineering, 2014. Ph.D. thesis, Technische Universität Dortmund.

44 S. Naujokat, J. Neubauer, T. Margaria, and B. Steffen (2016) Meta-level reuse for mastering domain specialization. In Margaria T. and Steffen B. (eds.), *Leveraging Applications of Formal Methods, Verification and Validation: Discussion, Dissemination, Applications* – 7th International Symposium, ISoLA 2016, Imperial, Corfu, Greece, October 10–14, 2016, Proceedings, LNCS vol. 9953, Springer, pp. 218–237.

45 B. Steffen and T. Margaria (1996) Tools get Formal Methods into Practice. Position statement for the Working Group on Formal Methods ACM Workshop on Strategic Directions in Computing Research, Boston, MA, June 1996, in ACM Computing Surveys 28A(4), December. Available at http://www.acm.org/surveys/1996/SteffenTools/.

46 B. Steffen, T. Margaria, A. Claßen, and V. Braun (1996) Incremental formalization: a key to industrial success. *Software: Concept and Tools*, **17** (2), 78-95.

47 A. Legay, B. Delahaye, and S. Bensalem (2010) Statistical model checking: an overview. Runtime Verification, LNCS 6418, pp. 122–135,

48 H. Raffelt, M. Merten, B. Steffen, and T. Margaria (2009) Dynamic testing via automata learning. *International Journal on Software Tools for Technology Transfer*, **11** (4), 307–324.

49 S. Windmüller, J. Neubauer, B. Steffen, F. Howar, and O. Bauer (2013) Active continuous quality control. 16th International ACM SIGSOFT Symposium on Component-Based Software Engineering, pp. 111–120.

50 M. Müller-Olm, D. Schmidt, and B. Steffen (1999) Model-checking: a tutorial introduction. Proceedings of the 6th International Symposium on Static Analysis (SAS '99), pp. 330–354.

51 B. Steffen and S. Naujokat (2016) Archimedean points: the essence for mastering change. LNCS Transactions for Mastering Change, no. 1.

52 J. Neubauer, S. Windmüller, and B. Steffen (2014) Risk-based testing via active continuous quality control. *International Journal on Software Tools for Technology Transfer*, **16**, 569–591.

53 T. Benedict, N. Bilodeau, P. Vitkus, E. Powell, D. Morris, M. Scarsig, D. Lee, G. Field, T. Lohr, R. Saxena, M. Fuller, and J. Furlan (2013) *Guide to the Business Process Management Common Body Of Knowledge*, 3rd edition, CreateSpace Independent Publishing Platform.

54 R.K.L. Ko S.S.G. Lee, and E.W. Lee (2009) Business process management (BPM) standards: a survey. *Business Process Management Journal*, **15** (5), 744–791.

55 J. Cardoso and W. van der Aalst (eds.), (2009) *Handbook of Research on Business Process Modeling*. IGI Publishing.

56 T. Margaria and B. Steffen (2009) Business process modelling in the jABC: the one-thing-approach. *Handbook of Research on Business Process Modeling*, IGI Global.

57 T. Margaria and B. Steffen (2006) Service engineering: linking business and IT. *IEEE Computer*, **39** (10), 45–55.

58 A.-L. Lamprecht and K. J. Turner (2016) Introduction to the special issue on "scientific workflows." *International Journal on Software Tools for Technology Transfer*, 1–6. doi: 10.1007/s10009-016-0428-z.

59 A.-L. Lamprecht (2013) *User-Level Workflow Design: A Bioinformatics Perspective*, LNCS 8311, Springer.

60 A.-L. Lamprecht and T. Margaria (eds.) (2014) *Process Design for Natural Scientists: An Agile Model-Driven Approach*. CCIS 500, Springer.

3

Intercomponent Dependency Issues in Software Ecosystems

Maëlick Claes,[1] Alexandre Decan,[2] and Tom Mens[2]

[1]COMPLEXYS Research Institute, University of Mons, Belgium
[2]COMPLEXYS Research Institute, Software Engineering Lab, Faculty of Sciences, University of Mons, Mons, Belgium

3.1 Introduction

Software engineering research has traditionally focused on studying the development and evolution processes of individual software projects. The omnipresence of the Internet gave rise to a wide range of collaborative software development tools, especially in the open-source development scene. This has led to bigger and more geographically distributed communities of developers, and made it possible to develop more complex software systems. It also gave rise to so-called *software ecosystems*, that is, "collections of software products that have some given degree of symbiotic relationships" [1].

Analyzing software projects from such an ecosystemic perspective can reveal new insights into why and how they evolve. Projects that are part of an ecosystem tend to be interdependent, and developers contributing to this ecosystem may be involved in multiple projects and share implicit or explicit knowledge across these projects. Hence, the evolution of a project may be affected to a certain degree by the changes in connected projects. This implies that project evolution should be studied in the context of its surrounding ecosystem. This view is shared by Lungu [2], who defined a software ecosystem as "a set of software projects that are developed and evolve together in the same environment."

One of the main reasons for dependencies between components in an ecosystem is software reuse, a basic principle of software engineering [3]. Software components often rely on (i.e., reuse) the functionality offered by other components (e.g., libraries), rather than reimplementing the same functionality. While this tends to reduce the effort from the point of view of a single component, it increases the overall complexity of the ecosystem through the need to manage

Software Technology: 10 Years of Innovation in IEEE Computer, First Edition.
Edited by Mike Hinchey.
© 2018 the IEEE Computer Society, Inc. Published 2018 by John Wiley & Sons, Inc.

these dependencies. This complexity can become the cause of many maintainability issues and failures in component-based software ecosystems [4]. For this reason, it is important to study dependency-related issues and to provide tools that would allow ecosystem maintainers to deal with these issues.

This chapter therefore discusses different types of maintenance issues related to component-based software ecosystems and how these issues impact maintainers and users of the ecosystem. We illustrate how these issues have been studied on two well-known *package-based* software ecosystems, Debian and R, both containing thousands of packages.

We show how analyzing these issues from the ecosystem point of view may help the ecosystem's maintainers to detect these issues better. This will allow them to decide more easily if and when the observed issues become problematic and to take decisions to fix the issue or prevent it from reappearing in the future.

3.2 Problem Overview

This section presents different types of issues related to intercomponent dependencies that can happen during the development and evolution of components of a software ecosystem. We provide a common vocabulary of the intercomponent dependency relationships we are interested in, discuss the possible problems caused by such interdependencies, and provide a summary of the state of the art of proposed solutions.

3.2.1 Terminology

Several researchers have proposed general models to study intercomponent dependencies [5–7]. Based on these models, this chapter uses the following vocabulary to describe the different types of intercomponent relationships that are relevant.

Components act as the basic software unit that can be added, removed, or upgraded in the software system. They provide the right level of granularity at which a user can manipulate available software. Components are typically organized in coherent collections called distributions, repositories, or archives. The set of components of a distribution that are actually used by a particular user is called her component status. To modify the component status, for example, by upgrading existing components or installing new ones, the user typically relies on a tool that is called the component manager. This manager uses component metadata in order to derive the context in which components may or may not be used. Examples of such metadata are component dependencies and conflicts. Component dependencies represent positive requirements (a component needs to be present for the proper functioning of another component), while component conflicts represent negative

(a)

```
Package: xul-ext-adblock-plus
Description: Advertisement blocking extension
             for web browsers
Source: adblock-plus
Version: 2.1-1+deb7u1
Replaces: adblock-plus (<< 1.1.1-2)
Provides: adblock-plus, iceape-adblock-plus,
    icedove-adblock-plus, iceweasel-adblock-plus
Depends: iceweasel (>= 8.0) | icedove (>= 8.0)
                             | iceape (>= 2.5)
Enhances: iceape, icedove, iceweasel
Conflicts: mozilla-firefox-adblock
```

(b)

```
Package: SciViews
Title: SciViews GUI API - Main package
Imports: ellipse
Depends: R (>= 2.6.0), stats,
         grDevices, graphics, MASS
Enhances: base
Version: 0.9-5
```

Figure 3.1 Two concrete examples of component metadata. (a) The Debian package `xul-ext-adblock-plus`. (b) The R package `SciViews`.

requirements (e.g., certain components or component versions cannot be used in combination). One of the most generic ways to express dependencies (although not supported by every component manager) is by means of a conjunction of disjunctions, allowing a choice of which component can satisfy a dependency.

Figure 3.1 provides a concrete example of how component dependencies and conflicts can be specified for packages in the Debian and R ecosystems, respectively. The Debian package `xul-ext-adblock-plus` depends on one of the three packages: `iceweasel`, `icedove`, or `iceape`. This is expressed by a disjunction (vertical bar |) of packages. The package conflicts with `mozilla-firefox-adblock`. The R package `SciViews` depends on version 2.6 of the R language as well as on packages `stats`, `grDevices`, `graphics`, and `MASS`. The notion of conflicts and the ability to express disjunctions of dependencies are not explicitly supported by R package metadata.

Some ecosystems allow components to depend on, or conflict with, an abstract component. In that case, the dependency (or conflict) is satisfied (or violated) by any component that provides features of that abstract component. For example, in Figure 3.1 the Debian package `xul-ext-adblock-plus` provides the features of the following abstract packages: `adblock-plus`, `iceape-adblock-plus`, `icedove-adblock-plus`, `iceweasel-adblock-plus`. Any dependency on `adblock-plus` would be satisfied if `xul-ext-adblock-plus`, or any other package providing `adblock-plus`, were installed.

Dependencies and conflicts can be restricted to specific versions of the target component. This is usually represented by a constraint on the version number. For example, in Figure 3.1 Debian package `xul-ext-adblock-plus` requires version 8.0 or higher of `iceweasel`. R package metadata does not support depending on specific package versions.

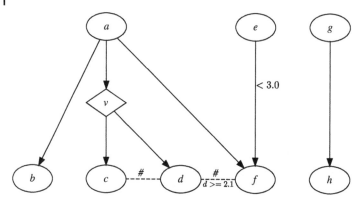

Figure 3.2 Example of a component dependency graph.

Figure 3.2 provides an example of a component graph showing the afore-mentioned relationships. Components are visualized by ellipses and abstract components by diamonds. Edges represent component dependencies and dashed lines represent component conflicts. Edge labels depict constraints on the component version. For example, abstract component v depends on two components c and d that are in mutual conflict. Component d is also in conflict with version 2.1 or superior of component f. Component e depends on a version lower than 3.0 of component f.

3.2.2 Identifying and Retrieving Dependency Information

Particular types of software ecosystems where dependencies play a central role are *package-based* ecosystems. Such ecosystems generally consist of collections of software projects bundled in packages that need to rely on other packages in order to function correctly. Well-known examples of such package-based ecosystems are Debian and R, both containing thousands of packages. LaBelle and Wallingford [8] showed that the package dependency graphs for the open-source Debian and FreeBSD distributions form a complex network with small-world and scale-free properties.

Extensive research has been conducted on two package-based ecosystems: Debian [5,9–16] and R [17–19]. Other software ecosystems make use of components comparable to packages such as plug-ins (e.g., the Eclipse software development environment [20]), modules (e.g., the NetBeans software development environment), libraries [21], extensions and add-ons (e.g. the Firefox web browser), and mobile app stores [22,23].

In *package-based* ecosystems, each package is generally required to provide *metadata* specifying package dependencies. Two examples of this were given in Figure 3.1. Sometimes, however, the metadata can be incomplete or inconsistent, or even entirely lacking. In particular, constraints on dependency versions are often missing or inaccurate, because the component metadata is not always updated if the source code of components is being modified. In those cases, it may still be possible to retrieve the information using automated configuration tools such as make, cmake, autoconf, ant, and maven.

Another way to retrieve the necessary metadata is through *static code analysis*. The source code of a software project usually contains the necessary information about which library or module is imported and which part of it is being used. A static analyzer can use this information to obtain all dependencies across components at the ecosystem level. This solution does have its limits however, since there is no guarantee that dependencies discovered in the source code will actually be used at runtime. For this, dynamic code analysis would be required. This is particularly so for dynamically typed languages where it is much harder to derive the call dependencies statically.

In order to facilitate retrieval of component dependencies, Lungu et al. [7] proposed *Ecco*, a framework to generically represent dependencies between software projects. It models an ecosystem as a set of projects containing entities, which are classes or methods. Entities can be of type provided, called or required. Lungu et al. used *Ecco* to compare different strategies to extract dependencies statically from dynamically typed Smalltalk source code. While some methods are more efficient than others, none is able to successfully recover the list of all existing dependencies.

As explained by Abate et al. [10], a direct dependency graph obtained by identifying the list of components required by each component of the ecosystem is not enough to characterize package interactions because those other components may have dependencies themselves. Because of this, they introduced the notion of strong dependencies of a component, which are the components that are always required, directly or indirectly, in order to successfully use the component depending on them. On top of this, they introduced a measure of component sensitivity in order to determine, by means of the strong dependency graph, how much a change to a component may impact the ecosystem. In the context of Debian for example, they noticed that the most extreme cases of sensitive packages would go unnoticed when relying solely on direct dependencies. Maintainers can use a sensitivity metric based on strong to decide whether or not a component should be upgraded or removed.

3.2.3 Satisfying Dependencies and Conflicts

Satisfying Dependency Constraints
Once the dependencies of each component of an ecosystem have been identified, one needs to verify if they can be satisfied. The presence of dependency constraints can make some dependencies unsatisfiable. Being unable to satisfy

dependencies will prevent a user from using a component, which would be highly undesirable. Based on the strong dependency graph, tools like `dis-tcheck` have been developed to detect those components that cannot satisfy their dependencies. Such tools have been used successfully in different ecosystems such as Debian, OPAM, and Drupal and have been shown to be useful to developers [24].

Satisfying Component Coinstallability
Conflicts may prevent a component to be used in a given context. If a component is in conflict with one of its strong dependencies, it will be unusable. When a conflict is declared (directly or indirectly) between two components, all components that strongly depend on both of them will not be able to work either. In a system where only one version of a component can be used at the same time, when two components need to depend (directly or indirectly) on two different versions of the same component, they will be unusable together. This problem is known for package-based ecosystems (and more particularly Debian) as the problem of coinstallability [11,13–15]. It can be generalized as the ability for two components to be used together.

We refer to strong conflicts as all components that are known to be always incompatible together. Just like the strong dependency graph can be used to satisfy dependency constraints, a strong conflict graph can be used to detect coinstallability problems between components. Such a graph enables to identify the most problematic components of an ecosystem.

It is important to stress that components may be in strong conflict "by design": They cannot be installed together because they were never meant to work together. If this is the case, developers and users can be made aware of this impossibility by documenting such "known" conflicts explicitly in the component metadata. An example of this is shown in Figure 3.1, where package `xul-ext-adblock-plus` is declared to be in direct conflict with `mozilla-firefox-adblock`.

In addition to such known conflicts, new and unexpected indirect strong conflicts may arise during component evolution without the maintainers being aware of them. These conflicts require specific tool support to cope with them, as will be explained in Section 3.3.

3.2.4 Component Upgrade

When developing software components, errors may be inadvertently introduced when changes occur in the software components one depends upon. When changes to a component cause the software to fail, it puts a heavy burden on the maintainers of the component that depend on this failing component. This is especially true in a large ecosystem where thousands of components are interdependent, and a single failure may affect a large fraction of the ecosystem.

Many researchers have studied the problem of component upgrades. Nagappan and Ball [25] effectively showed that software dependency metrics could be used to predict post-release bugs. Robbes et al. [26] studied the ripple effect of API method deprecation and revealed that API changes can have a large impact on the system and remain undetected for a long time after the initial change. Hora et al. [27] also studied the effects of API method deprecation and proposed to implement rules in static analysis tools to help developers adapt more quickly to a new API. McDonnell et al. [28] studied the evolution of APIs in the Android ecosystem. They found that while more popular APIs have a fast release cycle, they tend to be less stable and require more time to get adopted. Bavota et al. [29] studied the evolution of dependencies between Apache software projects and found that developers were reluctant to upgrade the version of the software they depend upon. In Ref. [4] they highlighted that dependencies have an exponential growth and must be taken care of by developers.

All these studies indicate that component upgrade is often problematic and that contemporary tools provide insufficient support to cope with them. One of the solutions to detect errors during the development process is continuous integration [30]. However, while continuous integration can help to detect changes that break the system, it does not provide information on which components can be safely upgraded. Developers would benefit from recommender tools specifically designed to help them making such decisions.

In the context of *package-based* ecosystems, Di Cosmo et al. [5] highlighted peculiarities of package upgrades and discussed that current techniques are not sufficient to overcome failures. They proposed solutions to this problem [9,12] and built a tool called `comigrate` to efficiently identify sets of components that can be upgraded without causing failures [16]. Similarly, Abate et al. [31] proposed a proof-of-concept package manager designed to allow the use of difference dependency solvers as plug-ins in order to better cope with component upgrade issues.

3.2.5 Inter-Project Cloning

One solution to avoid problems due to component dependencies would be to reuse code through copy–paste rather than depending on it. Indeed, some ecosystems consisting of distributed software for a specific platform do not allow components to depend one upon another. For example, the component manager for Android mobile apps only allows for apps to depend on the core Android platform, forcing app developers to include third-party libraries inside their own package. Mojica et al. [23] showed that this gives rise to very frequent code reuse across mobile apps.

Similarly, in ecosystems with intercomponent dependencies, developers may decide to reimplement (part of) a component they need in order to avoid depending on it. In some cases, the effort needed to reimplement the component may be smaller than if developers have to fix errors caused by dependency changes. Especially for open-source software, the development time can be significantly reduced by directly cloning the existing code as long as it does not violate software licenses.

In the context of a single software projects, the presence of software clones has been extensively studied and have shown to be beneficial or detrimental to software maintenance [32–35]. While there have been recent studies on inter-project cloning [36,37], insight on the causes and implications of inter-project software clones is still lacking. Although using cloning instead of a component manager to manage dependencies may help to avoid dependency upgrade problems from a user point of view, it forces each developer to choose which version of all their strong dependencies to include in their own component.

Additionally, we previously studied functions that were duplicated between different *CRAN* packages [38] and showed that most clones could not have been avoided by relying upon dependencies. While there is still a nonnegligible amount of cloned functions that could be removed, further work is required to understand why these functions have been cloned.

3.3 First Case Study: Debian

This section presents some of the intercomponent dependency issues raised in the previous section, for the concrete case of the Debian package-based ecosystem.

3.3.1 Overview of Debian

Debian is an open-source package distribution of the GNU/Linux operating system. Debian aims at providing an operating system that is as stable as possible. It uses a software package management system with a strict policy to achieve these goals (see www.debian.org/doc/debian-policy). Having existed for more than two decades, Debian is one of the oldest Linux distributions that is still maintained today. It contains several tens of thousands of packages, and its community spans over a thousand distinct developers. The development process of Debian is organized around three main package distributions: stable, testing, and unstable.

stable corresponds to the latest official production distribution, and only contains stable, well-tested packages. Table 3.1 summarizes the characteristics of the different releases of the stable distributions.

testing contains package versions that should be considered for inclusion in the next stable Debian release. A stable release is made by *freezing* the testing release for a few months to fix bugs and to remove packages containing too many bugs.

Table 3.1 Stable releases of Debian since 2005.

Version	Name	Freeze date	Release date	No. of packages
3.1	sarge	N/A	June 6, 2005	~15 K
4.0	etch	N/A	April 8, 2007	~18 K
5.0	lenny	July 27, 2008	February 15, 2009	~23 K
6.0	squeeze	August 6, 2010	February 6, 2011	~28 K
7.0	wheezy	June 30, 2012	March 4, 2013	~36 K
8.0	jessy	November 5, 2014	April 26, 2015	~ 43 K

unstable is a rolling release distribution containing packages that are not thoroughly tested and that may still suffer from stability and security problems. These releases contain the most recent packages but also the most unstable ones.

A major problem when analyzing strong package conflicts is the sheer size of the package dependency graph: There are literally thousands of different packages with implicit or explicit dependencies to many other packages. Vouillon and Di Cosmo [39] addressed this problem by proposing an algorithm and theoretical framework to compress such a dependency graph to a much smaller *coinstallability kernel* with a simpler structure but equivalent coinstall-ability properties. Packages are bundled together into an equivalence class if they do not have a strong conflict with one another, while the collection of other packages with which they have strong conflicts is the same.

As an example, the Debian i386 testing distribution on January 1, 2014 contained >38 K packages, >181 K dependencies, 1490 declared conflicts, and >49 K strong conflicts. The coinstallability kernel for the same data resulted in 994 equivalence classes and 4336 incompatibilities between these equivalence classes. The coinst tool (coinst.irill.org) was developed specifically for extracting and visualizing such coinstallability kernels.

Based on this tool and related research advances on strong dependency and strong conflict analysis [5,9–15], other tools have been created to determine appropriate solutions to package coinstallation problems; for example, comi-grate (coinst.irill.org/comigrate), coinst-upgrade, distcheck, and the dose tools for Debian Quality Assurance (qa.debian.org/dose/). These tools are actively being used by the Debian community. These solutions, however, do not take into account the evolution over time of strong conflicts.

In Ref. [40], we used coinst to study the evolution of strong conflicts on a period of 10 years for the Debian i386 testing and stable distributions. We aimed to determine to which extent these historical data provide additional

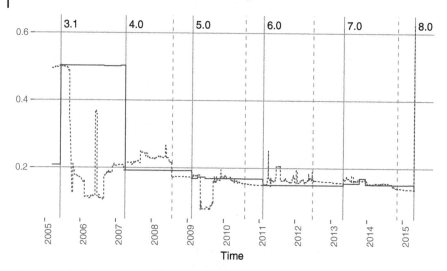

Figure 3.3 Ratio of strong conflicting packages in snapshots of Debian's `testing` distribution (dotted line) and `stable` distribution (solid line). The vertical lines correspond to the freeze date (dashed lines) and release date (straight lines) of each major `stable` release.

information to understand and predict how strong conflicts evolve over time and to improve support for addressing package coinstallation problems.

Figure 3.3 shows the evolution over time of the ratio of strong conflicting packages in a snapshot over all packages in that snapshot. We observe that starting from 2007 and with only a few exceptions, the ratio of the `testing` distribution remains between 15 and 25%. We also observe a slight decrease over time, despite the fact that the number of packages increases with each new major release. This shows that the Debian community actively strives to keep strong conflicts at a minimum. The `stable` distribution follows a comparable evolutionary behavior, combined with the presence of "plateaus" corresponding to different public releases of Debian. Finally, the `testing` distribution reveals a number of "trend breaks," that is, sudden increases in the number or ratio of strong conflicts that appear suddenly and disappear after some time.

3.3.2 Aggregate Analysis of Strong Conflicts

Some of the conflicts are present in the distribution "by design," but others may be harmful. Distinguishing the good from the bad ones is a complex task that has traditionally required a lot of manual investigation, with many issues going unnoticed for quite an extensive amount of time. A natural approach to identify potentially problematic packages is to look for trend breaks in the evolution of the absolute or relative number of strong conflicting packages in the distribution. Sudden increases hint that some problematic package(s) may have appeared, and sudden decreases indicate that some problematic package(s) have been fixed. Many such discontinuities are clearly visible in Figure 3.3, with peaks ranging from a few hundreds to over 4000 strong conflicts.

Using the `coinst-upgrade` tool [15] that identifies the root causes for the changes in conflicts between two repositories, we retrieved all trend breaks that added at least 500 strong conflicts. We manually inspected each trend break, and checked it against the information available from the Debian project, to determine the nature of the problematic packages and the degree of seriousness of the problem, and paired the events where each problematic package was first introduced and then removed.

We observed that a few trend breaks were *dayflies* that were fixed the day after their introduction, while several took a few weeks, three took hundreds of days to fix, two have been fixed in several phases, and two still remain unfixed today. Most of these issues would have been captured by the `comigrate` tool [16] if it would have been available at that time, and one issue could have been anticipated using the `challenged` [41] tool.

Interestingly, a few relevant trend breaks *are not identifiable by any of the existing tools*, while an inspection of the aggregate analysis (as presented here) would have drawn attention to them. This illustrates that there is a clear opportunity for improving current automated tool support.

3.3.3 Package-Level Analysis of Strong Conflicts

Once a trend break has been spotted, one still needs to identify manually what are the packages in the snapshot that are the root causes of the trend break. Some of these problematic packages are shown in boldface in Table 3.2.

This process can be automated by studying the characteristics of each package related to strong conflicts by resorting to three simple metrics:

- The *minimum* number of strong conflicts.
- The *maximum* number of strong conflicts.
- The number of *conflicting days over mean*, that is, the number of days the package has more strong conflicts than $\dfrac{\text{maximum} + \text{minimum}}{2}$.

These metrics allow one to focus on packages with a significant amount of strong conflicts, while at the same time ignoring those packages that have such a large number of conflicts only for a short time period. The latter case usually corresponds to transient problems, like the *dayflies* that we were able to identify in the previous aggregate analysis.

After ordering the packages with respect to the above three metrics, we obtain a list of potentially problematic packages, of which the top 10 are presented in

Table 3.2 Top 10 of potentially problematic packages identified by three simple metrics.

Potentially problematic package	Minimum conflicts	Maximum conflicts	Conflicting days over mean
libgdk-pixbuf 2.0-0	0	675	1349
libgdk-pixbuf 2.0-dev	0	3320	915
liboss4-salsa-asound 2	2963	3252	891
liboss-salsa-asound 2	1741	2664	862
klogd	3	502	709
sysklogd	3	719	639
ppmtofb	0	719	639
selinux-policy-default	0	719	633
aide	0	719	633
libpam-umask	0	720	546

Packages shown in boldface were manually identified as root causes of trend breaks during the aggregate analysis.

Table 3.2. Interestingly, most of the packages that we manually identified as root causes during the aggregate analysis (shown in boldface) are also revealed by the metrics, with the important advantage that the metrics-based approach can be automated and requires much less manual inspection.

3.4 Second Case Study: The R Ecosystem

3.4.1 Overview of R

There are many popular languages, tools, and environments for statistical computing. On the commercial side, among the most popular ones are SAS, SPSS, SPSS, Statistica, Stata, and Excel. On the open-source side, the R language and its accompanying software environment for statistical computing (www.r-project.org) are undeniably a very strong competitor, regardless of how popularity is being measured [42].

R forms a true *software ecosystem* through its package management system that offers an easy way to install third-party code and data sets alongside tests, documentation, and examples. The main R distribution installs a few *base* packages and *recommended* packages. The exact number of installed packages depends on the chosen version of R. (For R 3.2.2, there are 16 *base* packages and 15 *recommended* packages.) In addition to these main R packages, thousands of additional packages are developed and distributed through different repositories.

Precompiled binary distributions of the R environment can be downloaded from the Comprehensive R Archive Network (*CRAN*, see cran.r-project.org). *CRAN* constitutes the official R repository, containing the broadest collection of R packages. It aims at providing stable packages compatible with the latest version of R. Quality is ensured by forcing package maintainers to follow a rather strict policy. All *CRAN* packages are tested daily using the command-line tool R CMD check, which automatically checks all packages for common problems. The check is composed of over 50 individual checks carried out on different operating systems. It includes tests for the package structure, the metadata, the documentation, the data, the code, and so on. For packages that fail the check, their maintainer is asked to resolve the problems before the next major R release. If this is not done, problematic packages are archived, making it impossible to install them automatically, as they will no longer be included in *CRAN* until a new version is released that resolves the problems. However, it remains possible to install such archived packages manually.

Every R package needs to specify in its *DESCRIPTION* file the packages it depends upon (see Figure 3.1 for an example). We consider as dependencies the packages that are listed in the *Depends* and *Imports* fields of the *DESCRIPTION* file, as these are the ones that are required to install and load a package.

We have conducted multiple studies on the R ecosystem, focused on problems related to intercomponent dependencies mentioned in Section 3.2 [17,38,43–45]. We summarize our main findings in the following sections. First, we present the main repositories containing R packages and the difficulties encountered when trying to manage dependencies across these different repositories. Next, focusing on the *CRAN* repository, we show how a part of package maintenance effort needs to be dedicated to fixing errors caused by dependency upgrades. Finally, we study the presence of identical cross-package clones in *CRAN* packages and investigate their reason of existence.

3.4.2 R Package Repositories

Besides *CRAN*, R packages can also be stored on, and downloaded from, other repositories such as *Bioconductor* (bioconductor.org), *R-Forge* (r-forge.r-project.org), and several smaller repositories such as *Omegahat* and *RForge*. An increasing number of R packages can also be found on "general-purpose" web-based version control repositories such as *GitHub*, a web platform for Git version control repositories [45]. Table 3.3 provides a brief comparison of the four of the biggest R package repositories. It also provides an indication of the size of each repository, expressed in terms of the number of provided R packages.

Bioconductor focuses on software packages and data sets dedicated to bioinformatics. *Bioconductor* packages are not installed by default: Users must configure their R installation with a *Bioconductor* mirror. As in *CRAN*,

Table 3.3 Characteristics of considered R package repositories.

Repository	Year	No. of R packages (date)	Role	Package versions
CRAN	1997	6411 (March 19, 2015)	Distribution	Stable releases
BioConductor	2001	997 (March 19, 2015)	Distribution only	Stable releases
R-Forge	2006	1883 (March 18, 2015)	Mainly development	SVN version control
GitHub	2008	5150 (February 17, 2015)	Mainly development	Git version control

packages that fail the daily check will be dropped from the next release of *Bioconductor*. *R-Forge* is a software development forge specialized at hosting R code. Its main target is to provide a central platform for the development of R packages, offering SVN repositories, daily built and checked packages, bug tracking, and so on. *GitHub* is becoming increasingly popular for R package development. Both *R-Forge* and *GitHub* differ from *CRAN* and *Bioconductor* because they do not only *distribute* R packages but also facilitate the *development* of R packages, thanks to their integrated version control system.

Support for multiple repositories is built deeply into R. For example, the R function `install.packages` can take the source repository as an optional argument, or can be used to install older versions of a given package. While this works well for repositories such as *CRAN* and *Bioconductor*, it does not for development forges such as *GitHub* due to the lack of central index of all packages.

One of the easiest ways to install packages hosted on forges is by using the `devtools` package. It provides various functions to download and install a package from different sources. For example, the function `install_github` allows the installation of R packages directly from *GitHub*, while the function `install_svn` allows the installation from an SVN repository (such as the one used by *R-Forge*). By default, the latest package version will be installed, but optional parameters can be used to install a specific version. As such, there is theoretically no longer a strict need to rely on package distributions. Therefore, development forges must be considered an important and integral part of the R package ecosystem.

Figure 3.4 shows the overlap of R packages on different distributions and development forges. Between *Bioconductor* and the other package repositories, the overlap is very limited. A negligible amount of *Bioconductor* packages is present on *CRAN* or *R-Forge*. This can be explained by the highly specialized nature of *Bioconductor* (focused on bioinformatics) compared to the other package repositories.

(a)

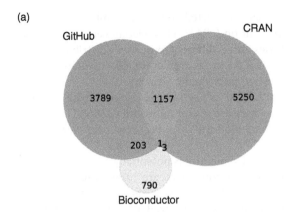

(b)

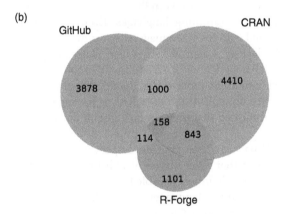

(c)

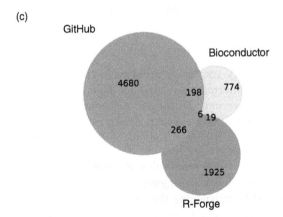

Figure 3.4 Number of R packages belonging to GitHub, CRAN, Bioconductor, and R-Forge (counted during the first trimester of 2015).

Around 18% of the *CRAN* packages are hosted on *GitHub*, while 22.5% of all R packages on *GitHub* are also present on *CRAN*. This overlap can be explained by the fact that both repositories serve different purposes (distribution and development, respectively). *Many* R packages are developed on *GitHub*, while stable releases of these packages are published on *CRAN*.

We observe that *R-Forge* has 12.3% of its packages in common with *GitHub*, while as much as 45.2% of its packages are in common with *CRAN*. This shows that *R-Forge* serves as a development platform for *some* of the packages that get distributed through *CRAN*.

While the usage of `devtools` and similar tools potentially provides a way to use forges as a rolling release distribution, there are limitations to such a solution. First, there might be no central listing of packages available on these forges. For *R-Forge* the problem could easily be solved as it contains relatively few SVN repositories. *GitHub*, however, contains millions of Git repositories filled with content from various programming languages. Even if we limit *GitHub* repositories to those tagged with the R language, the vast majority does not contain an R package. The lack of a central listing of packages prevents `devtools` to automatically install dependencies. An additional problem is that the same package can be hosted in multiple repositories, making the problem of dependency resolution even more difficult. Interviews with R package maintainers active on GitHub have confirmed that they are facing such problems in practice [46].

To address these problems, R package users and developers would benefit from a package installation manager that relies on a central listing of available packages on different repositories. It is definitely feasible to achieve such a tool, since popular package managers for other languages such as JavaScript (e.g., `bower` and `npm`) and Python (e.g., `pip`) also offer a central listing of packages, facilitating their distribution through several repositories including *GitHub*.

3.4.3 Interrepository Dependencies

How can we quantify the dependency resolution problem in the R package ecosystem by analyzing the extent of interrepository package dependencies? We previously observed that an R package might belong to different repositories (e.g., *GitHub* may store the development version, while *CRAN* may contain the stable release version of the package). Figure 3.5 shows the interrepository package dependencies. An edge $A \xrightarrow{x\%} B$ means that x% of the packages in repository A have a *primary* dependency belonging to repository B. This *primary* dependency is computed by privileging the distributed version of a package over its development version. For example, if package on *GitHub* depends on package belonging to both *CRAN* and *GitHub*, it will be counted as a primary dependency from *GitHub* to *CRAN*.

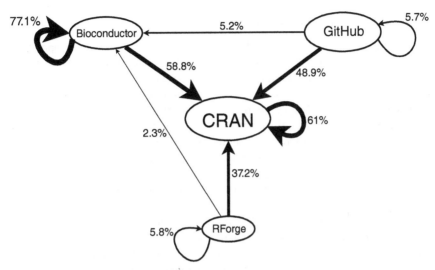

Figure 3.5 Percentage of packages per repository that depend on at least one package from another repository. The font size of the repository name is proportional to the number of packages it hosts.

We observed that *CRAN* is self-contained: Only 61% of *CRAN* packages have dependencies, and all those dependencies are satisfied by *CRAN* because this is imposed by *CRAN*'s daily R CMD check. *Bioconductor* depends primarily on itself and on *CRAN*: 58.8% of all *Bioconductor* packages depends on *CRAN* packages, while 77.1% of all *Bioconductor* packages depends on other *Bioconductor* packages. The situation for *GitHub* and *R-Forge* is very different: 48.9% of *GitHub* packages and 37.2% of *R-Forge* packages depend on a package from *CRAN*. This represents 87.1% (with respect to 86.4%) of all the dependencies in *GitHub* (with respect to *R-Forge*). Interestingly, the number of *GitHub* and *R-Forge* R packages having an intrarepository dependency is very low (less than 6%).

These observations strongly suggests that *CRAN* is at the center of the ecosystem and that it is nearly impossible to install packages from *GitHub*, *Bioconductor*, or *R-Forge* without relying on *CRAN* for the package dependencies. Because of *CRAN*'s central position, its longevity, and its important size in terms of packages, one might choose to distribute a new package only on *CRAN* and to depend only on *CRAN* packages.

On the other hand, we observed that more and more R packages are being developed and distributed on *GitHub* [45]. Combined with the problems that R package maintainers are facing [46], we believe that interrepository dependencies will become a major concern for the R community. A multirepository package dependency manager could address this.

3.4.4 Intrarepository Dependencies

Because *CRAN* is self-contained, it does not suffer from interrepository dependency problems. This does not mean, however, that *CRAN* does not suffer from package dependency upgrades. Interrepository package dependency upgrades are the cause of many errors, and therefore put a heavy burden on package maintainers. Despite the presence of continuous integration processes at the repository level (e.g., the R CMD check tool in *CRAN* or *Bioconductor*), a lot of maintenance effort remains required to deal with such errors.

For *CRAN* packages, the R CMD check is run on every package for different *flavors* of R. Each flavor corresponds to a combination of the operating system, compiler, and R version being used. While the check results can vary a lot depending on the chosen flavor, we concentrate our next analyses on the flavor based on stable releases of R for *Debian*. This choice of flavor avoids the noise introduced by portability issues or changes occurring in R itself. This flavor is among the best supported, it also contains the most *CRAN* packages and it exhibits a less error-prone environment (see Figure 3.6).

From September 3, 2013 to September 3, 2015, we took a daily snapshot of the results of the R CMD check (see cran.r-project.org/web/checks/). The snapshots associate with each *CRAN* package its reported status, which is either OK, NOTE, WARNING, or ERROR. There were 4930 available packages on *CRAN* at the beginning of this period, and 7235 at the end of this period. During the whole period, 19,517 pairs package-version were available for a total of 7820 different packages. We were only interested in the ERROR status because it can provoke package archival. Each time we found an ERROR, we identified the reason of this change among the following ones: because the package itself gets upgraded (PU); because of a strong dependency upgrade (DU); or due to other external factors (EF). In total, we identified 1320 occurrences of a status change

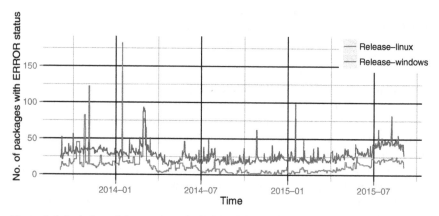

Figure 3.6 Evolution of the number of CRAN packages with ERROR status for two different flavors of the R CMD check.

Table 3.4 Identified reasons for status changes to and from ERROR.

Status changes	Number	Package update (PU)	Strong dependency upgrade (DU)	External factor (EF)
From . . . to ERROR	1310	30 (2.3%)	541 (41.3%)	739 (56.4%)
From ERROR to . . .	1288	346 (26.85%)	293 (22.75%)	649 (50.4%)

to ERROR, and 1288 occurrences of a status change from ERROR back to some other status. The results are summarized in Table 3.4.

We observe that most ERRORs are introduced (56.4%) and fixed (50.4%) without a version update from the package (PU) or an upgrade of one of its dependencies (DU). Looking at the ERRORs that were caused by a package update to a new version, we see that while very few packages (2.3%) failed when a new version of the package itself was released, more ERRORs were removed by the update of a package version (26.85%) than by the upgrade of a strong dependency (22.75%).

Of the 1288 ERRORs that were removed, 26 were introduced before we started extracting data. Only for the remaining 1262 ERRORs we could identify the cause of both their introduction and disappearance. We observed that most (45.7%) of the 514 ERRORs that were introduced by a DU were removed by another DU, while 32.7% disappeared because of a PU. We also observed that among the 334 ERRORs fixed by a PU, 50.3% were introduced by a DU and 44.9% by an EF. This is, more than half of the errors fixed by the package maintainers were introduced by changes in their package dependencies.

From the above, we can conclude that breaking changes in packages force dependent packages to be updated. This can require an important maintenance effort. A way to reduce this effort would be to allow package maintainers to specify the required versions of their dependencies. This is currently not possible because the *CRAN* policy imposes package maintainers to support the latest available version of each dependency. The R community would benefit from allowing packages to depend on different versions of other packages. It would give them the time needed to perform appropriate dependency upgrades without impacting the *validity* of other packages, and without impacting end users. The community could also benefit from specific tools that predict in advance what could become broken if a specific dependency were to be upgraded in incompatible ways.

3.5 Conclusion

This chapter presented different issues that are commonly encountered in evolving software ecosystems involving a large number of software components and interdependencies. We provided a common vocabulary inspired by the state of the art in this research domain. We discussed how each issue impacts component developers and presented solutions have been proposed in the research literature. We illustrated these issues in practice, although two case studies were carried out on two very popular open-source package-based software ecosystems.

For the Debian package ecosystem, we showed that despite the existence of multiple tools to solve many of the issues related to component dependencies, an historical analysis of strong conflicts allowed us to discover problems that could not be identified by current tools.

For the R package ecosystem, we presented the main repositories where R packages are developed and distributed and showed that, despite the rising popularity of *GitHub*, *CRAN* remains the most important package repository. Focusing on *CRAN*, we found that an important number of package errors are caused by dependency upgrades and developers need to fix the error by releasing a new version of their package. The R community would therefore benefit from more advanced tools that recommend package maintainers and users how to overcome problems related to package upgrades.

To conclude, while previous research has led to the creation of efficient tools to cope with dependency issues in component-based software ecosystems, there still is room for improvement. By historically analyzing the component dependency graph, more precise information can be obtained and used to detect the root causes of dependency issues and to provide better automated tool support for dependency management.

Acknowledgments

This research was carried out in the context of the research project AUWB-12/17-UMONS-3 "Ecological Studies of Open Source Software Ecosystems" financed by the Ministère de la Communauté française – Direction générale de l'Enseignement non obligatoire et de la Recherche scientifique as well as a research credit J.0023.16 "Analysis of Software Project Survival" financed by the Fonds de la Recherche Scientifique – FNRS, Belgium.

References

1 D.G. Messerschmitt and C. Szyperski (2003) *Software Ecosystem: Understanding and Indispensable Technology and Industry.* MIT Press.
2 M. Lungu (2008) Towards reverse engineering software ecosystems. International Conference on Software Maintenance (ICSM), pp. 428–431,

3 J. Sametinger (1997) *Software Engineering with Reusable Components*, Springer.

4 G. Bavota, G. Canfora, M. Di Penta, R. Oliveto, and S. Panichella (2015) How the Apache community upgrades dependencies: an evolutionary study. *Empirical Software Engineering*, **20** (5), 1275–1317.

5 R. Di Cosmo, S. Zacchiroli, and P. Trezentos (2009) Package upgrades in FOSS distributions: details and challenges. CoRR, abs/0902.1610.

6 D. M. German, J. M. Gonzalez-Barahona, and G. Robles (2007) A model to understand the building and running interdependencies of software. Working Conference on Reverse Engineering (WCRE), pp. 140–149.

7 M. Lungu, R. Robbes, and M. Lanza (2010) Recovering inter-project dependencies in software ecosystems. International Conference on Automated Software Engineering (ASE), pp. 309–312.

8 N. LaBelle and E. Wallingford (2004) Inter-package dependency networks in open-source software. CoRR, cs.SE/0411096.

9 P. Abate, R. Di Cosmo, R. Treinen, and S. Zacchiroli (2012) Dependency solving: a separate concern in component evolution management. *Journal of Systems and Software*, **85** (10), 2228–2240.

10 P. Abate, R. Di Cosmo, J. Boender, and S. Zacchiroli (2009) Strong dependencies between software components. International Symposium on Empirical Software Engineering and Measurement (ESEM), pp. 89–99.

11 C. Artho, K. Suzaki, R. Di Cosmo, R. Treinen, and S. Zacchiroli (2012) Why do software packages conflict? International Conference on Mining Software Repositories (MSR), pp. 141–150.

12 R. Di Cosmo, D. Di Ruscio, P. Pelliccione, A. Pierantonio, and S. Zacchiroli (2011) Supporting software evolution in component-based FOSS systems. *Science of Computer Programming*, **76** (12), 1144–1160.

13 R. Di Cosmo and J. Boender (2010) Using strong conflicts to detect quality issues in component-based complex systems. Indian Software Engineering Conference, pp. 163–172.

14 R. Di Cosmo and J. Vouillon (2011) On software component co-installability. ESEC/FSE, pp. 256–266.

15 J. Vouillon and R. Di Cosmo (2013) Broken sets in software repository evolution. International Conference on Software Engineering, pp. 412–421.

16 J. Vouillon, M. Dogguy, and R. Di Cosmo (2014) Easing software component repository evolution. International Conference on Software Engineering, pp. 756–766.

17 M. Claes, T. Mens, and P. Grosjean (2014) On the maintainability of CRAN packages. International Conference on Software Maintenance, Reengineering, and Reverse Engineering (CSMR-WCRE), pp. 308–312,

18 D. M. German, B. Adams, and A. E. Hassan (2013) The evolution of the R software ecosystem. European Conference on Software Maintenance and Reengineering (CSMR), pp. 243–252.

19 K. Hornik (2012) Are there too many R packages? *Austrian Journal of Statistics*, **41** (1), 59–66.

20 M. Wermelinger and Y. Yu (2008) Analyzing the evolution of eclipse plugins. International Conference on Mining Software Repositories, ACM Press, pp. 133–136.

21 D. Dig and R. Johnson (2006) How do APIs evolve? A story of refactoring. *Journal of Software Maintenance and Evolution: Research and Practice*, **18** (2), 83–107.

22 R. C. Basole and J. Karla (2012) Value transformation in the mobile service ecosystem: a study of app store emergence and growth. *Service Science*, **4** (1), 24–41.

23 I. J. Mojica, B. Adams, M. Nagappan, S. Dienst, T. Berger, and A. E. Hassan (2014) A large scale empirical study on software reuse in mobile apps. *IEEE Software*, **31** (2), 78–86.

24 P. Abate, R. Di Cosmo, L. Gesbert, F. Le Fessant, R. Treinen, and S. Zacchiroli (2015) Mining component repositories for installability issues. Working Conference on Mining Software Repositories (MSR), 24–33.

25 N. Nagappan and T. Ball (2007) Using software dependencies and churn metrics to predict field failures: an empirical case study. International Symposium on Empirical Software Engineering and Measurement (ESEM), pp. 364–373.

26 R. Robbes, M. Lungu, and D. Röthlisberger (2012) How do developers react to API deprecation? The case of a Smalltalk ecosystem. International Symposium on Foundations of Software Engineering,

27 A. Hora, R. Robbes, N. Anquetil, A. Etien, S. Ducasse, and M.T. Valente (2015) How do developers react to API evolution? The Pharo ecosystem case. International Conference on Software Maintenance (ICSME), p. 10.

28 T. McDonnell, B. Ray, and M. Kim (2013) An empirical study of API stability and adoption in the Android ecosystem. International Conference on Software Maintenance (ICSM), pp. 70–79.

29 G. Bavota, G. Canfora, M. Di Penta, R. Oliveto, and S. Panichella. (2013) The evolution of project inter-dependencies in a software ecosystem: the case of Apache. International Conference on Software Maintenance (ICSM).

30 B. Vasilescu, S. van Schuylenburg, J. Wulms, A. Serebrenik, and M.G.J. van den Brand (2014) Continuous integration in a social-coding world: empirical evidence from GitHub. International Conference on Software Maintenance and Evolution (ICSME), pp. 401–405.

31 P. Abate, R. Di Cosmo, R. Treinen, and S. Zacchiroli (2011) MPM: a modular package manager. International Symposium on. Component Based Software Engineering (CBSE), pp. 179–188,

32 E. Jürgens, F. Deissenboeck, B. Hummel, and S. Wagner (2009) Do code clones matter? International Conference on Software Engineering (ICSE), pp. 485–495.

33 C. Kapser and M. W. Godfrey (2008) 'Cloning considered harmful' considered harmful: patterns of cloning in software. *Empirical Software Engineering*, **13** (6), 645–692.

34 M. Kim, V. Sazawal, D. Notkin, and G. C. Murphy (2005) An empirical study of code clone genealogies. ESEC/FSE, pp. 187–196.

35 R.K. Saha, Muhammad Asaduzzaman, M.F. Zibran, C.K. Roy, and K.A. Schneider (2010) Evaluating code clone genealogies at release level: an empirical study. International Working Conference on Source Code Analysis and Manipulation (SCAM), pp. 87–96.

36 R. Koschke (2014) Large-scale inter-system clone detection using suffix trees and hashing. *Journal of Software: Evolution and Process*, **26** (8), 747–769.

37 J. Svajlenko, J.F. Islam, I. Keivanloo, C.K. Roy, and Mohammad M. Mia (2014) Towards a big data curated benchmark of inter-project code clones. International Conference on Software Maintenance and Evolution (ICSME), pp. 476–480.

38 M. Claes, T. Mens, N. Tabout, and P. Grosjean (2015) An empirical study of identical function clones in CRAN. International Workshop on Software Clones (IWSC), pp. 19–25.

39 J. Vouillon and R. Di Cosmo (2013) On software component co-installability. *ACM Transactions on Software Engineering and Methodology*, **22** (4), 34.

40 M. Claes, T. Mens, R. Di Cosmo, and J. Vouillon (2015) A historical analysis of Debian package incompatibilities. Working Conference on Mining Software Repositories (MSR), pp. 212–223,

41 P. Abate, R. Di Cosmo, R. Treinen, and S. Zacchiroli (2012) Learning from the future of component repositories. International Symposium on Component Based Software Engineering (CBSE), pp. 51–60.

42 R. A. München (2015) The popularity of data analysis software. http://r4stats.com/articles/popularity/.

43 M. Claes, T. Mens, and P. Grosjean (2014) maintaineR: a web-based dashboard for maintainers of CRAN packages. International Conference on Software Maintenance and Evolution (ICSME), pp. 597–600.

44 A. Decan, T. Mens, M. Claes, and P. Grosjean (2015) On the development and distribution of R packages: an empirical analysis of the R ecosystem. European Conference on Software Architecture Workshops (ECSAW), pp. 41:1–41:6.

45 A. Decan, T. Mens, M. Claes, and P. Grosjean (2016) When GitHub meets CRAN: an analysis of inter-repository package dependency problems. International Conference on Software Analysis, Evolution, and Reengineering,

46 T. Mens (2016) Anonymized E-Mail Interviews with R Package Maintainers Active on CRAN and GitHub. Technical Report, University of Mons, Belgium.

4

Triangulating Research Dissemination Methods: A Three-Pronged Approach to Closing the Research–Practice Divide

Sarah Beecham,[1] Ita Richardson,[1] Ian Sommerville,[2] Padraig O'Leary,[3] Sean Baker,[1] and John Noll[1,4]

[1]*Lero – The Irish Software Research Centre, University of Limerick, Limerick, Ireland*
[2]*School of Computer Science, University of St Andrews, Scotland, UK*
[3]*School of Computer Science, University of Adelaide, Australia*
[4]*University of East London, London, UK*

4.1 Introduction

Probably, it is no surprise that practitioners rarely look to academic literature for new and better ways to develop software. And why should they? Arguably, conducting such research is not their job. Academic literature is vast and necessarily full of rigor. It often has a style that is hard to penetrate, even for audiences with years of postdoctoral research experience. As researchers working closely with industry, we want to meet industry halfway: We are confident that we have something to communicate to practitioners that, given the right platform, they could find beneficial and of practical use. So how can we reach industry?

In this chapter, we explore various ways that researchers can share their findings with practitioners. We look not only at traditional methods such as publishing our work in journals, but also further afield, at more practical physical involvement with industry. We demonstrate that through initiatives such as workshops, action research, case studies, commercialization, and industry fellowships, we can build successful collaborations for mutual gain.

Empirical researchers often talk about triangulation as being a powerful technique to facilitate the validation of our data. When using triangulation, we strengthen the credibility in our findings by collecting our data (and cross-verifying) from two or more sources, and then we apply a combination of research methods in the study of the same phenomenon (Morse, 1991). Why

Software Technology: 10 Years of Innovation in IEEE Computer, First Edition.
Edited by Mike Hinchey.

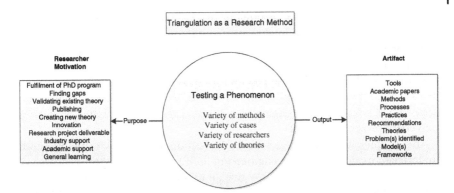

Figure 4.1 Triangulation as a research method.

not also take this broad approach in our dissemination process? In this chapter, we propose that researchers triangulate the approach to reaching out to our industry colleagues. If one way does not work, let us try another.

Figure 4.1 gives an overview of how triangulation is used as a research method. Figure 4.2 shows how we can adapt this approach to sharing our research with industry. This chapter focuses on the alternative methods as a means of reaching out to industry. The authors of this chapter all have first-hand experience in working with industry through one or more of these

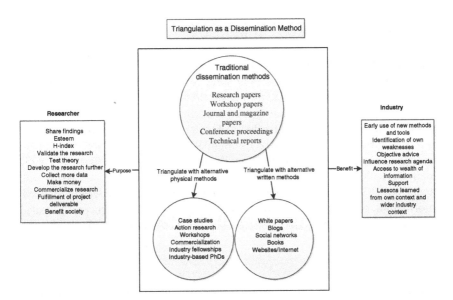

Figure 4.2 Triangulation as a dissemination method.

methods. While mostly positive, we also touch on some of the barriers to dissemination and how we might overcome them.

We present dissemination patterns in context to the software engineering activities of academics and suggest how researchers might be rewarded for developing tools and process models that industry value enough to support the development work financially. In other words, we look at commercialization opportunities for software engineering outputs that were initiated as part of university projects and Ph.D.

This chapter is organized as follows: In Section 4.2 we look at the research undertaken in global software engineering (GSE), as a subset of the vast area of software engineering research. We give an account of how practitioners view our research and where they go to for support. In this section we highlight some of the issues with traditional ways of disseminating our work through academic publications. In Section 4.3 we reflect on where practitioners go to for support, based on our empirical study. Section 4.4 looks at various paths to disseminating academic research output. In particular, we discuss how academics collaborate with industry through physical interaction and how some researchers straddle the research–practice divide by commercializing their research. It is in this Section 4.4 that we present some solutions to how researchers can meet practitioners halfway, for example, by holding workshops and conducting case studies. Section 4.5 looks at some barriers to commercializing our output, and Section 4.6 concludes this chapter with a summary of recommendations for future collaboration and improved sharing of research output.

4.2 Meeting the Needs of Industry

Our current examination into current research dissemination methods was triggered by a 12-month study we conducted to identify how we could make our research on GSE more accessible to practitioners (Beecham et al., 2013). We have been writing about this software engineering subject for well over a decade, and while the early literature tended to focus on problems, more recently we have developed solutions and recommendations for GSE. This is based on evidence, lessons learned, and direct engagement with industry (Beecham et al., 2010, 2011, 2012, 2014; Richardson et al., 2012; Deshpande et al., 2013; Noll et al., 2014). Furthermore, the wider literature provides a wealth of GSE information, where a quick search of the IEEEXplore digital library[1] revealed more than 2500 sources (see Table 4.1 for breakdown of content type).

---

1 We used search string: (((("Global Software Development") OR "Global Software Engineering") OR "Distributed Software Development") – (http://ieeexplore.ieee.org).

Table 4.1 IEEEXplore search results for publications on GSE (Jan 1999–Sep 2015).

Content type	Frequency
Conference and workshop proceedings	2219
Journals and magazines	267
Books and e-books	57
Early access	16
Total	2559

4.2.1 Commercialization Feasibility Study

We conjectured that one way to reach industry is to commercialize our research and package it in the form of a decision support system (DSS) where practitioners would have fast access to context-specific support. The idea of developing a DSS was motivated by our drive to support practitioners who typically do not have the time to search the academic literature for nuggets of information that fit their context. Our system aimed to capture recommended practices (on the basis of extensive practical research findings) (Beecham et al., 2010; Noll et al., 2010, 2014; Richardson et al., 2012) and provide users with a quick and easy way to find solutions to their specific development problems. As a starting point for delivering best practices via a DSS, we focused on the GSE process. Having collaborated extensively with distributed software development organizations, our team of researchers was well positioned to share lessons learned and recommended practices with the wider community.

However, moving from a conceptual model to a professional tool that practitioners would use (and pay for) is a complex process requiring major investment. Based on our experience, one way to commercialize research is shown in Figure 4.3. This innovation pipeline from research to commercialization for a business product based on software has five stages:

1) An initial idea surfaces from either a funded project with defined deliverables or through an investigation of gaps found in the research literature, a Ph.D. thesis, or some other external trigger.

Figure 4.3 The innovation pipeline.

2) From an initial idea, which may or may not be based on an identified business problem, a proof-of-concept demonstrator is produced. In universities, this may be created by Ph.D. students or by research staff, specifically employed to work on this development.

3) If the proof-of-concept demonstrator appears to have some commercial value, the next stage is to develop a prototype system that can demonstrate the wider functionality of the product is developed. This includes the user interface. In principle, this could be created by extending the proof-of-concept software; in practice, the proof-of-concept system is usually so corrupted by change that a complete rewrite is necessary.

4) If the prototype system appears to be commercially viable, a product development process can commence with the output of that process being a number of beta-versions of the software that are released for evaluation.

5) If that evaluation is positive, the first commercial release of the system is then produced (if there is funding to do so). Further releases are then created in response to customer feedback, competition, and technology changes.

Figure 4.3 shows the path followed by two of the authors to commercialize an invention. Before moving into a serious development phase, we conducted a feasibility study to explore whether there was a potential market for a DSS for GSE.[2] We produced a prototype DSS (Beecham et al., 2012) to test the market. Our initial goal was to explore practitioners' thoughts about GSE research and then assess their interest in the idea of GSE-focused DSS. We elaborate on the commercialization funding process in our Section 4.4 of this chapter.

We surveyed several practitioners engaged in GSE (Beecham et al., 2013, 2014). Our test group was an influential group of practitioners from organizations such as Google, KPMG, Microsoft, and Oracle, and we interviewed senior managers and project managers from these companies. We found that our practitioners were typical of the software engineering population as they recounted familiar issues with their global development activities. However, and arguably of more significance, while interviewing this group of practitioners, we gained some interesting insight into what practitioners really want regarding support.

4.2.2 Typical GSE Issues Were Reported

Respondents' candid responses revealed that their organizations were struggling with the kind of GSE challenges that we have been actively researching. Not surprisingly, they recounted problems in the following areas:

1) Culture including mismatched work ethics, languages, religions

---

2 Feasibility study funding is revisited in the Solutions Section 4.4.

2) Communication overhead resulting from the need to communicate with more people
3) Different time zones across sites
4) Tool mismatch
5) Vendor selection
6) Sourcing skills
7) Task allocation

Other recurring themes were members of the team being left out of relevant and timely conversations and the inability to roll out best practices across sites as intended. For those involved in outsourcing, concerns included dealing with vendor retention, the true cost of outsourcing, and how to build a good supplier–vendor relationship.

Given that both researchers and practitioners recognize these development problems and that research has solutions to match them, we asked practitioners in our study whether they were aware of such work. Participants indicated that though they perceive GSE research as potentially useful and that studying the subject would doubtlessly improve GSE performance, they did not read articles on GSE. Therefore, those practitioners in our sample had no insight into the GSE research that is being undertaken internationally.

4.2.2.1 Why Don't Practitioners Read the Academic Literature That Addresses Their Problems?

Practitioners do not read GSE domain-specific articles perhaps because GSE is viewed as mainstream software engineering. This certainly seems the case here, as controversially many practitioners interviewed did not view GSE as separate from general project management. A major barrier to industry implementing solutions offered by academia is that the gateway is often in the form of an academic publication, a medium viewed as "boring" (Taylor, 2010), lengthy, dense, impenetrable, inaccessible, and costly (requiring subscriptions), with an emphasis on theory and method rather than tangible outcomes. Finally, practitioners do not seem to want frameworks; they want patterns of context-specific help. In addition, ideally, help will come from people with practical experience, since experience-based advice seems to trump all.

4.3 The Theory–Practice Divide

Robert Glass drew attention to the theory–practice divide in his 1996 inaugural Practical Programmer column in *Communications of the ACM* (Glass, 1996). According to Glass, researchers simply did not have the required experience to make their theories the solution of choice. At the time of writing, Glass did not believe that there was a convincing body of research in certain areas and that "theorists who fail to evaluate their ideas in a practical setting before advocating them are of particular concern." Since then, with more than 15 years of research on GSE, Glass's point still seems to be valid; and although it would be rare to find a process solution or tool published in a top-tier conference or journal that has not gone through some form of validation, can we really expect practitioners to take a leap of faith and apply a theory that has not been proven in practice first?

However, on closer inspection, there are several weaknesses to how we validate our research. For example, when our tools and methods are tested with students rather than with practitioners, where according to Kitchenham and colleagues "the use of students as subjects" can affect the general validity of formal experiments (Kitchenham et al., 2002). Furthermore, in Runeson and Höst's guidelines for conducting case studies they observe that the academic preference for quantitative rather than qualitative studies is far removed from real practice: "The analytical research paradigm is not sufficient for investigating complex real life issues, involving humans and their interactions with technology" (Runeson and Höst, 2009).

Despite the need for more qualitative analysis, it seems that empirical research, particularly controlled experiments, is rare in computer science research as evidenced by two independent surveys performed by Sjøberg et al. (2005) and Ramesh et al. (2004) who searching for methods used across a broad range of publications found only a fraction of articles in computer science were based on case studies, experiments with human subjects or field studies. "The majority of published articles in computer science and software engineering provide little or no empirical validation and the proportion of controlled experiments is particularly low" (Sjøberg et al., 2005).

4.3.1 Making Research Accessible

Practitioners, when considering the relevance of academic research, look to findings that are relevant to their situation. Shari Lawrence Pfleeger clearly articulated the importance of relevance and contextualizing solutions when she noted that "practitioners, who are the audience for our evidence, must be able to understand our theories and findings in the context of their work and values" (Pfleeger, 1999). Ekrem Kocaguneli and his colleagues' first rule for researchers to communicate with practitioners is to report relevant results (Kocaguneli et al., 2013). Researchers should also remember to recheck their findings and reflect on their significance.

Fortunately there are many counter examples of how academia is researching jointly with industry (many of the examples in this chapter being a case in point). While we have identified that practitioners do not read academic papers, we need to identify "how" we can get those relevant research results into industry. This is the dilemma we face as researchers solving industry-relevant problems.

4.3.2 Where Do Practitioners Really Go for Support?

In addition to depending on their own experience to solve GSE problems, practitioners also consult books, blogs, colleagues, online video tutorials, forums, and short, one- to two-page experience reports. The main source of support comes from peers. Although participants acknowledged the academic literature and external consultancies, they never used them for GSE-related issues. Experience is a key factor to where practitioners go for help with their GSE issues, as noted by one participant: "We talk to other managers who run teams elsewhere in the world . . . that is where we get our advice." When practitioners cannot speak to peers directly, they use resources such as blogs, wikis, and their corporate intranets. When we look at Table 4.1, which shows where much of the GSE research is published, and compare it to where practitioners read about GSE solutions (summarized in Table 4.2), we see little overlap.

Although the study sample in our feasibility study was small and highly selective, these results are important because the participants are in project and senior management roles in a cross-section of organizations, and we suspect that they reflect the behavioral patterns of practitioners from other organizations. Despite the vast number of publications, process models, innovative tools, and guidelines on GSE – some developed by academia expressly to address problems experienced in practice – there appears to be little take-up from industry. "Publications in peer-reviewed journals continue to be the key performance indicator within academia: whether anyone reads them is a secondary consideration" (Biswas and Kirchherr, 2015). There is a caveat: we know there are many practitioners that do straddle the practice–research divide and play active roles in our community, chair our industry tracks, and

Table 4.2 Where practitioners go to for GSE support.

Source	Example
Books	Covering: Agile software development, GSE, outsourcing, and project management
Other practitioners (interactive networks)	LinkedIn, blogs, communities of practice, discussion forums, and peers
Web	Agile community web and the World Wide Web
Non-GSE articles	Publications on topics such as project management
Vendor material	White papers
Intranet	Internal knowledge databases
Service or product material	Book promotion article
GSE academic publications	None reported

give excellent presentations at our shared workshops and conferences, but none of these practitioners formed part of our sample.

4.4 Solutions: Rethinking Our Dissemination Methods

Looking then toward the relevant research that is conducted in academia, and our finding that not all practitioners read material published in the literature, we now turn our attention to alternative ways of dissemination.

It is our view that, while publications are seen, and are, much of a researcher's output, our research can reach industry in other ways. We in Lero have been active in conducting industry-based software engineering research and in developing training courses for industry based on our research. In addition, we are not unique in doing that. In this section, we discuss some of the strategies that we use to ensure that industry has access to and uses our research results. There is nothing particularly novel about these methods, but they are here to remind both researchers and practitioners that we have a raft of methods we can draw on.

4.4.1 Workshops, Outreach, and Seminars

To ensure the relevance and dissemination of research conducted in academia, researchers need to go directly to the coalface – to the software engineers on the ground. To facilitate this happening, our research group and others play a part in giving talks directly to companies. We run training courses and workshops and speak at seminars organized by national agencies such as Enterprise Ireland (EI) and research centers such as Lero. Through these activities, we give software engineers access to up-to-date research. In this subsection, we describe two such activities that took place as industry workshops.

For example, we conducted a 2-day workshop on GSE for a global media company. The objective of the workshop was to introduce research findings on effective practices for GSE and identify specific practices that the attendees could apply in their own development teams.

Seventeen project managers, developers, and senior managers participated in the workshop, representing teams or individuals based in Germany, Spain, France, and England. The workshop was held in Istanbul so that none of the participants would be in their usual location; this was to reduce distractions and encourage participants to get to know their peers through social events.

The workshop addressed nine topics through exercises and presentations:

1) Why an organization engages in GSE
2) (Measuring) global distance (in terms of cultural, temporal, and geographic distances)

3) Collaboration models (how life cycle tasks are shared across distributed teams)
4) Software engineer motivation (does working in virtual teams demotivate?)
5) Agile methods in GSE
6) The global teaming model (GTM) (process support)
7) GTM self-assessment
8) Self-assessment results – cost and impact analysis
9) The way ahead – GTM practices to implement

The workshop yielded benefits for both the attendees and the researchers who presented the workshop. The first benefit from the attendees' point of view was the opportunity to meet and get to know their counterparts at other locations. Meeting at a neutral location ensured that there were opportunities for this during meals and breaks.

A more concrete outcome was that, as a group, the attendees identified some fundamental project management practices that need improvement, through the GTM self-assessment exercise (Beecham et al., 2015). These were subsequently prioritized by cost-benefit as the second part of the exercise. Gaps in expertise were identified, especially the need for a "product owner" with both domain knowledge and technical expertise, to serve as bridge between customers and developers during requirements identification. Global distance, specifically cultural distance, was identified among sites. This was particularly interesting in that different sites viewed their cultural distance differently. For example, the Spanish team determined their distance from the London team was much higher than the London team thought was the distance to the Spanish team. Agile methods were identified as a possible way to address continually changing requirements; however, there was also a great deal of skepticism from some participants about the effectiveness of an Agile approach, especially concerning requirements specification.

An intangible aspect of the workshop did not go unnoticed: participants recognized and appreciated that the company was spending a lot, in terms of time and direct expense, to bring them all to Istanbul for 2 days.

The researchers who conducted the workshop also realized benefits in three areas: dissemination, new data collected, and topics for further research. Each of the topics presented during the 2 days was based on research conducted by the presenters and their colleagues; many, such as the GTM assessment and global distance calculation, were derived directly from publications. As such, the workshop served as an alternative dissemination channel for these publications. Many of the exercises, such as the software engineer motivation survey, GTM assessment, and global distance calculation, were based on previously developed research instruments. Consequently, these exercises provided additional research data as well as valuable insights for practitioners. The results of these exercises yielded almost immediate tangible benefits in the form of publications, including one conference paper on software engineer motivation, a technical report and publication on global distance, and a draft paper on GTM assessment.

Finally, the workshop revealed additional topics for further research, including issues regarding Agile methods and GSE, measuring global distance, and software engineer motivation (Beecham and Noll, 2015). Such workshops are valuable for practitioners providing "high bandwidth" dissemination: nine topics were presented in 2 days, all based on recent research results. Further, because attendees were team leaders, the impact likely extends beyond just the attendees.

While workshops themselves do not contribute directly to any conventional academic metrics, data collected resulted in two publications, two papers, and three topics for further research, along with data to support that research. Collecting such data would otherwise have required weeks or even months, being able to do so in 2 days more than justifies the effort required to prepare such a workshop. Plus the researchers involved gained first-hand experience of the problems that the practitioners were facing in GSE.

Another example is the Medical Software Quality Assurance program developed jointly by Lero researchers and academics at the University of Limerick. It is an approved course within the university and has been designed specifically to enable unemployed computer science, engineering and technician graduates, or equivalent with a software background to convert to the medical technology sector. This program was instigated by the Irish Medical Device Association (IMDA) Skillnet, to fill the gap within this industry domain in Ireland for software quality roles. The training takes place on a part-time basis, and is conducted by qualified researchers who have a background in this topic.

Developed from research carried out by Lero – the Irish Software Research Centre and ARCH (Applied Research in Connected Health Technology Centre) researchers, the program provides graduates with fundamental theoretical and practical skills, abilities and knowledge for assuring the quality of medical software applications in accordance with regulatory requirements and quality management systems. Graduates have demonstrated that they are capable of creating and executing test cases and tracking software issues from their diagnosis to resolution and generally ensuring the quality of developed software.

On successful completion of the training program, the participants receive a Medical Software Quality Assurance, NFQ Level 8 award and ISTQB (International Software Testing Qualification Board) qualification. After completing the initial course in April 2015, 81% of the graduates were in full-time employment, moved to further study or have obtained an internship. This course ran again in 2015/2016. An updated version for software engineers working in the medical device industry was held in 2017/2018, with plans to run this again in 2018/2019.

This course is an example of how we are meeting demands from a growing industry within Ireland. We have used the university structures to develop courses specifically for people who need to develop new skills to gain new opportunities. The research we have undertaken is fundamental to carrying out such education.

4.4.2 Case Studies

There are many examples where research is conducted by carrying out case studies. While the main purpose of such research is often to understand what is happening in industry, the results from an industrial perspective can be quite compelling. Practitioners who participate in case studies are often prompted to reflect on their work practices and processes through discussion and engagement with the researcher. This can, in itself, lead to change and education within industry. Once the case study has been completed and written-up, this helps the company management and employees to understand what is currently happening within their company and how it measures up against others in similar situations. Results from a case study will often include a model of best practice that is usually presented to the practitioners, and who may implement lessons learned within their own organization.

An example of case study research carried out within Lero is that of O'Leary (2010). The object of the research project was to define a framework for the structured approach to the derivation of products from a software product line (O'Leary et al., 2012).

The initial development of the framework entailed a literature review and a series of expert opinion workshops. During this stage of the research, the framework was iteratively developed based on best practices as identified in both the literature and from expert opinion.

Using the framework as a starting point, a case study was conducted with the automotive division of Robert Bosch GmbH. The case study was to serve as an empirical validation where the framework was mapped and compared to product derivation practices within the company. In conducting the case study, researchers analyzed internal company documentation, which illustrated the existing practices through completed projects. They conducted an onsite visit to the company including a 2-day workshop with the corporate research division. Attendees included selected product architects and developers from product line business units. After the workshop, a technical report (O'Leary et al., 2010), on the company's product derivation process, was created and validated through feedback with Bosch experts. The final technical report was presented to teams engaged in software product lines within the company.

This case study had a dual impact. In the first instance, researchers modeled the industrial practices of Robert Bosch GmbH and then updated the framework based on the observations. In the second instance, practitioners from Robert Bosch GmbH were able to reflect on both their internal practices and best practices from the literature.

Factors discussing the lack of industry engagement with research have been well described, yet dissemination is still seen as a one-way process where researchers produce knowledge that practitioners consume. However, the experience of the researchers from the above case study suggests that dissemination is more likely to be effective if it is based on a two-way transfer of knowledge between researcher and practitioner.

4.4.3 Action Research

Action research can be described as "social research carried out by a team that encompasses a professional action researcher, and the members of an organization, community or network ('stakeholders') who are seeking to improve the participants' situation" (Greenwood and Levin, 2006). Further, action research is stated to simultaneously assist in practical problem solving and expand scientific knowledge. "In action research, the emphasis is more on what practitioners do than on what they say they do" (Avison et al., 1999). Action research involves five phases (Baskerville, 1999): diagnosing, action planning, action taking, evaluating, and specifying learning. Despite the five individual phases, the action research process is not a collection of sequential steps to be executed one after another. Rather it is a circular process where phases are usually conducted iteratively (Baskerville, 1999).

A group of researchers based at the University of Eastern Finland took an action research approach to identifying how best to support small to medium enterprises (SMEs) in their software process optimization and how to help them visualize improvements in tacit knowledge (a need recognized by the collaborating organization as well as the general software process improvement (SPI) literature (Clarke and O'Connor, 2013). Typically, process improvement in software SMEs tends to be moderate in nature since these small companies cannot afford to employ dedicated quality improvement personnel, and existing employees, being fully stretched, are unable to take on secondary tasks (Richardson and Gresse von Wangenheim, 2007). Hence, the process improvement approach in SMEs should be well focused, cost-effective, and suitable for process optimization and visualizing improvements (Richardson and Gresse von Wangenheim, 2007; Clarke and O'Connor, 2013). This focus can be difficult to achieve since process improvement activities in smaller software companies are often varied, to include both primary software development and support services (Pino et al., 2008).

The output from this group of researchers provided industry with a new way to document ideas, discussions, awareness, and accumulate learning experienced in software SMEs in the form of LAPPI – a process modeling technique that evolved through close collaboration with industry (Raninen et al., 2013). LAPPI filled a much needed gap for industry as there is a lack of SPI guidance for SMEs.

The main goal of this particular research was to explore how to practically and cost-effectively improve the processes of a small software company developing commercial off-the-shelf products. Action research was an ideal method to use here, as the researchers' involvement was highly participatory. A Ph.D. was completed on the back of this research where the student became practically a part of the company for over four years, "in which time the liaisons were very close and confidential" (Raninen, 2014). The research was conducted through getting to know the company and gaining the company's trust.[3] By taking an action research approach, The LAPPI modeling technique was shown to successfully identify opportunities for improvement in the development process, documentation handling, testing, and even the customer support process (Raninen et al., 2015).

Additionally, researchers were able to track the effect of the intervention. This successful collaboration between research and industry led to the organizations identifying several problems with the current processes that were subsequently streamlined. The process was validated through a customer satisfaction survey, demonstrating that the LAPPI intervention provided industry with significant improvement in customer response times and in customer support request resolution.

Action research, though requiring total immersion with industry for a prolonged period, is an effective way for researchers to engage with industry. In this particular case, the researchers gained by having access to real-world problems and working with industry to solve them. The researchers also gained by writing up the process and publishing the experience as both a Ph.D. and several journal and conference publications.

4.4.4 Practitioner Ph.D.'s

In our research, we have found that an effective method of involving industry, and in creating synergies between companies, has been to develop Ph.D. projects within industry. We ensure that not only are practitioners actively

---

3 The student needed to also become familiar with the research area's literature, define the research problem, perform the research steps, analyze, generate, and eventually try to generalize the results.

involved in carrying out research and in developing results, but that they publish these results for use by other companies. These may take the format of Case Study (as in solution 4.2) or Action Research (as in solution 4.3). In Ireland, funding has been forthcoming for such projects by relevant bodies such as Science Foundation Ireland, Irish Research Council, and EI.

One such example was the Ph.D. research undertaken by a practitioner, John Burton, based at a medical device company in Ireland. The focus of Burton's research was to understand how software processes could be implemented within the quality unit for which he was responsible, ensuring that regulation was taken into account (Burton, 2008). As an exemplar, Burton analyzed the Capability Maturity Model Integrated (CMMI$^©$) (2006) (CMMI, 2006), comparing it to medical device regulations and standards – FDA, ISO14971 (2007) (ISO, 2007), and IEC 62304:2006 (2008) (IEC, 2008) as summarized in Figure 4.4 (McCaffery et al., 2010).

Figure 4.4 illustrates that neither the CMMI$^©$ nor the medical device regulations can stand alone. Rather, they must be combined before good software is developed. From this, the Risk Management Capability Maturity Model was developed (Burton et al., 2008). This combines the software engineering requirements from risk management within the CMMI$^©$ with medical device regulations. Through this project, this research had a significant effect on a medical device company, ensuring that it achieved FDA regulation.

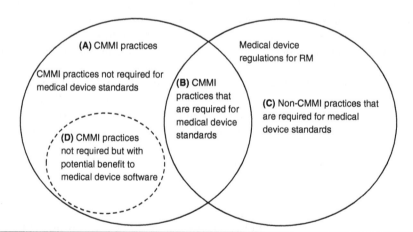

A- CMMI$^©$ Practices that are not mandatory for MD standards.
B- CMMI$^©$ Practices that are required for MD standards.
C- Non-CMMI$^©$ Practices that are required for MD standards.
D- CMMI$^©$ Practices that are not mandatory for MD standards but, if performed, could contribute to the safety of the MD software or enhance the company's RM practices.

Figure 4.4 Composition of the RMCM.

The research has been published widely, and, through our funding partners, we have been enabled to present it to a number of industry audiences. Additionally, it has been a stepping stone to Lero developing a strong portfolio of industry-based medical software quality research, and to the practitioner in securing a promotion.

4.4.5 Industry Fellowships

In Ireland, there is a focus on funding research that has impact from the industry perspective. Within our research centers, there is a requirement to involve industry, and in addition, there are specific funds that allow us to work directly with industry. One of this chapter's authors (Richardson) was involved in one such initiative in 2015–2016 – the Science Foundation Ireland Industry Fellowship. This provides academics and researchers with funding for up 1-year full-time and 2-year part-time to work in industry, becoming involved in the activities within the company, and undertaking research activities in conjunction with company employees.

The overall aim of this fellowship is, through the use of Action Research (see Section 4.3), to research, develop, and evaluate a Medical Device Software Quality Management System that will increase the effectiveness and efficiency of Medical Device Software Development within industry. Access to the company provides an "industrial working laboratory" to the researcher. For the company, participation in this action research project will provide them with an evaluated quality management system, contributing to the long-term growth and sustainability of the business. From the research perspective, this Medical Device Software Quality Management System will be published and will become available to other companies. It is possible that other researchers will take this system and further evolve it for use in other industry domains, such as automotive or finance.

This fellowship provides benefits to the company through access to an experienced researcher in their domain who has direct links to the University of Limerick, Lero – the Irish Software Research Centre, and to the Applied Research in Connected Health Technology Centre. Due to the company's most recent business focus, that of providing technical and software solutions to the connected health market, the company is now operating in a medical device regulated environment. Therefore, they are required to develop software solutions in compliance with international standards – both clinical and software. These include ISO standards such as ISO12207 (2008) (ISO/IEC, 2008) and IEC62304 (2008) (IEC, 2008) that will need to be introduced from a software perspective, and Food and Drugs Authority regulations from a clinical perspective.

From a software perspective, models and methods have been evolving as software engineering developed as a discipline in its own right. This emerging connected health software market requires expertise about these models and methods within companies, and companies need to have this expertise to be competitive. This fellowship will give the company an opportunity to implement models such as the Capability Maturity Model Integrated (2006) (CMMI, 2006), Agile software development, which is now being used in some medical device and healthcare situations (Fitzgerald et al., 2013), and Lean Software Development, which may also be used to develop medical device software (Cawley et al., 2011). Solutions need to be efficient and effective to maintain company competitiveness. Implementing these requirements in a growing competitive international market requires the development and implementation of a Medical Device Software Quality Management System (MD-SQMS). The research being carried out can be leveraged for these purposes through which the company will benefit.

While currently, employees within the company are well-versed in regulation, the expansion into medical device and connected health software requires that they now focus on software regulation as well as developing an understanding of software development standards and processes. Employees need to understand how to implement software processes and then how to convert regulations and quality requirements from their market place into tangible processes within their organization. These systems will ultimately help the company to build and implement medical devices and connected health solutions. Company growth and success will depend on this. This fellowship will also support the required upskilling of employees.

4.4.6 Commercializing Research

Another way to reach industry from a researcher perspective is to commercialize higher education research in the software engineering field. In this manner, the years of study that go into creating process models and tools as part of Ph.D. or research projects can not only fill a gap (or need) but can also benefit the inventors and bodies that funded the original research.

Conducting a feasibility study ideally needs the initial idea in the innovation pipeline (see Figure 4.3) to move past a conceptual phase so that there is something tangible to demonstrate to potential customers of the product. Enterprise Ireland's model of funding a commercialization feasibility study (where a sum of typically €10 000–15 000 is granted over a maximum period of 3 months) is cost-effective for research funding bodies. They limit the risk, where full commercialization funding (of typically between €130 000–300 000) is only granted when there is clear evidence that the new tool meets a real need that people are likely to pay for.

Our experience of participating in two feasibility studies indicates that marketing consultants are the recipients of the majority of the feasibility study funding, and the researchers are at liberty to select the consultants most suited to their development domain adhering to procurement fair trading rules where at least three consultants bid for the contract. Sourcing suitable consultants can be problematic since consultants with knowledge of both the market and the new technology being developed are scarce. Also, the fees charged by consultants means that the funding will only pay for around 13 days consultancy, all of which means that the researchers need to invest a lot of their own time to work with the consultants to fill in knowledge gaps and create needed documentation and marketing material such as a slide deck or video demo.

Enterprise Ireland takes a very inclusive view of what constitutes a product with potential for commercialization, and it provides support for researchers making applications. Our experience has been very positive where we benefited from a dedicated EI representative who worked with us to ensure had the best chance of being funded (providing the invention meets the key criteria relating to novelty and need). We managed the process from initial application through to approval within a six-month period.

Enterprise Ireland's Commercialization Fund Programme aims to convert the outputs of state-funded research into innovative new products, services, and companies. This program supports researchers in higher education institutions and research performing organizations to undertake research that has the potential to result in the commercialization of new innovations by way of licenses to improve the competitiveness of Irish industry or through the spin out of new startup ventures. Figure 4.5 summarizes the feasibility support given by EI, and Figure 4.6 describes the full commercialization project funding.

A **Commercial Case Feasibility Grant** goes toward investigating, scoping, and developing a commercial case for innovations or project ideas. Researchers, in partnership with their Technology Transfer Office (or equivalent office), can apply for this grant to:

- Perform market analysis and validation
- Profile the competitor landscape
- Perform patent landscaping and develop the IP strategy
- Investigate potential routes to exploitation to the economic benefit of Ireland
- Understand relevant regulatory issues or other barriers/hurdles to commercialization
- Create a small demonstration or early prototype

Figure 4.5 Commercial Case Feasibility Grant (according to EI).

A **Commercialisation Fund Project Support** is available to develop and commercialize research innovations. Researchers are given funding to undertake research projects that address a gap or need in the market by developing innovations that:

- can be commercialized in Ireland
- will be licensable ideally within 2–5 years
- can lead to the establishment of a startup company

Figure 4.6 Commercialisation Fund Project Support (according to EI).

In 2015, two of the authors of this chapter received funding to commercialize a training tool that had reached the stage of being a demonstrator. The tool[4] was originally developed as part of a Ph.D. program of research (Monasor, 2014). In Ireland, researchers are encouraged to seek commercialization funding that is available from EI and the European Regional Development Fund.[5]

4.5 Obstacles to Research Relevance

Not surprisingly, evolving a demonstrator to a tool that industry might use in practice requires a great deal of investment, in time devoted to technical development, project management, and marketing. This is a balancing act, and the reality of spending time on real development and marketing will doubtless impact on publishable output over the period of the commercialization project. On the other hand, while we have seen our research develop to a point where industry is showing genuine interest, turning that interest into actual economic rewards is quite a hurdle.

4.5.1 The (IR)Relevance of Academic Software Engineering Research

The vast majority of papers on software engineering are anything but rigorous. They often use self-selecting participants (or worse, students), they do not isolate them or attempt to find a representative sample, and they do not provide enough information for the research to be repeated. This will not change – simply because achieving rigor is so incredibly expensive that it is practically impossible.

However, this is not the reason why practitioners do not use and learn from research results. As noted above, the sources that practitioners use are even less rigorous and are often heavily biased toward commercial interests. The real

---

4 http://venture.lero.ie.
5 http://www.enterprise-ireland.com/en/funding-supports/Researcher/Funding-to-Commercialise-Research/.

problem is that researchers are neither incentivized nor funded to make their work relevant and practical.

The metrics for research success are based on publications. Thus, researchers have to publish early and often if they are to acquire a research reputation and continuing funding. Spending time making research "relevant and accessible" is wasted time, especially when compared to colleagues who are climbing the career ladder more quickly by publishing more papers, giving talks at conferences, and building their academic community reputation.

Also, there is a big gap between research results and practice, and to fill that gap and make research convincing to practitioners requires industrial scale experiments. This often means building properly engineered systems (not research prototypes), which is expensive, takes a lot of time, and does not generate many papers. If research sponsors want industry to use research, they have to fund this kind of work. This rarely happens, and so it is rarely possible to demonstrate the real potential of what seems to be high-quality research. The situation will not change until we address these problems, yet academia appears to have neither the will nor the resources to do so.

While it is clear that industry pays little attention to software engineering research, it is not clear whether this matters to practitioners. Industry has the resources to help change this situation, but industrial research funding is limited.

4.5.2 Barriers to Research Commercialization

In this section, we consider the wider question of "Why are there not more academic millionaires?" We do this by examining the challenges to commercializing software research as a route to dissemination.

Across the world, governments are encouraging universities to exploit their research to create new businesses, innovative products and, it is hoped, economic growth. In areas such as engineering, pharmacy and biotechnology, links between successful companies and universities are well-established and university research is often a starting point for new products, product improvements, and even government policy.

One might think that an area where there is huge potential for economically exploitable research is in software-related areas such as software engineering, artificial intelligence, and computer graphics. However, while some university researchers have been spectacularly successful in creating software companies (Google being the preeminent example), the vast majority of computing-related research has no direct commercial impact. There are two fundamental reasons for this:

First, in spite of their public commitment to research exploitation, universities do not value research commercialization activities as highly as research. Second, outside of areas such as engineering and biotechnology, academics and university management do not really understand what is involved in turning practical research into a successful product. The latter issue is a learning problem; the first, however, is a cultural and economic issue that is much more difficult to address.

4.5.3 Academic Barriers to Commercialization

Academics do not get promoted or secure tenure by commercializing their research. The advent of international university league tables such as the Times Higher Education World Rankings,[6] and national league tables in countries such as the United Kingdom means that universities adapt their strategy to perform as well as possible in these tables. The major factor in most of these tables is research performance, as measured by publications, citations, and research income awarded. Consequently, these are the metrics that are used to assess the performance of researchers.

Academics realize, often before getting a permanent appointment, that research is what really matters, and consequently they adjust their behavior so that research is prioritized. The metrics for research success are based around *publications*, so that researchers have to publish early and often if they are to acquire a research reputation and continuing funding. The general mindset in universities is research first, then teaching, then esteem, with *commercialization* coming a long way behind (if at all). The only way to change academic behavior is change the success metrics so that commercialization is given equal parity with research.

However, this is incredibly difficult, both culturally and practically. Culturally, the majority of disciplines in universities do not have scope to commercialize their research. Promotion and tenure committees include representatives from these disciplines, and these representatives will know little about the reality of commercialization. They will not be able to make an effective comparison of a researcher with well-cited publications to a researcher who has worked with industry to commercialize research.

Furthermore, commercialization is not an individual effort, and the success or otherwise of a commercialization activity is only partly related to the underlying research. An excellent piece of research with commercial potential may fail because the companies involved do not invest enough in the work; it may fail because the economic climate makes venture capital funding difficult; and it may fail because a competitive product comes to market earlier. How can a tenure committee take these things into account?

More established professors have fewer concerns about promotion or tenure so perhaps they are better positioned to pursue commercialization. Leaving aside the fact that personnel at this level often have administrative

---

6 https://www.timeshighereducation.com/world-university-rankings.

responsibilities, the reality is that many senior academics are unlikely to have had any experience in industry. The reason for this is obvious – they have been promoted because they are good researchers – and to establish a research track record, they have to spend most of their time working in universities on research projects. In short, academics lack "skin in the game" (Monasor et al., 2013).

4.5.4 Business Barriers to Commercialization

The adoption of new technologies is often more influenced by business issues than the actual functionality provided by the new technology. Key factors that influence industry take-up of technology include:

Compatibility. How does the technology fit with the software, hardware, and business processes used in a company? Technology that requires existing infrastructures to change will be harder to exploit. (Since the amount of work needed to adapt the technology to fit with other software is often unknown.)

Trust. Is the new technology supplied by a company that is an existing supplier or a company with at least a national reputation? This is important because companies have to trust their suppliers of new technology. For this reason and for reasons of compatibility, it may make sense to develop new technologies in partnership with an existing company. However, many academics are reluctant to do this because it means giving up at least some control of the development. Knowledge exchange or technology transfer offices in universities are also wary of transferring university IP to an external organization.

Reliability. If the new technology has been built as part of a funded project or Ph.D. research program, how can industry be assured that the new technology will be maintained past the lifetime of the project? What incentives are there for the academic team to continue to work on the development once the funding stops?

Risk. Adopting new technology may create new business risks that are not well-understood. Middle management personnel, who are often the decision makers in a business, are particularly averse to risk as it threatens their position. They therefore tend to be conservative and prefer well-tried rather than novel technologies.

Usefulness. Is a product actually useful to a business? If a company (rightly or wrongly) does not think they have the problems that the technology addresses, it is difficult to convince them to adopt it. The new tool needs to address some pain point for the industry to convince them to make the investment (Monasor et al., 2013).

Usability. Many researchers see usability as an "add-on" and focus on the functionality of their innovation. However, if it is not obvious within a few minutes how a product can be used in a particular setting, it is unlikely to be adopted.

Cost-effectiveness. Researchers tend to focus on problems that they see as interesting, rather than issues that have the most effect on business costs. Creating a new tool or process that leads to a 20% improvement in a process that represents 5% of the total development cost of a system is unlikely to be successful, irrespective of the merits of the innovation. Yet, process is important, and business success is positively correlated to organizations continually reflecting on and adapting their processes in response to changing situational contexts (Clarke et al., 2015).

Fashion and blind prejudice. Although they may claim to be objective, decision makers are influenced by fashion and prejudice and an innovation that is seen as addressing "old problems" is likely to be less well-received than one that addresses problems that managers have read about recently.

An important consequence of these factors from a university innovation perspective is that the value of some new technology to business is likely to be significantly less than a valuation that is based on the functionality of a technology. All too often, academics claim their technology to be better than existing technology and so its value should be comparable to or greater than that technology. They are disillusioned when they discover that the rest of the world does not share their views.

4.5.5 Organizational Barriers to Commercialization

Of course, universities recognize that their academics lack industry experience and marketing expertise, and virtually all universities now have innovation offices and technology transfer offices whose ostensible role is to support academics in taking their research to market. The personnel in these offices are supposed to have a better understanding of how to commercialize research; they are mandated to work with the academic research "owner" to reduce the time she needs to spend away from her academic work.

The experience of the authors, who worked as academics in several universities in the United Kingdom, Ireland, and the United States, was that these offices were ineffective and often hindered rather than supported innovation. There were several reasons for this:

Few, if any, staff in these offices had a background in computing or software engineering. They did not understand the innovation pipeline for software, the importance of bringing new software-based technologies to market quickly, the importance of the people involved to the value of an innovation, and exploitation models such as open-source software (Kogut and Metiu, 2001).

The lack of understanding of the software industry meant that innovation office staff had no experience in valuing software research, and so tended to base value on what a user would have to spend to replicate the work rather than on the business value of an innovation.

The initial response to any new approach in these offices was IP protection, through patents and other risk elimination tactics. This inevitably introduces significant delays and costs into the process.

The metrics through which innovation offices are judged tend to be process metrics such as the number of potential users consulted, rather than financial metrics such as the number of successful spin-outs or licensing agreements.

The way around these issues is to ensure that researchers can access innovation support within their own discipline, from people who have experience of the software industry. This is impractical in small departments, but there is evidence that this approach is effective: the Edinburgh School of Informatics has in-house innovation support and is one of the most successful in research exploitation in the United Kingdom, through startups and spin-outs. Similarly, Lero – the Irish Software Research Centre, has at the time of this writing employed a dedicated person whose role is to facilitate commercialization of the research produced in Lero's research projects.

4.5.6 Funding Barriers to Commercialization

Apart from these internal barriers to the exploitation of software-related research, the nature of the innovation process means that there is a critical funding gap between research results and the development of a convincing industrial prototype system. Figure 4.7 shows how existing government and venture capital funding fits into this innovation pipeline.

The problem faced by academic innovators is the funding gap between the development of a proof-of-concept demonstrator (in the second step) and the funding of early versions of a product (in the fourth step). Research funding bodies take ideas and fund proof-of-concept systems (stages 1 and 2). Venture capitalists take prototypes and fund product development (stages 3–5).

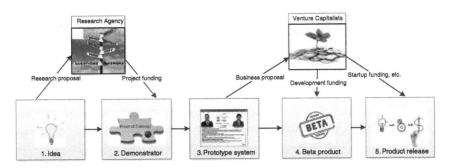

Figure 4.7 Funding the innovation pipeline.

However, there are few funders for the crucial central prototype development stage (as shown in), which shows the commercial rather than the technical viability of an innovation. It is not research, so not in the remit of the research funding bodies; venture capitalists hesitate to support such early-stage work because of the risks that the work is not commercially viable.

Routes to funding this development of research include angel investors, who will take on risky projects for a large percentage of equity and university innovation funds who may have short-term funding available. However, obtaining such funding is typically a time-intensive and sometimes bureaucratic process.

Furthermore, even if funding is available, university processes may make it difficult to develop and deliver a prototype system quickly. Typically, universities are large organizations with formal, often bureaucratic, hiring processes. Appointing new staff, even to temporary positions, is often a prolonged process. Sometimes this takes so long that it is impossible to retain the researchers involved in the initial demonstrator development so new staff take longer to get up to speed and understand what they are doing. This has indeed been the case with our own project VENTURE (www.venture.lero.ie), where the original Ph.D. student who developed the demonstrator could not wait for the uncertainty of funding coming through, and as an excellent developer was quickly hired by a leading software company.

All this means that academic researchers are often reluctant to engage in commercialization processes. They do not contribute directly to academic career metrics and they involve activities that, put simply, are not much fun. It is not surprising that they often prefer to move onto a new idea rather than continue the development of a demonstrator system.

Does all this mean that the commercial exploitation of research in computer science and software engineering is a lost cause? We believe that, with the current system, encouragement is not enough and unless there is significant change, then we will not see significant commercialization of research from universities. Changes that we think are essential are mentioned as follows:

1) The establishment of a separate career path in universities for researchers, which is based on research exploitation. Critically, individual assessment of "success" within this career path has to be based on peer review not on some arbitrary metrics, and there should not be direct comparisons with other career paths. Researchers should be able to move to and from the research career path but should not be put in a position where they have to be researchers as well as exploiters of that research.

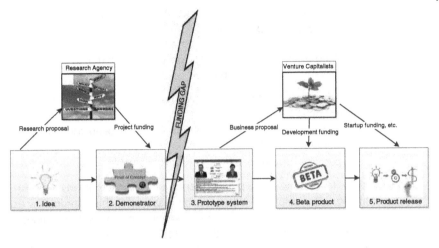

Figure 4.8 The prototype funding gap.

2) The co-location of researchers on this path with research support officers who have recent industrial experience and an understanding of the technology being exploited. There should not be unrealistic expectations of commercial success and there has to be cross-funding from successful to unsuccessful projects.

3) Universities must be realistic about IP ownership and give ownership of the IP to the researchers. Researchers engaged in exploitation are then working for themselves and are more likely to be motivated to succeed. Of course, this means that if the work is commercially successful, universities will not have a legal basis for sharing in that financial success. However, experience in the United States is that successful researchers are often major donors to endowment funds so, indirectly, benefits may accrue to the university from the work.

4) There must be funding mechanisms to bridge the "prototype gap" as discussed above (see Figure 4.8). Either universities or research agencies should provide limited seed funding so that convincing prototypes can be developed and demonstrated. It would be perfectly reasonable to expect a successful company to repay this funding so that the supporting funds can be self-sustaining.

Box 4.1: The Practice–Research Paradox

There are several arguments that illustrate the potential value that practitioners could receive from the research community.

- Problems mentioned by practitioners are well-known and well-studied by the research community.
- Many empirically based and validated solutions have been identified to address the problems raised by practitioners.
- Practitioners perceive that research is potentially valuable.

Despite these facts, none of the practitioners in our sample regularly looks to academic literature for solutions. What are the reasons for this paradox?

The first is *accessibility*. Practitioners do not have time to read and digest academic publications to extract potentially relevant solutions to their specific problems. Also, practitioners must interpret these research results in the context of their own organizations. Peer-reviewed articles are also expensive (few are open access).

The second is *credibility*. Robert Glass's assertion of the practice–research gap (Glass, 1996) is nicely reflected in practitioner preference for advice from people with "skin in the game."

Last is *relevance*. Academic publications are written to satisfy academic standards of scientific rigor and follow conventions appropriate for academic discourse. As such, even if the subject discussed is relevant, much of the content of a typical academic publication is not relevant to a manager seeking, for example, an introduction to GSE issues or solutions to a specific problem.

4.6 Conclusion

Returning to GSE research as an example, we find that although researchers address relevant problems, that relevance is often buried in the detail. Also, to address the question of whether the published solutions are reaching their intended audience, we can confidently say "no". Why? Because research results often are inaccessible, lack credibility, and are irrelevant (see Box 4.1).

When researching, we have collaborated with industry partners on many projects at many different levels. During this time, we have established our checklist for researchers and the wider community to consider when promoting stronger ties between research and industry (see Table 4.3).

Table 4.3 Checklist for researchers conducting industry relevant research.

Question	Recommendations
Why?	Ensure that the research addresses a business problem as well as a technical problem, reflects the needs of practice, and you can confidently declare the reason for conducting the research.
What?	To accompany the academic publication, write shorter (two page) evidence-based papers using accessible, nonacademic language, where findings are validated from a business perspective, to ensure their credibility.
Who?	Researchers and practitioners should work more closely together, collaborating in both conducting and reporting research (e.g. Industry Fellowships, Industry Ph.D.'s, Action research).
Where?	Researchers need to disseminate their work more widely – venture into the "gray" literature, and use social networks, blogs, and wikis as well as alternative media, such as videos, to reach a wide audience. Also through workshops or commercialization activities.
How?	Work with industry and funding agencies to secure funding to develop research, and help industry understand the importance of publications to academic recognition.

4.6.1 Research and Practice Working Together to Innovate

Innovation is at the heart of our work – it is through launching new tools, applications, etc. that businesses thrive. It is the new ideas that academics gain their reputation. Therefore, how can we work together to achieve our mutual goals? Perhaps one way is that when we as researchers put forward our novel ideas, they must resonate with the needs of the community: "to engage industry in technology transfer, we cannot just present technical solutions but must also relate these to the real needs of the business" (Sommerville and Ransom, 2005).

The impact software engineering research has on practical business is subtle (Grier, 2014). In some cases, we can clearly trace the new ideas that began in universities, where the ideas get tested "in the rigors of a laboratory, are published in academic journals and then move forth into the world where they become the foundation for products and services" (Grier, 2014). For example the first Google server was built by Sergey Brin and Larry Page in a Stanford University lab.

How can we trace the course of any significant theoretical concept from abstract formulation to actual use in industrial operations? Grier fears that over the years the interests of business and research are moving further apart, especially since any university-based research that has a substantial impact on industry is "almost always difficult to separate from other parts of organizational life"(Grier, 2014).

4.6.2 Final Thoughts

If research sponsors want industry to use research, they have to fund the building of properly engineered systems (not flaky research prototypes). This type of research is expensive, takes a lot of time, and does not generate many papers.

However, once the tools, technologies, and methods derived from research have been applied in practice, researchers should be well placed to publish their development activities as case studies.[7] Technical reports and white papers can be converted, with a little creativity, into academic papers. Researchers could be doubly rewarded by (a) seeing their ideas move from theory/prototype to practice and a fully functioning tool, and (b) moving up the academic ladder by publishing their validated research in good venues, and being cited for their original work. In accordance with our dissemination message, the authors of this chapter are all now going to triangulate this dissemination: we will blog about this research and produce a summarized version of the paper presented as a white paper. We will continue to give seminars in our specific fields, participate in industry workshops, and spend time with industry with our fellowships and action research initiatives. We may even move completely into the practitioner sphere should our commercialization efforts succeed in becoming a spin-out.

Acknowledgments

We thank all the practitioners who gave of their time and agreed to be interviewed. EI supported this work through its Commercialization Fund Programme under Commercial Case Feasibility (support contract number CF20122753Y), through its Commercialization Fund and the European Regional Development Fund (support contract number CF 2014 4348, 2015), and through grant 10/CE/I1855 to ARCH – Applied Research for Connected Health.

This work was also supported, in part, by Science Foundation Ireland grant 13/RC/2094 and co-funded under the European Regional Development Fund through the Southern & Eastern Regional Operational Programme to Lero – the Irish Software Research Centre (www.lero.ie).

References

D.E. Avison, F. Lau, M.D. Myers, and P.A. Nielsen (1999) Action research. *Communications of the ACM*, **42** (1), 94–97 0001–0782.

R.L. Baskerville (1999) Investigating information systems with action research. *Communications of the Association for Information Systems (AIS)*, **2** (4), 1–32.

---

7 Need to ensure that any nondisclosure agreements setup between collaborating parties allows for this.

S. Beecham, N. Carroll, and J. Noll (2012) *A decision support system for global team management: expert evaluation* REMIDI – International Workshop on Tool Support Development and Management in Distributed Software Projects co-located with 7th IEEE International Conference on Global Software Engineering (ICGSE '12) PUCRS, Porto Alegre, Brazil, August 27–30, IEEE Computer Society.

S. Beecham and J. Noll (2015) What Motivates Software Engineers Working in Global Software Development? *16th International Conference on Product-Focussed Software Process Improvement (Profes'15), Bolzano, Italy, 2–4 December,* Springer.

S. Beecham, J. Noll, and I. Richardson (2014) *Using Agile Practices to Solve Global Software Development Problems – A Case Study. In: Methods and Tools for Project/Architecture/Risk Management.* Globally Distributed Software Development Projects PARIS Workshop (ICGSEW'14), co-located with ICGSE, Fudan University, Shanghai, China August 18–21, IEEE Computer Society.

S. Beecham, J. Noll, and I. Richardson (2015) Assessing the Strength of Global Teaming practices: A pilot study. *IEEE International Conference on Global Software Engineering (ICGSE'15), Castilla-la Mancha, Spain,* IEEE Computer Society.

S. Beecham, J. Noll, I. Richardson, and N. Ali (2010) *Crafting a global teaming model for architectural knowledge management.* IEEE International Conference on Global Software Engineering (ICGSE'10), Princeton, New Jersey, USA, 23–26 August.

S. Beecham, J. Noll, I. Richardson, and D. Dhungana (2011) *A decision support system for global software development.* Sixth IEEE International Conference on Global Software Engineering Workshop (ICGSEW), IEEE 1457718391.

S. Beecham, P. O'Leary, S. Baker, I. Richardson, and J. Noll (2014) Making software engineering research relevant. *IEEE Computer,* **47** (4), 80–83.

S. Beecham, P. OLeary, I. Richardson, S. Baker, and J. Noll (2013) *Who are we doing Global Software Engineering research for?* IEEE 8th International Conference on Global Software Engineering (ICGSE) IEEE.

A.K. Biswas and J. Kirchherr (2015) Prof, no one is reading you. *The Straits Times,* Singapore, SPH Digital News/Copyright © 2015 Singapore Press Holdings Ltd. Co. Regn. No. 198402868E.

J. Burton (2008) A Software Risk Management Capability Model for Medical Device Software, PhD Thesis, University of Limerick.

J. Burton, F. McCaffery, and I. Richardson (2008) Improving software risk management practices in a medical device company. In: Q. Wang, D. Pfahl, D.M. Raffo (eds) *Making Globally Distributed Software Development a Success Story. ICSP 2008. Lecture Notes in Computer Science,* vol **5007**, Springer, Berlin, Heidelberg.

O. Cawley, X. Wang, and I. Richardson (2011) *Medical Device Software Development – A Perspective from a Lean Manufacturing Plant.* Software

Process Improvement and Capability determination Conference, Dublin, Ireland, 30 May–1 June.

P. Clarke and R. V. O'Connor (2013) An empirical examination of the extent of software process improvement in software SMEs. *Journal of Software: Evolution and Process*, **25** (9), 981–998 2047–7481.

P. Clarke, R. V. O'Connor, B. Leavy, and M. Yilmaz (2015) Exploring the relationship between software process adaptive capability and organisational performance. *IEEE Transactions on Software Engineering*, **41** (12), 1169–1183.

CMMI Product Team (2006) Capability Maturity Model® Integration for Development, Version 1.2 (CMMI). Technical Report CMU/SEI-2006-TR-008, Carnegie Mellon University.

S. Deshpande, S. Beecham, and I. Richardson (2013) Using the PMBOK Guide to Frame GSD Coordination Strategies. *IEEE 8th International Conference on Global Software Engineering (ICGSE)*, IEEE.

B. Fitzgerald, K. Stol, R. O'Sullivan, and D. O'Brien (2013) *Scaling Agile Methods to Regulated Environments: An Industry Case Study*. Proceedings of the 35th International Conference on Software Engineering (Software Engineering in Practice track), San Francisco, USA.

R. Glass (1996) The relationship between theory and practice in software engineering. *Communications of the ACM*, **39** (11) 11–13.

D.J. Greenwood and M. Levin (2006) *Introduction to action research: Social research for social change*, SAGE publications, ISBN: 1483389375.

D.A. Grier (2014) Practice and theory. *Computer*, (2), 104–104, 0018–9162.

IEC 62304:2006 (2008) Medical device software – Software life cycle processes, International Standards Organization.

ISO 14971 (2007) Medical devices – Application of risk management to medical devices, 2nd Edition, International Standards Organization.

ISO/IEC 12207:2008 (2008) Systems and software engineering – Software life cycle processes, International Standards Organization.

B. Kitchenham, S. L. Pfleeger, L. Pickard, P. Jones, D. Hoaglin, K. El Emam, and J. Rosenberg (2002) Preliminary guidelines for empirical research in software engineering. *IEEE Transactions on Software Engineering*, **28** (8), 721–734.

E. Kocaguneli, T. Zimmermann, C. Bird, N. Nagappan, and T. Menzies (2013) *Distributed Development Considered Harmful? A Case Study of Reporting Research to Industry*. Proceedings of the 35th International Conference on Software Engineering (ICSE 2013 Software Engineering In Practice (SEIP) Track), San Francisco, CA, USA, May.

B. Kogut, and A. Metiu (2001) Open-source software development and distributed innovation. *Oxford Review of Economic Policy*, **17** (2), 248–264.

F. McCaffery, J. Burton, and I. Richardson (2010) Risk Management Capability Model (RMCM) for the development of medical device software. *Software Quality Journal*, **18** (1), 81–107 DOI: 10.1007/s11219-009-9086-7.

M.J. Monasor (2014) A framework for interaction training in Global Software Development. PhD Thesis, University of Castilla-La Mancha.

M.J. Monasor, A. Vizcaíno, M. Piattini, J. Noll, and S. Beecham (2013) *Simulating Global Software Development Processes for Use in Education: A Feasibility Study. Systems, Software and Services Process Improvement*, Springer Berlin Heidelberg, pp. 36–47, ISBN: 3642391788.

M.J. Monasor, A. Vizcaíno, M. Piattini, J. Noll, and S. Beecham (2013) Simulating global software development processes for use in education: A feasibility study. *Systems, Software and Services Process Improvement*, 36–47.

J.M. Morse (1991) Approaches to qualitative-quantitative methodological triangulation. *Nursing Research*, **40** (2), 12–123, 0029–6562.

J. Noll, S. Beecham, and I. Richardson (2010) Global software development and collaboration: Barriers and solutions. *ACM Inroads*, **1** (3), 66–78, 2153–2184.

J. Noll, I. Richardson, and S. Beecham (2014) *Patternizing GSD Research: Maintainable Decision Support for Global Software Development*. Ninth IEEE International Conference on Global Software Engineering (ICGSE'14), Fudan University, Shanghai, China, August 18–21, IEEE Computer Society.

P. O'Leary (2010) Towards a Product Derivation Process Reference Model for Software Product Line Organisations. PhD Thesis, University of Limerick, Ireland.

P. O'Leary, E.S.D. Almeida, and I. Richardson (2012) The pro-pd process model for product derivation within software product lines. *Information and Software Technology*, **54** (9), 1014–1028.

P. O'Leary, S. Thiel, and I. Richardson (2010) Experience Report on Industrial Product Derivation Practices within a Software Product Line Organisation. Lero Technical Reports: Limerick, Ireland. Lero-TR-2010-03.

S.L. Pfleeger (1999) Albert Einstein and empirical software engineering. *IEEE Computer*, **32** (10), 32–37.

F.J. Pino, F. García, and M. Piattini (2008) Software process improvement in small and medium software enterprises: a systematic review. *Software Quality Journal*, **16** (2), 237–261, DOI: 10.1007/s11219-007-9038-z.

V. Ramesh, R. L. Glass, and I. Vessey (2004) Research in computer science: an empirical study. *Journal of Systems and Software*, **70** (1–2), 165–176. DOI: http://dx.doi.org/10.1016/S0164-1212(03)00015-3 0164–1212.

A. Raninen (2014) Practical Process Improvement: SPI Enablers for Small Product-Focused Software Companies. PhD, University of Eastern Finland.

A. Raninen, J. Ahonen, H. M. Sihvonen, P. Savolainen, and S. Beecham (2013) LAPPI: A light-weight technique to practical process modelling and improvement target identification. *Journal of Software: Evolution and Process (JSEP)*, **25**, 915–933.

A. Raninen, H. Merikoski, J.J. Ahonen, and S. Beecham (2015) Applying software process modeling to improve customer support processes. *Journal of Software: Evolution and Process (JSEP)*, **27**, 274–293, DOI: 10.1002/smr.1713.

I. Richardson, V. Casey, F. McCaffery, J. Burton, and S. Beecham (2012) A process framework for global software engineering teams. *Information and Software Technology*, **54** (11), 1175–1191, 0950–5849.

I. Richardson and C. Gresse von Wangenheim (2007) Guest Editors' introduction: why are small software organizations different? *IEEE Software*, **24** (1), 18–22, 0740–7459.

P. Runeson and M. Höst (2009) Guidelines for conducting and reporting case study research in software engineering. *Empirical Software Engineering*, **14** (2), 131–164, 1382–3256.

D.I.K. Sjøberg, J.E. Hannay, O. Hansen, V. B. Kampenes, A. Karahasanovic, N. K. Liborg, and A. C. Rekdal (2005) A survey of controlled experiments in software engineering. *IEEE Transactions on Software Engineering*, **31** (9), 733–753.

I. Sommerville and J. Ransom (2005) An empirical study of industrial requirements engineering process assessment and improvement. *ACM Transactions on Software Engineering and Methodology*, **14** (1), 85–117.

R.N. Taylor (2010) Enabling innovation: a choice for software engineering. Proceedings of the FSE/SDP workshop on Future of software engineering research. Santa Fe, New Mexico, USA, ACM: 375–378.

Part II

Autonomous Software Systems

5

Apoptotic Computing: Programmed Death by Default for Software Technologies

Roy Sterritt[1] and Mike Hinchey[2]

[1]*School of Computing, and Computer Science Research Institute, Ulster University, County Antrim, Northern Ireland*
[2]*Lero – The Irish Software Research Centre, University of Limerick, Limerick, Ireland*

5.1 Biological Apoptosis

The biological analogy of autonomic systems has been well discussed in the literature, including Refs [1–3]. While reading this the reader is not consciously concerned with their breathing rate or how fast their heart is beating. Achieving the development of a computer system that can self-manage without the conscious effort of the user is the vision and ultimate goal. Another typical biological example is that the touching of a sharp knife results in a reflex reaction to reconfigure the area in danger to a state that is out of danger (self-protection, self-configuration, and, if damage is caused, self-healing) [4].

If one cuts oneself and starts bleeding, one treats it and carries on with one's tasks without any further conscious thought (although pain receptors will induce self-protection and self-configuration to use the other hand!). However, often, the cut will have caused skin cells to be displaced down into muscle tissue [5]. If they survive and divide, they have the potential to grow into a tumor. The body's solution to deal with this situation is cell self-destruction (with mounting evidence that some forms of cancer are the result of cells not dying fast enough, rather than multiplying out of control, as previously thought).

It is believed that a cell knows when to commit suicide because cells are programmed to do so – self-destruct (sD) is an intrinsic property. This sD is delayed due to the continuous receipt of biochemical retrieves. This process is referred to as apoptosis [6,7], pronounced either as *APE-oh-TOE-sls* or *uh-POP-tuh-sis* and stands for "to fall off" or "drop out," used by the Greeks to refer to the Fall/Autumn dropping of leaves from trees; that is, loss of cells that ought to die in the midst of the living structure. The process has also been nicknamed "death by default" [5], where cells are prevented from putting an end to themselves due to constant receipt of biochemical "stay alive" signals. The key aspect of apoptosis is that the cell's self-destruction takes place in a programmed and controlled way; the suicidal cell starts to shrink, decomposes internal structures, and degrades all internal proteins. Thereafter, the cell breaks into small membrane-wrapped fragments (*drop-off*) that will be engulfed by phagocytic cells for recycling. Necrosis, is the unprogrammed death of a cell, involving inflammation and toxic substances leaking to the environment [6].

Further investigations into the apoptosis process [7] have discovered more details about the self-destruct program. Whenever a cell divides, it simultaneously receives orders to kill itself. Without a reprieve signal, the cell does indeed self-destruct. It is believed that the reason for this is self-protection, as the most dangerous time for the body is when a cell divides, since if just one of the billions of cells locks into division the result is a tumor, while simultaneously a cell must divide to build and maintain a body.

The suicide and reprieve controls have been compared to the dual key on a nuclear missile [8]. The key (chemical signal) turns on cell growth but at the same time switches on a sequence that leads to self-destruction. The second key overrides the self-destruct [8].

5.2 Autonomic Agents

The name *autonomic* is suggestive of an analogy to the biological nervous system and properties of homeostasis and responsiveness. The general properties of an autonomic, or self-managing, system can be summarized by four objectives – and four attributes [9,10]. Essentially, the objectives represent broad system requirements, while the attributes identify basic implementation mechanisms. An autonomic system's objectives are as follows:

- *Self-Configuration*. The system must be able to readjust itself automatically, either to support a change in circumstances or to assist in meeting other system objectives.
- *Self-Healing*. In reactive mode, the system must effectively recover when a fault occurs, identify the fault, and, when possible, repair it. In proactive mode, the system monitors vital signs to predict and avoid health problems, or reaching undesirable levels.
- *Self-Optimization*. The system can measure its current performance against the known optimum and has defined policies for attempting improvements. It can also react to the user's policy changes within the system.

- *Self-Protection.* The system must defend itself from accidental or malicious external attacks, which requires an awareness of potential threats and the means to manage them.

To achieve these self-managing objectives, a system must be

- *self-aware*–aware of its internal state;
- *self-situated*–aware of current external operating conditions and context;
- *self-monitoring*–able to detect changing circumstances; and
- *self-adjusting*–able to adapt accordingly.

Thus, a system must be aware of its available resources and components, their ideal performance characteristics, and current status. It must also be aware of interconnection with other systems, as well as rules and policies for adjusting as required. A system's ability to operate in a heterogeneous environment requires relying on open standards to communicate with other systems. These mechanisms do not exist independently. For example, to successfully survive an attack, the system must exhibit self-healing abilities, with a mix of self-configuration and self-optimization. This not only ensures the system's dependability and continued operation, but also increases self-protection from similar future attacks. Self-managing mechanisms must also ensure minimal disruption to users.

Autonomic computing is dependent on many disciplines for its success; not least of these is research in agent technologies. There are no assumptions that agents have to be used in an autonomic architecture, but their properties such as adaptability, autonomy, cooperation, and so on complement very well the objectives of the paradigm. In addition, as in complex systems there are arguments for designing the system with agents [11], as well as providing inbuilt redundancy and greater robustness [12], through to retrofitting legacy systems with autonomic capabilities that may benefit from an agent approach [13].

Emerging research suggests that the autonomic manager may be an agent itself; for instance, an agent termed as self-managing cell (SMC) [14] containing functionality for measurement and event correlation and support for policy-based control.

In Figure 5.1, the autonomic manager (AM) may be considered to be a stationary agent managing a component. The autonomic communications channel implies that AMs communicate through such means as event messages. However, it is feasible for mobile agents to play a role here. The proclaimed mobile agent advantages, such as the ability to reduce network load, overcome network latency, encapsulate protocols, execute asynchronously, execute autonomously, adapt dynamically, reflect natural heterogeneity, maintain robustness and fault-tolerance, would facilitate autonomic managers within different systems cooperating via agents (Figure 5.2) as well as self-* event messages to manage the system.

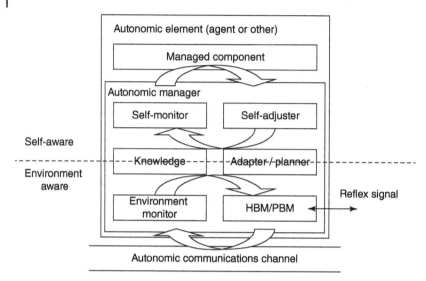

Figure 5.1 Autonomic element: managed component plus autonomic manager. (Reproduced from Ref. [15] with permission from IEEE.)

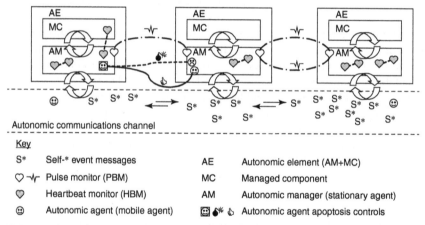

Figure 5.2 An autonomic environment consisting of autonomic elements with autonomic agents (stationary and mobile), HBMs (I am alive), PBMs (I am healthy), and Apoptosis (stay alive). (Reproduced from Ref. [16] with permission from Springer.)

5.3 Apoptosis within Autonomic Agents

Agent destruction has been proposed for mobile agents, in order to facilitate security measures [17]. Greenberg et al. highlighted the scenario simply by recalling the situation where the server omega.univ.edu was decommissioned, its work moving to other machines. When a few years later a new computer was assigned the old name, to the surprise of everyone, email arrived, much of it 3 years old [17]. The mail had survived "pending" on Internet relays waiting for omega.univ.edu to come back up.

Greenberg encourages consideration of the same situation for mobile agents; these would not be rogue mobile agents – they would be carrying proper authenticated credentials. This work would be done totally out of context due to neither abnormal procedure nor system failure. In this circumstance, the mobile agent could cause substantial damage, for example, deliver an archaic upgrade to part of the network operating system, resulting in bringing down the entire network.

Misuse involving mobile agents comes in the form of misuse of hosts by agents, misuse of agents by hosts, and misuse of agents by other agents. From an agent perspective, the first is through accidental or unintentional situations caused by that agent (race conditions and unexpected emergent behavior), the latter two through deliberate or accidental situations caused by external bodies acting upon the agent. The range of these situations and attacks have been categorized as damage, denial-of-service, breach-of-privacy, harassment, social engineering, event-triggered attacks, and compound attacks.

In the situation where portions of an agent's binary image (e.g., monetary certificates, keys, information, etc.) are vulnerable to being copied when visiting a host, this can be prevented by encryption. However, there has to be decryption in order to execute, which provides a window of vulnerability [17]. This situation has similar overtones to our previous discussion on biological apoptosis, where the body is at its most vulnerable during cell division [15].

Figure 5.2 represents a high level view of an autonomic environment (much of the detail is extracted for simplicity, showing only 3 AEs (*autonomic elements*) whereas a system may have in the hundreds, thousand to millions of managed components). Each of the AEs is an abstract view of figure and in this scenario the *managed component* (MC) represents a self-managing computer system. Note that each of these autonomic elements (self-managing computer system) may have many other lower level AEs (for instance an autonomic manager for the disk drive) while at the same time the AEs in Figure 5.2 may reside within the scope of a higher level AM (system-wide local area network domain's AE).

Within an AM, vital processes may be safeguarded by heartbeat monitors (I am alive) to ensure their continued operation, and to have an immediate indication if any fail (note in Figure 5.2 that all three AEs have HBMs within their AMs). An AM has a control loop continually monitoring (and adjusting if necessary) metrics within the MC, yet vital processes within the MC may also be safeguarded by a HBM with it emitting a heartbeat as opposed to being polled by the AM to ensure its continued operation, resulting in avoiding lost time (time to next poll) for the AM to notice it has failed when it does fail (note in Figure 5.2 that the left-hand AE has a HBM between the AM and a process on the MC).

Since each AM is in a key position to be aware of the health of its computer-based system (through the continuous control loop with the MC), it may share this health indication through a pulse (I am un/healthy) to another AM (for instance, in Figure 5.2 the left-hand AE to the middle AE) this not only allows self-managing options if the machines are, for instance, sharing workload as a cluster but protects the AM itself as the pulse also acts as a HBM from one AM to another. As such, if the vital process of the AM itself fails, the neighboring AM will immediately become aware and, for instance, pursue a restart of the failed AM and/or initiate a failover to another AM. This pulse signal may also act as a reflex signal (more direct than the AM processing lots of event messages to eventually determine an urgent situation) between AMs warning of an immediate incident. Since AMs also monitor the external environment (the second control loop) they have a view of how healthy the environment is in their locality. This *environment health* may also be encoded into the pulse signal along with that *self health* (just as our hearts have a double beat – lubb-dupp). This is represented by the double pulse signals between the right-hand and center AEs in Figure 5.2.

It has been highlighted that the AMs communicate and cooperate through self-managing event messages and pulse signals. Mobile agents may also be used to assist in the self-managing tasks where one AM dispatches an agent to work on its behalf, for example to update a set of policies. The apoptosis (stay alive/self-destruct mechanism) may be utilized in this scenario as self-protection, to withdraw authorization to continue operation, for example, if the policies become out-of-date (Figure 5.2 left-hand AE to the middle AE depicts both scenarios, one agent is to self-destruct the other still has an authorization "stay alive" signal to continue). Note that the self-destruct scenario is indicated by a dotted line, as in the case of *strong* apoptotic computing it is the actual absence of the stay alive signal that will result in the self-destruction (death by default). *Weak* apoptotic computing may send an explicit (self-destruct) signal to trigger the destruction (see Section 5.5.1).

There exists a concern in certain circumstances over denial-of-service (DoS) attacks being used to prevent stay alive signals reaching where they need to be and as such inducing unintentional self-destruct – a hackers dream. Likewise, DoS is an issue for weak apoptotic computing preventing terminate signals potentially leaving dangerous scenarios. We need to develop DoS immune architecture as part of the next-generation self-managing systems.

5.4 NASA SWARM Concept Missions

Space Exploration Missions, through necessity, have been incorporating more and more autonomy and adaptability. Autonomy may be considered as self-governance of one's own tasks/goals. NASA is investigating the use of swarm technologies for the development of sustainable exploration missions that will be autonomous and exhibit autonomic properties [15]. The idea is that biologically inspired swarms of smaller spacecraft offer greater redundancy (and, consequently, greater protection of assets), reduced costs and risks, and the ability to explore regions of space where a single large spacecraft would be impractical.

ANTS (Autonomous NanoTechnology Swarm) is a NASA concept mission, a collaboration between NASA Goddard Space Flight Center and NASA Langley Research Center, which aims at the development of revolutionary mission architectures and the exploitation of artificial intelligence techniques and the paradigm of biological inspiration in future space exploration [18]. The mission concept includes the use of swarm technologies for both spacecraft and surface-based rovers, and consists of several sub-missions:

- *SARA: The Saturn Autonomous Ring Array* will launch 1000 pico-class spacecraft, organized as ten sub-swarms, each with specialized instruments, to perform in situ exploration of Saturn's rings, by which to understand their constitution and how they were formed. The concept mission will require self-configuring structures for nuclear propulsion and control. Additionally, autonomous operation is necessary for both maneuvering around Saturn's rings and collision avoidance.
- *PAM: Prospecting Asteroid Mission* will also launch 1000 pico-class spacecraft, but here with the aim of exploring the asteroid belt and collecting data on particular asteroids of interest for potential future mining operations.
- *LARA: ANTS Application Lunar Base Activities* will exploit new NASA-developed technologies in the field of miniaturized robotics, which may form the basis of remote landers to be launched to the moon from remote sites, and may exploit innovative techniques to allow rovers to move in an amoeboid-like fashion over the moon's uneven terrain.

In terms of ANTS, missions' autonomy, for instance, results in a worker having responsibility for its goals. To achieve these goals, many self-* properties such as self-configuration will be necessary, as well as utilization of HBM, PBM, and reflex reactions within AMs. NASA missions, such as ANTS, have mission control and operations in a trusted private environment. This eliminates many of the wide range of agent security issues discussed earlier, just leaving the particular concerns; namely, is the agent operating in the correct context and exhibiting emergent behavior within acceptable parameters, whereupon apoptosis can make a contribution.

The ANTS architecture is itself inspired by biological low-level social insect colonies with their success in the division of labor. Within their specialties, individual specialists generally outperform generalists, and with sufficiently efficient social interaction and coordination, the group of specialists generally outperforms the group of generalists. Thus, systems designed as ANTS are built from potentially very large numbers of highly autonomous, yet socially inter-active, elements. The architecture is self-similar in that elements and subelements of the system may also be recursively structured as ANTS [19], and as such the self-management architecture with at least an AM per ANT craft can abstractly fit with that portrayed in Figure 5.2.

The revolutionary ANTS paradigm makes the achievement of such goals possible through the use of many small, autonomous, reconfigurable, redundant element craft acting as independent or collective agents [20].

Let us consider the role of the self-destruct property, inspired by apoptosis, in the ANTS mission: Suppose one of the worker agents was indicating incorrect operation, or when coexisting with other workers was the cause of undesirable emergent behavior, and was failing to self-heal correctly. That emergent behavior (depending on what it was) may put the scientific mission in danger. Ultimately, the stay alive signal from the ruler agent would be withdrawn [21].

If a worker, or its instrument, were damaged, either by collision with another worker, or (more likely) with an asteroid, or during a solar storm, a ruler could withdraw the stay alive signal and request a replacement worker. Another worker could self-configure to take on the role of the lost worker; that is, the ANTS adapt to ensure an optimal and balanced coverage of tasks to meet the scientific goals.

If a ruler or messenger were similarly damaged, its stay alive signal would also be withdrawn, and a worker would be promoted to play its role.

5.5 The Evolving State-of-the-Art Apoptotic Computing

5.5.1 Strong versus Weak Apoptotic Computing

In our opinion apoptotic computing and the use of apoptosis are "death by default" requiring periodic "stay alive" signals to prevent self-destruction/suicide. Although this may seem at first a subtle difference from sending a self-destruct signal/trigger to induce self-destruction, it is fundamental. Only an inherent built in default death can guarantee safety for the scenarios touched on here. For instance, relying on sending a self-destruct signal/trigger to an agent containing system password updates that is now in a hostile environment – that signal will never get through. Likewise, a robot with adaptive capabilities may learn behavior to ignore such a trigger. To boot, consider garbage collection first used in Lisp and many languages since or the destructor method in OO, is a death trigger for programmed death in principle any different? The true apoptosis is death by default with stay alive signals. That said we recognize not all circumstances will require the extreme death by default mechanism and as such we have utilized (also the biologically cell inspired) quiescence (self-sleep) as a less drastic measure. As such programmed death triggered by a death signal may also be appropriate in some circumstances, although we believe many using it under the apoptosis descriptor should really be using death by default. To distinguish the difference we refer to death by default with stay alive signs as *strong* apoptotic computing and programmed death with death trigger as *weak* apoptotic computing.

5.5.2 Other Research

The apoptotic computing paradigm and apoptosis concept has been investigated by other researchers. Tschudin proposed utilizing apoptosis (programmed death) in highly distributed systems [22], "once triggered by some external event, a termination signal will propagate." Riordan and Alessandri proposed apoptosis (programmed death) as a means to automatically counter the increasing amount of security vulnerabilities published and which hackers make use of before systems administrators can close of the published vulnerability [23]. They proposed an apoptosis service provider that states "should a vulnerability be found in *name, secret* is released into the environment to trigger various preconfigured responses (presumably to shut down *name* or to warn a responsible party). Lilien and Bhargava [24] utilize apoptosis as a means to protect the security of data, where it is activated when detectors determine a credible threat of a successful attack on the bundle (atomic bundle of private data as an agent or object) by any host, including the destination guardian of a bundle being transmitted. Burbeck [25] essentially presents a tutorial on parallels between biology and computing, and evolves four interconnected principles for multicellular computing; one being apoptosis (programmed death), mentioning that a familiar example in computing is the Blue Screen of Death, which is a *programmed* response to an unrecoverable error. A civilized metazoan (comparing with biological metazoan cell) computer should sense its own rogue behavior, for example, download of uncertified code, and disconnect itself from the network. Olsen et al. have developed a multiagent system (named HADES) that is capable to control and protect itself via life protocols and a rescue protocol. Its life protocols control the replication, repair, movement, and self-induced death that govern each agent in the system [26]. Saudi et al. [27] essentially discuss apoptosis for security systems, specifically focusing on network problems, recovering ground highlighted in Burbeck [25], and go on to apply that to addressing worms [28]. Jones [29], in his master's dissertation, implemented apoptotic self-destruct and stay alive signaling specifically investigating memory requirements of inheritance versus an abstract-oriented approach (AOP). The majority of these works may be considered to fall into the *weak* apoptotic computing (programmed death & termination signals) area yet could benefit from utilizing *strong* apoptotic computing (programmed death by default and stay alive signals).

5.6 "This Message Will Self-Destruct": Commercial Applications

Although not necessarily referred to under the apoptotic computing tag, many popular software-based applications have emerged over the last decade utilizing an apoptotic mechanism.

One class of applications provides self-destruct text message services, such as Snapchat, iDelete [30], and Apple providing it for iMessage [31]. These are growing beyond social networking and increasingly finding ground in the security arena not just for messages but self-destructing data in general [30], for instance, self-deleting phones if an incorrect password is entered repeatedly.

Wickr is one such that focus on the security aspect, and allows users to text, send images, videos, and pdfs to individuals or groups and time limit access to those communications. Wickr allows the sender to set the self-destruct time from between 1 s and 5 days. Wickr uses forensic deletion techniques to ensure that messages and other media are irrecoverable once they have self-destructed [30].

This self-destructor has also moved into the digital rental application; where on apps such as BBC iPlayer and Sky Go digital content viewers, programs can be downloaded that automatically delete after a time period.

5.7 Conclusion

The human body regulates vital bodily functions, such as telling the heart how fast to beat, monitors and adjusts blood flow, allows cells to die, and so on, all without conscious effort. We need to develop computer-based systems that can perform similar operations on themselves, without requiring constant human intervention.

The current state of success includes inspiring applications of apoptotic computing for data objects, highly distributed systems, services, agents, and swarm systems. In addition to further applied research of the paradigm to other areas, the challenges ahead orient around trust, and not least of which for users trusting a computer-based systems with self-destruct capabilities! Standards need to be developed with an immediate challenge to develop a DoS immune architecture as part of the next-generation self-managing systems.

We have made the case previously that all computer-based systems should be autonomic [32]. Likewise, there resides a very strong argument that all CBS' *should be apoptotic*, especially as we increasingly move into a vast pervasive and ubiquitous environment. This should cover all levels of interaction with technology from data, to services, to agents, to robotics. With recent headline incidents of credit card and personal data loses by organizations and governments to the Sci-Fi nightmare scenarios now being discussed as possible, programmed death by default is a necessity.

The *apoptotic computing* project, first started back in 2002 [9,21,33–35] involves working toward the long-term goal of developing *Programmed Death by Default for Computer-Based Systems* to provide for this foreseen future. It is essentially biologically inspired by the apoptosis mechanisms in multicellular organisms. It may be considered as a subarea of bioinspired computing, natural computing, or autonomic systems (providing the self-destruct property).

We are rapidly approaching the time when new autonomous computer-based systems and robots should undergo tests, similar to ethical and clinical trials for new drugs, before they can be introduced, the emerging research from apoptotic computing may offer that safeguard.

Acknowledgments

This work is partially supported by the Ulster University's Computer Science Research Institute (CSRI) and SFI's Lero – The Irish Software Engineering Research Centre. Parts of the work were carried out while Roy Sterritt was a visiting researcher at NASA GSFC between 2004–2007 (SEL Code 501) and Mike Hinchey was employed at NASA GSFC as Director of the Software Engineering Lab (Code 501). Technologies in this chapter are patented (US Patents 7,627,538 and 7,765,171) by NASA and assigned to the US Government. The chapter is mainly based on the IEEE Computer article [36] and column [2].

References

1 J. Kephart and D. Chess (2003) The vision of autonomic computing. *IEEE Computer*, **36** (1), 41–52.
2 M.G. Hinchey and R. Sterritt (2006) Self-managing software. *Computer*, **39** (2), 107–109.
3 S. Dobson, R. Sterritt, P. Nixon, and M. Hinchey (2010) Fulfilling the vision of autonomic computing. *IEEE Computer*, **43** (1), 35–41.
4 R. Lockshin and Z. Zakeri (2001) Programmed cell death and apoptosis: origins of the theory. *Nature Reviews Molecular Cell Biology*, **2**, 542–550.
5 Y. Ishizaki, L. Cheng, A.W. Mudge, and M.C. Raff (1995) Programmed cell death by default in embryonic cells, fibroblasts, and cancer cells. *Molecular Biology of the Cell*, **6** (11), 1443–1458.
6 M. Sluyser (ed.) (1996) *Apoptosis in Normal Development and Cancer*, Taylor & Francis, London.
7 J. Klefstrom, E.W. Verschuren, and G.I. Evan (2002) c-Myc augments the apoptotic activity of cytosolic death receptor signaling proteins by engaging the mitochondrial apoptotic pathway. *Journal of Biological Chemistry*, **277**, 43224–43232.

8 J. Newell (1994) Dying to live: why our cells self-destruct, Focus, Dec.

9 R. Sterritt (2002) Towards autonomic computing: effective event management. Proceedings of 27th Annual IEEE/NASA Software Engineering Workshop (SEW), Maryland, USA, December 3–5, IEEE Computer Society, pp. 40–47.

10 R. Sterritt and D.W. Bustard (2003) Autonomic computing: a means of achieving dependability? *Proceedings of IEEE International Conference on the Engineering of Computer Based Systems (ECBS'03), Huntsville, Alabama, USA, April 7–11*, IEEE CS Press, pp. 247–251.

11 N.R. Jennings and M. Wooldridge (2000) Agent-oriented software engineering, in *Handbook of Agent Technology*, J. Bradshaw (ed.), AAAI/MIT Press, Cambridge.

12 M.N. Huhns, V.T. Holderfield, and R.L.Z. Gutierrez (2003) Robust software via agent-based redundancy. Proceedings of the Second International Joint Conference on Autonomous Agents & Multiagent Systems, AAMAS 2003, July 14–18, Melbourne, Victoria, Australia, pp. 1018–1019.

13 G. Kaiser, J. Parekh, P. Gross, and G. Valetto (2003) Kinesthetics eXtreme: an external infrastructure for monitoring distributed legacy systems. Proceedings of the Autonomic Computing Workshop – IEEE Fifth Annual International Active Middleware Workshop, Seattle, USA, June.

14 E. Lupu et al. (2003) EPSRC AMUSE: Autonomic Management of Ubiquitous Systems for e-Health.

15 R. Sterritt and D.W. Bustard (2003) Towards an autonomic computing environment. Proceedings of IEEE DEXA 2003 Workshops: 1st International Workshop on Autonomic Computing Systems, Prague, Czech Republic, September 1–5, pp. 694–698.

16 R. Sterritt and M.G. Hinchey (2004) Apoptosis and self-destruct: a contribution to autonomic agents? *Proceedings of Third NASA-Goddard/IEEE Workshop on Formal Approaches to Agent-Based Systems (FAABS III), Washington DC, April 26–27, 2004*, LNAI 3228, Springer pp. 262–270. doi: 10.1007/978-3-540-30960-4_18.

17 M.S. Greenberg, J.C. Byington, T. Holding, and D.G. Harper (1998) Mobile Agents and Security. *IEEE Communications*, **36**, 76–85.

18 NASA ANTS Online http://ants.gsfc.nasa.gov/ (accessed November 2010).

19 S.A. Curtis, J. Mica, J. Nuth, G. Marr, M. Rilee, and M. Bhat (2000) ANTS (Autonomous Nano-Technology Swarm): an artificial intelligence approach to asteroid belt resource exploration, Curtis, International Astronautical Federation, 51st Congress, October 2000.

20 P.E. Clark, S. Curtis, M. Rilee, W. Truszkowski, J. Iyengar, and H. Crawford (2001) ANTS: a new concept for very remote exploration with intelligent software agents, Presented at 2001 Spring Meeting of the American Geophysical Union, San Francisco, Dec. 10–14 2001; EOS Trans. AGU, 82 (47).

21 R. Sterritt and M.G. Hinchey 2005 Engineering ultimate self-protection in autonomic agents for space exploration missions, Proceedings of IEEE Workshop on the Engineering of Autonomic Systems (EASe 2005) at 12th Annual IEEE International Conference and Workshop on the Engineering of Computer Based Systems (ECBS 2005), Greenbelt, MD, USA, April 3–8, 2005, pp. 506–511.

22 C. Tschudin (1999) Apoptosis: the programmed death of distributed services, in *Secure Internet Programming: Security Issues for Mobile and Distributed Objects*, J. Vitek and C. Jensen (eds.), Springer, pp. 253–260.

23 J. Riordan and D. Alessandri (2000) Target naming and service apoptosis, in *Recent Advances in Intrusion Detection (LNCS 1907)*, H. Debar, L. Mé, and S. Wu (eds.), Springer, pp. 217–225.

24 L. Lilien and B. Bhargava (2006) A scheme for privacy-preserving data dissemination. *IEEE Transactions on Systems, Man and Cybernetics, Part A: Systems and Humans*, **36** (3), 503–506.

25 S. Burbeck (2007) Complexity and the Evolution of Computing: Biological Principles for Managing Evolving Systems. Whitepaper (V2.2).

26 M.M. Olsen, N. Siegelmann-Danieli, and H.T. Siegelmann (2008) Robust artificial life via artificial programmed death. *Artificial Intelligence*, **172**, 884–98.

27 M.M. Saudi, M. Woodward, A.J. Cullen, and H.M. Noor (2008) An overview of apoptosis for computer security. Proceedings of the International Symposium on Information Technology ITSim 2008.

28 M.M. Saudi, A.J. Cullen, M.E. Woodward, H.A. Hamid, A.H. Abhalim An overview of STAKCERT framework in confronting worms attack. 2nd IEEE International Conference on Computer Science and Information Technology, 2009, ICCSIT 2009, Aug. 8–11, pp. 104–108. doi: 10.1109/ICCSIT.2009.5234764.

29 D. Jones (2010) Implementing biologically-inspired apoptotic behaviour in digital objects: an aspect-oriented approach, M.Sc. dissertation, Open University UK, March.

30 C. Kotfila (2014) This message will self-destruct: the growing role of obscurity and self-destructing data in digital communication. *Bulletin of the Association for Information Science and Technology*, **40** (2), 12–16.

31 M. Prigg (2014) Apple takes on Snapchat with a text self-destruct button: latest software destroys messages, Daily Mail Online. Available at http://www.dailymail.co.uk/sciencetech/article-2646338/Apple-gears-launch-iOS-8-turn-iPhone-remote-control.html (accessed Feb. 28, 2017).

32 R. Sterritt and M.G. Hinchey, (2005) Why computer-based systems should be autonomic. Proceedings of the 12th Annual IEEE International Conference and Workshop on the Engineering of Computer Based Systems (ECBS 2005), Greenbelt, MD, USA, April 3–8, 2005, pp. 406–414.

33 R. Sterritt and M.G. Hinchey 2010 "SPAACE IV: self-properties for an autonomous & autonomic computing environment – part IV a newish hope", Proceedings of AA-SES-IV: 4th IEEE International Workshop on Autonomic and Autonomous Space Exploration Systems (at SMC-IT), Pasadena, CA, USA, June 2009, in *"Proceedings of the Seventh IEEE International Conference and Workshops on Engineering of Autonomic and Autonomous Systems (EASe 2010)"*, IEEE CS Press, Pages 119–125.

34 R. Sterritt and M.G. Hinchey 2005 From here to autonomicity: self-managing agents and the biological metaphors that inspire them. Proceedings of Integrated Design & Process Technology Symposium (IDPT 2005), Beijing, China, June 13–17, pp. 143–150.

35 R. Sterritt and M.G. Hinchey 2006 Biologically-inspired concepts for autonomic self-protection in multiagent systems. *Proceedings of 3rd International Workshop on Safety and Security in Multi-Agent Systems (SASEMAS 2006) at AAMAS 2006, Hakodate, Japan,* in M. Barley et al. (eds.), Safety and Security in Multi-Agent Systems: Research Results from 2004–2006, LNCS 4324, Springer, pp. 330–341.

36 R. Sterritt (2011) Apoptotic computing: programmed death by default for computer-based systems. *Computer,* **44**, 59–65. doi: 10.1109/MC.2011.5.

6

Requirements Engineering for Adaptive and Self-Adaptive Systems

Emil Vassev and Mike Hinchey

Lero – The Irish Software Research Centre, University of Limerick, Limerick, Ireland

6.1 Introduction

Autonomic systems are systems that are aware of their behavior and can modify it to reflect changes in the operating environment. An autonomic system must be designed with both an understanding of the need for self-adaptation and monitoring as well as of the system's inability to monitor everything. Practice has shown that developers initially tackle such issues with requirements engineering, which focuses on what a system should do and the constraints under which it must do it.

The autonomy requirements engineering (ARE) approach addresses what adaptations are possible in a system and, ultimately, how to realize those adaptations. In a joint project with the European Space Agency (ESA), Lero – The Irish Software Research Centre has developed ARE as an approach that combines special *generic autonomy requirements* (GAR) with *goal-oriented requirements engineering* (GORE). Using this approach, software engineers can determine what autonomic features to develop for a particular software-intensive system as well as what artifacts that process might generate, for example, goals models, requirements specification.

The rest of this entry is organized as follows. Section 6.2 presents a short overview of ARE. Section 6.3 provides details about the system goals and how ARE frames those in goals models. Section 6.4 discusses in great detail how ARE handles the realization of the system objectives through the fulfillment of special autonomy-assistive requirements. Furthermore, Section 6.5 tackles both the recording and formalization of the autonomy requirements. Finally, Section 6.6 concludes the chapter with a brief summary and roadmap.

Software Technology: 10 Years of Innovation in IEEE Computer, First Edition.
Edited by Mike Hinchey.

6.2 Understanding ARE

The first step in developing any new software-intensive system is to determine the system's functional and nonfunctional requirements. The former requirements define what the system will actually do, while the latter requirements refer to its qualities, such as performance, along with any constraints under which the system must operate. Despite differences in application domain and functionality, all autonomous systems extend upstream the regular software-intensive systems with special *self-managing objectives* (self-* objectives). Basically, the self-* objectives provide the system's ability to automatically discover, diagnose, and cope with various problems. This ability depends on the system's degree of autonomicity, quality and quantity of knowledge, awareness and monitoring capabilities, and quality characteristics such as adaptability, dynamicity, robustness, resilience, and mobility. Basically, this is the basis of the ARE approach [1–4]: Autonomy requirements are detected as self-objectives backed up by different capabilities and quality characteristics outlined by the GAR model.

Currently, this approach is the only complete and comprehensive solution to the problem *of autonomy requirements elicitation and specification.* Note that the approach targets exclusively the *self-* objectives* as the only means to explicitly determine and define autonomy requirements. Thus, it is not meant to handle the regular functional and nonfunctional requirements of the systems, presuming that those might by tackled by the traditional requirements engineering approaches, for example, use case modeling, domain modeling, constraints modeling. Functional and nonfunctional requirements might be captured by our ARE approach only as part of the self-* objectives elicitation, that is, some of the GAR's requirements might be considered as functional and nonfunctional requirements.

The ARE approach starts with the creation of a *goals model* that represents system objectives and their interrelationships for the mission in question. For this, we use GORE where ARE goals are generally modeled with intrinsic features such as *type, actor,* and *target,* with links to other goals and constraints in the requirements model. Goals models might be organized in different ways copying with the mission specifics and engineers' understanding about the mission goals. Thus, we may have (1) hierarchical structures where goals reside at different level of granularity; (2) concurrent structures where goals are considered as concurrent; and so on. The goals models are not formal and we use natural language along with UML-like diagrams to record them.

The next step in the ARE approach is to work on each one of the system goals along with the elicited environmental constraints to come up with the self-* objectives providing the autonomy requirements for this particular system's behavior. In this phase, we apply our GAR model to a mission goal to derive autonomy requirements in the form of goal's supportive and alternative self-*

objectives along with the necessary capabilities and quality characteristics. In the first part of this phase, we record the GAR model in natural language. In the second part though, we use a formal notation to express this model in a more precise way. Note that, this model carries more details about the autonomy requirements, and can be further used for different analysis activities, including requirements validation and verification. ARE could be used at several stages in the workflow from initiating a mission concept through to building and launching a spacecraft.

- As has been demonstrated in a case study for the BepiColombo mission [2,3], high-level mission goals can be used in conjunction with a fairly general GAR model to generate a high-level model incorporating the autonomy requirements (self-* objectives). This model could be combined with a reasoning engine to establish whether or not all the requirements are mutually compatible. It could also be used to communicate the requirements as long as the engineers can see what alternative behavior is required when the mission is following a goal and under what circumstances.
- The model could be used to assist in the compilation of the autonomy requirements (AR) section of the System Requirements Specification document. The goals model along with the autonomy requirements elicited per goal will form such a section. This eventually will help to easily derive some of the functional and nonfunctional requirements – related to the monitoring activities, knowledge, and AR (autonomy requirements) quality attributes. As mentioned already, the formal part can be omitted and instead we may write down the detailed ARs in natural language.
- The process of writing the ARs could also be used to add further details to the ARE model.
- If the formal model is required, with the necessary tool support it should be possible to formally validate and verify the ARs. It should be also possible with appropriate tools to derive from the formal model ARs written in natural language
- Eventually, if both the ARs written in a natural language and the formal model are made available together to the software design engineers, it should help to ensure more accurate implementation of the software with fewer bugs.

6.3 System Goals and Goals Models

Goals have long been recognized to be essential components involved in the requirements engineering (RE) process [5]. To elicit system goals, typically, the system (for ESA, along with the mission where the system is going to be used) under consideration is analyzed in its organizational, operational, and technical settings; problems are pointed out and opportunities are identified; high-level goals are then identified and refined to address such problems and meet the opportunities; requirements are then elaborated to meet those goals.

Goal identification is not necessarily an easy task [6–8]. Sometimes goals can be explicitly stated by stakeholders or in preliminary material available to requirements engineers, for example, mission description. Often though, they are implicit so that goal elicitation has to be undertaken. The preliminary analysis of the current system (and the mission to be accomplished by that system) is an important source for goal identification. Such analysis usually results in a list of problems and deficiencies that can be formulated precisely. Negating those formulations yields a first list of goals to be achieved by the system-to-be. In our experience, goals can also be identified systematically by searching for intentional keywords in the preliminary documents provided, for example, mission description. Once a preliminary set of goals and goal-related constraints is obtained and validated with stakeholders, many other goals can be identified by *refinement* and by *abstraction*, just by asking HOW and WHY questions about the goals/constraints already available [9]. Other goals are identified by resolving conflicts among goals or obstacles to goal achievement. Furthermore, such goals might be eventually defined as self-* objectives. Goals are generally modeled by *intrinsic features* such as their type and attributes, and by their *links* to other goals and to other elements of a requirements model. Goals can be hierarchically organized and prioritized, where high-level goals (e.g., mission objectives) might comprise related, low-level subgoals that can be organized to provide different alternatives of achieving the high-level goals. In ARE, goals are registered in plain text with characteristics like *actors, targets,* and *rationale.* Moreover, intergoal relationships are captured by goals models putting together all goals along with associated constraints. ARE's *goals models* are presented in UML-like diagrams. *Goals models* can help us to consecutively assist in capturing autonomy requirements in several ways [1–4]:

1) An ARE goals model might provide the starting point for capturing autonomy requirements by analyzing the environment for the system-to-be and by identifying the problems that exist in this environment as well as the needs that the system under development has to address to accomplish its goals.
2) ARE goals models might be used to provide a means to represent *alternative ways* where the objectives of the system can be met and analyze and rank these alternatives with respect to *quality concerns* and other constraints, for example, environmental constraints:
   a) This allows for exploration and analysis of alternative system behaviors at design time.
   b) If the alternatives that are initially delivered with the system perform well, there is no need for complex interactions on autonomy behavior among autonomy components.

c) Not all the alternatives can be identified at design time. In an open and dynamic environment, new and better alternatives may present themselves and some of the identified and implemented alternatives may become impractical.

d) In certain situations, new alternatives will have to be discovered and implemented by the system at runtime. However, the process of discovery, analysis, and implementation of new alternatives at runtime is complex and error-prone. By exploring the space of alternatives at design time, we are minimizing the need for that difficult task.

3) ARE goals models might provide the traceability mechanism from design to requirements. When a change in requirements is detected at runtime (e.g., a major change in the global mission goal), *goal models can be used to reevaluate the system behavior alternatives with respect to the new requirements and to determine if system reconfiguration is needed*:

a) If a change in requirements affects a particular goal in the model, it is possible to see how this goal is decomposed and which parts of the system implementing the functionality needed to achieve that goal are in turn affected.

b) By analyzing a goals model, it is possible to identify how a failure to achieve some particular goal affects the overall objective of the system.

c) Highly variable goals models can be used to visualize the currently selected system configuration along with its alternatives and to communicate suggested configuration changes to users in high-level terms.

4) ARE goals models provide a unifying view of the system by relating goals to high-level system objectives and quality concerns:

a) High-level objectives or quality concerns serve as the *common knowledge* shared among the autonomous system's parts (or components) to achieve the global system optimization. In this way, the system can avoid the pitfalls of missing the globally optimal configuration due to only relying on local optimizations.

b) Goals models might be used to identify part of the knowledge requirements, for example, actors or targets.

Moreover, goals models might be used to manage conflicts among multiple goals including self-* objectives. Note that by resolving conflicts among goals or obstacles to goal achievement, new goals (or self-* objectives) may emerge.

6.4 Self-* Objectives and Autonomy-Assistive Requirements

ARE uses goals models as a basis to help to derive self-* objectives per a system (or mission) goal by applying a model for GAR to any system goal [2]. The self-*

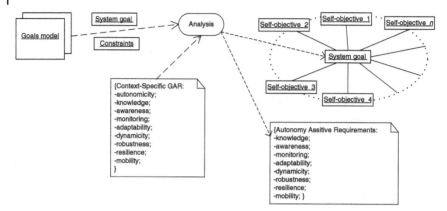

Figure 6.1 The ARE process of deriving self-* objectives per system goal.

objectives represent *assistive* and eventually *alternative goals* (or objectives) the system may pursue in the presence of factors threatening the achievement of the initial system goals. The diagram presented in Figure 6.1 depicts the process of deriving the self-* objectives from a goals model of the system-to-be. Basically, a context-specific GAR model provides some initial self-* objectives, which should be further analyzed and refined in the context of the specific system goal to see their applicability. For example, the context-specific GAR models for the different classes of space missions [1] define a predefined set of self-* objectives for each class of space missions. These self-* objectives cope with both constraints and challenges spacecraft must overcome while performing a mission of specific class. For example, GAR defines the following self-* objectives for the class of Polar Low Earth Orbit Satellite Missions [1]:

- *Self-Orbit* (autonomously acquire the target orbit; adapt to orbit perturbations)
- *Self-Protection* (autonomously detect the presence of radiation and move to escape)
- *Self-Scheduling* (based on operational goals and knowledge of the system and its environment, autonomously determine what task to perform next)
- *Self-Reparation* (implies operations replanning based on performance degradation or failures)

As shown in Figure 6.1, in addition to the derived self-* objectives, the ARE process also produces *autonomy assistive requirements*. These requirements (also defined as adaptation-assistive attributes) are initially defined by the GAR model [1] and are intended to support the achievements of the self-* objectives. The *autonomy assistive requirements* might be defined as following:

- *Knowledge*. Basically data requirements that need to be structured to allow efficient reasoning.

- *Awareness.* A sort of functional requirements where knowledge is used as an input along with events and/or sensor signals to derive particular system states.
- *Resilience* and *Robustness.* A sort of soft goals. For example, such requirements for Geostationary Earth Orbit (GEO) Missions [1] are defined as *"robustness: robust to communication latency"* and *"resilience: resilient GEO positioning."* These requirements can be specified as soft goals leading the system toward *"reducing and copying with communication latency"* and *"keeping GEO positioning optimal."* A soft goal is satisfied rather than achieved. Note that specifying soft goals is not an easy task. The problem is that there is no clear-cut satisfaction condition for a soft goal. Soft goals are related to the notion of satisfaction. Unlike regular goals, soft goals can seldom be accomplished or satisfied. For soft goals, eventually, we need to find solutions that are "good enough" where soft goals are satisfied to a sufficient degree. Thus, when specifying robustness and resilience autonomy requirements we need to set the desired degree of satisfaction.

Monitoring, mobility, dynamicity, and *adaptability* – might also be defined as soft goals, but with *relatively high degree of satisfaction.* These three types of autonomy requirements represent important *quality requirements* that the system in question needs to meet to provide conditions making autonomicity possible. Thus, their degree of satisfaction should be relatively high. Eventually, adaptability requirements might be treated as hard goals because they determine what parts of the system in question can be adapted (not how).

6.4.1 Constraints and Self-* Objectives

In addition to the self-* objectives derived from the context-specific GAR model, more self-* objectives might be derived from the constraints associated with the targeted system goal. Note that the Analysis step in Figure 6.1 uses the context-specific GAR model and elaborates on both system goal and constraints associated with that goal. Often environmental constraints introduce factors that may violate the system goals and self-* objectives will be required to overcome those constraints. Actually, constraints represent obstacles to the achievement of a goal. Constructing self-* objectives from goal constraints can be regarded as a form of *constraint programming*, in which a very abstract logic sentence describing a goal with its actors and targets (it may be written in a natural language as well) is extended to include concepts from *constraint satisfaction* and *system capabilities* that enable the achievement of the goal. *Task Analysis* [10] is proposed as a good methodology for identify system capabilities. Task analysis can be defined as the study of what a system is required to do, in terms of actions and/or cognitive processes in order to achieve a given goal. Hierarchical task analysis, specifically, is a method of decomposing a high-level capability down to its lowest levels in order to enumerate every capability required of a system. In ARE, the capabilities are actually abstractions of system operations that need to be performed to maintain the goal fulfillment along with constraint satisfaction. In this approach, we need to query the provability of the targeted goal, which contains constraints, and then if the system goal cannot be fulfilled due to constraint satisfaction, a self-* objective is derived as an assistive system goal preserving both the original system's goal targets and constraint satisfaction. A good example demonstrating this process can be found in the ARE-BepiColombo case study [2,3]. In this example, both high temperature and irradiation are environmental constraints that helped to determine variants of the self-protection objective assisting the scientific objectives of BepiColombo. Note that constraints influence the definition of *policies* and *scenarios* when specifying or recording in natural language self-* objectives.

6.4.2 Mission Analysis and Self-* Objectives

Considering the Space Missions domain, the analysis performed to determine self-* objectives might be part of the Space Mission Analysis, which is an activity that takes aspects such as *payload operational requirements* and *spacecraft system constraints* as inputs, and generates as an output a mission specification. A key aspect of this process is the selection of mission parameters, for example, trajectory parameters. Note that *the mission specification leads to design requirements on the spacecraft systems and subsystems*. The Space Mission Analysis and Design (SMAD) Process consists of the following steps [11,12]:

- Define objectives:
  - Define broad objectives and constraints
  - Estimate quantitative mission needs and requirements
- Characterize the mission:
  - Define alternative mission concepts
  - Define alternative mission architectures
  - Identify system drivers for each architecture
  - Characterize mission concepts and architectures
- Evaluate the mission:
  - Identify critical requirements
  - Evaluate mission utility
  - Define baseline mission concept
- Define requirements:
  - Define system requirements
  - Allocate requirements to system elements

Typical Functional requirements are related to the following:

- *Performance.* Factors impacting this requirement include the primary mission objective, payload size, orbit, and pointing

- *Coverage.* Impacting factors include orbit, number of satellites, and scheduling
- *Responsiveness.* Impacting factors include communications architecture, processing delays, operations
- *Secondary Mission* (if applicable)

Typical operational requirements are as follows:

- *Duration.* Factors impacting this requirement include nature of the mission (experimental or operational), level of redundancy, orbit (e.g., altitude)
- *Availability.* Impacting factors include level of redundancy
- *Survivability.* Impacting factors include orbit, hardening, electronics
- *Data Distribution.* Impacting factors include communications architecture
- *Data Content, Form and Format.* Impacting factors include user needs, level, and place of processing, payload
- *Ground Station Visibility*
- *Eclipse Duration.* Consider the eclipse period for spacecraft in an Earth orbit
- *Launch Windows.* The time of launch of a spacecraft is often constrained by dynamic aspects related to reaching the mission orbit, or by system requirements.

Typical constraints are as follows:

- *Cost.* Factors impacting this constraint include number of spacecraft, size and complexity, orbit
- *Schedule.* Impacting factors include technical readiness, program size
- *Political.* Impacting factors include sponsoring organization (customer), if international program
- *Interfaces.* Impacting factors include level of user and operator infrastructure
- *Development Constraints.* Impacting factors include sponsoring organization.

Ideally, SMAD might integrate the ARE process of deriving self-* objectives per system goal as long as SMAD helps to identify the system goals, functionality, and constraints. In this approach, the analysis step of that process (see Figure 6.2) might also use other inputs such as quantitative mission needs, alternative mission concepts, mission utility, performance and other constraints, and operational requirements (e.g., duration, availability, survivability). Note that despite the different input parameters, the global invariant driving the analysis step is always defined as *"What the system (spacecraft on a mission) should do when the system goals (or mission objectives) cannot be achieved by simply following the operational instructions?"*

Along with the SMAD input provided to the analysis step (see Figure 6.2), SMAD can also be used to provide information for deriving additional self-* objectives related to the following:

- *Accuracy* Goals. Nonfunctional goals requiring the state of the system components and environmental objects to accurately reflect the state of

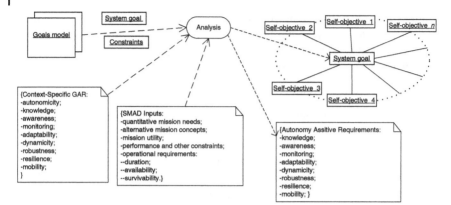

Figure 6.2 The ARE process of "deriving self-* objectives per system goal" as part of SMAD.

the corresponding monitored/controlled objects in both the system and environment. Note that such goals are often overlooked in the RE process and their violation may be responsible for major failures [13].

- *Performance Goals.* Specialized into time and space performance goals, the former being specialized into *response time* and *throughput* goals [12].
- *Security Goals.* Specialized into *confidentiality, integrity,* and *availability* goals [14]. Note that the latter can be specialized in turn until reaching domain-specific security goals.
- *Satisfaction Goals.* Concerned with satisfying agent requests (human operators or system components).
- *Information Goals.* Concerned with keeping specific agents informed about other objects' states.
- *Achieve (cease) Goals.* Concerned with system behavior related to certain required properties that should be *eventually satisfied* in some future state (denied)
- *Maintain (avoid) Goals.* Concerned with system behavior related to certain required properties that should be *permanently satisfied* in every future state (denied) unless some other property holds.
- *Optimize Goals.* Compare behaviors to favor those that better ensure some soft target property.

6.5 Recording and Formalizing Autonomy Requirements

To record autonomy requirements, ARE relies on both natural language and formal notation. In general, a more detailed description in a natural language may precede the formal specification of the elicited autonomy requirements. Such description might be written as a scenario describing both the conditions and sequence of actions needed to be performed in order to achieve the self-* objective in question. Note that a self-objective could be associated with multiple scenarios. The combination of a self-* objective and a scenario ARE forms an *ARE requirements chunk* (RC). A requirements chunk can be recorded in a natural language as follows [2].

6.5.1 ARE Requirements Chunk

- *Self-protection_1*: Autonomously detect the presence of high-solar irradiation and protect (eventually turn off or shade) the electronics and instruments on board.
  - *Assisting System Goals:* BepiColombo Transfer Objective.
  - *Actors:* BepiColombo transfer module, the Sun, base on Earth, BepiColombo composite module (MPO and MMO), solar irradiation, shades, power system.
  - *Targets:* Electronics and instruments.
- *Scenario*: If the solar radiation level is less than 90 Sv, then the MMO spacecraft shades the instruments and turns off the electronics onboard. In case the radiation level is equal to or higher than 90 Sv, MMO performs one of the following operations: (1) move the spacecraft to an upper orbit; (2) move the spacecraft to a lower orbit; and (3) the spacecraft decides what to do on its own.

RCs associate each goal with *scenarios* where the *goal–scenario pairs* can be assembled together through *composition, alternative, and refinement* relationships.

The next step, is the requirements specification, which can be considered as a form of *formal specification*. The formal notation to be used for requirements recording must cope with ARE, that is, it should be expressive enough to handle both the goals models produced by GORE and the requirements generated by GAR. KnowLang [15] is formal method having all the necessary features required to handle such a task. The process of requirements specification with KnowLang goes over a few phases:

1) Initial knowledge requirements gathering. Involves domain experts to determine the basic notions, relations, and functions (operations) of the domain of interest.
2) Behavior definition. Identifies situations and behavior policies as "control data" helping to identify important self-adaptive scenarios.
3) Knowledge structuring. Encapsulates domain entities, situations, and behavior policies into KnowLang structures like concepts, properties, functionalities, objects, relations, facts, and rules.

When specifying autonomy requirements with KnowLang, an important factor to take into consideration is to know how the KnowLang framework handles these requirements at runtime. KnowLang comes with a special KnowLang Reasoner [15] that operates on the specified requirements and provides the system with awareness capabilities. The reasoner supports both logical and statistical reasoning based on integrated Bayesian networks. The KnowLang Reasoner is supplied as a component hosted by the system (e.g., the BepiColombo's MMO spacecraft) and thus, it runs in the system's operational context as any other system's component. However, it operates in the knowledge representation context (KR Context) and on the KR symbols (represented knowledge). The system talks to the reasoner via special ASK and TELL Operators allowing for knowledge queries and knowledge updates. Upon demand, the KnowLang Reasoner can also build up and return a self-adaptive behavior model as a chain of actions to be realized in the environment or in the system itself [15].

6.6 Conclusion

This chapter has presented the autonomy requirements engineering approach. ARE relies on GORE to elicit and define the system goals, and uses a GAR model to derive and define assistive and eventually alternative goals (or objectives) of the system. The system may pursue these "self-*" objectives" in the presence of factors threatening the achievement of the initial system goals. Once identified, the autonomy requirements including the self-* objectives can be further formalized, for example, specified with the KnowLang formal method.

Future work is mainly concerned with development of tools for the ARE model. An efficient ARE Tool Suite incorporating an autonomy requirements validation approach is the next logical step needed to complete the ARE framework. Moreover, an efficient ARE framework shall adopt KnowLang as a formal notation and provide tools for specification and validation of autonomy requirements.

Runtime knowledge representation and reasoning shall be provided along with monitoring mechanisms to support the autonomy behavior of a system at runtime. Moreover, we need to build an ARE Test Bed tool that will integrate the KnowLang Reasoner and will allow for validation of self-* objectives based on simulation and testing. This will help engineers validate self-* objectives by evaluating the system's ability to perceive the internal and external environment and react to changes. Therefore, with the ARE Test Bed tool, we shall be able to evaluate capabilities that might manifest system awareness about situations and conditions.

Acknowledgments

This work was supported by ESTEC ESA (Contract No. 4000106016), by the European Union FP7 Integrated Project Autonomic Service-Component Ensembles (ASCENS), and by Science Foundation Ireland Grant 03/CE2/I303_1 to Lero – The Irish Software Research Centre at University of Limerick, Ireland.

References

1 E. Vassev and M. Hinchey (2013) On the Autonomy Requirements for Space Missions. Proceedings of the 16th IEEE International Symposium on Object/Component/Service-oriented Real-time Distributed Computing Workshops (ISCORCW 2013). IEEE Computer Society.

2 E. Vassev and M. Hinchey (2013) Autonomy requirements engineering: a case study on the BepiColombo mission. Proceedings of C* Conference on Computer Science & Software Engineering (C3S2E '13), ACM, pp. 31–41.

3 E. Vassev and M. Hinchey (2013) Autonomy requirements engineering. Proceedings of the 14th IEEE International Conference on Information Reuse and Integration (IRI '13), IEEE Computer Society, pp. 175–184.

4 E. Vassev and M. Hinchey (2013) Autonomy requirements engineering. *IEEE Computer*, **46** (8), 82–84.

5 D.T. Ross and K.E. Schoman (1977) Structured analysis for requirements definition. *IEEE Transactions on Software Engineering*, **3** (1), 6–15.

6 A. van Lamsweerde, R. Darimont, and Ph. Massonet (1995) Goal-directed elaboration of requirements for a meeting scheduler: problems and lessons learnt. Proceedings of the 2nd International IEEE Symposium on Requirements Engineering. IEEE, pp. 194–203.

7 P. Haumer, K. Pohl, and K. Weidenhaupt (1998) Requirements elicitation and validation with real world scenes. *IEEE Transactions on Software Engineering*, Special Issue on Scenario Management, **24**, 1036–1054.

8 C. Rolland, C. Souveyet, and C.B. Achour (1998) Guiding goal-modeling using scenarios. *IEEE Transactions on Software Engineering*, Special Issue on Scenario Management, **24**, 1055–1071.

9 A. van Lamsweerde (2000) Requirements engineering in the year 00: a research perspective. Proceedings of the 22nd International Conference on Software Engineering (ICSE'2000). ACM, pp. 5–19.

10 B. Kirwan and L.K. Ainsworth (1992) *A Guide to Task Analysis*, CRC Press.

11 P. Fortescue, G. Swinerd, and J. Stark (eds.) (2011) *Spacecraft Systems Engineering*, 4th Edition, John Wiley & Sons, Ltd., Chichester.

12 B.A. Nixon (1993) Dealing with performance requirements during the development of information systems. Proceedings of the 1st International IEEE Symposium on Requirements Engineering (RE'93), pp. 42–49.

13 A. Lamsweerde and E. van Letier (2000) Handling obstacles in goal-oriented requirements engineering. *IEEE Transactions on Software Engineering*, Special Issue on Exception Handling, **26** (10), 978–1005.

14 E.J. Amoroso (1994) *Fundamentals of Computer Security*, Prentice-Hall.

15 E. Vassev and M. Hinchey (2013) Knowledge representation and reasoning for self-adaptive behavior and awareness. *TCCI: Special Issue on ICECCS 2012*, Springer.

7

Toward Artificial Intelligence through Knowledge Representation for Awareness

Emil Vassev and Mike Hinchey

Lero – The Irish Software Research Centre, University of Limerick, Limerick, Ireland

7.1 Introduction

The concept of artificial intelligence is built upon four fundamental elements: data, information, knowledge, and wisdom [1]. In this "quadruple", data takes the form of measures and some sort of representations of the world, for example, raw facts and numbers. Furthermore, information is obtained from data by assigning relevant meaning, such as a specific context where data has been obtained. Knowledge is a specific interpretation of information. And finally, wisdom is the ability to apply relevant knowledge to a particular problem. Thus, wisdom requires awareness, judgment, rules, and eventually experience. Note that it also helps create new knowledge.

When developing intelligent software, designers and software engineers employ different kinds of knowledge to derive models of specific domains of interest. Basically, the problem domain determines what kinds of knowledge shall be considered and what models might be derived from that knowledge. For example, knowledge could be internal (about the system itself) or external (about the system environment). Knowledge could also be a priori (initially given to a system) or from experience (gained from analysis of tasks performed during the system's lifetime). Other kinds of knowledge might relate to the application domain, the system's structure, problem-solving strategies, the system's ability to communicate with other systems, and so on.

The rest of this chapter is organized as follows. Section 7.2 presents a short state of the art of knowledge representation. Section 7.3 presents KnowLang, a new method for knowledge representation that emphasizes the self-adaptive behavior of intelligent systems. Section 7.4 discusses awareness as a key factor to the development of advanced intelligent systems and presents an awareness

Software Technology: 10 Years of Innovation in IEEE Computer, First Edition. Edited by Mike Hinchey.

model based on KnowLang and its reasoning capabilities. Finally, Section 7.5 concludes the chapter with a brief discussion about the challenges along with a brief roadmap.

7.2 Knowledge Representation

Intelligent system designers can use different elements to represent different kinds of knowledge. Knowledge representation (KR) elements could be primitives such as rules, frames, semantic networks and concept maps, ontologies, and logic expressions. These primitives might be combined into more complex knowledge elements. Whatever elements they use, designers must structure the knowledge so that the system can effectively process and easily perceive the results.

7.2.1 Rules

Rules organize knowledge into premise–conclusion pairs, in which the premise is a Boolean expression and the conclusion a series of statements. The premise is wrapped in an IF . . . THEN block and consists of one or more clauses, with multiple clauses connected by logical operators such as AND, OR, and NOT. For example, *IF it's lunchtime OR I'm hungry THEN I shall go to the restaurant.*

A major advantage of rule-based KR is its extreme simplicity, which makes it easy to understand the knowledge content. Rules that fire under specific conditions readily demonstrate the reasoning. However, a rule-based KR model can grow very large, incorporating thousands of rules and requiring extra effort and tools to maintain their consistency.

7.2.2 Frames

Frames represent physical entities, such as objects or persons, or simple concepts via a collection of information, derivation function calls, and output assignments, and can contain descriptions of semantic attributes as well as procedural details. Frames contain two key elements: *slots* are sets of attributes of the described entity, with special daemons often included to compute slot values, and *facets* extend knowledge about an attribute.

7.2.3 Semantic Networks and Concept Maps

Knowledge is often best understood as a set of related concepts. A semantic network is a directed graph consisting of nodes, which represent concepts and are connected by edges, which represent semantic relations between those concepts. There is no standard set of relations between concepts in semantic networks, but the following relations are common:

- instance: X is an instance of Y if X is a specific example of the general concept Y
- isa: X isa Y if X is a subset of the more general concept Y
- haspart: X haspart Y if the concept Y is a part of the concept X

Inheritance is a key notion in semantic networks and can be represented naturally by isa relations. Essentially, a computer-based semantic network uses metadata (data describing data) to represent the meaning of different information. Intelligent systems that recognize the meaning of information – for example, data stored in a warehouse – become immeasurably more intelligent. Extensible Markup Language (XML) and Resource Description Framework (RDF) are common content management schemes that support semantic networks.

Concept maps are similar to semantic networks, but they label the links between nodes in very different ways. They are considered more powerful than semantic networks because they can represent fairly complex concepts. For example, a hierarchy of concepts with each node constituting a separate concept. Concept maps are useful when designers want to use an intelligent system to adopt a constructivist view of learning.

7.2.4 Ontologies

Ontologies inherit the basic concepts provided by rules, frames, semantic networks, and concept maps. They explicitly represent domain concepts, objects, and the relationships among those concepts and objects to form the basic structure around which knowledge can be built [2]. The main idea is to establish standard models, taxonomies, vocabularies, and domain terminology and use them to develop appropriate knowledge and reasoning models.

An ontology consists of hierarchies of concepts – for example, an "objects" concept tree or a "relations" concept tree. Each concept has properties, which can be regarded as a frame. The relationships among the concepts form semantic networks, and rules and constraints impose restrictions on the relationships or define true statements in the ontology (facts).

Figure 7.1 shows an ontology that represents the concept of a coffee machine (CM). CM has properties such as height, weight, coffee bean hopper, touch screen, container. A semantic network defines the relationships between CM and the rest of the concepts in the ontology and includes the following properties: CM requires E (electricity), CM requires A (action), CM requires C (coffee), CM requires W (water), and CM makes CD (coffee drink). Some rules expressed with the ontology concepts add new knowledge about the coffee machine.

7.2.5 Logic

To achieve the precise semantics necessary for computational purposes, intelligent system designers often use logic to formalize KR. Moreover, logic is relevant to

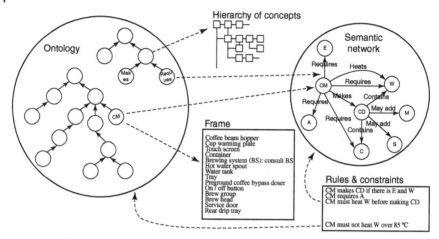

Figure 7.1 Ontology representing the concept of a coffee machine (CM).

reasoning (inferring new knowledge from existing knowledge), which in turn is relevant to entailment and deduction [3]. The most prominent logical formalism used for KR is *first-order logic* (FOL). FOL helps to describe a knowledge domain as consisting of objects, and construct logical formulas around those objects. Similar to semantic networks, statements in natural language can be expressed with logic formulas describing facts about objects using predicate and function symbols.

Extensions of FOL such as *second-order logic* and *temporal logics* strive to improve the logic formalism by increasing expressiveness. The problem with FOL is that it can quantify over individuals, but not over properties and time – we can thus specify a property's individual components, but not an individual's properties. With SOL, for example, we can axiomatize the sentence "component A and component B have at least one property in common, such as sharing at least one interface," which we cannot do with FOL. Temporal logics make it possible to model knowledge either as linear time or branching time temporal models, and can be used to describe and formalize complex reasoning patterns prescribing inference steps operating over temporal knowledge models.

Another prominent formalism is *description logic*, which evolved from semantic networks. With DL, we represent an application domain's knowledge by first defining relevant concepts in TBox and then using ABox to specify properties of objects. While less expressive than FOL, DL has a more compact syntax and better computational characteristics.

7.2.6 Completeness and Consistency

No KR model can provide a complete picture of the domain of interest. Domain objects are often real-world entities that cannot be described by a finite set of symbolic structures; moreover, such objects do not exist in isolation but in unlimited contexts. Intelligent systems consequently must rely on reasoning to infer missing knowledge. Knowledge consistency is critical for efficient reasoning. The degree to which systems achieve this efficiency is determined by whether they assume that the operational world is complete and closed or incomplete and open:

- *Closed-World Assumption* (CWA). Unless an atomic sentence is known to be true, it can be assumed to be false
- *Open-World Assumption* (OWA). Any information not explicitly specified, or that cannot be derived from known data, is considered unknown.

The following example illustrates the difference between these two assumptions:

- Given: Gloria drives a Mazda.
- Question: Does Gloria drive a red Mazda?
- Answer: (CWA) No.
- (OWA) Unknown. (Gloria's Mazda could be red.)

Although more restrictive than OWA, CWA maintains consistency in knowledge because it does not allow adding new facts, which can lead to inconsistency. Intelligent systems can also employ consistency rules and constraints, such as "no negation," to preserve knowledge consistency. There could be constraints for knowledge acquisition, retrieval, updating, and inferences.

7.2.7 Reasoning

When an intelligent system needs to decide on a course of action and there is no explicit knowledge to guide this decision, the system must reason – that is, figure out what it needs to know from what it already knows. There are two basic types of reasoning:

- *Monotonic.* New facts can only produce additional beliefs
- *Nonmonotonic.* New facts will sometimes invalidate previous beliefs

Current reasoning mechanisms are far from efficient, which is partially due to KR's inherently challenging task. FOL- or DL-based inferential engines usually do computations, acting on existing knowledge to produce new knowledge.

7.2.8 Technologies

FOL-based inferential engines use automated-deduction algorithms to prove theorems and build finite models, often in parallel. Theorem proving can help find contradictions or check for new information, while finite model building is a complementary inference task. The problem with FOL-based inferences is that the logical entailment for FOL is semidecidable – that is, if the desired conclusion follows from the premises, then eventually resolution refutation will find a contradiction. As a result, queries often unavoidably do not terminate.

Inference engines based on DL are extremely powerful when reasoning about taxonomic knowledge, as they can discover hidden subsumption relationships among classes. However, their expressive power is restricted to reduce computational complexity and to guarantee the decidability of their deductive algorithms. This restriction effectively prevents the wide application of taxonomic reasoning to heterogeneous domains. To make reasoning more efficient, intelligent systems should also include mechanisms capable of sifting context-aware knowledge from the overwhelming amount of information that is irrelevant to the current context.

7.3 KnowLang

Following a self-adaptation paradigm, software-intensive systems can respond to changing operational contexts, environments, or system characteristics and thus achieve greater versatility, flexibility, and resiliency, and also become more robust, energy efficient, and customizable. Consequently, developing self-adaptive systems with an eye toward knowledge representation and reasoning (KR&R) has been an area of increasing interest over the years: examples include research in semantic mapping, aspects of planning and control, and, most notably, human–robot interaction (HRI). In general, KR&R methodologies strive to solve complex problems characteristic of nondeterministic operational environments and of systems that must reason at runtime to discover missing answers.

Decision-making is a complex process, often based on more than just logical conclusions. In representing degrees of belief about knowledge that is necessarily uncertain or changing, probability and statistics can provide the basis for reasoning. For example, statistical inferences might help us draw conclusions about a city's overall traffic patterns based on data obtained from relatively few streets. Bayesian networks are often used to represent a *belief probability*, which summarizes a potentially infinite set of possible circumstances. Belief probability influences decision-making based on a system's past experiences, associating future success with prior actions generated in the execution environment. Maintaining an execution history for such actions helps the system compute and recompute the success probability of action execution. In this way, the system may learn (that is, infer new knowledge) and adapt so as not to execute actions that traditionally have had a low-success rate.

To operate efficiently and reliably in open-ended environments, systems must have some initial knowledge as well as the ability to learn based on knowledge processing and awareness. Moreover, a system's knowledge must be structured to provide an essential awareness of both its internal and external worlds. To meet these and other challenges, Lero – The Irish Software Engineering Center, has developed the KnowLang framework within the ASCENS Project mandate [4]. KnowLang [5,6] is a KR&R framework for efficient and comprehensive knowledge structuring that is intended to support both logical and statistical reasoning. At its very core, the framework is a formal specification language providing a comprehensive, yet multitier model where knowledge can be presented at different levels of abstraction and grouped by following both hierarchical and functional patterns. Knowledge specified with KnowLang takes the form of a knowledge base (KB) incorporating an ontology using concepts organized through concept trees, object trees, relations, and predicates. Each concept is specified with particular properties and functionality and is hierarchically linked to other concepts. For reasoning purposes, every concept specified with KnowLang has an intrinsic "state" attribute that can be associated with a set of possible state expressions. Moreover, concepts and objects can be connected via relations. Relations are binary and can have *probability distribution* attributes. Probability distribution, which is used to support probabilistic reasoning, presents a belief probability about relations between different knowledge concepts – time, situation, action, event, and so forth – that are often in competition. By specifying KnowLang relations through their probability distributions, we are actually creating Bayesian networks that connect concepts and objects within the ontology.

7.3.1 Modeling Knowledge with KnowLang

Modeling knowledge with KnowLang occurs in the following three stages:

1) *Initial Knowledge Gathering.* When domain experts determine the interest domain's basic notions, relations, and functions or operations
2) *Behavior Definition.* During which domain-specific situations and behavior policies are identified as control data to help determine important self-adaptive scenarios
3) *Knowledge Structuring.* To encapsulate the identified domain entities, situations, and behaviors into KnowLang structures – that is, concepts, objects, relations, facts, and rules.

This knowledge modeling process results in KnowLang's multitier specification model, illustrated in Figure 7.2.

KnowLang provides a formal language that integrates ontologies with rules and Bayesian networks based on logical and statistical reasoning to build a knowledge base (KB) via the following three main tiers [6]:

1) A knowledge corpus that explicitly represents domain concepts and relationships

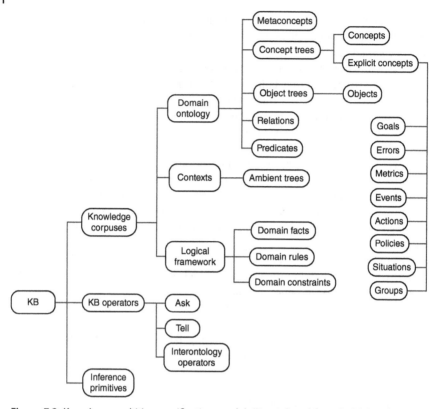

Figure 7.2 KnowLang multitier specification model. (Reproduced from Ref. [6] with permission of Springer.)

2) KB operators that represent particular and general factual knowledge
3) Inference primitives that use additive probabilities to represent degrees of belief in uncertain knowledge

A KB specified with KnowLang outlines a KR (knowledge relationship) context that is specific to the targeted system's domain. A special KnowLang Reasoner operates in this context to allow for knowledge querying and update. The KnowLang Reasoner is conceived as a component hosted by a self-adaptive system; thus, it runs in the system's operational context as any other system component does. By operating on the KB, the reasoner can *infer* special self-adaptive behavior. KnowLang provides a predefined set of "ask" and "tell" operators that allow communication with the KB [7]. Tell operators feed the KR context important information – driven by errors, executed actions, new sensory data, and the like – thus helping the KnowLang Reasoner update the KR with recent changes in both the system state and the execution environment. The system uses ask operators to elicit recommended behaviors, with prior knowledge compared to current outside input to generate appropriate actions that comply with determined goals and beliefs. In addition, ask operators may provide the system with awareness-based conclusions about the current system and environment states and, ideally, with behavior models for self-adaptation.

7.3.2 Knowledge Representation for Self-Adaptive Behavior

In summary, KnowLang employs special knowledge structures and a reasoning mechanism to model *self-adaptive behavior* [8]. Such behavior can be expressed via KnowLang's structure policies: events, actions, and situations, as well as relations between policies and situations. Policies are at the core of any KR for self-adaptive behavior. Ideally, KnowLang policies are specified in a way that will allow a system to pursue a specific goal within a specific situation via actions generated in the environment or in the system itself. Specific conditions determine the specific actions to be executed. These conditions often differ from the past situations triggering a policy. Thus, self-adaptive behavior depends not only on the specific situations a policy is specified to handle, but also on additional conditions and probabilistic beliefs.

In order to initiate self-adaptive behavior, relations must be specified between policies and situations vis-à-vis a belief probability: a policy may be related to multiple situations and vice versa. A belief probability supports probabilistic reasoning, helping the KnowLang Reasoner choose the most probable situation–policy "pair" – that is, the most probable policy to be applied to a particular situation. Thus, we might specify several different relations connecting a specific situation with various policies that may be undertaken when the system is in that situation; the probability distribution should help the Reasoner decide which policy to choose in each case.

At runtime, the KnowLang Reasoner maps situations to policies [5–8], and, for any actual situation, applies the policy with the highest possible belief probability. When a policy is applied, the Reasoner checks it against the particular conditions to be met and then performs actions that meet these particular conditions. Although initially specified, the belief probability is recomputed after any action is executed. Furthermore, the Reasoner maintains a history of these action executions, and recomputation is based on the consequences of the action execution, which allows for *reinforcement learning* within the system.

7.3.3 Case Study

To illustrate self-adaptive behavior based on this approach, imagine a robot carrying items from point *A* to point *B* using two possible routes, route one and

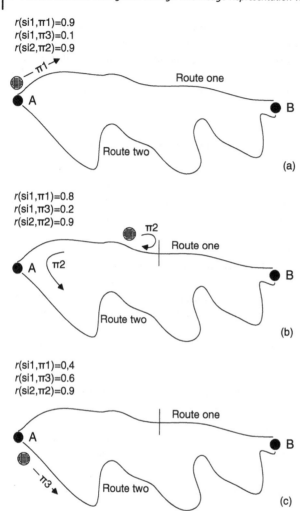

Figure 7.3 Robot's self-adaptive behavior.

route two, as shown in Figure 7.3. In this case study, through self-adaptive behavior based on applying KnowLang framework policies, a robot programmed to carry items from point A to point B via route one (a) will alter its course when route one is blocked (b) and instead follow route two (c). If route one is blocked in the future, the higher probabilistic belief rate regarding route two will lead the robot to change its behavior, choosing route two as its primary route.

Situation si1: "robot is at point A loaded with items" triggers policy π1: "go to point B via route one" if the relation $r(si1,\pi1)$ has a higher probabilistic belief rate than other possible relations (for example, such a belief rate has been initially established for this relation because route one is shorter). Whenever the robot is in si1, it will continue applying the π1 policy. However, when the robot finds itself in situation si2: "route one is blocked," it will no longer apply that policy; si2 will trigger policy π2: "go back to si1 and then apply policy π3," with policy π3 defined as: "go to point B via route two." The unsuccessful application of policy π1 will decrease the probabilistic belief rate of relation $r(si1,π1)$, and the eventual successful application of policy π3 will increase the probabilistic belief rate of relation $r(si1,π3)$. Thus, if route one continues to be blocked in the future, relation $r(si1,π3)$ will come to have a higher probabilistic belief rate than relation $r(si1,π1)$, and the robot will change its behavior by choosing route two as a primary route. It is also possible for the situation to change in response to external stimuli, for example, the robot receives a "route two is blocked" message or "route one is obstacle-free" message.

Any long-running self-adaptive system must change behavior in response to stimuli from the execution environment, and all such environments are subject to uncertainty due to potential evolution in requirements, business conditions, available technology, and the like. Thus, it is important to capture and plan for uncertainty as part of the development process. Failure to do so may result in systems that are overly rigid for their purpose, an eventuality of particular concern for domains that typically use self-adaptive technology, such as unmanned space flight. We hypothesize that KnowLang, by allowing developers to model uncertainty and create mechanisms for managing it as part of knowledge representation and reasoning, will lead to systems that are expressive of the real world, more fault tolerant because they can anticipate fluctuations in requirements and conditions, and highly flexible in managing dynamic change.

7.4 Awareness

A successful intelligent system employs its knowledge to become more self-aware. To achieve this self-awareness, system designers develop more sophisticated KR models and reasoning capabilities (e.g., KnowLang), drawing on research in ontologies, data mining, intelligent agents, autonomic computing, knowledge processing, and many other areas.

Conceptually, awareness is a product of knowledge and monitoring. A large class of software-intensive systems – including those for industrial automation, consumer electronics, airplanes, automobiles, medical devices, and civic infrastructure – must interact with the physical world. More advanced systems, such as unmanned autonomous systems, do not just interact but also perceive important structural and dynamic aspects of their operational environment. To become interactive, an autonomous software system must be aware of its physical environment and whereabouts, as well as its current internal status. This ability helps intelligent software systems sense, draw inferences, and react.

Closely related to artificial intelligence, awareness depends on the knowledge we transfer to software systems so they can use it to exhibit intelligence. In addition to knowledge, artificial awareness also requires a means of sensing changes so that the system can perceive both external and internal worlds through raw events and data. Thus, self and environmental monitoring are crucial to awareness: To exhibit awareness, software-intensive systems must sense and analyze their internal components and the environment in which they operate. Such systems should be able to notice a change and understand its implications. Moreover, an aware system should apply both pattern analysis and pattern recognition to determine normal and abnormal states.

Ideally, awareness should be part of the cognitive process that underlies learning. An efficient awareness mechanism should also rely on both past experience and new knowledge. Awareness via learning is the basic mechanism for introducing new facts into the cognitive system – other possible ways are related to interaction with a human operator who manually introduces new facts into the knowledge base. Here, we clarify the nature of artificial awareness and its impact on contemporary software-intensive systems.

7.4.1 Classes of Awareness

Awareness generally is classified into two major areas: *self-awareness*, pertaining to the internal world; and *context-awareness*, pertaining to the external world. Autonomic computing research defines these two classes [9]:

- A self-aware system has detailed knowledge about its own entities, current states, capacity and capabilities, physical connections, and ownership relations with other systems in its environment.
- A context-aware system knows how to sense, negotiate, communicate, and interact with environmental systems and how to anticipate environmental system states, situations, and changes.

Perhaps a third class could be *situational awareness*, which is self-explanatory; other classes could draw attention to specific problems, such as operational conditions and performance (operational awareness), control processes (control awareness), interaction processes (interaction awareness), and navigation processes (navigation awareness). Although classes of awareness can differ by subject, they all require a subjective perception of events and data "within a volume of time and space, the comprehension of their meaning, and the projection of their status in the near future" [10].

To better understand the idea of awareness in software-intensive systems, consider an exploration robot. Its navigation awareness mechanism could build a map on the fly, with landmarks represented as part of the environment knowledge, so that navigation becomes simply a matter of reading sensor data from cameras and plotting the robot's position at the time of observation. Via repeated position plots, the robot's course and land-reference speed can be established [11].

7.4.2 Structuring Awareness

Recent research efforts have focused on awareness implementations in software-intensive systems. For example, commercially available server-monitoring platforms, such as Nimbus [12] and Cittio's Watch Tower [13], offer robust, lightweight sensing and reporting capabilities across large server farms. Such solutions are oriented toward massive data collection and performance reporting, so they leave much of the final analysis and decision-making to a human administrator. Other approaches achieve awareness through model-based detection and response based on offline training and models constructed to represent different scenarios that the system can recognize at runtime.

To function, the mechanism implementing the awareness must be structured to take into consideration different stages – for example, it might be built over a complex chain of functions such as raw data gathering, data passing, filtering, conversion, assessment, projection, and learning. As Figure 7.4 shows, ideally, all the awareness functions could be structured as an awareness pyramid, forming the mechanism that converts raw data into conclusions, problem prediction, and eventually learning.

The pyramid levels in Figure 7.4 represent awareness functions that can be grouped into four specific tasks. The first three levels include monitoring tasks; the fourth, recognition tasks; the fifth and sixth, assessment tasks; and the last, learning tasks [11]:

- *Monitoring.* Collects, aggregates, filters, manages, and reports internal and external details such as metrics and topologies gathered from the system's internal entities and its context

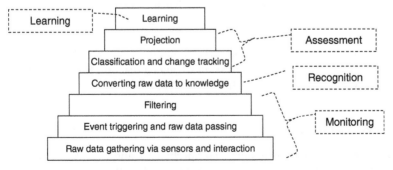

Figure 7.4 The awareness pyramid. (Reproduced from Ref. [11] with permission of Awareness Magazine.).

- *Recognition.* Uses knowledge structures and data patterns to aggregate and convert raw data into knowledge symbols
- *Assessment.* Tracks changes and determines points of interest, generates hypotheses about situations involving these points, and recognizes situational patterns
- *Learning.* Generates new situational patterns and maintains a history of property changes

Aggregation can be included as a subtask at any function level; it is intended to improve overall awareness performance. For example, it can pull together large amounts of sensory data during the filtering stage or recognition tasks can apply it to improve classification. The awareness process is not as straightforward as it might seem. Rather, it is cyclic, with several iterations over the various awareness functions. Closing the chain of awareness functions can form an awareness control loop in which different awareness classes can emerge [11]. The process's cyclic nature is why awareness itself is so complex, with several levels of exhibition and degrees of perception. The levels can be related to data readability and reliability, that is, they might include noisy data that must be cleaned up and eventually interpreted with some degree of probability.

Other levels might include *early awareness*, which is a product of one or two passes of the awareness control loop, and *late awareness*, which should be more mature in terms of conclusions and projections. Similar to humans who react to their first impression but then find that a later and better realization of the situation shifts their reaction, an aware software system should rely on early awareness to react quickly to situations when fast reaction is needed and on late awareness when more precise thinking is required.

The long-term impact of awareness-related research and development is a road map leading to artificial intelligence. Machine intelligence depends on the ability to perceive the environment and react to changes in it. The awareness mechanism uses raw data gathered via system's sensors to recognize objects, project situations, track changes, and learn new facts. A successful awareness mechanism can exhibit awareness at different levels of maturity and relevance. Noisy data can affect awareness relevance, which can lead to awareness results gradually changing over time and data input. Ideally, the awareness mechanism should help intelligent systems behave like humans, realizing situations and reacting progressively: The first impression triggers a reaction that can change based on progressive realization of the current situation.

7.4.3 Implementing Awareness

The four awareness functions require a comprehensive and well-structured KB to hold KR symbols that can express the system itself with its proper internal structures and functionality as well as the environment (see Section 7.3).

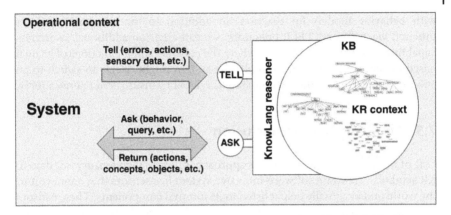

Figure 7.5 Implementing awareness with KnowLang. (Reproduced from Ref. [6] with permission of Springer.).

Building an efficient awareness mechanism requires properly integrating the awareness pyramid within the implemented software system.

The goal is to provide a means of monitoring and KR with a reasoner supporting awareness reasoning. KR adds a new open-world KR context to the program, and the reasoner operates in this context, taking into account the monitoring activities that drive the awareness control loop and deliver awareness results to the system itself.

Figure 7.5 depicts the KnowLang approach to the awareness problem. In this approach, KnowLang provides the constructs and mechanisms for specifying knowledge models at the ontology and logic foundation levels [6]. To specify knowledge with KnowLang, we need to think about domain concepts and their properties and functionalities, important states of major concepts, objects as realizations of concepts, relations that show how concepts and objects connect to each other, self-adapting scenarios for the system in question, remarkable behavior in terms of policies driving the system out of specific situations, and other important specifics that can be classified as concepts (see Section 7.3).

As Figure 7.5 shows, the KB comprises KR structures such as concept trees, object trees, and concept maps. The system talks to the KnowLang reasoner via a predefined set of TELL and ASK operators [7,8], forming a communication interface that connects both the system and the KB. TELL operators feed the KB with important information driven by errors, executed actions, new sensory data, and so forth, thus helping the KnowLang reasoner update the KR context with recent changes in both the system and execution environment. The system uses ASK operators to receive recommended behavior, where knowledge is used against perception to generate appropriate actions in compliance with specific goals and beliefs. In addition, ASK operators can provide awareness-based conclusions about the system or environment's current state and ideally with behavior models for reaction. In addition to the awareness abilities initiated via ASK and TELL operators, we can envision additional awareness capability based on self-initiation, where the reasoner initiates actions of its own based on state changes. For example, the system might decide to switch to an energy-saving mode if the current state is related to insufficient energy supply.

7.5 Challenges and Conclusion

One of the biggest challenges in this approach is how to map sensory raw data to KR symbols. An aware software-intensive system has sensors that connect it to the world and eventually help it listen to its internal components. These sensors generate raw data that represent the world's physical characteristics. The problem is that these low-level data streams must be converted to programming variables or more complex data structures that represent collections of sensory data, and those programming data structures must be labeled with KR symbols.

Another considerable challenge is how to express states and reason about them. KnowLang introduces an explicit STATES attribute [5,6] that helps us specify concepts with a set of important states in which the concepts instances can be. Thus, we explicitly specify a variety of states for important concepts, for example, "operational" and "nonoperational" for a robot's motion system. Furthermore, a state in KnowLang is specified as a Boolean expression where we can use event activation, action execution, or property changes to build a state's Boolean expression. To facilitate complex state evaluation, the reasoner can use special predicates in which complex system states are evaluated as the product of other states.

The long-term impact of knowledge representation and awareness-related research and development is a road map leading to artificial intelligence. Machine intelligence depends on the ability to perceive the environment and react to changes in it. The awareness mechanism uses raw data gathered via system's sensors to recognize objects, project situations, track changes, and learn new facts. A successful awareness mechanism can exhibit awareness at different levels of maturity and relevance. Noisy data can affect awareness relevance, which can lead to awareness results gradually changing over time and data input. Ideally, the awareness mechanism should help intelligent systems behave like humans, realizing situations and reacting progressively: The first impression triggers a reaction that can change based on progressive realization of the current situation.

References

1 P. Makhfi (2008) MAKHFI – Methodic Applied Knowledge to Hyper Fictitious Intelligence. Available at http://www.makhfi.com/.

2 W. Swartout and A. Tate (1999) Ontologies. IEEE Intelligent Systems, Jan./ Feb. pp. 18–19.

3 R. J. Brachman and H. J. Levesque (2004) *Knowledge Representation and Reasoning*, Elsevier.

4 ASCENS – Autonomic Service-Component Ensembles (2015) http://www .ascens-ist.eu/.

5 KnowLang – Knowledge Representation and Reasoning for Adaptive Systems (2015) http://knowlang.lero.ie.

6 E. Vassev and M. Hinchey (2015) Knowledge representation for adaptive and self-aware systems. *Software Engineering for Collective Autonomic Systems*, LNCS, vol. 8998, Springer, Heidelberg, pp. 221–247.

7 E. Vassev (2012) Operational semantics for KnowLang ASK and TELL operators. Technical report, Lero-TR-2012-05, Lero, University of Limerick, Ireland.

8 E. Vassev, M. Hinchey, and B. Gaudin (2012) *Knowledge Representation for Self-Adaptive Behavior. Proceedings of C* Conference on Computer Science & Software Engineering (C3S2E '12)*, ACM Press, New York, pp. 113–117.

9 IBM (2001) Autonomic Computing: IBM's Perspective on the State of Information Technology, IBM Autonomic Computing Manifesto. Available at www.research.ibm.com/autonomic/manifesto/auto nomic_computing.pdf.

10 M.R. Endsley (1995) Toward a theory of situation awareness in dynamic systems. *Human Factors*, 37 (1), 32–64.

11 E. Vassev (2012) Building the pyramid of awareness. Awareness Magazine - Self-awareness in Autonomic Systems, July

12 Nimbus. www.nimbusproject.org (accessed February 2016).

13 Cittio's Watch Tower. (2006) www.networkcomputing.com/dataprotection/ cittios-watchtower-30/229611534.

Part III

Software Development and Evolution

8

Continuous Model-Driven Engineering

Tiziana Margaria,[1] Anna-Lena Lamprecht,[1] and Bernhard Steffen[2]

[1]*Department of Computer Science and Information Systems, University of Limerick, and Lero – The Irish Software Research Centre, Limerick, Ireland*
[2]*Fakultät für Informatik, TU Dortmund University, Dortmund, Germany*

8.1 Introduction

Agility has become an increasing necessity for application software, particularly when business-critical issues are concerned. In companies, software systems drive and coordinate how product planning, production, marketing, and sales are approached, and how these relate to the (software) ecosystems [1,2] of customers and suppliers. In organizations, the same happens for the IT that supports the organization's management, communication, and evolution. Such software systems are gaining strategic importance, embodying an increasing portion of a company's distinctive know-how and culture. At the same time, they must be continuously updated and adapted to meet the ever-changing market conditions and the inevitable technological change, often driven by globalization that forces them to move toward integration and harmonization. Additional change factors complicate this process. For instance, the increased intermediation in software production leads to the widespread use of off-the-shelf components and software, outsourcing, open-source software development practices, and even inner sourcing [3,4], which resorts within the company to the same methods as open sourcing. The adoption of services such as X-as-a-service [5], in which X can be various factors such as software, hosting, and accounting, also intermediates and shields hardware and software toward a utility-like model of fruition. Other change factors include decreased intermediation in the hierarchy of responsibility, such as making CEOs and CTOs/CIOs personally liable for mishaps such as compliance and governance-level mistakes. These are typically rooted in the software systems that run the

Software Technology: 10 Years of Innovation in IEEE Computer, First Edition.
Edited by Mike Hinchey.

company and manage its communication with its operational environment and ecosystems. Thus, companies feel a growing need to tightly control their own business and with it also its strategies, processes, rules, and regulations. This faster pace of change and deep reaching dependencies require application and business experts to continuously oversee and steer the entire scenario from their unique perspective.

Mastering this increasingly fluid and interdependent situation requires a new software development paradigm, tailored to reliably keep up with the pace of innovation. In particular, the increasing acceleration and entanglement mandate introducing means for establishing adequate degrees of freedom. They should be strong enough to serve as guidance, yet flexible enough to allow all necessary changes and provide easy-to-use push-button methods for validation at both design time and runtime. Ultimately, this new landscape should lead to a situation where application experts themselves can directly participate as first-class and integral actors in the software development process. This is way beyond the UX paradigm [6,7] that allows users to participate, but as "other" from the developers.

State-of-the-art design methods and development technologies offer only partial support to bridge the technology/application gap in this fashion:

1) Domain-specific languages ease the software development by providing derived functionality that allows concise solutions [8,9]. They typically address advanced programmers and are not suitable as a means of communication with non-IT application experts.
2) Model-driven design [10,11] shifts the attention and the design activities from the programming level to the modeling level, but still remains within the IT realm of models. Even at the platform-independent level, the typically UML-based MDD and model-driven architecture approaches provide varieties of model structures that focus on different technical issues/aspects. Mastering such technologies is a special art requiring both IT knowledge and a good sense of dealing with abstraction.
3) Aspect orientation [12,13] organizes/modularizes the realization of different cross-cutting concerns. This way, it supports the reuse of the so-called aspect code, and also helps to deal individually with each aspect by delegating the correct positioning to a separately designed weaving mechanism. Particularly for highly distributed implementations, aspect orientation is a powerful programming paradigm to cover, for example, factors such as quality of service, exception handling, or even roles, rights, and permissions.
4) eXtreme Programming (XP) [14,15] directly aims at continuously involving customer and application experts via frequent prototypes and the "test first" paradigm: Functionalities are prioritized and added one by one, giving the customer the opportunity to review them individually and control the progress. Unfortunately, this approach does not scale easily, failing

particularly when the focus of typical business applications should be on their global interplay.

5) Service-oriented approaches try to overcome the typical problems of traditional "programming in the large" by abandoning the construction of complex monolithic applications and replacing them with suites of services or service-like artifacts programmed in the small [16–19].

6) This approach supports agility but addresses neither the problem of orchestration nor the management of evolution.

7) Process modeling [20–23] aims at providing a formal basis for application and business experts to formulate their intents unambiguously. This approach works quite well in the rare cases where the business expert fully knows what he needs and how to express it in process notation. Otherwise, the visual nature of process diagrams can easily lead to wrong interpretations, suggesting deceptive safety or agreement understandings among stakeholders, while even totally senseless process descriptions often survive lengthy review meetings, where only some of the participants truly master the formalism's semantics. Thus, process models are often used as "better" forms of documentation, still to be "correctly" interpreted by the IT personnel.

8) Agile and lean software development [24–26] focus on speed and frugality in the design and realization of software. They are powerful meta-level approaches, but need to be fielded by grounding onto some design method or paradigm, as they are merely organizational frameworks, that neither imply nor exclude a specific way of designing and implementing a system.

All these approaches contribute in different fashions and from different perspectives to closing the gap between the technical and the application experts, but currently there is no satisfactory solution to allow business experts to continuously oversee and steer their business scenarios from their own perspective. Moreover, even though there exists a wealth of methods for quality assurance covering both design time and runtime, today's validation technology is still far from addressing the needs of today's agile development.

8.2 Continuous Model-Driven Engineering

Continuous Model-Driven Engineering (CMDE) aims at establishing a holistic view that transparently and consistently joins all the pieces together in order to establish a consistent dialogue between all the involved stakeholders. In particular, it aims at providing the following:

- *Application-Level Control* – the continuous involvement of the customer and application expert along the entire systems' life cycle, including software maintenance and evolution.

- *Continuous and Ongoing Quality Assurance* with different means at different levels and phases: requirement validation, simulation, verification, data flow analysis, testing, and monitoring.
- *Specific Service-Oriented Support* for integrating new technologies in an easy and noninvasive fashion.

Conceptually, CMDE borrows ideas from the seven software and system development paradigms already mentioned. The combination of eXtreme Programming, model-driven design, and process modeling forms the backbone of what we call eXtreme Model-Driven Design (XMDD) [18,23,27], an approach based on the elaboration and refinement of abstractly executable application and business models, called the *application logic* models. The way it is managed, it is then itself agile and lean.

XMDD's user-centric perspective derives from process modeling, clearly privileging the business-first perspective. Its analysis, verification, and refinement techniques resemble those used in model-driven design, while its devotion to a direct and continuous user experience via model execution provides a feedback-driven eXtreme flavor. Depending on the development stage, execution might mean a simple step-through in terms of if-then games, document browsing, simulation, full execution, or mixtures thereof.

In XMDD, developers continue the elaboration and refinement of the application logic until it reaches a predetermined case-specific level, at which point the classical requirement–implementation gap becomes a service-oriented realization of user- and application-level functionalities. Thus, rather than building highly complex software architectures, XMDD manages complex hierarchical models that orchestrate user- and application-level functionality in an agile, bazaar-like fashion, and in this way it eliminates or substitutes more rigid cathedral-style approaches [28]. In this sense, the model/code border is flexible and can be moved at need. Whenever an external system is hit, its API becomes a set of functionalities to be called as services.

The agility is not only in the speed of development, where models can be created and validated with regard to the application logic well before any code is written, but also in the robustness concerning the evolution of technical platforms or of the IT landscape in a company, organization, or its ecosystem.

CMDE solidifies this model-at-the-center perspective via the One-Thing Approach (OTA) [23,29], which combines the simplicity of waterfall development with maximum agility. Key to OTA is viewing the entire development process as a cooperative, hierarchical, evolving, and interactive decision process, which is organized by building and refining one comprehensive model, the "one thing." Figure 8.1 contrasts this idea with the Rational Unified Process [30]: Textual process descriptions, use case diagrams, and other UML diagrams are all aggregated into one single model that reflects their imposed constraints on the eventual solution (illustrated in Figure 8.2). This one-thing model in

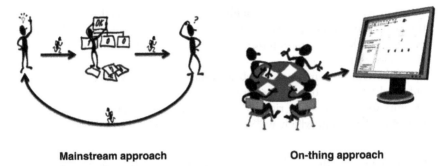

Mainstream approach   **On-thing approach**

Figure 8.1 The mainstream approach versus the One-Thing Approach.

practice nearly automatically reveals inconsistencies and misunderstandings: Whenever two stakeholders or two parts of the system do not harmonize, the mismatch is pretty evident in terms of interfaces, decompositions, or constraints. With this approach, each stakeholder – including the application expert – can continuously place decisions in terms of constraints, and each development step or evolution can be regarded simply as a transformation or reification of this set of constraints. Typical constraints might comprise many aspects and touch on several forms of knowledge and can adequately be expressed through the following:

- Temporal logic formulas, which can express the application's intentions, internal policies, legal constraints, or technical frame conditions.

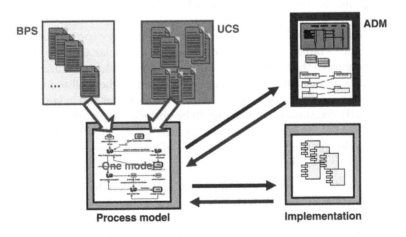

Figure 8.2 The One-Thing Approach.

- Loose process models, which roughly specify the distributed workflow from the management perspective, without concerning technicalities like type correctness, location, or interoperability that are taken care of elsewhere at a more technical level.
- Symbolic type information, which is sufficient to imply executability. It is enforced later by synthesis technology.
- Definitions of roles and rights, timing and localization constraints, and exception handling, which will be integrated during aspect-oriented code generation.

In this framework, the development process's waterfall character focuses on the chosen decision hierarchy: who can decide or modify what, the binding power assigned to decisions, and how conflicts should be resolved. This approach lets all the stakeholders monitor globally and at any time the development or evolution process via constraint checking, along the structure of knowledge and expertise and along the organizational aspects and the responsibility distribution. At the same time, this approach imposes by construction a kind of decision hierarchy by mapping areas of competencies to individuals' roles that are then asked to identify required actions and avoid constraint violation.

Like XP for programming in the small, this approach revolutionizes process and application development. It replaces the typically long intervals between contract-and-requirements time and delivery-and-acceptance time – with all the associated pitfalls – by a continuous, cooperative development process that reveals misconceptions early, so that they can be addressed as soon as they arise. This is the key to a good design, and to early validation. This way, serious logical flaws are typically revealed already at modeling time, which reduces the required iterations between the testing and the development team prior to customer deployment.

The better and shared understanding of the application under construction – the user experience – builds naturally along the way. In particular, this new view of cooperation between the customer and the contractor/developer reduces the need for complex and expensive specification documents. These all too often impose early technical or design decisions, before the customer can judge their impact. Such early decisions often turn out to be obstacles when adjusting the project in the overall context. In contrast, and as Figure 8.2 illustrates, the cooperative development and evolutionary style of CMDE supports the agile adjustment through the following:

- *Continuous Customer Update* The impact of each design decision on the application logic becomes apparent via the One-Thing Approach, which provides customers with a continuously updated user experience. In this sense, the approach is viable also for dev-ops teams [31], because it naturally brings together at the One-Thing Table all the stakeholders along the development chain.

- *Focus on Application Logic* This trait lets developers repair and modify at the same level where the need appears. Following the service-oriented paradigm additionally makes noninvasive exchange or integration of third-party functionality easy.
- *Constraint Analysis* At any stage, developers can verify the formulated constraints via local checking and data-flow analysis to ensure parameterization and configuration constraints. They can also use model checking [32,33] to ensure global properties concerning protocols, version compatibility, policies, or legal process requirements [34].
- *Code Generation* Once all required elementary services are implemented, stand-alone code is generated to fully match the tracer behavior [35,36]. It also manages aspects like role specifications, rights, permissions, security, load balancing, and long-running transactions management.
- *Testing and Test-Based Modeling* In order to validate user-level functionality of the running application, active automata learning is employed to realize the paradigm of test-based modeling [37]. This provides user-level graphical models that can be inspected by the application expert for their actual runtime behavior. Additionally, these models provide the basis for (customer-side) online monitoring.
- *Monitoring and Lifelong Learning* Our runtime environment tracks resource consumption and availability as well as the progress of individual process instances according to their defining models. This monitoring process is enhanced by active automata learning that continuously updates the available (monitoring) model on the basis of monitoring-based observation: Whenever the monitoring reveals a discrepancy to the monitoring model, this discrepancy is translated into a counter-example trace that can then be used to progress in the lifelong learning process.

8.3 CMDE in Practice

CMDE reveals its power in the context of formal methods-based tooling with the jABC, our corresponding development and execution framework (Figure 8.3) [38,39]. jABC provides application-level tracing and simulation models that are executable in a mode tailored to the current development stage. Figure 8.2 illustrates which of its parts and plug-ins come into play in the different phases of the development process. The jABC framework has been instrumental to the success of several scientific and industrial projects, spanning telecommunication services, supply chain management, bioinformatics, logistics, and healthcare. In all these cases, agility at the customer, user, and application level proved to be the key to aligning and linking business and IT [40].

Five larger, intertwined research projects illustrate the character of our approach:

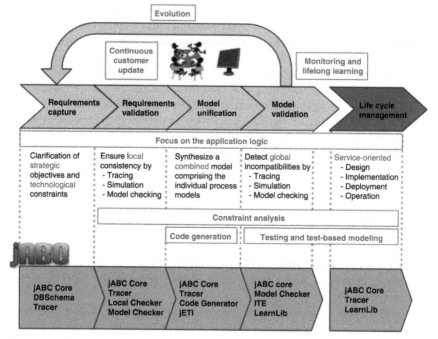

Figure 8.3 The development process with CMDE and jABC.

- A systematic large-scale case study in bioinformatics [41].
- A dedicated investigation of simplicity as a driver to support innovation [42–44].
- A smooth integration of data-flow handling that even enables a higher order parameter transfer where processes and services can be passed around just like data [45,46].
- A constraint-oriented technology for supporting variability and evolution [47].
- A dynamic approach to organize quality assurance along the process life cycle on the basis of active automata learning [48,49].

All these projects were built on top of the jABC framework following the CMDE paradigm and helped to strengthen jABC's technological basis in a bootstrapping fashion.

The bioinformatics domain is characterized by a plethora of freely available, distributed, and at the same time very heterogeneous services for all kinds of data retrieval and analysis tasks. The application of the technologies described in this book laid the foundation for the Bio-jETI framework [50,51], which facilitates the integration of the different existing bioinformatics services as lightweight workflow building blocks and their use for the design and implementation of complex and continuously evolving analysis processes. It has been used in several bioinformatics workflow projects and has served as the technical basis for systematic case studies on user-level workflow design in this field [41,52].

Design for Simplicity aims at fighting the often unexpectedly high longer term costs for maintenance, adaptation, migration, and so on. Guided by the questions "What is really required?," "What is provided in terms of standards solutions?," and "Which parts really need to be newly developed?" [53], a number of projects have been realized, which comprise the above-mentioned projects of bioinformatics, a plug-in framework enhancing the functionality of the jABC framework [54], a synthesis-based approach to service-oriented programming [55], and a learning-based testing approach [56].

Higher order parameter transfer enables a dynamic framework for binding and execution of (business) process models in a way that provides graphical ad hoc processes modeling. It flexibly combines functionality from third-party services discovered in the Internet with synthesized process chains that solve situation-specific tasks. Key to this approach is the introduction of type-safe stacked second-order execution contexts that allow higher order process modeling [45,46,57]. Tamed by our underlying strictly service-oriented notion of abstraction, this approach is tailored also to be used by application experts with little technical knowledge: Users can select, modify, construct, and then pass (component) processes during process execution as if they were data. The most advanced feature of this framework is the combination of online synthesis with the integration of the synthesized process into the running application. This ability leads to a particularly flexible way of implementing self-adaptation and to a particularly concise and powerful way of achieving variability not only at design time but also at runtime.

Constraint-based variability modeling is a flexible, declarative approach to managing solution-space variability [47,58]. Product variants are defined in a top-down manner by successively restricting the admissible combinations of product artifacts until a specific product variant is determined. Methods range from applying model checking to manually designed variants to applying synthesis technology [59,60] for the fully automatic generation of product variants that satisfy all given constraints. This technology underlies the loose programming approach [55], where incomplete specifications are turned into running programs via synthesis. Moreover, it can be even combined with the above-mentioned concept of higher order processes [46] to realize a very flexible form of runtime adaptability.

Incremental active automata learning technology [61–63] enables to periodically infer evolving behavioral automata of complex applications in order to monitor the evolution of applications throughout their whole life cycle with minimum manual effort [48]. The underlying approach of test-based modeling overcomes the typical bottleneck of model-based testing, because it does not require any *a priori* test models [64]. This technology profits from the higher order modeling approach described above [56], and it can be nicely adapted to risk-based testing [48].

8.4 Conclusion

Domain specificity is a key success factor for CMDE: The more the structures the application domain imposes on the dedicated development environment, the more easy it is to involve the application expert.

Besides adequate visual representation, this requires in particular tailored component libraries that allow application expert to compose the intended functionality using intuitive, domain-specific building blocks. The service-oriented library concept underlying the jABC is specifically designed for this kind of user-level modeling: Building blocks can be easily constructed using third-party components, renamed, graphically represented by expressive icons, structured in domain-specific taxonomies, and additionally constraint using temporal logic formulas in order to provide a domain-specifically guided graphical modeling experience. This has been very successful for applications where flow graph-like modeling is adequate. In other cases, for example, for modeling of complex ontologies, "graphical hacks" are required.

To overcome this limitation, our most recent framework extension comprises meta-modeling-based definitions of graphical languages from which application-specific modeling tools can automatically be generated [65–67]. This does not only allow us to flexibly adapt to common graphical conventions but also to elegantly specify and automatically enforce complex structural constraints complementing our current temporal logic-based constraint technology. We are planning to illustrate the power of this approach by generating a product line of PMN tools that allows one to provide each user with a modeling tool for exactly the fragment of BPMN she desires [67]. One instance of such a tool will be used to enhance our framework with process or project management for overseeing development and evolution. It will include deadline management and progress reports, automatically informing all relevant parties when certain actions are required, managing different versions and product lines, and automatically steering the build and quality management process. In fact, this development is another example of CMDE bootstrapping, a phenomenon we repeatedly observe since we consequently follow this paradigm.

Acknowledgment

This work was supported, in part, by Science Foundation Ireland Grant 13/RC/ 2094 and cofunded under the European Regional Development Fund through the Southern & Eastern Regional Operational Programme to Lero – the Irish Software Research Centre (www.lero.ie).

References

1 D. Messerschmitt and C. Szyperski (2003) *Software Ecosystem: Understanding an Indispensable Technology and Industry*, MIT Press.
2 S. Jansen, S. Brinkkemper, and M.A. Cusumano (2014) *Software Ecosystems: Analyzing and Managing Business Networks in the Software Industry*, Edward Elger Publishing.
3 K.-J. Stol and B. Fitzgerald (2015) Inner source – adopting open source development practices in organizations: a tutorial. *Software*, 32, 60–67.
4 K.-J. Stol, P. Avgeriou, Muhammad A. Babar, Y. Lucas, and B. Fitzgerald (2014) Key factors for adopting inner source. *ACM Transactions on Software Engineering and Methodology*, 23 (2). doi: 10.1145/2533685
5 J. Dixon (2014) CloudTech. http://www.cloudcomputing-news.net/news/ 2014/aug/18/x-as-a-service-xaas-what-the-future-of-cloud-computing-will-bring/ (accessed August 2014).
6 M. Hassenzahl User experience and experience design. In: *The Encyclopedia of Human–Computer Interaction*, 2nd ed. Interaction Design Foundation.
7 D.L. Scapin, B. Senach, B. Trousse, and M. Pallot (2012) User experience: buzzword or new paradigm? The Fifth International Conference on Advances in Computer–Human Interactions (ACHI 2012), Valencia, pp. 338–341.
8 M. Fowler (2010) *Domain-Specific Languages*, Addison-Wesley.
9 M. Mernik, J. Heering, and A.M. Sloane (2005) When and how to develop domain-specific languages. *ACM Computation Surveys*, 37 (4), 316–344,
10 M. Völter, T. Stahl, J. Bettin, H. Arno, and S. Helsen (2013) *Model-Driven Software Development: Technology, Engineering, Management*, John Wiley & Sons, Inc., New York.
11 G. Mussbacher et al. (2014) The relevance of model-driven engineering thirty years from now. Proceedings of the 17th International Conference on Model Driven Engineering Languages and Systems (MODELS'14), LNCS 8767, pp. 183–200.
12 G. Kiczales et al. (2006) Aspect-oriented programming. ECOOP'97 – Object-Oriented Programming, LNCS 1241, pp. 220–242.
13 S. Clarke and E. Baniassad (2005) *Aspect-Oriented Analysis and Design*, Addison-Wesley Professional.
14 K. Beck (2000) *Extreme Programming Explained: Embrace Change*, Addison-Wesley.
15 M. Stephens and D. Rosenberg (2003) *Extreme Programming Refactored: The Case Against XP*, Apress.

16 M.N. Huhns and M.P. Singh (2005) Service-oriented computing: key concepts and principles. *IEEE Internet Computing*, **9**, 75–81.

17 T. Erl (2007) *SOA: Principles of Service Design*, Prentice Hall.

18 T. Margaria and B. Steffen (2012) Service-orientation: conquering complexity with XMDD. In: *Conquering Complexity*, Springer, London, pp. 217–236.

19 T. Margaria, B. Steffen, and M. Reitenspiess (2005) Service-oriented design: the roots. Proceedings of the 3rd International Conference on Service-Oriented Computing (ICSOC 2005), LNCS 3826, pp. 450–464.

20 L. Osterweil (1987) Software processes are software too. Proceedings of the 9th International Conference on Software Engineering, pp. 2–13.

21 W. van der Aalst and K. van Hee (2002) *Workflow Management: Models, Methods, and Systems*, MIT Press.

22 J. Cardoso and W. van der Aalst (Eds.) (2009) *Handbook of Research on Business Process Modeling*, IGI Publishing.

23 T. Margaria and B. Steffen (2009) Business process modelling in the jABC: the One-Thing approach. In: *Handbook of Research on Business Process Modeling*, IGI Global.

24 K. Beck et al. (2001) Manifesto for Agile Software Development.

25 R.C. Martin (2003) *Agile Software Development: Principles, Patterns, and Practices*, Prentice Hall.

26 M. Poppendieck and T. Poppendieck (2003) *Lean Software Development: An Agile Toolkit*, Addison-Wesley Professional.

27 G. Jung et al. (2008) SCA and jABC: bringing a service-oriented paradigm to web-service construction. In: *Leveraging Applications of Formal Methods, Verification and Validation: Third International Symposium (ISoLA 2008)*, CCIS 17, Springer, pp. 139–154.

28 E.S. Raymond (1999) The cathedral and the bazaar: musings on Linux and Open Source by an accidental revolutionary.

29 B. Steffen and P. Narayan (2007) Full life-cycle support for end-to-end processes. *IEEE Computer*, **40** (11), 64–73.

30 P. Kruchten (2004) *The Rational Unified Process: An Introduction*, 3rd ed. Addison-Wesley Professional.

31 M. Loukides (2012) What is DevOps?

32 E.M. Clarke, O. Grumberg, and D.A. Peled (1999) *Model Checking*, MIT Press.

33 M. Müller-Olm, D. Schmidt, and B. Steffen (1999) Model-checking: a tutorial introduction. Proceedings of the 6th International Symposium on Static Analysis (SAS'99), pp. 330–354.

34 M. Bakera, T. Margaria, C. Renner, and B. Steffen (2009) Tool-supported enhancement of diagnosis in model-driven verification. *Innovations in Systems and Software Engineering*, **5**, 211–228.

35 S. Jörges, T. Margaria, and B. Steffen (2008) Genesys: service-oriented construction of property conform code generators. *Innovations in Systems and Software Engineering*, **4** (4), 361–384.

36 S. Jörges (2013) *Construction and Evolution of Code Generators: A Model-Driven and Service-Oriented Approach*, LNCS 7747, Springer.

37 J. Neubauer et al. (2012) Automated continuous quality assurance. Formal Methods in Software Engineering, Rigorous and Agile Approaches (FormSERA), pp. 37–43.

38 B. Steffen, T. Margaria, R. Nagel, S. Jörges, and C. Kubczak (2007) Model-driven development with the jABC. In: *Hardware and Software: Verification and Testing*, LNCS 4383, pp. 92–108.

39 M. Hörmann et al. (2008) The jABC approach to rigorous collaborative development of SCM applications. In: *Leveraging Applications of Formal Methods: Verification and Validation*, CCIS 17, pp. 724–737.

40 T. Margaria and B. Steffen (2006) Service engineering: linking business and IT. *IEEE Computer*, **39** (10), 45–55.

41 A.-L. Lamprecht (2013) *User-Level Workflow Design: A Bioinformatics Perspective*, LNCS 8311, Springer.

42 T. Margaria and B. Steffen (2010) Simplicity as a driver for Agile innovation. *IEEE Computer*, **43** (9), 90–92.

43 T. Margaria and B. Steffen (2011) Special session on "Simplification through Change of Perspective". 34th IEEE Software Engineering Workshop (SEW), pp. 67–68.

44 T. Margaria and B. Steffen (2018) Simplicity as a driver for Agile innovation. This Volume.

45 J. Neubauer and B. Steffen (2013) Plug-and-play higher-order process integration. *IEEE Computer*, **46** (11), 56–62.

46 J. Neubauer, B. Steffen, and T. Margaria (2013) Higher-order process modeling: product-lining, variability modeling and beyond. *Electronic Proceedings in Theoretical Computer Science*, **129**, 259–283.

47 S. Jörges, A.-L. Lamprecht, T. Margaria, I. Schaefer, and B. Steffen (2012) A constraint-based variability modeling framework. *International Journal on Software Tools for Technology Transfer*, **14** (5), 511–530.

48 S. Windmüller, J. Neubauer, B. Steffen, F. Howar, and O. Bauer (2013) Active continuous quality control. 16th International ACM SIGSOFT Symposium on Component-Based Software Engineering, pp. 111–120.

49 J. Neubauer, S. Windmüller, and B. Steffen (2014) Risk-based testing via active continuous quality control. *International Journal on Software Tools for Technology Transfer*, **16**, 569–591.

50 T. Margaria, C. Kubczak, and B. Steffen (2008) Bio-jETI: a service integration, design, and provisioning platform for orchestrated bioinformatics processes. *BMC Bioinformatics*, **9** (Suppl. 4), S12.

51 A.-L. Lamprecht, T. Margaria, and B. Steffen (2009) Bio-jETI: a framework for semantics-based service composition. *BMC Bioinformatics*, **10** (Suppl. 10), S8.

52 A.-L. Lamprecht and T. Margaria (Eds.) (2014) *Process Design for Natural Scientists: An Agile Model-Driven Approach*, CCIS 500, Springer.

53 M. Merten and B. Steffen (2013) Simplicity driven application development. *Journal of Integrated Design and Process Science (SDPS)*, **17** (3), 9–23.

54 S. Naujokat et al. (2013) Simplicity-first model-based plug-in development. *Software: Practice and Experience*, **44** (3), 277–297.

55 A.-L. Lamprecht, S. Naujokat, T. Margaria, and B. Steffen (2010) Synthesis-based loose programming. Proceedings of the 7th International Conference on the Quality of Information and Communications Technology, pp. 262–267.

56 B. Steffen and J. Neubauer (2011) Simplified validation of emergent systems through automata learning-based testing. 34th IEEE Software Engineering Workshop (SEW), pp. 84–91.

57 J. Neubauer (2014) Higher-order process engineering, PhD thesis, Technische Universität Dortmund, Germany.

58 A.-L. Lamprecht, S. Naujokat, and I. Schaefer (2013) Variability management beyond feature models. *IEEE Computer*, **46** (11), 48–54.

59 B. Steffen, T. Margaria, and B. Freitag (1993) Module configuration by minimal model construction. *Fakultät für Mathematik und Informatik*, Universität Passau.

60 T. Margaria and B. Steffen (2007) LTL-guided planning: revisiting automatic tool composition in ETI. Proceedings of the 31st Annual IEEE/NASA Software Engineering Workshop (SEW 2007), pp. 214–226.

61 M. Isberner, F. Howar, and B. Steffen (2014) Learning register automata: from languages to program structures. *Machine Learning*, **96** 65–98.

62 B. Steffen, F. Howar, and M. Merten (2011) Introduction to active automata learning from a practical perspective. In: *Formal Methods for Eternal Networked Software Systems*, LNCS 6659, Springer, pp. 256–296.

63 F. Howar, B. Steffen, and M. Merten (2011) Automata learning with automated alphabet abstraction refinement. In: *Verification, Model Checking, and Abstract Interpretation*, Springer, LNCS 6538, pp. 263–277.

64 H. Raffelt, M. Merten, B. Steffen, and T. Margaria (2009) Dynamic testing via automata learning. *International Journal on Software Tools for Technology Transfer*, **11** (4), 307–324.

65 S. Naujokat, L.-M. Traonouez, M. Isberner, B. Steffen, and A. Legay (2014) Domain-specific code generator modeling: a case study for multi-faceted concurrent systems. Proceedings of the 6th International Symposium on Leveraging Applications of Formal Methods, Verification and Validation, Part I (ISoLA 2014), LNCS 8802, pp. 463–480.

66 S. Naujokat, M. Lybecait, D. Kopetzki, and B. Steffen (2017) CINCO: a simplicity-driven approach to full generation of domain-specific graphical modeling tools. *International Journal on Software Tools for Technology Transfer*. doi: 10.1007/s10009-017-0453-6

67 B. Steffen and S. Naujokat (2016) Archimedean points: the essence for mastering change. Transactions on Foundations for for Mastering Change, Lecture Notes in Computer Science, vol. 9960, Springer, Cham, Switzerland.

9

Rethinking Functional Requirements: A Novel Approach Categorizing System and Software Requirements
Manfred Broy

Institut für Informatik, Technische Universität München, München, Germany

9.1 Introduction

There is a substantial amount of thought, discussion, disagreement, perhaps even confusion about adequately categorizing requirements in software and systems engineering. The certainly most common general classification of requirements is by distinguishing between "functional" and "nonfunctional" requirements.

The community tends to agree on the notion of "functional" requirements. For nonfunctional requirements, things get more complicated. The obvious understanding to call every requirement that cannot be called "functional" a "nonfunctional" requirement is overly simplistic and not a very helpful classification anyhow. However, even if assuming that the term "functional" has a clear meaning, the set of nonfunctional requirements gathers a too broad spectrum of quite different types of requirements that should not be collected under one large umbrella. It is more adequate to characterize more explicitly and directly in which sense "functional" and "nonfunctional" requirements should be understood and how they can be further categorized and classified.

In fact, even the meaning of the term "functional" proves to be less clear after a short, more careful reflection, since the notion of "function" is less clear and commonly less well understood than some people might assume. There is a broad spectrum of interpretations what the term "function" means starting with the mathematical notion of a function (a mapping between two sets), and more management related notions of "function" referring to concepts such as task, role, job, duty, or purpose. As a matter of fact, the term "functional requirement" has many different connotations depending on the way the terms "function" and "functional" are understood.

In the end, the challenge to characterize classes of functional and nonfunctional requirements strongly depends on characterizations of the different kinds of

Software Technology: 10 Years of Innovation in IEEE Computer, First Edition.
Edited by Mike Hinchey.

observations made about systems, captured and formalized in terms of adequate system models. Strictly speaking, there is a wide range of models and views capturing viewpoints onto systems and their behavior. One view refers to functional behavior in terms of the system's interface behavior. Others aim at more operational views such as state transition behavior or interactive behavior between the components of architectures. To make these categories precise, we suggest more structured views onto systems. In particular, we need to differentiate a number of viewpoints and levels of abstraction. One level addresses a functional view that is adequate to model functional requirements. Other levels address more implementation-oriented, technical views onto systems, which then might help to address implementation-specific properties. In fact, we may distinguish between behavioral properties, which refer to the black box behavior shown at the interface of systems, and those that refer to the behavior of the architecture or to behavior in terms of states of systems, which means that we introduce behavioral glass box views that go beyond properties subsumed under the heading functional behavior.

There are several complementary ways to model behavior. We suggest distinguishing two classes of behavioral requirements. One class addresses what we call logical behavioral properties, the other one addresses probabilistic behavioral properties. A behavioral property is called logical, if it is a property that addresses sets of observations, but not quantitative probabilistic measures for these sets of observations. This distinction will be made more precise in the following. For both logical and probabilistic behavior models, we distinguish black box ("interface") views and glass box ("internal") views onto systems.

The goal of this chapter is the categorization of requirements on the basis of a scientific sufficiently precise notion and adequate models of systems. We choose an approach, different to characterizations found so far in literature. We understand functional requirements as properties in terms of the functional behavior of systems, where we assume that the behavior of systems including timing aspects can be described by sets of finite or infinite behavioral observations about systems at their interfaces including probabilistic views. Each observation collects the users' actions, the interactions, and system's reactions for some instances of usage of the system. This idea is very much along the lines of the concept of use cases. The interface behavior view addresses classical notions of functional behavior and behavioral correctness.

In the literature, there exist a number of proposals toward classifying requirements. Glinz [1] provides a stimulating discussion; however, we do not fully agree to his conclusions for categorizing requirements. In contrast to Glinz, we come up with a more rigorous approach. We suggest rethinking the term "functional" as a classification and suggest using "functional" in the sense of "interface behavior" where we introduce two categories of interface behavior: logical and probabilistic ones. Furthermore, we distinguish between system-level (interface) behavior (which is close to what is traditionally called "functional") and architectural-level behavior. Then, the term "functional" in the sense of the functionality offered by the system is most adequately addressed by the logical and probabilistic interface behavior of systems, since this way the function of a system in the sense of purpose is captured.

In the traditional view, there is a rich class of properties that are not called functional. However, some of the so-called nonfunctional "quality" requirements of systems, such as requirements about safety or security properties, address requirements captured by interface behavior. In fact, these are typically formulated as probabilistic system properties that are formalized by probabilistic behavior models of systems. Accordingly, we come up with the conclusion that what is traditionally and commonly called "functional requirements" in our approach and our terminology is called "logical interface behavior requirements." This includes timing properties – at least as long as timing is of functional importance as in hard real-time systems. Moreover, several further categories of requirements traditionally called nonfunctional are in our view probabilistic interface behavior requirements – and thus as well in the suggested novel categorization of functional requirements.

Besides logical behavior requirements that specify which patterns of observed behavior and interactions are called logically correct, there is the wide field of probabilistic behavioral requirements given in terms of probabilities of certain behavioral patterns, which relate to notions like reliability, functional safety, and to a large extent also to security. Even fields like usability belong to some extent to probabilistic behavioral interface requirements. As a result of including probabilistic notions of behavior, only a restricted number of the so-called quality requirements (in the sense of quality in use) then are related to nonbehavioral issues or issues of behaviors beyond the interface view.

Our approach to classifying requirements is strictly based on a structured system reference model. The justification of this approach is the fact that requirements refer to properties of a product or system. But how can we formulate properties about systems without a clear notion and concept of system? To be more precise, we introduce a generic formal system model and use it as a basis to classify and specify requirements. In addition to logical views onto behavior, we introduce probabilistic views that specify the probabilities of certain sets of observations. We use a comprehensive architectural model of systems with a functional, a logical subsystem, or a state-based and a technical view.

Other requirements address properties not referring to behavior but related to the syntactic or physical representation of systems. These are properties like for instance "readability." Readability of code may depend not only on the complexity of the functionality, but also on its specific syntactic representation and structuring.

The remainder of the chapter is as follows: first, we discuss approaches found in literature to classify requirements and lay the foundations for the contributions of this chapter. Then, we introduce as a reference a general formal modeling and architectural framework for systems. Based on this framework that allows for categorization of system properties, we outline a proposal for categorizing requirements and relate the framework to existing classifications, before concluding the chapter with a summary.

9.2 Discussion: Classifying Requirements – Why and How

In this section, we briefly discuss existing approaches to the classification of requirements. We argue why such classifications are useful, how well-defined existing approaches are, and discuss different forms of classifications.

There are several useful approaches to the categorization of requirements: One possibility is to structure requirements according to stakeholders, but then it is difficult to get a generic categorization of requirements, because different systems have different groups of stakeholders. Moreover, for quite a number of requirements, the requirements of the stakeholders are overlapping such that we cannot relate requirements uniquely to just one stakeholder.

9.2.1 On Classifying Requirements as Being Functional

The term function carries many different meanings. In general, speaking for a system or, more generally, for an object about "its function" refers to its purpose and to what something does or what it is used for. There is a wide spectrum of notions associated with the term "function":

- In mathematics, a function is a mapping between two sets.
- In engineering, a function refers to the purpose of a system or of a certain part thereof.
- In organization, a function refers to a professional or official position or a role of a person or a department.
- In biology, a function refers to the role of a specific species in an ecological system.
- In medicine, a function denotes the physiological activity of an organ or body part.
- In chemistry, a function refers to the characteristic behavior of a chemical compound.
- In anthropology, a function aims at the role of a social practice in the continued existence of a group of humans.

In systems engineering, generally, the term function refers to the aim, intention, purpose, use, or role of a system and its behavior and effect. In a more restrictive usage, we speak about a function offered by the system to express that the system can be used for a specific purpose. Systems today usually offer sets of functions. Then, they are called *multifunctional* and their functionality can be structured into a hierarchy of subfunctions [2].

Often a function offered by a multifunctional system is called a *feature*, or more precisely, a *functional feature*. Sometimes, the term *service* is used, too. We distinguish between the requirement that a system provides a particular functional feature meaning that it can be used in particular ways for particular purposes (e.g., adaptive cruise control for a car) and a more detailed description and specification of the interaction with the system if used for that purpose (e.g., a detailed description how the adaptive cruise control function works in terms of interactions between the system and its operational context, in terms of user interactions and input via sensors and output via actuators). Thus, there is a close connection between the concept of a function and that of a use case. More precisely, use cases describe sets of scenarios of usage of systems that correspond to the usage of functions offered by the systems.

Thus, in our terminology a functional feature is an intentional term expressing that a system offers a certain behavior such that it can be used for a specific purpose. A specification of a feature is the specification of a function of a system given by a detailed description of the interaction between the system and its operational context (users, neighbor systems, sensors, and actuators connected to the physical environment) to provide that feature. Generally, there are several ways to realize functional features by patterns of interaction and thus by concrete functions.

In connection with systems, for us a "functional requirement" of a system expresses that

- a system shall offer a particular functional feature such that the systems can be used for a specific purpose (perhaps in terms of a use case illustrated by scenarios), or
- a function (a specific instance of a functional feature) of a system having a particular property – that may be a logical property or a probabilistic one – characterizing part of the interface behavior of the system, specified by the interaction between the system and its operational context.

Therefore, a functional requirement describes that and with what quality a system can be used for a certain purpose in terms of behavioral properties of systems at their interfaces – that manifest functionality and may be captured in terms of logical or probabilistic specification of interface behavior.

9.2.2 "Nonfunctional" Requirements and Their Characterization

There is a lot of discussion and disagreement on the term nonfunctional requirements. A simplistic view would claim that all requirements that are not functional are nonfunctional. However, then it becomes obvious that what is called nonfunctional requirements forms a large heterogeneous set of very different categories of requirements and properties, more difficult to characterize in a more constructive and explicit way than simply by negation of the term "functional."

In response to this missing agreement, Glinz has provided a rich discussion on the state of terminology with respect to the notion of nonfunctional requirements in [1]. He writes *"Although the term non-functional requirements has been in use for more than twenty years, there is no consensus in the requirements engineering community what non-functional requirements are and how we should elicit, document and validate them"*. He gives a number of good arguments and examples how different and incompatible various interpretations of the notion "nonfunctional" are and that in many publications the presented definitions are not overly convincing. Although he has fostered valuable discussions on the notion of nonfunctional requirements, in the end his own particular definition remains unfortunately equally imprecise and fuzzy. According to his definition, a nonfunctional requirement is an "attribute of" or a "constraint on" a system. This is unsatisfactory as a definition, because it reduces the fuzzy term "nonfunctional" requirement to the equally fuzzy and general terms such as "attribute" or "constraint." It does not become evident why system functionality and functional requirements should not also be described by attributes or constraints. More helpful is certainly his taxonomy of nonfunctional requirements that he presents, but even this representation remains quite informal, imprecise, and fuzzy in the end.

As a matter of fact, there are different options to capture the term nonfunctional requirement and to choose structuring principles for them. In the approach of Glinz, the chosen structuring principle is not completely clear, not overly precise, and not explicit. His structuring principle remains organized in the form of fuzzy terms like "functional" requirement, "attribute," and "constraint." The subcategorization of attributes into performance requirements and specific quality requirements is even more vague and arbitrary; For instance, what exactly is a "specific quality requirement"? However, for this chapter, we use the valuable starting point provided by Glinz and provide the next step on the categorization of functional and nonfunctional requirements.

We postulate that a term like nonfunctional requirements for systems can only be made precise based on an appropriate formalization in terms of an adequate modeling concept for systems. A promising approach is to use a system reference model, which provides a structured description of a system in terms of modeling concepts. Then, we are able to relate requirements to certain parts and concepts of the system model. This provides a more explicit and more precise structuring guideline.

9.2.3 Limitations of Classification Due to Heterogeneity and Lacking Precision

In any case, we have to keep in mind another problem: The more general requirements are, the more abstract they are, and the more difficult it is to make them precise the more difficult it is to categorize them. For instance, high-level abstract requirements may be very general and, thus, on one hand comprise a number of subrequirements, which may belong to different categories. Thus, a high-level requirement can perhaps be made precise and refined into a selection of essentially different more concrete and precise requirements, which may belong to different categories.

An example of this problem is found in Glinz's paper [1], where he writes about a specific security requirement. The abstract requirement is *"The system shall prevent any unauthorized access to the customer data"*. As Glinz points out that such a requirement could be either made more concrete by talking about the probability of successful access by unauthorized persons or by functional requirements that require the introduction of a password mechanism. Essentially, both these more concrete requirements are possible refinements of the given requirement. In fact, there might be even more concrete requirements, because if the user's name and password is used to protect data against unauthorized usage, then the crucial question is what are the procedures of the users choosing and handling their passwords. Therefore, in addition to functional requirements, there might be assumptions about the operational context specifying how people choose their passwords and which rules they follow to protect their passwords. Given enough information about the users, their habits, and their context, we might be able to estimate and to calculate probabilities measuring how secure the chosen password mechanism is for preventing unauthorized access.

One difficulty in the rigorous classification of requirements lies to a large extent often in the insufficient precision or a lack of concreteness of the formulation of requirements. Imprecise informal requirements cannot be understood as precise logical predicates about systems with an unbiased meaning. There are generally several different ways to make the meaning of an informally stated requirement precise, and concrete, which may lead to slightly and sometimes essentially different formalizations resulting in different system properties. As a consequence, given informal requirements may be classified differently depending on the decisions which of the different choices leading into precision and formalization are taken. To avoid this additional difficulty when categorizing requirements, which has its source in missing precision, we concentrate in the following on requirements that are sufficiently precisely formulated or even formalized. Using formalized system models facilitates the formalization of requirements significantly. Even more, it may allow a direct formulation of requirements in a formal way.

A second difficulty in categorizing is due to heterogeneous properties representing a conjunction of properties from different categories. Even if we have introduced clean categories for system assertions there exist requirements formulated by assertions that include properties from different categories. Also in this case a straightforward categorization is not possible. Then, a decomposition of requirements into a set of properties with homogeneous categories is a way out. Let Q1 and Q2 be assertions representing requirements from clearly different categories, then the requirement of the property Q = Q1 ∧ Q2 cannot be categorized to belong to exactly one category. We call Q then a *heterogeneous, composite* requirement addressing different categories. An open question is whether we can usefully decompose every requirement into a conjunction of subrequirements each of which belongs to exactly one category.

In the remainder of this chapter, we aim at requirements that are sufficiently precise and decomposed such that they can be uniquely classified. We are aware that in practical projects this is often not the case. However, we aim a strictly foundational view as a firm basis for more pragmatic approaches.

9.2.4 Approach: System Model-Based Categorization of Requirements

For categorizing requirements, we follow strictly a system-structuring and modeling-oriented approach. In essence, it uses two modeling frameworks:

- A system notion and a system modeling theory, supporting several fundamental system views such as the *interface view*, the *architecture view*, and the *state view*. For these behavioral views, we distinguish between
  - a logical view in terms of sets of observations/sets of instances of behaviors; we speak of a logical view since it is two valued. An instance of behavior is either in the set or not.
  - a probabilistic view – complementary to the logical one – in terms of probabilities of observations and instances of behaviors.
- A comprehensive system architecture, comprising a context view, a functional view, an architectural subsystem view, and a technical view including aspects of software, hardware, and mechanics as well as physical realizations.

These two elements of the considered framework are complementary: the elements of the modeling theory are applied to capture the concepts of the comprehensive system model and architecture. All requirements are categorized in terms to these two subframeworks. This approach does – only implicitly – address one of the fundamental problem of requirements in practice, which is contradictory or conflicting requirements. As soon as requirements are made precise or even formalized in terms of models, a clear notion of consistency is available.

9.2.4.1 Fundamentals on Requirements and System Models

Requirements address system properties (and in addition context properties and sometimes development process properties). A collection of system requirements defines a set of system properties. The conjunction over these properties results in a system requirements specification. Viewed as a comprehensive system property, requirement specifications describe sets of systems.

Strictly speaking, however, the term "set of systems" requires a more careful reflection. If the term "set" is used in a mathematical and not in a pragmatic, informal way, then systems have to be mathematical elements, since only mathematical elements (with a clearly defined notion of equality) can be members of mathematical sets. In a pragmatic perspective, systems are real-world objects and not mathematical elements. We may carry out experiments and make observations about real-world systems and relate properties (in terms of models) to these observations to judge upon their validity.

To be able to deal with systems as mathematical elements, we introduce *system models*. Strictly speaking, we have to distinguish between systems as part of the physical world and mathematical or logical system models. Given a universe of mathematical system models it makes sense to speak about a set of (models of) systems. The postulation of a universe of system models has a second remarkable effect. Only having such models available we can precisely talk about requirements in terms of properties of systems, where properties are represented by logical predicates referring – strictly speaking – not to real-world systems but to their hopefully sufficiently adequate mathematical models. Note that the choice of the system model then has a strong impact on the formulation of requirements.

The formulation of requirements in terms of system models implies that only a restricted collection of system properties can be expressed depending on the expressive power of the system model. This shows that the choice of the universe of system models is crucial – both for their expressive power in requirements engineering as well as for the categorization of requirements.

Models and their formalization support the precise definition of key concepts in requirements engineering such as completeness and consistency, which otherwise would be difficult or not possible at all. A requirements specification is *consistent* in a logical sense, if the set of systems that fulfill the requirements specification is not empty. It is *complete*, if the system (more precisely an instance in the set of system models) is uniquely determined – this does not exclude nondeterminism. However, a requirement specification is practically never complete in a comprehensive way. Only the specification of certain views and models may be complete. In requirements engineering, we are rather interested in a relative subjective completeness – requirements should be complete in the sense that all acceptable stakeholders' expectations are captured and documented.

9.2.4.2 Pragmatic vs. Model-Based Formulation of Requirements

Following the line of thought of the previous section, it becomes clear that we have to distinguish between

- requirements formulated in a pragmatic way in terms of observations about real-world physical systems and

- requirements formulated in terms of properties of a predefined universe of system models such that they can be formalized in terms of mathematics and logics.

The distinction between pragmatic requirements (formulated in terms of observations about real-world systems) and formal requirements (in terms of an appropriate system modeling concept) is complemented by the following distinction for requirements:

- *Intentional Requirements* they are formulated in (prescriptive) intentional terms, often called goals; they can be very general and comprehensive (and nearly superficial) such as "the system should be safe" or more specifically "the airbag must not be activated in situations that are not severe crashes." Also in the second example, a concrete explanation is not given what it means that a situation is called "a severe crash."
- *Concrete Requirements – System Specifications* they are formulated in terms of very concrete expected properties of system behavior such as "if the water temperature as measured by the water temperature sensor gets over 80 °C, then the gas supply valve is closed in less than 50 ms."

Only concrete requirements can be formally verified. They are typically formulated with certain system models in mind.

9.3 The System Model

For making requirements more concrete, more precise, and also making them more formal, a classical way is to refer to a formalized structured model of systems. To this end, we suggest working with a formalized model of a system as we find it typically not only for general software systems but also for embedded systems.

We base our approach on a system model that has been developed at the Technical University of Munich over several decades. It suggests structuring systems using three levels of abstractions expressed by a specific modeling theory with the notion of interface behavior as its key concept (Figure 9.1). This model framework has been and is in use for a number of purposes in theory and practice in software and systems engineering.

9.3.1 The Basics: System Modeling Ontology

The key and starting point for our approach of categorization of system properties and requirements is the fundamental concept of a system. We suggest a modeling framework providing system modeling concepts and a reference architecture comprising adequate levels of abstraction:

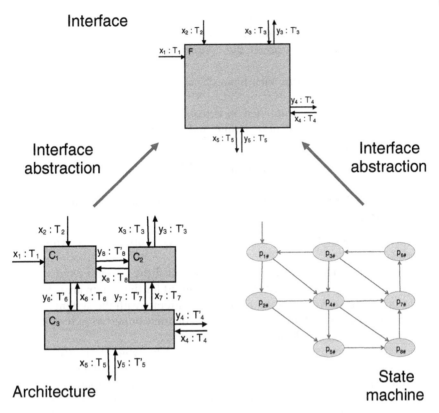

Figure 9.1 Relationship between the views: architecture and state machines and their interface abstractions.

- The modeling framework consists of a family of mathematical and logical modeling concepts for systems addressing the notion of interface, state, and architecture:
  - *Logical Model:* a system is described by sets of behaviors in terms of interface, architecture, and state. We distinguish between the interface view (black box view) and a logical glass box view on internal properties.
  - *Probabilistic Model:* a system is described in terms of fundamental probabilities of its behaviors, more precisely probability distributions over sets of logically possible behavior in terms of interface behavior, architectural behavior, and probabilistic state machines.
- The reference architecture consists of a structured set of views in terms of levels of abstraction – sometimes called comprehensive system architecture; it comprises the following views:
  - *Functional View: (Structured System Interface Behavior Specification) and Corresponding Operational Context* structuring of the system functionality

into a hierarchy of system functions with modes to capture their dependencies (see, Ref. 3) and the specification of properties of their context in terms of assumptions about the context and related guarantees of the system [4].

– *Subsystem Architecture: View* hierarchical structure of subsystems ("logical components").
– *Technical and Physical: View* structured into the disciplines electronic hardware, software at design time and run time, mechanics and their connections.

The two modeling frameworks are related and shortly described in the following.

The model addresses a specific notion of discrete system with the following characteristics and principles.

• A *system* has a well-defined boundary (called its "scope") that determines its *interface*.
• Everything outside the system boundary is called the system's *environment*. Those parts of the environment that are relevant for the system are called the system's *context*. Actors in the context that interact with the system such as users, neighbored systems, or sensor and actuators connected to the physical environment are called the *operational context*.
• By a discrete system's interface it is indicated by which steps the system interacts with its operational context. The *syntactic interface* defines the set of actions that can be performed in interaction between the system and its context over its boundary. In our case, syntactic interfaces are defined by the set of input and output channels together with their types. The input channels and the types determine the input actions for a system while the output channels and then types determine the output actions for a system.
• We distinguish between *syntactic interface*, also called *static interface*, which describes the set of input and output actions, which can take place over the system boundary, and the *interface behavior* (also called *dynamical interface*), which describes the system's *functionality* in terms of the input and output actions; the interface behavior is captured by the causal relationship between streams of actions captured in input and output *histories*. This way we define a logical behavior as well as a probabilistic behavior for systems.
• The logical interface behavior of systems is described by logical expressions, called *interface assertions*, by *state machines*, or it can be further decomposed into *architectures*.
• A system has an *internal structure* and some internal *behavior* ("glass box view"). This structure is described by its state space with state transitions and/ or by its decomposition into subsystems forming its architecture; by an architecture the system is decomposed into a number of subsystems, which interact and also provide the interaction with the system's operational

context. The state machine and the architecture associated with a system are called its state view and its structural or architectural view, respectively.

- Complementary, the behaviors of systems can be described by sets of *traces*, which are sets of scenarios of input and output behavior of systems. We distinguish between finite and infinite scenarios.
- Moreover, systems operate in real time. In our case, we use discrete time, which seems, in particular, adequate for discrete systems.
- Systems interact with their operational context and subsystems operate concurrently within the system's architectures.

This gives a highly abstract and at the same time quite comprehensive model of systems. This model is formalized in the following by a specific modeling theory [5].

9.3.1.1 Data Models – Data Types
Data models define a set of data types and some basic functions for them. A *(data) type* T is a name for a data set for which usually a family of operations is available. Let TYPE be the set of all data types.

9.3.1.2 Interface Behavior
Systems have *syntactic interfaces* that are described by their sets of input and output channels attributed by the type of messages that are communicated over them. Channels are used to connect systems to be able to transmit messages between them. A set of typed channels is a set of channels with types given for each of its channels.

Definition. Syntactic interface Let I be the set of typed input channels and O be the set of typed output channels. The pair (I, O) characterizes the syntactic interface of a system. The *syntactic interface* is denoted by (I▶O).

Figure 9.2 shows the syntactic interface of a system F by a graphical representation by a data flow node with its syntactic interface consisting of

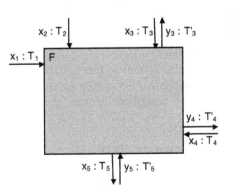

Figure 9.2 Graphical representation of a system F as a data flow node.

the input channels $x_1, \ldots$ of types $T_1, \ldots$ and the output channels $y_1, \ldots$ of types $T'_1, \ldots$.

Definition. Timed Streams   Given a message set M of data elements of type T, we represent a *timed stream* s of type T by a mapping

$$s : IN\backslash\{0\} \to M^*$$

In a timed stream s a sequence $s(t)$ of messages is given for each time interval $t \in IN\backslash\{0\}$. In each time interval an arbitrary, but finite sequence of messages may be communicated. By $(M^*)^\infty$ we denote the set of timed streams.

A (timed) channel history for a set of typed channels C assigns to each channel $c \in C$ a timed stream of messages communicated over that channel.

Definition. Channel History   Let C be a set of typed channels; a (total) *channel history* x is a mapping (let IM be the universe of all messages)

$$x : C \to (IN\backslash\{0\} \to IM^*)$$

such that $x(c)$ is a timed stream of messages of the type of channel $c \in C$. $\vec{C}$ denotes the set of all total channel histories for the channel set C.

The behavior of a system with syntactic interface (I▶O) is defined by a mapping that maps the input histories in $\vec{I}$ onto output histories in $\vec{O}$. This way we get a functional model of a system interface behavior.

Definition. I/O-Behavior   A mapping $F: \vec{I} \to \mathcal{P}(\vec{O})$ is called an *I/O-behavior*. By IF[I▶O] we denote the set of all (total and partial) I/O-behaviors with syntactic interface (I▶O) and by IF the set of all I/O-behaviors.

Interface behaviors model system functionality. For systems we assume that their interface behavior F is total, formally $F(x) \neq \varnothing$ for all $x \in \vec{I}$. In [5] additional logical constraints are introduced to call a function F a behavior such as strong causality and realizability. Behaviors F may be deterministic (in this case, the set $F(x)$ of output histories has at most one element for each input history x) or nondeterministic.

9.3.1.3 State Machines by State Transition Functions

State machines with input and output describe system implementations in terms of states and state transitions. A state machine is defined by a state space and a state transition. State machines can be described by state transition diagrams as shown in Figure 9.3.

Definition. State Machine with Syntactic Interface (I▶O)   Given a state space Σ, a state machine (Δ, Λ) with input and output according to the syntactic interface (I▶O) consists of a set $\Lambda \subseteq \Sigma$ of initial states as well as of a

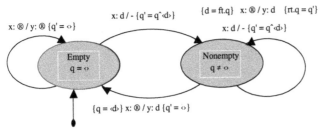

Figure 9.3 A Simple state machine – described by a state transition diagram.

nondeterministic state transition function

$$\Delta : (\Sigma \times (I \to M^*)) \to \mathcal{P}(\Sigma \times (O \to M^*))$$

For each state $\sigma \in \Sigma$ and each valuation a: $I \to M^*$ of the input channels in I by sequences of input messages every pair $(\sigma', b) \in \Delta(\sigma, a)$ defines a successor state σ' and a valuation b: $O \to M^*$ of the output channels consisting of the sequences produced by the state transition. (Δ, Λ) is a *Mealy machine* with possibly infinite state space. If in every transition the output b depends on the state σ only but never on the current input a, we speak of a *Moore machine.*

As shown in [5], every state machine has a unique interface abstraction in terms of an interface behavior associated to the state machine.

9.3.1.4 Systems and Their Functionality

In the introduced formal model, systems interact with their operational contexts via the channels of their syntactic interfaces. We identify both systems by names. A system named k has an interface, consisting of a syntactic interface (I▶O) and an interface behavior

$$F_k : \vec{I} \to \mathcal{P}(\overline{O})$$

The behavior may be a combination of a larger number of more elementary subfunction behaviors. Then, we speak of a *multifunctional* system (see [3]). Let SID be the set of system names. A system named $k \in$ SID is called *statically interpreted* if only a syntactic interface $(I_k▶O_k)$ is given for k and *dynamically interpreted* if an interface behavior $F_k \in IF[I_k▶O_k]$ is specified for k.

9.3.1.5 Architectures

An architecture structure decomposes a system into a family of subsystems as shown in Figure 9.4. In the following we assume that each system used in an architecture as a subsystem has a unique identifier k. Let K be the set of identifiers for the subsystems of an architecture.

Definition. Syntactic and Interpreted Architecture A syntactic architecture (K, ξ) defines a syntactic interface $\xi(k)$ for each component identifier $k \in K$. An

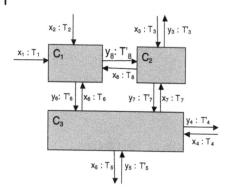

Figure 9.4 A simple architecture – described by a data flow graph.

interpreted architecture (K, ψ) for a syntactic architecture (K, ξ) associates an interface behavior $\psi(k) \in IF[I_k \blacktriangleright O_k]$ for the syntactic interface $\xi(k) = (I_k \blacktriangleright O_k)$ with every component identifier $k \in K$.

In [5], syntactic conditions are given for the well-formedness of an architecture in terms of the composability of its components. Moreover, a composition operator $\otimes$ is introduced that describes the composition $\otimes \{\psi(k): k \in K\}$ of an interpreted architecture yielding the interface behavior of the system with that architecture.

A syntactic architecture can be specified by its set of subsystems (called components) and their communication channels and an interface specification for each of its components.

9.3.1.6 Probabilistic Interface View

As an extension of the logical model of system interface behavior, we introduce a probabilistic model (see [6]). Given a set of typed channels C, we define a probability distribution for a set of histories $H \subseteq \vec{C}$ by the function

$$\mu : H \to [0 : 1]$$

Let $m[\vec{C}]$ denote the set of all probability distributions over sets of histories $H \subseteq \vec{C}$.

Given a functional behavior

$$F : \vec{I} \to \mathcal{P}(\vec{O})$$

a probabilistic behavior is defined by a function

$$D_F : \vec{I} \to m(\vec{O})$$

where for every input history $x \in \vec{I}$ by

$$D_F(x)$$

we get a probability distribution for every input history $x \in \vec{I}$ over the set of possible output histories:

$$\mu_x : F(x) \rightarrow [0 : 1]$$

We get a probability $\mu_x(Y)$ by the function μ for every measurable set $Y \subseteq F(x)$ of output histories. This shows that μ defines for every input history, $x \in \vec{I}$ a probability distribution μ_x *on the set F(x) of possible output histories*.

The probabilistic view, as introduced here for the interface model is in a straightforward manner extended to architecture and state machines (see [6]). A probabilistic state machine is represented by a state transition function with a probability distribution for the set of pairs of successor states and output. An architecture is modeled probabilistically by given probabilistic interface behaviors for each of its sub-systems.

9.3.2 System Views and Levels of Abstractions

The comprehensive architectural system model that we suggest consists of two levels of abstraction and a number of views, which make the architecture tractable to manage. It provides a systematic approach for a comprehensive description of the architecture of embedded software systems and the functionality provided by them. We consider the following two levels of abstraction:

- *Conceptual Architecture* consisting of the *functional view* (structural interface view) usage level, given by a function hierarchy, specified as result of the requirements engineering) and the *subsystem architecture* (describing the interaction logic between local subsystems) as well as *context view*, both with an additional probabilistic view onto the functional behavior.
- *Technical Architecture* consisting of the *software* (software architecture, consisting of the code architecture, the task architecture of executable and schedulable units, and the scheduling and deployment on the runtime platform, communication architecture including the bus scheduling), the *hardware* and the *deployment mapping* of the software tasks onto the hardware, the concrete physical implementation of HMI, and reactions in terms of *physical devices*.

The principle of the two levels decouples the development of the application in terms functionality and the logics of its implementation from its technical architecture in terms of the concrete devices. The goal is a precise specification and modeling as well as a verification of the implemented application, irrespectively of the details of the technical architecture. Furthermore, the application-independent components of the technical architecture (hardware and platform) can be specified, modeled, implemented, verified, and refined independently of the chosen specific implementation.

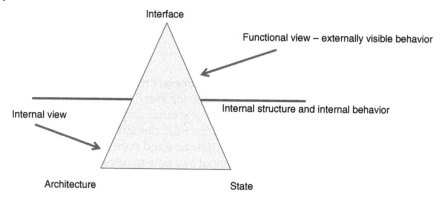

Figure 9.5 Iceberg of system views.

9.3.3 Structuring Systems into Views

In principle, functional observations are related to interface behavior. Hence, a functional perspective for a system addresses interface behavior. Observations and properties that refer to interface behavior of a system are to be called *functional*.

The system views and their relationships shown in Figure 9.5 can be abstracted into the "iceberg" of system views shown in Figure 9.6.

The functional view sees only the top of the iceberg of behavior – see Figure 9.5 – namely interface behavior which is of particular interest in Requirements Engineering.

In contrast, properties of the structuring of systems into architectures and properties of their components are not to be called functional, in general, since they aim at internal architectural aspects. Nevertheless, these nonfunctional properties address behavioral requirements referring to system architecture with its subsystems and their local interface behaviors. Such views lead to behavioral glass box views onto systems in terms of their subsystems and their behaviors or their states and state transitions. We get glass box views that way, which are behavioral, too. They can again be captured in terms of logical or probabilistic models.

9.4 Categorizing System Properties

Systems and their models are fundamentally characterized as follows: a system has a scope and a boundary, which clearly separates it from its operational context, with which it interacts over its interface determined by its system boundaries. This view leads to the concept of system interface, structured into a syntactic and a behavioral part. This system model induces a structure on the system properties that can be used for a categorization of requirements.

9.4.1 System Behavior: Behavioral Properties

Behavioral views address the interface behavior of systems but also their "internal" behavior in terms of their architecture and state transitions that is hidden from the interface view by information hiding. There are two principal ways to describe the internal behavior of software systems: state machines and architectures. In both cases we get behavioral views onto the system interior talking about the system's internal structure, its state space, its state transitions, and its structuring into its subsystems, their connection, relationship, and interaction – which at the architecture and state perspective can again be captured both from a logical and from a probabilistic point of view. In the state view, we describe the states, given by the state space, which the system can take, the state transitions, and the probability that certain state transitions are taken. Both descriptions could and should be used side by side.

This way, we model system behavior by the interface, the architecture, and the state view. For each of these views, we can take both a logical and a probabilistic perspective (Table 9.1).

The glass box behavior view is not part of the functional view since it talks not directly about the functionality of systems, but rather about implementation related aspects describing how the systems is internally structured and behaves, which internal states are used such that the required functionality is implemented.

Note: Logical and Probabilistic Views onto Behavior The term logical behavior refers to the fact that propositional logic is two-valued. From a logical

Table 9.1 Overview of behavioral categories.

		Syntactic part	Behavior	
			Logical	Probabilistic
"External" black box view	Functional view	Syntactic interface	Logical interface behavior	Probabilistic interface behavior
"Internal" glass box view	Architecture view	Hierarchical data flow graph of subsystems	Subsystems and their logical interface behavior	Subsystems and their probabilistic interface behavior
	State view	State space structure (Attributes) I/O messages	Logical state machine logical state transitions	Probabilistic state machine probabilistic state transitions

perspective, an instance of behavior such as a history is either part of a system behavior or not. In contrast, the term "probabilistic" refers to a spectrum of values in the interval [0:1]. Besides probabilistic views, we may introduce other quantitative concepts for requirements such as fuzzy logic, measure theory, or metric distances.

For the interpretation, validation, and evaluation of probabilistic requirements, we have to distinguish between two subtle ways to interpret probabilistic requirements. If requirements speak about a set of product instances (e.g., one million cars of a specific model), then we have to distinguish for a statement "the behavior X occurs with probability P" between the following two interpretations

- for each individual car this probability is guaranteed.
- for all the cars produced this probability is guaranteed in a statistical average.

This shows that care is advised when stating requirements in probabilistic manner to express precisely in which way the probabilistic statements should be interpreted and understood.

9.4.1.1 Functional Properties: Logical and Probabilistic Interface Behavior
The functional view talks about the functionality of systems as it manifests itself by the interface behavior of the system. It is described by the interface behavior of the system and may include both logical and probabilistic views. As a result we understand how the system cooperates with its environment exclusively considering issues of interactions. In both these views, we get the information, which interactions are possible in principle and what their probabilities are.

In a structured functional view along [3], we structure a system into a hierarchy of functional features and describe each feature by specifications of functions on input and output streams as well as their dependencies by modes of operations. In the probabilistic perspective, we define probability distributions for these functions in terms of their sets of output behavior.

9.4.1.2 Behavioral Glass Box View: Logical and Probabilistic Behavior
Glass box views address the internal structure and properties of systems. There are basically two complementary instances of glass box views: the architectural view and the state view. They are complementary in the sense, that one describes a system's architecture in terms of its set of subsystems with their behavior and interaction and the other describes the system's state space and state transitions. If a state machine description for each of the components of the architecture is given, by composition (in terms of the described architecture) of these state machines given for each of the components a (composed) state machine for the overall system is constructed [5].

9.4.1.2.1 Architectural View: Structure, Logical, and Probabilistic Behavior
A more involved issue is, of course, the glass box behavior from an architectural point of view. In the architectural view, a system is decomposed into a

hierarchy of subsystems forming its components. It is described in the architecture how the components are connected and their behavior is described by the interface behaviors of the components in terms of their interactions. By the description of the behaviors of its components and the structure of the architecture the behavior of the architecture is specified from which the interface behavior of the system can be deduced. In the architectural perspective, we get a view onto the behavior of a system in terms of its subsystems – more precisely the interface behavior of its subsystems in the logical and also in the probabilistic sense.

The interface behavior of the components includes again both logical and probabilistic views. As a result we understand how the components interact with each other and with the system's operational context exclusively considering issues of interactions. In this view, we get the information, which interactions are in principle possible and what their probabilities are.

9.4.1.2.2 *State View: Logical and Probabilistic State Transitions*
In a state view, a system is described by a state machine. For doing that we describe its state space and specify a state transition relation including input and output. This yields a Mealy machine extended to possibly infinite state space. The machine represents the logical state view.

In the probabilistic view, we specify a probability distribution for the state transitions and thus the probability that in given states certain state transitions are chosen. State machines provide a logical and a probabilistic a glass box view onto the system behavior in terms of state transitions.

9.4.2 Variations in Modeling System Behavior

The illustrated perspectives, models, and structures show the possibility for a comprehensive documentation of systems and their structural and behavioral properties. The following aspects are essential:

- *System Scope and Boundary:* system border, for instance in the case of embedded systems at the sensors / actuators, at the buses, at the controllers, at the software
- *Granularity of Interaction and Time:* time (discrete or continuous) and messages (discrete or continuous, with fine grained or coarse grained modeling of interactions)
- *Logical and/or Probabilistic Views*
- *Abstraction Level:* technical or functional (in the sense of the application domain)

It is important to fix these aspects in a requirements specification, particularly in relation to the properties as captured by the model. A dimension of classification refers to different levels of abstraction of architectures and state machines as introduced before.

9.4.3 System Context: Properties of the Context

For the introduced system model, the concept of system scope and context is essential. A system has to be clearly separated from its context. The notion of context comprises everything what is not inside the system's boundary. However, of course, we are mainly interested in context aspects in connection with the system requirements that are relevant for the system, its properties, its behavior, and its requirements. In requirements engineering, we capture therefore "facts" about the context – as far as they are relevant for the system under development. These facts serve as assumptions in requirements specifications (see [7]).

It is helpful to classify the elements of the context beyond the characterization given before. A straightforward characterization yields following categories of context:

- *Operational Context:* systems, users, and physical environment in the context with which the system under development interacts possibly as part of business processes (Figure 9.6). The behavior of systems (and even of users) in the context may be captured to some extent again by the interface model.
- *Usage Context:* scale of usage, number of users, and time of usage (in the sense of "duration").
- *User Interface Context:* issues of user interface have to be captured, related to the type of user. This is an extended usage context. Logical and physical

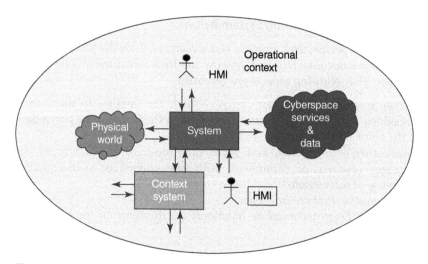

Figure 9.6 System and its operational context.

(interaction modalities) aspects of user interfaces have to be distinguished and described independently.

- *Business Context:* marketing the system in use, issues of the system related to business and marketing. This may be the number of system instances sold, issues of contracts, price, and so on. This category may include questions about the cost and value of a system or its parts. It is important, for example, for prioritizing requirements and system properties or even for formulating requirements.
- *Problem Domain:* terminology, notions, rules, and concepts of the application domain – as far as of interest for requirements engineering.
- *Development Context:* development processes, requirements addressing properties of the development process. Typical examples are the choice of the life cycle model or certain standards of certification.
- *Execution Context:* hardware and execution platform.

These context elements have to be captured in sufficient detail during requirements engineering to the extent they are needed for reflecting and documenting requirements. Strictly speaking, the properties of the context are not requirements but assumptions on which the requirements specifications rely on.

The operational context is described also by a syntactic interface and its interface behavior as illustrated in Figure 9.6.

In the following we concentrate on systems and their operational context, mainly.

9.4.4 Nonbehavioral System Properties: System Representation

Besides behavioral properties, there are nonbehavioral properties of systems that refer to properties not related to behavior. Specific properties refer to the syntactic representation of systems. These are quality attributes such as the readability of code. A rich class of such properties is found in the technical views onto systems; for instance, this covers properties such as material, temperature, or geometry.

Systems and their parts have to be represented syntactically. For example, programs ("code") are syntactic representations of software systems. Representations can be given by technical (code that describes software) or by logical (formulas that describe the behavior of software) means. In the behavioral categories, we describe by which modeling concept a system part is represented. For software, we may require the representation in a specific programming language or a specific coding standard. Also the technical view refers to a large extent to the question how a system is represented. Therefore, certain technical standards or specific devices might be suggested or even strictly required.

The system model with its logical and probabilistic models of behavior leads to a clear separation and classification of properties into the following two categories of system properties:

- *Behavioral Properties* including probabilistic and logical behavior addressing interface, architectural, state transition, and technical views onto systems.
- *Representation-Related Properties* that talk about the way the system is syntactically or technically represented, described, structured, implemented, and executed (such as which programming languages are used, etc.). Of course, from representations parts of the behavior can be deduced but not vice versa, in general.

Some traditional categories of requirements may lie in-between behavioral and representation-specific requirements. Examples might be questions of security and safety, which speak about behavioral properties but also about issues that are related to the syntactic representation and architectural structuring of systems.

A nonbehavioral viewpoint onto systems is to look at them as syntactic entities being representations by syntactic structure – such as for instance program code. Certain requirements address syntactic structure and properties. Typical examples would be readability, appropriate structuring of the architecture, or requiring program code following certain coding standards.

Other properties such as understandability and modifiability may both depend on issues of behavior and issues of syntactic representation. Furthermore, there are properties, which do not just refer to the representation of software systems as such, but also to the platforms on which code is executed or to skills of the developers. Examples are properties addressing portability or migration. These are properties that refer to the larger system context.

9.5 Categorizing Requirements

We aim at a systematic structuring of requirements according to the classification of properties of systems into categories, as well as the description of properties of their context, and their development process. We distinguish following categories of requirements and information relevant for requirements: assumptions about the operational context of the system – its behavior in terms of logic and probability, system properties (system requirements), development process properties (process requirements), properties of the wider system context such as the system in operation, its evolution, its business aspects, and marketing.

For the remainder, we concentrate mainly on behavioral and structural system properties and requirements to express those and do not consider requirements in detail that refer to the context or the development process. We structure and categorize the requirements of systems according the classification of properties of systems and to the views resulting from chosen viewpoints. We use three fundamental behavioral views:

- functional (properties in terms of the interface behavior),
- (logical) subsystem structuring – logical and probabilistic properties at the level of architecture – including state views in terms of state spaces and state transitions, and
- in addition to the behavioral view, we deal with a representation view that includes technical, physical, syntactical representation, structuring, and implementation details.

Each view is captured by modeling techniques taken from a basic set of system modeling concepts:

- Interface and interface behaviors in terms of the interaction over the system boundaries.
- Architecture and architectural behavior in terms of structuring a system into a set of subsystems and their connection by communication channels and the logical and probabilistic interaction between the components and over the system boundaries.
- State and state transition behavior in terms of describing the state space of a system, and its state transitions triggered by interaction.

For behavior, we distinguish in any case always between

- logical behavior in terms of sets of patterns of interaction and
- probabilistic behavior in terms of the probabilities for the patterns of interaction.

These different aspects of behavior apply to all three modeling concepts interface, state, and architecture.

9.5.1 A Rough Categorization of Requirements

In the end, the challenge to characterize different classes of functional and subclasses of nonfunctional requirements depends very much on a categorization of the observations we make about systems. To do a classification, we need several structural views onto systems. Thus, we take a functional viewpoint that is good enough to model all the functional requirements (in sense of logical and probabilistic interface behavior) at a well-chosen level of abstraction and we have, in addition, more detailed viewpoints onto a system, which then might help to study nonfunctional properties and, in particular, system quality properties.

First of all, we categorize requirements and additional context information roughly as follows:

- *System-Specific Requirements:* these are requirements that refer to the system, its behavior, its structure and representation, and its properties (including quality issues).
    - Properties of the behavior of the system in terms of logic (sets of behaviors) and probability
        - ○ *Black Box System* interface – logical and probabilistic
        - ○ *Glass Box* architecture and state – logical and probabilistic
    - Properties of the syntactic and technical representation of systems.
    - Structuring of the systems – architecture and state.
- *Operational Context Properties:* these are properties of the operational context with emphasis on its behavior; strictly speaking these are not requirements but descriptions of facts called assumptions (see [4]). These may be seen as part of the requirements where they are considered as assumptions, the requirements may rely on.
- *Usage-Specific Requirements:* these are requirements that address specific usage issues such as properties of MMI. They can be seen as special cases of system-specific requirements or operational context properties.
- *Problem Domain Modeling:* capturing properties of the application domain relevant for requirements engineering of the system under development.
- *Development Process Properties:* these are properties required for the development process. Some may include or imply system specific requirements and vice versa – some system specific requirements may include or imply requirements for the development process.
- *Business-Specific Requirements*: these are requirements that deal with costs and marketing.

A second characterization deals with the question to what extent a requirement is abstract and general or concrete and precise such that it can be implemented and verified without discussions about its exact interpretation or the way it should be realized.

We distinguish four levels of goals and requirements:

1) *Goals* formulate general intentional properties to achieve. For example, "*The system has no vulnerabilities concerning security*"
2) *Abstract Requirements* formulate system properties without giving a concrete measure to judge or verify to what extent a system has that property. For example, "*Private user data have to be protected against access by the system administrator*"
3) *Concrete Requirements* give specific properties that can be measured and verified defining ways making abstract requirements concrete. For example, "*All private user data is encrypted by a key chosen by the user but hidden to the administrator.*"

4) *Specifications* are descriptions of system behavior and functionality in terms of concrete system models and their behavior in terms of interactions. For example, *"During login, the user is asked for his/her encryption key before she/he can get access to his/her data."*

Those four stages of requirements refer to the refinement of goals to abstract and further to concrete requirements and finally to system specifications.

Another dimension of classifying and evaluating requirements is their preciseness of description and their formality as well as the chosen level of abstraction.

Requirements may be composed from a set of more elementary requirements. If these more elementary requirements all belong to the same category the requirement is called *homogenous* otherwise *heterogeneous*.

9.5.1.1 Functional Requirements: Logic, Time, and Probability

Functional requirements are requirements that address properties of the black box view (users' perspective) onto systems. This view captures logical and probabilistic interface behavior including timing properties especially in the case of real-time systems.

Example A Short Example about Logic, Time, and Probability   To explain the different categories we introduce a short example of an airbag with a number of properties/requirements about the timing of the airbag:

1) The airbag has to be activated after the crash sensor indicates a crash within the interval of 160–180 ms.
2) The probability that the airbag fails to fulfill specification 1) is less than 0.01%.
3) The probability that the airbag is activated within an interval of 170 ± 5 ms after the crash sensor indicated a crash is above 90%.
4) The probability that the airbag gets activated without a signal coming from the crash sensor is below 10^{-8}%.

The first property is a logical interface requirement, the second a reliability and also a safety requirement, while the third one is a performance and also a safety requirement, and the fourth one is a probabilistic safety property. Note that all these requirements can be expressed in terms of logical and probabilistic system interface behavior. Therefore, they are functional requirements in our terminology.

To deal with safety properties more detailed models are needed. For instance, in addition to the system interface behavior model an interface model extended by hazards that capture safety critical mishaps and probabilities about their occurrence. Also the architectural and the state model are extended by defects, fault, failure, and error cases such that their interface abstraction is the extended functional interface model capturing safety critical defects.

Finally, we come up with the following bottom line: what is traditionally called functional requirements is in our approach and terminology called logical behavioral interface requirements that do not refer to time. More generally, probabilistic interface behavior requirements cover the wide field of notions like reliability, functional safety, and to a large extent security. Even fields like usability then can be positioned to some extent as probabilistic behavioral requirements often related to assumptions about the operational context such as behavioral properties and capabilities of the specific users.

9.5.1.2 Actually Nonfunctional Requirements: Internal Behavior and Representation

Nonfunctional requirements about systems are requirements that address properties of representation and behavioral properties in the glass box view onto systems. This view comprises logical and probabilistic behavior at the level of architecture and state.

There is a variety of requirements addressing this glass box behavior, such as a reduced interaction between subsystems, referring to the bandwidth of the middleware. Moreover, safety issues as considered in FMEA and FTA or in security analysis have to look at behavioral properties at the architectural or even more detailed at the technical implementation level. This illustrates once more that there are behavioral aspects of systems that are not functional.

In security requirements, for instance, we find a mixture of behavioral properties, in particular, such as, for example, the probability that passwords are chosen that they cannot be guessed with a sufficiently high probability or requirements such that middleware is used that cannot be cracked by hackers.

Similar situations apply for functional safety. In functional safety to a large extent investigations (in terms of FMEA) are carried out to analyze whether malfunctions of certain subsystems might lead to hazardous ("unsafe") behaviors of systems (visible in terms of hazards in the operational context due to failures in system interface behavior). These are usually behavioral properties of components at the level of the logical or the technical architecture; to analyze those we often need an extension of behavior from regular to exceptional cases.

To speak about what traditionally is called nonfunctional quality requirements such as for instance safety or security we have to speak about requirements that have to do with behavior – to large extent interface behavior. Actually, these are requirements captured in terms of probabilistic behavior.

9.5.1.3 Quality Requirements

There is a rich number of publications on software and system quality models. Quality requirements for systems comprise (following [8]) among others a large amount of quality factors (also known as "quality attributes") such as

- Functional suitability
- Usability
- Reliability
- Security

- Safety
- Performance
- Efficiency
- Maintainability
- Reusability
- Releasability
- Executability

We do not consider further factors in the following that need a wider development context such as maintainability, reusability, or properties related to operation such as releasability, executability, or supportability.

Based on the factors and our categorization, we may identify specific requirement categories as expressed in quality models in Table 9.2. We keep the quality model small and simple – just detailed enough to demonstrate the idea.

We explain the introduced quality categories by indicating which of the rough categories have to be considered for them. Black indicates very strong relationship, dark grey strong, light grey some, and white indicates no relationship.

As the table suggests certain system properties are not referring to behavior directly but to aspects of representation such as readability, which is an important attribute for maintainability and reusability. Finally, there is a rich class of requirements that are mixtures of properties from several categories.

Only a restricted set of the traditionally called nonfunctional requirements then is related exclusively to nonbehavioral issues when using the richer behavioral system model including probabilistic behavior.

9.5.2 A Novel Taxonomy of Requirements?

In requirements engineering, we gather, specify, analyze, and decide about the requirements – required properties of the system under development – also in relationship to its context. What we suggest implies a quite rigorous rethinking of categorizations of requirements. This rethinking has to go hand in hand with more elaborate models of system behavior including probability but also more elaborate models of nonbehavioral aspects of systems. The result is a more detailed novel categorization framework for requirements. An important question is, of course, how far such a novel categorization framework actually helps in requirements engineering or even more so in the design of requirements engineering methods.

In fact, the categorization may help in any case for a better clarification and more consequent definition of the different categories of requirements. A lot of literature in requirements engineering – including textbooks – so far still is quite confusing and not very systematic. Many authors do not provide a

Table 9.2 Intensity of relationship between quality attributes and modeling views (black indicates very strong relationship, dark grey strong, light grey some, and white indicates no relationship).

	Interface			Architecture			State			Representation
Functional properties	Syntactic	Logical	Probabilistic	Syntactic	Logical	Probabilistic	Syntactic	Logical	Probabilistic	
Functional suitability	black	black	dark grey	white	white	white	white	white	white	white
Usability	white	light grey	white	white	white	white	white	white	white	black
Reliability	black	light grey	black	white	white	dark grey	white	white	white	white
Security	dark grey	dark grey	dark grey	light grey	white	light grey	white	white	white	light grey
Safety	black	dark grey	black	white	white	dark grey	white	white	white	white
Performance	black	dark grey	black	white	white	white	white	white	white	white
Maintainability	dark grey	dark grey	light grey	dark grey	dark grey	white	dark grey	dark grey	white	black
Reusability	dark grey	white	white	black	black	white	black	black	white	dark grey
Releasability	white	white	white	white	white	white	white	white	white	black
Executability	white	white	white	white	white	white	white	white	white	black
Supportability	white	white	white	white	white	white	white	white	white	black

rigorous and sharp distinction between the essential categories of behavioral properties such as logical and probabilistic behavior and black box vs. glass box views and the nonbehavioral aspects that are related to system representation – be it at the level of interface specification, design, or at the level of code.

A challenging and interesting question is the relationship between behavioral views and quality views. Should quality views be rather related to behavioral interface views such as the functional view or to the subsystem view?

The introduced system model addresses only requirements that directly speak about systems and their operational context. However, there are further requirements that address the role and properties of systems in a wider context. This context includes the following main areas:

- Operational context (structure and behavior)
- Problem (application) domain properties
- Users and usage properties and requirements
- Business and economy
- Society and sustainability
- Development process

Moreover, requirements may be formulated at various levels of generality, granularity, and formality:

- Comprehensive goals (business, technical, methodological, etc.)
- Specific goals
- Abstract requirements
- Concrete requirements
- System specification

The introduction of probabilistic behavioral views brings in a new dimension into the categorization of requirements. The relationship between architectural concepts and modeling techniques poses fruitful questions and brings in new ideas for structuring requirements.

The following perspective aims at an additional helpful categorization of requirements:

- System in use
- System in operation
- System in development and in evolution
- System in business

It is also helpful to speak about groups of stakeholders. In some sense, this is orthogonal to the categorization we introduced so far. For instance, which features a system offers is usually relevant more or less for all these categories. Different categorizations can be included by adding respective attributes to requirements.

A bottom line of our discussion is as follows:

- Complex and general abstract requirements such as goals may be decomposed into a number of concrete requirements belonging to different categories.
- Abstract vague, imprecise requirements can be and have to be decomposed and refined and made more concrete and precise; this can be done in different ways and therefore may lead to concrete requirements in different categories depending on the choice of their refinement. System models are helpful on this road for making requirements precise and formalizing them.

This shows that, in general, only requirements that are sufficiently concrete, detailed, and precise can be uniquely categorized as long as they are not heterogeneous requirements composed of subrequirements from different categories.

An ideal categorization of requirements should lead into a taxonomy that can be understood as a tree of classifications – in fact, as a taxonomy. In our case, categories allow us to decompose every property and thus every requirement R into a composed requirement $R_1 \wedge \ldots \wedge R_n$ such that every requirement R_i is a member of exactly one fundamental homogeneous category (note that we do not consider here the form $R_1 \vee \ldots \vee R_n$ where $R_1, \ldots, R_n$ are from different categories).

9.6 Summary

A careful categorization of requirements is a prerequisite for any systematic requirements engineering. As demonstrated in this chapter, a comprehensive system model is helpful to work out such a systematic approach that is less ad hoc than existing approaches.

To categorize requirements, we distinguish between behavioral and non-behavioral aspects. Behavioral aspects are divided into logical and probabilistic views and, moreover, into external (interface) and internal views. Probabilistic properties talk about the set of all observations. This has some similarity to closed world assumptions.

In the light of our discussion, we suggest to redefine the term "functional requirement" to requirements that speak about the syntactic interface as well as the logical or probabilistic system interface behavior. This leads to a more general notion of functional behavior.

The basis for our discussion of requirements is a formal system modeling framework. The modeling approach is supported by

- a comprehensive theory,
- a set of modeling concepts,

- a development method, and
- tools.

The result is a more practical approach with high potential for system automation and reuse not only in requirements engineering.

Acknowledgments

It is a pleasure to acknowledge helpful discussions with Martin Glinz, Michael Jackson, Bran Selic, and my colleagues, in particular, Jonas Eckhardt, Mario Gleirscher, Daniel Mendez Fernandez, Birgit Penzenstadler, and Andreas Vogelsang.

References

1 M. Glinz (2007) On non-functional requirements. In: *15th IEEE International Requirements Engineering Conference (RE '07)*, IEEE.

2 M. Broy (2010) Multifunctional software systems: structured modeling and specification of functional requirements. *Science of Computer Programming*, **75**, 1193–1214.

3 M. Broy (2010) Multifunctional software systems: structured modeling and specification of functional requirements. *Science of Computer Programming*, **75**, S1193–1214.

4 M. Broy (2011) Towards a theory of architectural contracts: schemes and patterns of assumption/promise based system specification. in: M. Broy, Ch. Leuxner, T. Hoare (eds.), *Software and Systems Safety: Specification and Verification – Volume 30 NATO Science for Peace and Security Series - D: Information and Communication Security*, IOS Press, pp. 33–87.

5 M. Broy (2010) A logical basis for component-oriented software and systems engineering. *The Computer Journal*, **53** (10), S1758–1782.

6 P. Neubeck (2012) A Probabilitistic theory of interactive systems. Ph. D. dissertation, Technische Universität München, Fakultät für Informatik, December.

7 M. Broy 2017 Theory and methodology of assumption/commitment based system interface specification and architectural contracts. In: *Formal Methods in System Design*, Vol. 42, Issue 1, Springer US, pp. 33–87.

8 K. Lochmann and S. Wagner A quality model for software quality. Internal Report. Technische Universität München.

10

The Power of Ten—Rules for Developing Safety Critical Code[1]

Gerard J. Holzmann

JPL Laboratory for Reliable Software, NASA, Pasadena, CA, USA

10.1 Introduction

We introduced the Power of Ten coding rules in a column that appeared in June 2006, in *IEEE Computer*. Two years later, the rules became part of the official institutional coding standard that JPL adopted for mission-critical flight software development. Since then, this set of rules has been used for the development of two large space exploration missions, and a number of smaller ones. The first of the larger projects was the Mars Science Lab mission that safely landed the Curiosity Rover on the surface of Mars in August 2012. The flight software for that mission alone reached about three million lines of code: more than all missions to Mars that preceded it combined.

Each mission achieved their design objectives with unusually low residual error rates. Whether or not the adoption of the Power of Ten rules contributed to the low-error rates is difficult to tell with certainty. The added rigor that was imposed by the introduction of the rules, though, must have had a positive effect, as did the matching code review process that made use of static source code analyzers to check mechanically for any possible rule violations. The rules put a new emphasis on risk avoidance and code safety that in part changed the culture of software development at JPL.

With the benefit of close to a decade's worth of hindsight, we discuss the ten original rules, and we will consider some of the objections that have been raised against individual rules. For some of the rules we will also show where the

---

1 The research described in this chapter was carried out at the Jet Propulsion Laboratory, California Institute of Technology, under a contract with the National Aeronautics and Space Administration.

particulars of rule enforcement were modified somewhat in response to feedback from developers and mission managers.

10.2 Context

All serious software development projects use coding guidelines, and rightly so. The guidelines are meant to state what the ground rules are for the software to be written: how it should be structured and which language features should or should not be used.

Curiously, despite the importance of using these types of guidelines, there continues to be little consensus on what a good coding standard is. Among the many that have been proposed there are remarkably few patterns to discern, except that each new proposal tends to be longer than the one before it. The result is that most standards contain well over a hundred rules, sometimes with questionable justification. Some rules, especially those that try to stipulate the use of whitespace in programs, are based only on personal preference; others are meant to prevent very specific and unlikely types of defects that may have plagued an earlier coding effort within the same organization. Not surprisingly, until fairly recently, existing coding standards tend to have little effect on how developers actually wrote code. The most dooming aspect of many of the standards was that they rarely allowed for comprehensive tool-based compliance checking. Tool-based checking is important, since it is often infeasible to manually review the hundreds of thousands of lines of code, or worse, that are written for large applications.

The benefit of the bulky coding standards from the past has therefore often been very small, even for safety critical applications. A verifiable set of well-chosen coding rules can, however, make critical software components more thoroughly analyzable, also for properties that go beyond mere compliance with the set of rules itself. To be effective, though, the set of coding rules should be small and focused on risk reduction, and it must be easily understood and remembered. As noted, it is a considerable advantage if compliance with the rules can be checked mechanically. This, for instance, rules out the use of "weasel" words in the rules like "A function should not be *too long*" or rules that start with phrases like "*Try to avoid . . .*"

Instead of the hundreds of somewhat vague rules that usually crowd coding standards, we have argued that we can get significant benefit by restricting to just 10 well-chosen rules. Of course, such a small set cannot be all-inclusive, but it can give us a foothold to achieve measurable effects on software reliability and verifiability. To support strong checking, the rules are strict – one might even say that they are borderline draconian. The trade-off, though, will be clear. When it really counts, especially in the development of safety critical code, it may be worth going the extra mile and accept stricter limits than one would use for routine software development. In return, we should be able to demonstrate more convincingly than before that critical software will indeed work as intended.

10.3 The Choice of Rules

The purpose of the Power of Ten coding rules is to reduce risk. That is, to make it less likely that common coding errors find their way into the code and escape testing to cause havoc later. More specifically, the rules we propose here try to get us closer to four specific targets that we believe are correlated with reduced risk. They are as follows:

1) Full *language compliance*
2) Achieving and maintaining *code clarity*
3) Securing a *predictable execution*
4) Applying *defensive coding* strategies

Let us consider language compliance first. Our target is to have all code be compliant with a specific C standard (we often choose C99), without reliance on any hidden undefined, unspecified, or implementation-defined behavior. The rationale for this is clear. If we go outside the language definition, we end up relying on the particular choices of that compiler writers made to optimize code generation. When a language feature is undefined, the compiler writer is free to do whatever seems best, which does not necessarily match what a developer might assume. From one version or brand of the compiler to the next, those choices may well be made differently.

Especially for embedded systems code, this issue is far from trivial. Most compilers do not warn for noncompliant code, and most even support it explicitly, for instance, through the use of compiler-specific pragma directives. Often efforts are made to reuse code from one application to the next, where old choices that worked well in the earlier application may work very differently in the new context, when compiled with a different compiler for perhaps a different CPU target. None of those concerns exist if the code is maintained to be strictly language compliant. Noncompliance is an area of risk that can simply be eliminated.

Our second of the four targets is to improve code clarity. As a small example of the lack of code clarity, consider the following declaration. Even though this code is fully language compliant, do you really know what it means precisely? And if you do, how long did you have to stare at it to be sure?

```
int (*(*foo)(const void *))[3];
```

I have taken this example from the cdecl.org website, which provides a great tool for decoding and explaining constructs like these. And just in case you started worrying about this, the declaration means foo is declared to be a pointer to a function that takes a pointer to a constant of type `void` as an argument, and returns a pointer to an array of three integers.

We can admire C for providing such a terse formalism for defining complex things. Then again, if we can find less complex ways of achieving the same goal we can make our code more easily accessible to others. This includes peer reviewers and testers today, and your future colleague who will have to debug the code many years after you have left.

The third target we would like to achieve is to secure a predictable execution. The two key resources we worry about are naturally time and memory. We would like to be able to calculate precisely, before a system execution even begins, how much stack memory is maximally needed for the code to execute safely even under adverse conditions. We would also like to be able to derive an upper-bound for the execution time of any function in the system: the worst-case execution time (WCET).

Unless certain precautions are taken, this will not be possible. The small rule set we propose here though allows us to provide those guarantees by, for instance, restricting the use of dynamic memory allocation, eliminating recursion, and placing upper-bounds on the number of iterations of every loop.

The final target is defensive coding. Although the general principle that is followed here will be clear, it is not quite as easy to succinctly capture it in a few rules. A defensive coding strategy asks the programmer to make as few assumptions as reasonably possible about the context in which code is executed. If a calling function passes a pointer parameter that must be dereferenced, we would like to make sure that that pointer cannot accidentally be null. If an array index is provided, we would like to make sure that it cannot be negative, and that it cannot be larger than the array size allows. Similarly, if our code calls another function that is outside our own domain, we should check that it does not return an error code. We would also like to include a reasonable number of self-checks in the code that check for the sanity of an execution. Note that when an anomaly occurs in some remote part of the system, be it hardware or software related, bizarre things may start happening in our part of the world. The sooner we can detect that we have left the intended execution state, the easier it will be to restore sanity and diagnose the root cause of the anomaly.

We could leave our advice to programmers of embedded safety critical systems there, but this would be comparable to replacing a driving test with the advice: "when you go out on the road, be very careful." Although the sentiment will be appreciated and readily understood, its effect on the safety of subsequent driving, or in our case on the safety of software, will likely be nil. So we would like to make things a little more specific, without getting overly pedantic by trying to regulate where you put your spaces and how many you are allowed to use.

Every rule that follows can allow exceptions in rare cases, provided that each exception is carefully justified, thoroughly documented, and agreed to by your peers.

10.4 Ten Rules for Safety Critical Code

The choice of programming language that is used for the development of safety critical code is itself a key consideration, but we will not debate it here. At many organizations, JPL included, all safety and mission-critical code is written in the C programming language. With its long history, there is extensive tool support for this language, including the availability of strong source code analyzers, logic model extractors, metrics tools, debuggers, test support tools, and a choice of mature and stable compilers. The language is simpler than many of its descendants, which can make it significantly easier to analyze. C is also the target of the majority of coding guidelines that have been developed. For fairly pragmatic reasons, then, our coding rules target C and attempt to optimize our ability to check the reliability of critical applications written in C. Many of the rules we discuss, though, can also be applied to code written in comparable languages, such as C++, C#, or Java.

We discuss each of the rules, with a brief rationale for its inclusion in the Power of Ten rule set.

1) *Rule:* Restrict to simple control flow constructs – do not use *goto* statements, *setjmp* or *longjmp* constructs, and do not use direct or indirect *recursion*.

   Rationale: Simpler control flow enables stronger capabilities for analysis and often results in improved code clarity. The banishment of recursion is perhaps the biggest surprise here. Without recursion, though, we are guaranteed to have an acyclic function call graph, which can be exploited by code analyzers, and can directly help to prove that all executions that should be bounded are in fact bounded. Specifically, this rule does not require that all functions have a single point of return. There are many cases where an early error return simplifies code structure much better than the maintenance of a single point of return.

   Discussion: Ruling out the use of *goto* statements is surprisingly uncontroversial. Most programmers agree that code structure improves if the temptation to quickly patch code with *goto* statements is resisted. Sometimes the right solution is to add a function, sometimes it is to add a Boolean flag to a *for* or a *while* loop.

   Setjmp and *longjmp* can be useful in isolated cases to save and restore context, but they also make it virtually impossible to thoroughly test or analyze code. Similarly, in object-oriented languages, the use of exception-handling mechanisms can seriously befuddle code clarity and make it especially hard to thoroughly test all possible control flow paths through the code. Especially, for safety critical code one tends to spend far more time reviewing, testing, and analyzing code than writing it, the trade-offs are generally clear.

   Many developers have found the banishment of recursion the hardest to accept. It should be noted, though, that the rules are meant for the development of safety critical code in embedded systems, and not for general software development without comparable resource limits. Recursive functions can indeed simplify code structure, but in doing so they hide critical aspects of resource use from view. The use of recursive functions allows us to imagine that we have unlimited stack space. This is rarely a problem in general, but it is different in embedded systems.

We know that *every* recursive function can be rewritten as a nonrecursive function, using loops. Recursion, therefore, offers a convenience, but no additional expressive power. By avoiding recursion we avoid the implicit memory consumption on the stack, and make it explicit. This then allows us to set clear bounds on stack use for both nominal and off-nominal program executions. There is a close connection here with the next rule, which is meant to avoid runaway code.

2) *Rule:* All loops must have a fixed upper-bound. It must be possible for a checking tool to *prove* statically that a preset upper-bound on the number of iterations of a loop cannot be exceeded. If the loop-bound cannot be proven statically, the rule is considered violated.

Rationale: The absence of recursion and the presence of loop bounds suffice to prevent runaway code. This rule does not, of course, apply to iterations that are *meant* to be nonterminating (for instance, when used in a process scheduler). These types of loops are generally in a small minority, and should carry a comment that indicates that they are nonterminating. It is always best to use a fixed pattern for writing nonterminating loops, to make their intent clear to reviewers and testers.

Discussion: Most loops that appear in code easily comply with this rule. A typical for-loop, for instance, will iterate over a range of values of an index value. If we make sure that the index variable is not modified in the body of the loop, establishing loop termination is trivial. If the loop must follow a different pattern, for instance, if it is used to traverse a linked list of uncertain length, we can secure compliance with the rule by providing an explicit upper-bound that is well beyond what can reasonably be the maximum number of iterations. When that upper-bound is exceeded, an assertion failure can then be triggered, or the function containing the failing loop can be made to return an error code. (See Rule 5 about the use of assertions.)

The upper-bound can be any positive integer, for instance, we can use the predefined integer value for the given word size of the machine we are using. They key here is to prevent an *infinite* loop, so any finite number will do. Often, the bound can be set much tighter than this, by making a reasonable estimate of the maximum number of iterations that should be possible. When traversing a linked list, for instance, resource limits will generally limit the number of elements that could possibly end up in the list. We can multiply that number by a safety factor to define the bound. A violation of the bound at runtime can then reveal when the linked list has accidentally become corrupted and has become circular.

The evaluation of the loop bound on every iteration does of course impose some additional overhead. Where this is problematic, for instance, in the inner loop of a computationally challenging routine, a different method to secure loop termination will need to be found. In many embedded systems this can, for instance, be done with a watchdog timer that interrupts the computation when it exceeds a known limit.

3) *Rule:* Do not use dynamic memory allocation after initialization.

Rationale: The banishment of dynamic memory allocation is surprisingly common in safety critical software applications and it appears in most coding guidelines. The reasons are simple. First, memory allocators and garbage collectors often have unpredictable behavior that can significantly impact performance. Second, accidentally using memory that was freed or overshooting an allocated area of memory can corrupt a computation in ways that can be exceptionally difficult to diagnose and repair. Third, forgetting to free memory leads to memory leaks that slowly deprive a system of its resources, degrading performance until only a reboot can restore normal behavior. Finally, on systems with virtual memory, attempting to allocate more memory than physically available, can lead to trashing where the system is forced to spend most of its time swapping in core memory segments to disk and back.

Discussion: Forcing applications to live within a fixed, preallocated area of memory can eliminate many of these problems and make it easier to verify memory use, and guarantee the availability of sufficient resources to all tasks. Note that the only way to dynamically claim memory in the absence of heap memory allocation is to use stack memory. In the absence of recursion (Rule 1), an upper-bound on the use of stack memory can be derived statically, thus making it possible to prove that an application will always live within its preallocated memory means. Checking compliance with this rule is quite simple. We can check the code for any call to known memory allocators (*malloc* and friends). More precisely, we can also check the final executable for the presence of memory allocation routines. For added security, it is also possible to force linkage of the code with special routines that map all calls to, for instance, *malloc, calloc, realloc, alloca, brk,* or *sbrk* to assertion failures.

4) *Rule:* No function should be longer than what can be printed on a single sheet of paper in a standard reference format with one line per statement and one line per declaration. Typically, this means no more than about 60 lines of code per function.

Rationale: Each function should be a logical unit in the code that is understandable and verifiable as a unit. It is much harder to understand a logical unit that spans multiple pages when printed, or multiple screens when viewed on a display. Excessively long functions are often a sign of poorly structured code.

Discussion: This rule is meant to preserve code clarity. There are exceptions we can claim to this rule where splitting up a function into smaller pieces would jeopardize rather than enhance clarity. A good example is a function that contains a standard switch statement that covers all cases of an enumeration type. Even with just three statements per case, including the break statement (each of which should appear on a separate line) it would take less than 20 cases to reach the maximum function length. What if there are 30 cases to cover? An exception would be reasonable in cases like these. But, what if there are 50 or more cases? Here the best answer is likely to be different. In cases like these, code clarity may be improved with the use of a data-driven approach. Instead of using a switch statement with 50 cases, we can store the information in a table with 50 entries, and do a lookup of the case to be processed with a bounded for-loop. In some cases, the best solution is to store a fixed function pointer in the table for the detailed handling of each case. We will return to this in the discussion for Rule 9, which puts limits on the use of function pointers.

5) *Rule:* Our original Power of Ten rule required that all safety critical code should include a minimum of two assertions per function. Many functions are very simple though, and requiring the use of assertions in all would tend to have the undesirable effect of discouraging the use of short functions, which in turn can negatively affect code clarity. We have, therefore, revised this rule to require that the *average assertion density* over all codes, and over every major module of the code, is at least 2%. All assertions must be provably side effect free and defined as Boolean tests.

Rationale: Assertions allow us to write self-checking code. The assertion rule encourages an increased use of self-checking in complex functions, rather than in routine code. When assertions are side effect free, the less critical ones can selectively be disabled during execution. The disabling of assertion, though, is generally not recommended since it removes a layer of protection for safe execution.

Discussion: An overview of the use and benefits of assertions in source code can be found in, for instance, the study done by Clarke and Rosenblum [1]. There is a strong evidence that an increased use of assertions lowers the number of residual defects in code. Such a link was, for instance, shown in a study done at Microsoft in 2006 [2]. It should be noted that assertions are *not* meant to catch routine error conditions. There are other mechanisms for that, like returning an error code to the caller.

Assertions are meant to be used only for catching anomalous conditions that should *never* happen in a real-life execution. When an assertion fails, an explicit recovery action must be taken, which is often to initiate a recovery procedure or a complete restart of a module or of the entire system. Statistics for commercial code development indicate that unit tests often find at least one defect for every 10–100 lines of code written. The odds of intercepting those defects increase dramatically with even small increase in the overall assertion density of the code. The use of assertions is part of a defensive coding strategy. Assertions can be used to verify pre- and postconditions of functions, parameter values, return values of functions, and loop invariants.

It can be tempting to attempt to rule out the use of assertions for which a static checking tool can prove that they can never fail, but except for some obvious cases (e.g., *assert(true)*) this could be very difficult for cases where assertions are used to catch precisely the "cannot happen" cases in an execution that require some data or code corruption elsewhere to become feasible.

6) *Rule:* Data objects must be declared at the smallest possible level of scope.

   Rationale: This rule supports a basic principle of data hiding. Clearly, if an object is not in scope, its value cannot be referenced or corrupted. Similarly, if an erroneous value of an object has to be diagnosed, the fewer the number of statements where the value could have been assigned, the easier it is to diagnose the problem. The rule discourages the reuse of variables for multiple, incompatible purposes, which can complicate fault diagnosis.

   Discussion: One objection that has been raised against this rule is that it limits not just the visibility and accessibility of data in program executions, but also in the symbol table. This can make it more difficult to investigate the state of an embedded system when an anomaly has occurred. Note that this applies only to objects that are declared file static, to prevent that they become globally accessible (and corruptible).

   A simple solution, adopted for flight software development at JPL, is to mark all file static data objects with an uppercase macro STATIC. When we analyze the code, and check if the scope rule has been followed, we define the macro as its lowercase equivalent and make sure that the code can still be compiled. When the symbol table is generated for an anomaly investigation, the macro can be defined to be empty, which makes the data objects globally visible and accessible for debugging.

7) *Rule:* The return value of nonvoid functions must be checked by each calling function, and the validity of parameters must be checked inside each function.

   Rationale: This rule is meant to support the principles of locality and least surprise. We should be able to look at each function in a program as a logical unit and determine whether it is safe to execute or not. If, for example, the function dereferences one of its arguments, there should really be a protection in place against callers that pass a null pointer – whether or not this actually can happen in the current version of the code. It is always better to avoid long chains of brittle reasoning that depend critically on one particular version of the code, under assumptions that may be long forgotten by the time the code is updated years later.

Discussion: This is possibly the most debated and most frequently violated rule, and therefore, a little more suspect as general guidance for reliable code development. In its strictest form, this rule means that even the return value of every *close* statement or *memcpy* statement should be checked. One can make a case, though, that if the response to an error would rightfully be no different than the response to success, there is little point in checking a return value. In cases like these, it is acceptable to cast the function return value to (*void*) – thereby, indicating that the programmer explicitly and not accidentally decided to ignore the return value. In more dubious cases, a comment should be present to explain why a return value is irrelevant.

In most cases, though, the return value of a function should not be ignored, especially, if error return values must be propagated up the function call chain. Standard libraries famously violate this rule with potentially serious consequences. You may want to check, for instance, what happens if you accidentally execute *strlen(0)* or *strcat(s1, s2, -1)* with the standard C string library – it is almost certainly not what you want. By keeping the general rule, we make sure that exceptions must be justified, with mechanical checkers flagging violations. Often, it will be easier to comply with the rule than to explain why noncompliance might be acceptable.

You can compare this to a stop sign that is placed at an intersection of two deserted country roads. Should you always stop, even when you can see for miles each way that no other car is coming, or is it okay to simply drive through? Clearly, if you drive through, you can be ticketed, irrespective of whether it was safe to do so or not. The rule for stop signs could be reformulated to allow for each possible exception – but that would weaken the rule considerably. If it is easier to comply with a rule than to document a detailed argument why you should not, the rule will in most cases be followed – which is the effect we would like to achieve.

8) *Rule:* The use of the preprocessor must be limited to the inclusion of header files and simple macro definitions. Token pasting, variable argument lists, and recursive macro calls are not allowed. Preprocessor macros must always expand into complete syntactic units, and never redefined key-words. The use of conditional compilation directives is often also dubious, because it makes it much harder to test all possible ways in which code could be compiled and executed. The one exception to this rule is the use of a single conditional compilation directive to prevent the repeated inclusion of header files. There should rarely be justification for other uses of conditional compilation directives even in large software development

efforts. Each such use should be flagged by a tool-based checker and justified convincingly in the code.

Rationale: The C preprocessor is a powerful obfuscation tool that can destroy code clarity and befuddle many text-based checkers. The effect of constructs in unrestricted preprocessor code can be extremely hard to decipher, even with a formal language definition in hand. In a new implementation of the C preprocessor, developers often have to resort to using earlier implementations as the referee for interpreting complex defining language in the C standard. The rationale for the caution against conditional compilation is equally important. Note that with just 10 conditional compilation directives, there could be up to 2^{10} possible versions of the code, each of which would have to be tested – causing a huge increase in the required test effort.

Discussion: As an example of the difficulty of interpreting preprocessing rules, consider the following small example:

```
#define xy          hello
#define ab          goodbye
#define m(a,b,ab)   #   a##b   #ab
```

The example uses both the stringification operator (a single # symbol) and the token pasting operator (a double ## symbol). Now, try to answer how the following macro call will expand:

```
m(x,y,world)
```

Depending on the order in which the various operations are applied, you could end up with the result "hello" "world" (by first applying token pasting of x and y, then stringification of world and finally the stringification of hello), or with "x"y "world" (by starting with the stringification of x, followed by token pasting the result to y and finally stringifying world). Determining which expansion is the correct one is exceedingly difficult. Most C preprocessors will return the second expansion.

Many compilers support the use of a preprocessor pragma directive #pragma once to make sure that a header file is not expanded more than once. The Power of Ten rules, though, do not permit the use of any pragma directives because they are strictly defined outside the language proper, and their interpretation is compiler dependent. (It could, for instance, be that the compiler used during development and testing supports it, but the platform-specific compiler for the target platform does not.)

9) *Rule:* The use of pointers should be restricted. Specifically, there should be a limit on the maximum number of dereferencing operators per expression.

If a pointer dereference operation appears in a macro definition or *typedef* declaration, the name must have a suffix *_ptr* to indicate this. Function pointers are not permitted unless it can be statically determined at each point in the program which function is pointed to.

Rationale: Pointers are easily misused, even by experienced programmers. They can make it hard to follow or analyze the flow of data in a program, especially by tool-based static analyzers. Function pointers, similarly, can seriously restrict the types of checks that can be performed by static analyzers and should only be used if there is a strong justification for their use, and ideally alternative means are provided to assist tool-based checkers determine flow of control and function call hierarchies. For instance, if function pointers are used, it can become impossible for a tool to prove absence of recursion, so alternate guarantees would have to be provided to make up for this loss in analytical capabilities.

Discussion: The original version of this rule was considerably stricter than the version we ended up adopting, shown here. Originally, we required no more than one dereference operator per expression, and completely ruled out the use of dereference operators in macros or *typedef*s, and we ruled out all uses of function pointers. This put the bar a few notches too high for most software development efforts. Keeping in mind that the rules are meant to enhance code clarity and analyzability, it has been relatively easy to come up with a more workable alternative.

Constant function pointers, for instance, stored in lookup tables, pose no risk to safe execution or code analysis. Similarly, allowing macro names or *typedef* declarations with a *_ptr* suffix avoids that dereference operations can be hidden from view in the target code, and obscure critical code fragments. What is a reasonable limit on the number of dereference operators per expression? Clearly, code clarity is affected by overuse. For flight software development, we set the limit at two dereference operators per expression, before a justification must be given for deviating from this rule.

10) *Rule:* All code must be compiled, from the start of development, with compiler warnings enabled at the compiler's highest warning level. All code must compile with these setting without warnings. Once the code can pass this test, warnings should be mapped to compilation errors and abort a compilation if they occur. All code must be checked on every full build of the software with at least one, but preferably more than one, state-of-the-art static source code analyzer. It should pass the static analyses with zero warnings.

Rationale: There are several effective static source code analyzers on the market today, and a number of reasonable freeware tools as well.[2] There simply is no excuse for any serious software development effort not to

---

2 For an overview see, for instance, http://spinroot.com/static/index.html.

leverage this capability. It should be considered routine practice, even for noncritical code development.

Note that the rule of zero warnings applies even in cases where the compiler or the static analyzer gives an erroneous warning: If the compiler or the static analyzer gets confused, the code causing the confusion should be rewritten so that it becomes more trivially valid. Many developers have been caught in the assumption that a warning was surely incorrect, only to realize much later that the message was in fact valid for less obvious reasons. Older static analyzers used to have a bad reputation due to the imprecision of the early technology, but this is no longer the case. The best static analyzers today are fast and customizable, and they produce accurate messages. Their use should not be negotiable.

Discussion: The main flaw of this rule is perhaps that we should have listed it as the first, and not the last, rule. We did so in the longer coding standard that JPL adopted based on this rule set. It is possibly the most important rule in the set, and following it can have meaningful impact on code quality throughout development.

The recommended compiler settings, for example, for the gcc compiler, include the runtime flags `-Wall -Wextra -Wpedantic -std=c99`, and once the number of warnings is close to zero also `-Werror` to map warnings to errors. Additionally recommended settings include `-Wstrict-overflow`, `-Wshadow`, and `-fno-strict-aliasing` to catch additional classes of flaws that can be very hard to trace down if they are missed. For embedded software systems, we also require that all data types used explicitly state the precision. That is, instead of using just plain char or int, the requirement is to use `int8_t` or `int32_t` where the corresponding type definitions as available (e.g., in the system header files `stdint.h`). Where not available, the required types must be pre-defined explicitly within the application itself. The reason is that the native types like int and long hide a platform dependency on a machine's word size that can affect the correctness of a computation.

For coding style, we generally only require that all compound statements are enclosed in curly braces, which has a notable impact on code clarity. The simplest way to make sure this rule is consistently followed is to use a automatic code formatter, for example, clang-format.

10.5 Synopsis

The first two rules from the Power of Ten set are meant to guarantee the creation of a clear and transparent control flow structure that is easy to build, test, and analyze. The absence of dynamic memory allocation that is required by the third rule eliminates a class of problems related to the allocation and freeing of memory, and the use of stray pointers. The next four rules are fairly broadly accepted as standards for good coding style. Some benefits of other coding styles that have been advanced for safety critical systems, for example, the discipline of "design by contract" can partly be found in Rules 5–7.

At JPL these ten rules are taken into account in the writing of all safety- and mission-critical software, with very positive results. After overcoming a healthy initial reluctance to live within such strict confines, developers often find that compliance with the rules does tend to improve their code, and reduce the number of issues that need to be chased down later. The rules lessen the burden on the developer and tester to establish key properties of the code (termination or boundedness, safe use of memory and stack, etc.) by other means.

Exceptions to the rules should be rare, but they are of course possible. The main purpose of the Power of Ten rule set is that all exceptions must be justified convincingly. The need for justification is intended to cause a developer to pause and reflect on the issue at hand more carefully. Sometimes it is easier to just comply with a rule than having to explain why this may be unnecessary in a particular case.

When we first introduced the rules, the response was strongly positive, yet almost everyone who responded made an exception for at least one of the rules as going just a little too far. Curiously, each of the ten rules received an equal number of "votes" for being the exception. This may be an indication that the rule set is reasonably balanced.

If the rules seem draconian at first, bear in mind that they are meant to make it possible to check code where very literally your life may depend on its correctness: code that is used to control the airplane that you fly on, the nuclear power plant a few miles from where you live, or the spacecraft that carries astronauts into orbit and perhaps sometime soon to a neighboring planet in the solar system. The rules act like the seat belt in your car: initially, perhaps, a little uncomfortable, but after a while its use becomes second nature and not using them becomes unimaginable.

References

1 L.A. Clarke and D.S. Rosenblum (2006) A historical perspective on runtime assertion checking in software development. *ACM SIGSOFT Software Engineering Notes*, **31** (3), 25–37.

2 G. Kudrjavets, N. Nagappan, and T. Ball (2006) Assessing the relationship between software assertions and code quality: an empirical investigation, Microsoft technical report MSR-TR-2006-54.

11

Seven Principles of Software Testing

Bertrand Meyer

E.T.H. Zürich, Zurich, Switzerland

11.1 Introduction

While everyone knows the theoretical limitations of software testing, in practice we devote considerable effort to this task and would consider it foolish or downright dangerous to skip it. Other verification techniques such as static analysis, model checking, and proofs have great potential, but none is ripe for overtaking tests as the dominant verification technique. This makes it imperative to understand the scope and limitations of testing and perform it right.

The principles that follow emerged from experience studying software testing and developing automated tools such as AutoTest (http://se.inf.ethz.ch/research/autotest).

11.2 Defining Testing

As a verification method, testing is a paradox. Testing a program to assess its quality is, in theory, akin to sticking pins into a doll – very small pins, very large doll. The way out of the paradox is to set realistic expectations.

Too often the software engineering literature claims an overblown role for testing, echoed in the Wikipedia definition (http://en.wikipedia.org/wiki/Software_testing): "Software testing is the process used to assess the quality of computer software. Software testing is an empirical technical investigation conducted to provide stakeholders with information about the quality of the product or service under test, with respect to the context in which it is intended to operate." In truth, testing a program tells us little about its quality, since 10 or even 10 million test runs are a drop in the ocean of possible cases.

Software Technology: 10 Years of Innovation in IEEE Computer, First Edition.
Edited by Mike Hinchey.

There are connections between tests and quality, but they are tenuous: A successful test is only relevant to quality assessment if it previously failed; then it shows the removal of a failure and usually of a fault. (I follow the IEEE standard terminology: An unsatisfactory program execution is a "failure," pointing to a "fault" in the program, itself the result of a "mistake" in the programmer's thinking. The informal term "bug" can refer to any of these phenomena.)

If a systematic process tracks failures and faults, the record might give clues about how many remain. If the last three weekly test runs have evidenced 550, 540, and 530 faults, the trend is encouraging, but the next run is unlikely to find no faults, or 100. (Mathematical reliability models allow more precise estimates, credible in the presence of a sound long-term data collection process.)

The only incontrovertible connection is negative, a falsification in the Popperian sense: A failed test gives us evidence of nonquality. In addition, if the test previously passed, it indicates regression and points to possible quality problems in the program and the development process. The most famous quote by Edsger Dijkstra about testing expressed this memorably: "Program testing can be used to show the presence of bugs, but never to show their absence!"

Less widely understood (and probably not intended by Dijkstra) is what this means for testers: the best possible self-advertisement. Surely, any technique that uncovers faults holds great interest for all "stakeholders," from managers to developers and customers.

Rather than an indictment, we should understand this maxim as a definition of testing. While less ambitious than providing "information about quality," it is more realistic, and directly useful.

Principle 1: Definition
To test a program is to try and make it fail.

This keeps the testing process focused: Its single goal is to uncover faults by triggering failures. Any reference about quality is the responsibility of quality assurance but beyond the scope of testing. The definition also reminds us that testing, unlike debugging, does not deal with correcting faults, only finding them.

11.3 Tests and Specifications

Test-driven development, given prominence by agile methods, has brought tests to the center stage, but sometimes with the seeming implication that tests can be a substitute for specifications. They cannot. Tests, even a million of them, are instances; they miss the abstraction that only a specification can provide.

Principle 2: Tests versus specs
Tests are no substitute for specifications

The danger of believing that a test suite can serve as specification is evidenced by several software disasters that happened because no one had thought of some extreme case. Although specifications can miss cases too, at least they imply an effort at generalization. In particular, specifications can serve to generate tests, even automatically (as in model-driven testing); the reverse is not possible without human intervention.

11.4 Regression Testing

A characteristic of testing as practiced in software is the deplorable propensity of previously corrected faults to resuscitate. The hydra's old heads, thought to have been long cut off, pop back up. This phenomenon is known as regression and leads to regression testing: Checking that what has been corrected still works. A consequence is that once you have uncovered a fault it must remain part of your life forever.

Principle 3: Regression Testing
Any failed execution must yield a test case, to remain a permanent part of the project's test suite.

This principle covers all failures occurring during development and testing. It suggests tools for turning a failed execution into a reproducible test case, as have recently emerged: Contract-Driven Development (CDD), ReCrash, JCrasher.

11.5 Oracles

A test run is only useful if you can unambiguously determine whether it passed. The criterion is called a *test oracle*. If you have a few dozen or perhaps a few hundred tests, you might afford to examine the results individually, but this does not scale up. The task cries for automation.

Principle 4: Applying oracles
Determining success or failure of tests must be an automatic process.

This statement of the principle leaves open the *form* of oracles. Often, oracles are specified separately. In research such as ours, they are built in, as the target software already includes contracts that the tests use as oracles.

Principle 4 (variant): Contracts as oracles
Oracles should be part of the program text, as contracts. Determining test success or failure should be an automatic process consisting of monitoring contract satisfaction during execution.

This principle subsumes the previous one but is presented as a variant so that people who do not use contracts can retain the weaker form.

11.6 Manual and Automatic Test Cases

Many test cases are *manual*: Testers think up interesting execution scenarios and devise tests accordingly. To this category, we may add cases derived – according to Principle 3 – from the failure of an execution not initially intended as a test run. It is becoming increasingly realistic to complement these two categories by *automatic* test cases, derived from the specification through an automatic test generator. A process restricted to manual tests underutilizes the power of modern computers.

The approaches are complementary.

Principle 5: Manual and Automatic Test Cases
An effective testing process must include both manually and automatically produced test cases.

Manual tests are good at depth: They reflect developers' understanding of the problem domain and data structure. Automatic tests are good at breadth: They try many values, including extremes that humans might miss.

11.7 Testing Strategies

We now move from testing practice to research investigating new techniques. Testing research is vulnerable to a risky thought process: You hit upon an idea that seemingly promises improvements and follow your intuition. Testing is tricky; not all clever ideas prove helpful when submitted to objective evaluation.

A typical example is random testing. Intuition suggests that any strategy using knowledge about the program must beat random input. However, objective measures, such as the number of faults found, show that random testing often outperforms supposedly smart ideas. Richard Hamlet's review of random testing [1] provides a fascinating confrontation of folk knowledge and scientific analysis. There is no substitute for empirical assessment.

Principle 6: Empirical assessment of testing strategies
Evaluate any testing strategy, however attractive in principle, through objective assessment using explicit criteria in a reproducible testing process.

I was impressed as a child by reading *The Life of the Bee* [2] by Maurice Maeterlinck (famous as the librettist of Debussy's *Pelléas et Mélisande*) what happens when you put a few bees and a few flies in a bottle and turn the bottom toward a light source. As Figure 11.1 shows, bee, attracted by the light get stuck

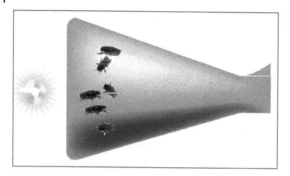

Figure 11.1 Smarter is not always better. Maeterlinck observed that if you put bees and files into a bottle and turn the bottom toward the lights source, the supposedly clever bees, attracted by the light, get stuck and die, while apparently stupid flies get out within a couple of minutes. Is this a metaphor for testing strategies?

and die of hunger or exhaustion; flies do not have a clue and try all directions – getting out within a couple of minutes.

Maeterlinck was a poet, not a professional biologist, and I do not know if the experiment holds up. But it is a good metaphor for cases of apparent stupidity outsmarting apparent cleverness, as happens in testing.

11.8 Assessment Criteria

In applying the last principle, the issue remains of which criteria to use. The testing literature includes measures such as "number of tests to first failure."

For the practitioner this is not the most useful: We want to find all faults, not just one. Granted, the idea is that the first fault will be corrected and the criterion applied again. But successive faults might be of a different nature; an automated process must trigger as many failures as possible, not stop at the first.

The *number* of tests is not that useful to managers, who need help deciding when to stop testing and ship, or to customers, who need an estimate of fault densities. More relevant is the *testing time* needed to uncover the faults. Otherwise, we risk favoring strategies that uncover a failure quickly but only after a lengthy process of devising the test; what counts is total time. This is why, just as flies get out faster than bees, a seemingly dumb strategy such as random testing might be better overall.

Other measures commonly used include test coverage of various kinds (such as instruction, branch, or path coverage). Intuitively, they seem to be useful, but there is little actual evidence that higher coverage has any bearing on quality. In fact, several recent studies suggest a negative correlation; if a module has higher test coverage, this is usually because the team knew it was problematic, and indeed it will often have more faults.

More than any of these metrics what matters is how fast a strategy can produce failures revealing faults.

Principle 7: Assessment criteria
A testing strategy's most important property is the number of faults it uncovers as a function of time.

The relevant function is fault count against time, fc(t), useful in two ways: Researchers using a software base with known faults can assess a strategy by seeing how many of them it finds in a given time; project managers can feed fc(t) into a reliability model to estimate how many faults remain, addressing the age-old question "when do I stop testing?"

11.9 Conclusion

We never strayed far from where we started. The first principle told us that testing is about producing failures; the last one is a quantitative restatement of that general observation, which also underlies all the others.

References

1 R. Hammett (1994) *Encyclopedia of Software Engineering*, J.J. Marciniak, (ed.), Wiley-Interscience, pp. 970–978.
2 M. Maeterlinck (1901) *The Life of the Bee*, Dodd, Mead.

12

Analyzing the Evolution of Database Usage in Data-Intensive Software Systems

Loup Meurice,[1] Mathieu Goeminne,[2] Tom Mens,[2]
Csaba Nagy,[1] Alexandre Decan,[2] and Anthony Cleve[1]

[1]*PReCISE Research Center on Information Systems Engineering, Faculty of Computer Science, University of Namur, Namur, Belgium*
[2]*COMPLEXYS Research Institute, Software Engineering Lab, Faculty of Sciences, University of Mons, Mons, Belgium*

12.1 Introduction

The August 2010 *IEEE Computer* column [1] reported on four important challenges that developers of evolving *data-intensive software systems* (DISS) are confronted with. By *data-intensive* we understand any *software system* (i.e., a collection of programs implementing the business logic) that strongly interacts with a *database* (containing the business data, e.g., customers, invoices, shipments, that form an accurate image of the business). While the software system is implemented in one or more programming languages (e.g., Java), the business data is managed by a (often relational) database management system (DBMS). The database is structured according to a schema that faithfully models the business structure and its rules.

It is widely known that any software system is subject to frequent changes [2]. These changes can have many causes, including requirements changes, technological changes (e.g., new technology or new languages), and structural changes that aim to improve quality (in either the programs or the data). While both the software and database engineering research communities have addressed such evolution problems separately, the challenge is how to cope with the coevolution of the software system and its data system.

The link between the software part and the data part of a data-intensive system is ensured through some API, library, or framework that takes care of connecting the program code to the database. In the simplest case, the code will contain embedded database queries (e.g., SQL statements) that will be

Software Technology: 10 Years of Innovation in IEEE Computer, First Edition.
Edited by Mike Hinchey.
© 2018 the IEEE Computer Society, Inc. Published 2018 by John Wiley & Sons, Inc.

dynamically built by the application programs and then interpreted by the DBMS. In more complex cases, especially for object-oriented programming languages such as Java, object-relational mappings (ORM) will be provided to translate the concepts used by the program (e.g., classes, methods, and attributes) into concepts used by the database (e.g., tables, columns, and values).

While an ORM mainly serves to tackle the so-called *object-relational impedance mismatch* [3], this comes at a certain cost. For instance, ORM middleware provides programmers an external, object-oriented view on the physical, relational database schema. Both schemas can evolve asynchronously, each at their own pace, often under the responsibility of independent teams. Severe inconsistencies between system components may then progressively emerge due to undisciplined evolution processes. In addition, the high level of dynamicity of current database access technologies makes it hard for a programmer to figure out which SQL queries will be executed at a given location of the program source code, or which source code methods access a particular database table or column. Things may become even worse when multiple database access technologies coexist within the same software system. In such a context, coevolving the database and the program requires mastering several different languages, frameworks, and APIs.

This chapter reports on the research progress we have recently achieved in this domain, and situates it in the light of the achievements of other researchers. Our research has been focused on Java projects, because Java is one of the most popular object-oriented programming languages today, and because it offers a wide variety of frameworks and APIs for providing an ORM or other means of communication with a DBMS. To better understand how the use of such technologies within software projects evolves over time, we carried out empirical studies at different levels of granularity. At a coarse-grained level, we analyzed and compared the evolution of database technologies used in the source code of thousands of Java projects. At a fine-grained level, we studied the coevolution between database schema changes and source code changes, focusing on a limited number of Java systems and database technologies.

This chapter is structured as follows. Section 12.2 presents the state of the art in research on the evolution of data-intensive software systems, and puts our own research into perspective. Section 12.3 provides an overview of the empirical approach that we have been following to study the coevolution of Java-based software systems interacting with relational database systems. Section 12.4 presents some of the findings based on a coarse-grained empirical analysis of several thousands of systems. Section 12.5 explores three such systems at a fine-grained level of detail, studying the coevolution between their software and database parts, taking into account the ORM that relates them. Section 12.6 concludes the chapter and Section 12.7 presents some open avenues of further research.

12.2 State of the Art

While the literature on database schema evolution is very large [4], few authors have proposed approaches to systematically *observe* how developers cope with database evolution in practice. Sjøberg [5] presented a study where the schema evolution history of a large-scale medical application is measured and interpreted. Curino et al. [6] focused on the structural evolution of the Wikipedia database, with the aim to extract both a micro- and a macroclassification of schema changes. Vassiliadis et al. [7] studied the evolution of individual database tables over time in eight different software systems. They also tried to determine whether Lehman's laws of software evolution hold for evolving database schemas as well [8]. They conclude that the essence of Lehman's laws remains valid in this context, but that specific mechanics significantly differ when it comes to schema evolution.

Several researchers have tried to identify, extract, and analyze database *usage* in application programs. The purpose of the proposed approaches ranges from error checking [9–11], over SQL fault localization [12], to fault diagnosis [13]. More recently, Linares-Vasquez et al. [14] studied how developers *document* database usage in source code. Their results show that a large proportion of database-accessing methods is completely undocumented.

Several researchers have also studied the problem of database schema evolution *in combination* with source code evolution. Maule et al. [15] studied a commercial object-oriented content management system to statically analyze the impact of relational database schema changes on the source code. Chen et al. [16] proposed a static code analysis framework for detecting and fixing performance issues and potential bugs in ORM usage. Their analysis revealed that the modifications made after analysis caused an important improvement of the studied systems' response time. Qiu et al. [17] empirically analyzed the coevolution of relational database schemas and code in 10 open-source database applications from various domains. They studied specific change types inside the database schema and the impact of such changes on PHP code. Karahasanović [18] studied how the maintenance of application consistency can be supported by identifying and visualizing the impacts of changes in evolving object-oriented systems, including changes originating from a database schema. However, he focused on object-oriented databases rather than relational databases. Lin and Neamtiu [19] studied the so-called *collateral* evolution of applications and databases, in which the evolution of an application is separated from the evolution of its persistent data, or from the database. They investigated how application programs and database management systems in popular open-source systems (Mozilla, Monotone) cope with database schema changes and database format changes. They observed that collateral evolution can lead to potential problems.

From a less technical point of view, Riaz et al. [20] conducted a survey with software professionals in order to determine the main characteristics that predict maintainability of relational database-driven software applications. It would be interesting to see to which extent these subjective opinions obtained from professionals, correspond to the actual maintainability problems that can be observed by analyzing the evolution history of the source code and database schemas directly.

12.2.1 Our Own Research

Our own research focuses on the empirical analysis of the coevolution of object-oriented code and relational database schemas, restricted mainly to open-source Java systems and ORM technologies, and studying both the technical and social aspects.

In Ref. [21], we empirically analyzed the evolution of the usage of SQL, Hibernate, and JPA in *OSCAR*, a large and complex open-source information system that has been implemented in Java. We observed a migration to ORM and persistence technologies offered by Hibernate and JPA, but the practice of using embedded SQL code still remains prevalent today. Contrary to our intuition, we did not find a specialization of developers toward specific database-related activities: the majority of developers appeared to be active in both database-unrelated and database-related activities during the considered time period. As a parallel research track, we validated on the *OSCAR* system a tool-supported method for analyzing the evolution history of legacy databases [22]. We extracted the logical schema for each system version from the SQL files collected from the versioning system. Then, we incrementally built a historical schema that we visualized and analyzed further. This analysis focused on the database and did not consider the application code. In Ref. [23], we studied both the database schema and the application code in order to identify referential integrity constraints. We demonstrated our approach on the Oscar system by searching foreign key candidates. We analyzed the database schema, the embedded SQL statements in the Java code, and the JPA object model. In Ref. [24], we presented a tool-supported technique allowing to locate the source code origin of a given SQL query in hybrid data-intensive systems that rely on JDBC, Hibernate, and/or JPA to access their database.

Complementing the research of Ref. [21], in Ref. [25] we carried out a coarse-grained historical analysis of the usage of Java relational database technologies (primarily JDBC, Hibernate, Spring, JPA, and Vaadin) on several thousands of open-source Java projects extracted from a GitHub corpus consisting of over 13K active projects [26]. Using the statistical technique of survival analysis, we explored the survival of the database technologies in the considered projects. In particular, we analyzed whether certain technologies co-occur frequently, and whether some technologies get replaced over time by others. We observed that some combinations of database technologies appeared to complement and reinforce one another. We did not observe any evidence of technologies disappearing at the expense of others.

With respect to tool support, we developed DAHLIA, a tool to visually analyze the database schema evolution [27]. DAHLIA provides support for both 2D and 3D visualization. The 2D mode proposes an interactive panel to investigate the database objects (e.g., tables, columns, foreign keys, and indexes) of the historical schema and query their respective history. The 3D mode makes use of the city metaphor of CodeCity [28].

12.3 Analyzing the Usage of ORM Technologies in Database-Driven Java Systems

For the current chapter, we limited ourselves to mine historical information from large *open-source Java systems*. The choice for Java is because it is the most popular programming language today according to different sources such as the TIOBE Programming Community index (August 2015). In addition to this, a large number of technologies and frameworks have been provided to facilitate database access from within Java code.

The choice for open-source systems is motivated by the accessibility of source code. The source code development history for the chosen systems was extracted from the project repositories available through the Git distributed version control system. This enables us to analyze the evolution over time of the project activity and the database usage by the considered systems.

A large-scale empirical analysis, carried out in Ref. [25], revealed that a wide range of frameworks and APIs are used by open-source Java projects to facilitate relational database access. These technologies operate on different levels of abstraction. For example, as illustrated in Figure 12.1, a developer can simply choose to embed character strings that represent SQL statements in the source code. The SQL queries are sent to the database through a connector like JDBC, which provides a low-level abstraction of SQL-based database access.

Interaction with the database can also be realized using an ORM library. These libraries offer a higher level of abstraction based on a mapping between Java classes and database tables. The mapping can take many different forms, as illustrated in Figure 12.2. The first example shows the use of Hibernate configuration files (i.e., .hbm.xml). The second example illustrates the use of Java annotations based on JPA, the standard API in Java for ORM and data persistence management. Such a mapping may allow direct operations on objects, attributes, and relationships instead of tables and columns. This is commonly referred as the *active record pattern*.

Some ORM libraries also provide SQL-inspired languages that allow to write SQL-like queries using the mappings defined before. The third example in Figure 12.2 illustrates the Hibernate Query Language (HQL) and the fourth

Source code and libraries

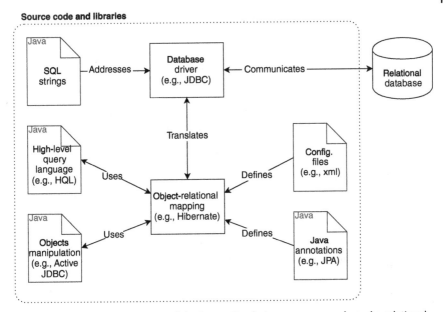

Figure 12.1 Schematic overview of the interaction between source code and a relational database.

example uses ActiveJDBC, a Java implementation of the ActiveRecord ORM from Ruby on Rails.

There are also popular web application frameworks with database access APIs among their features. For instance, the *Spring* framework provides interfaces to make it easier to use JPA or to access a database through JDBC. It offers solutions for resource management, data access object (DAO) implementations, or transaction handling. Typically, it supports the integration with popular ORM frameworks such as Hibernate.

12.3.1 Coevolution

The plethora of different database access technologies available for Java systems, combined with the omnipresence of relational SQL-based database technologies, inspired us to study the problem of coevolution from two different points of view.

From a coarse-grained, general point of view, we want to understand if and how different database access technologies for Java are used together and how this evolves over time. Do some technologies reinforce one another? Do newer technologies tend to replace older ones? Since the use of database access technologies may differ significantly from one Java system to another, an answer to such questions requires a large-scale longitudinal study over several

Example of using Hibernate configuration files:

```
1  <hibernate-mapping>
2    <class name="Customer" table="AppCustomers">
3      <id name="id" type="int" column="id"/>
4      <property name="name" column="name" type="String"/>
5    </class>
6  </hibernate-mapping>
```

Example of using JPAannotations:

```
1  @Entity
2  @Table(name="AppCustomers")
3  public class Customer {
4    @Id
5    private int id;
6    String name;
7    [...]
8  }
```

Example of using Hibernate Query Language (HQL):

```
1  public List<Customer> findAllCustomers(){
2    String hql = "select c from Customer c";
3    return executeQuery(hql);
4  }
5  public List executeQuery(String hql){
6    return session.createQuery(hql).list();
7  }
8  public Customer findCustomer(Integer id){
9    return (Customer) session.get(Customer.class, id);
10 }
```

Example of direct object manipulation using ActiveJDBC:

```
1  List<Customer> customers = Customer.where("name = 'John Doe'");
2  Customer john = customers.get(0);
3  john.setName("John Smith");
4  john.saveIt();
```

Figure 12.2 Four examples of Java ORM usage.

hundreds or thousands of Java projects in order to come to conclusive, statistically relevant results. This is what we will present in Section 12.4.

From a fine-grained, system-specific point of view, we also want to determine how database tables and columns evolve over time, and how given database tables and columns are accessed by the program's source code (e.g., through which technologies, in which classes and methods, through which queries, etc.). Addressing such questions is highly useful in the context of data-intensive systems maintenance; in particular to achieve a graceful coevolution of the database and the programs. The answers to those questions being system specific, they cannot be generalized. Therefore, Section

12.5 will focus on automated fine-grained analysis of three particular data-intensive systems.

12.4 Coarse-Grained Analysis of Database Technology Usage

Despite the fact that database technologies are crucial for connecting the source code to the database, a detailed study of their usage and their evolution is generally neglected in scientific studies. At a coarse-grained level of abstraction, we wish to understand how existing open-source Java systems rely on relational database technologies, and how the use of such technologies evolves over time.

By doing so, we aim to provide to developers and project managers a historical overview of database technologies usage that helps them to evaluate the risks and the advantages of using a technology or a combination of technologies. In particular, empirical studies can help to determine if (and which) database technologies are often replaced and if they can remain used in Java projects for a long time before becoming completed with or substituted by another technology.

12.4.1 Selected Java Projects and Relational Database Technologies

In order to carry out such a coarse-grained empirical study, we extracted Java projects from the *Github Java Corpus* proposed by Allamanis and Sutton [26]. In total, we studied 13,307 Java projects that still had an available Git repository on March 24, 2015. By skimming recent scientific publications, Stack Exchange, and blog posts, we identified 26 potential relational database technologies for Java. As a constraint, we imposed that the chosen technologies need to have at least a direct means of accessing a relational database. They also need to be identifiable by static analysis. We determined the presence of each of these technologies in each of the 13,307 projects by analyzing the import statements in Java files, as well as the presence of specific configuration files. For the first commit of each month of each considered Java project, we retraced a historical view of the files that can be related to a particular technology or to a particular framework.

This left us with 4503 Java projects using at least one of the considered database technologies. Based on this first collection of Java projects and database technologies, we narrowed down our selection to consider only the most popular technologies. We identified four technologies that were each used in at least 5% of all considered Java projects in our collection: JDBC (used in

Table 12.1 Selected Java database technologies.

Used technology	URL	Occurs if the project contains at least a file	#projects
JDBC	www.oracle.com/ technetwork/java/ javase/jdbc	Importing java.sql	2008
JPA	www.tutorialspoint .com/jpa	Importing javax.persistence or java. persistence, or whose filename is meta-inf/persistence.xml	1075
Spring	projects.spring.io/ spring-framework	Importing org.springframework or whose name is spring-config.xml or beans.xml	759
Hibernate	hibernate.org	Importing org.hibernate or whose filename ends with .hbm.xml	718

15.1% of all 4503 projects), JPA (8.1%), Spring (5.7%), and Hibernate (5.4%). The results are summarized in Table 12.1.

Of all considered Java projects in our collection, only 2818 of them used at least one of these four technologies at least once. In the remainder of this section, we will, therefore, focus only on these four technologies and the 2818 Java projects that use them.

Table 12.2 presents some size and duration metrics over these 2818 Java projects. We observe that the distribution of metrics values is highly skewed, suggesting evidence of the Pareto principle [29].

12.4.2 Evolution of Database Technology Usage

Since our goal is to study the evolution of database technology usage over time in Java projects, Figure 12.3 visualizes the evolution over time of the occurrence

Table 12.2 Characteristics of the 2818 considered Java projects.

	Mean	Standard deviation	Minimum	Median	Maximum
Number of days between first and last considered commit	950.8	999.3	0	701	6,728
Number of commits	1245.1	5781.6	1	123.5	174,618
Number of distinct contributors	12.1	29.6	1	4	1,091
Number of files in latest version	1001.2	3384.1	1	195	103,493

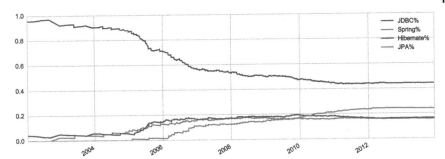

Figure 12.3 Evolution of the share of each technology T ∈ {JDBC, Hibernate, JPA, Spring}.

of the retained technologies in the considered projects. For each technology, T ∈ {JDBC, Hibernate, JPA, Spring}, the y-axis shows the fraction

$$\frac{\text{number of projects using technology T}}{\text{number of projects using any of the 4 considered technologies}}$$

Intuitively, Figure 12.3 reveals the relative importance (in terms of number of projects) of one technology over another one. (The sum of shares is sometimes greater than 1 because some projects use multiple technologies simultaneously.)

We observe that **JDBC was and remains the most frequent technology**, which is not surprising since it provides the basic means for connecting to a database and handling SQL queries. Nevertheless, **the share of JDBC appears to be decreasing since 2008**, which coincides with the emergence of JPA. We also observe that Hibernate and Spring obtained their maximum before 2010 and since then their shares are slowly decreasing. We hypothesize that this is due to JPA becoming more popular and partially overtaking the other technologies. Indeed, of the four considered technologies, **only JPA's share continues to grow over the considered timeframe.**

12.4.3   Co-Occurrence of Database Technologies

Considering the four selected relational database technologies, which combinations of them frequently co-occur in our selection of Java projects? Such information would reveal which technologies are complementary, and which technologies are used as supporting technologies of other ones.

Let us consider the technologies appearing at least once in the entire lifetime of each considered project. Figure 12.4 shows the number of projects in which a combination of technologies has been detected. A first observation is that **JDBC is the sole technology in 62% of all projects** (1239 out of 2008). A possible interpretation is that, in many cases, the services provided by JDBC are considered as sufficient by the developers, and the advantages provided by

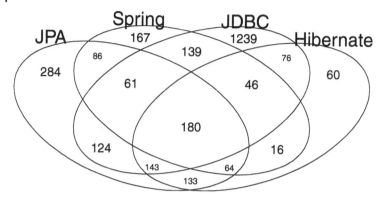

Figure 12.4 Number of projects for each combination of database technologies.

more advanced technologies do not justify the *cost* of their introduction. On the other hand, we observe that **a large proportion of projects that make use of another technology also make use of JDBC.** For instance, Hibernate is used alone in only 8% of all projects (60/718), and a majority (62%) of all projects that make use of Hibernate also make use of JDBC (but not necessarily at the same time in their history).

Something similar can be observed for JDBC and JPA. JPA occurs in isolation in 26% of all projects, while almost half (47%) of all projects that make use of JPA also make use of JDBC. Considering the four selected technologies, **38% of all projects used at least two technologies over their observed lifetime.**

These high numbers could be due to the fact that some technologies are used as supporting or complementary technologies for others. More specifically, the low-level JDBC is probably punctually used to express complex queries that cannot be expressed – or are difficult to express – with higher level technologies. However, the reason why 180 of the 2818 considered projects have used all of the four technologies simultaneously remains unknown.

While Figure 12.4 shows that most projects use several database technologies over their lifetime, it does not provide information about their actual co-occurrences. We therefore compared, for each project, the overall number of detected technologies through the entire lifetime and the maximum number of simultaneously present (i.e., *co-occurring*) technologies. Table 12.3 presents the detected co-occurrences of technologies. We observed that **in more than 80% of all cases, different database technologies tend to co-occur together in a project.** This represents 887 co-occurrences for 1068 projects with at least two technologies in their whole lifetime.

While the four technologies present comparable numbers of projects in which they co-occur, these numbers are proportionally very different. For example, **while only 37% of the occurrences of JDBC coincide with another technology, 91% of the occurrences of Hibernate coincide with another technology.**

Table 12.3 Number of projects in which a technology was used (column 2); absolute and relative number of projects in with the technology co-occurred with one of the 3 other technologies (column 3); absolute and relative number of projects in which a specific pair of database technologies co-occurs (columns 4–7).

Technology	# Projects	Co-occurrences with any of the three other technologies	Co-occurrences with			
			JDBC	Spring	Hibernate	JPA
JDBC	2008	743 (37%)	–	363 (49%)	396 (53%)	454 (61%)
Spring	759	582 (77%)	363 (62%)	–	278 (48%)	358 (62%)
Hibernate	718	652 (**91%**)	396 (61%)	278 (43%)	–	502 (**77%**)
JPA	1075	771 (72%)	454 (59%)	358 (46%)	502 (65%)	–

If we zoom in closer, **we observe a co-occurrence with JPA for 77% of all projects in which Hibernate occurs**. This is the highest observed percentage of co-occurrences. On the opposite side of the spectrum, we find that only 43% of all projects in which Hibernate occurs, co-occur with Spring. This is the lowest observed percentage of co-occurrences. Of all considered pairs of technologies, **Spring and Hibernate are used together the least frequently**.

12.4.4 Introduction and Disappearance of Database Technologies

Introducing a new database technology in a software project comes at a certain cost. Therefore, a common policy is to introduce a new technology only if the expected benefits outweigh the expected cost. Examples of such benefits are more efficient services, increased modularity, and a simpler implementation or maintenance.

For each project, we analyzed at what moment in the project's lifetime each occurring database technology got introduced or disappeared. We observed that the answer was strongly related to the duration and size of the considered projects. To take into account the effect of project duration, we normalized the lifetime of each project into a range of values between 0 (the start of the project) and 1 (the last considered commit). To study the effect of project size, we split our project corpus into two equally sized subsets containing the small and the large projects, respectively. Project size was measured as number of files in the latest revision (see Table 12.2). All small projects contained less than 195 files.

(a)
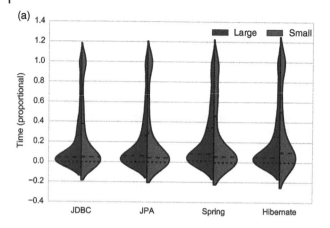

(b)
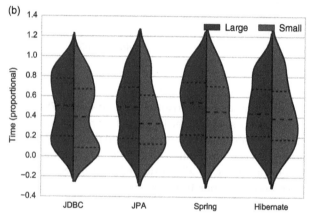

Figure 12.5 Relative time of introduction and disappearance of database technologies. Horizontal dashed lines represent the quartiles of the distribution.

Figure 12.5 shows the relative moment in the project history where each of the considered technologies has been introduced (Figure 12.5a) or removed (Figure 12.5b). Projects in which the considered technology did not disappear before the last observable commit have been disregarded. For both small and large projects, **over 50% of the introductions of a technology are done very early in the projects' life** (in the first 15% of their lifetime). This is what one would expect, since a database (and by extension, a database access technology) is usually part of a project specification since its beginning.

In Figure 12.5, the distribution of the time of technology removal is much less skewed than the distribution of the time of technology introduction. We do not observe particular difference across technologies. Overall, **technologies tend to disappear faster in small than in large projects**, especially for JDBC and JPA.

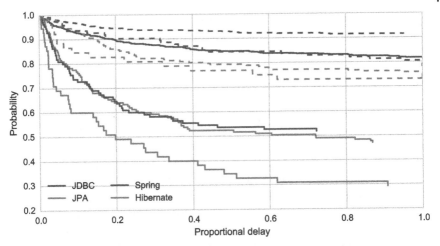

Figure 12.6 Probability that a technology remains the last introduced technology over time.

As many projects use multiple technologies, either simultaneously or one after the other, it is useful to study how the introduction of a new technology can affect the presence of a previous one. We used the statistical technique of *survival analysis* to study this question. This technique creates a model estimating the *survival rate* of a population over time, considering the fact that some elements of the population may leave the study, and for some other elements the event of interest does not occur during the observation period. In our case, the observed event is the introduction of a second technology after the introduction of a previously occurring one.

Figure 12.6 presents the results of the survival analysis, distinguishing the small projects (dashed lines) from the large ones (straight lines). The survival rates of technologies in large projects are significantly lower than for small projects, implying that **new technologies are introduced more often and more quickly in large projects than in small ones**. The survival rates are also significantly higher for JDBC than for the other technologies, both for small and large projects. This indicates that **JPA, Spring, and Hibernate rarely succeed JDBC and, if they do, it happens later and more uniformly**. Among the possible explanations, JDBC may be sufficient to satisfy the initial requirements of most projects, while new technologies are only introduced as these requirements change and grow over time.

Figure 12.6 also reveals that Hibernate has a much lower survival rate than the other technologies. Both small and large **projects tend to complete or to replace Hibernate more often than any other technology**. Finally, we observe that during the first 10% of the projects' lifetime, the survival rates of Hibernate decrease by 15% (with respect to 40%) that represents a more important decrease than for the other technologies, which means that **Hibernate is usually quickly followed or complemented by another technology.**

12.4.5 Discussion

We collected and analyzed data for more than 13 K Java projects. Of these, 4503 projects used at least one out of 26 identified Java relational database technologies. Among these technologies, JDBC, JPA, Hibernate, and Spring were the most widely used, covering 2818 of all Java projects. We, therefore, analyzed the evolution and co-occurrences of those four technologies in order to get a high-level view of their usage in Java projects. As projects often make use of these technologies either simultaneously or one after the other, we deepened our analyses to identify the most frequently co-occurring pairs of technologies, and to determine how fast a technology tends to be replaced by or completed by another one. This coarse-grained analysis allowed us to observe some interesting global trends concerning the four considered technologies (highlighted in **boldface** in the previous sections).

While a coarse-grained analysis may help to identify such global trends, a more fine-grained analysis is required to target more specific research questions. How and why do developers decide to introduce new database technologies to complement existing ones? How and where are particular technologies used in the source code? Are the same database schema elements covered by different technologies? Do particular code files involve different technologies?

In addition to this, a fine-grained analysis may help to reveal whether the use of particular technologies is in line with the evolution of the database schema. Are some parts of the code out-of-date with respect to the database schema? Is it easier to detect and address these inconsistencies with some of the technologies? Which typical workflows can we observe in the usage of those technologies? Can we quantify and compare the impact on the code of a database change? These are the types of questions that will be targeted in Section 12.5.

12.5 Fine-Grained Analysis of Database Technology Usage

12.5.1 Analysis Background

In our fine-grained analysis, we investigate in the source code and the database schema how some measurable characteristics of database usage in data-intensive systems evolve over time. Our objective is to understand, at a fine-grained level, how the systems evolve over time, how the database and code coevolve and how several technologies may coexist in the same system.

Table 12.4 Main characteristics of the selected systems.

System	Description	KLOC	Start date
OSCAR	EMR system	>2000	11/2002
OpenMRS	EMR system	>300	05/2006
Broadleaf	E-commerce framework	>250	12/2008

We studied the evolution of three large open-source Java systems (*OSCAR*, *OpenMRS*, and *Broadleaf Commerce*) that have been developed for more than 7 years, and rely on the database access technologies that we studied in the coarse-grained analysis of Section 12.4. Two of these systems are popular, electronic medical record (EMR) systems and the third one is an e-commerce framework. All three use a relational database for data persistence and deal with a large amount of data. Hence, they are real representatives of data-intensive software systems. Table 12.4 presents an overview of the main characteristics of the selected software systems.

OSCAR (oscar-emr.com) is an open-source EMR information system that is widely used in the health care industry in Canada. Its primary purpose is to maintain electronic patient records and interfaces of a variety of other information systems used in the health care industry. *OSCAR* has been developed since 2002. The source code comprises approximately two million lines of code. *OSCAR* combines different ways to access the database because of the constant and ongoing evolution history of the product: the developers originally used JDBC, then Hibernate, and more recently JPA. We empirically confirmed these findings in Ref. [21].

OpenMRS (openmrs.org) is a collaborative open-source project to develop software to support the delivery of health care in developing countries (mainly in Africa). It was conceived as a general-purpose EMR system that could support the full range of medical treatments. It has been developed since 2006. *OpenMRS* uses a MySQL database accessed via Hibernate and dynamic SQL (JDBC).

Broadleaf (www.broadleafcommerce.org) is an open-source, e-commerce framework written entirely in Java on top of the Spring framework. It facilitates the development of enterprise-class, commerce-driven sites by providing a robust data model, services, and specialized tooling that take care of most of the "heavy lifting" work. *Broadleaf* has been developed since 2008. It uses a relational database accessed by the source code via JPA.

For all the systems, we performed a static analysis on the source code of selected revisions from the version control systems. First, we picked the initial commits and then we went on through the next revisions and selected those which were at least 15 days from the last selected revision and contained at least

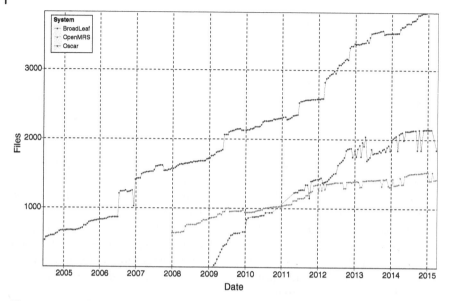

Figure 12.7 Evolution over time of the number of files in each system.

500 modified lines. As a result, we have a snapshot of the state of each system in every 2–3 weeks of its development. This extraction process is detailed in Refs [24] and [27]. As is customary for many open-source projects, the number of code files of each system grows more or less linearly over time (see Figure 12.7).

12.5.2 Conceptual Schema

We developed static analyzers to compute size metrics of the source code and the database schema. We also identified the database access points in the source code where the database is accessed through JDBC, Hibernate, or JPA. These access points could be simple CRUD (create, read, update, or delete) operations, or locations where the system queries the database with native SQL or HQL queries.

We used the gathered information to build a generic conceptual schema of all the different artifacts that can be analyzed historically in a given data-intensive system. This schema is presented in Figure 12.8 (it was created using DB-Main tool [30]). The central element is Version, which assigns a unique version identifier to the other artifacts, in order to be able to analyze the evolution of each program component and data component of the system over time. The green elements in the figure represent the source code components (e.g., File, Class, Method, and Attribute – each of them has its own definition at a

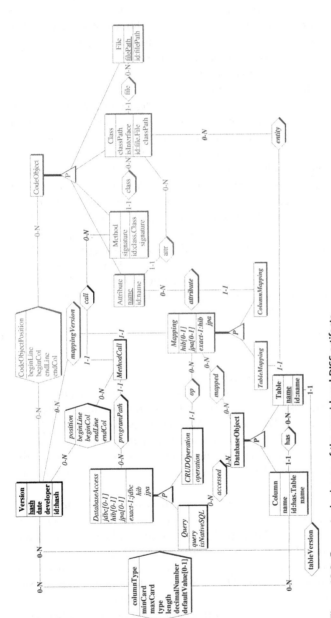

Figure 12.8 Conceptual schema of the considered DISS artifacts.

particular position in the code, expressed as a couple of coordinates: a begin line and column, and an end line and column). The text in bold represents the database components (e.g., Table and Column). The text in italic represents the DatabaseAccess (e.g., Query and CRUDOperation). Such database accesses appear in the program code as MethodCall to particular methods (at a particular position in the code) that are part of the API, library of framework that takes care of the database access. Database queries (e.g., SQL queries) may be embedded in the code and provide a direct access to some DatabaseObject. Alternatively, the database access may take place through some ORM Mapping (shown by the bold italic text in the figure).

Let us illustrate the use of our conceptual schema. Figure 12.2 shows a sample of Java code using Hibernate for accessing the database in a given system version. In that piece of code, in particular in the third example, one easily detects the presence of two database accesses: line 9 retrieves the customer corresponding to a given id, whereas line 3 executes an HQL query selecting all the customers recorded in the system. The first access makes use of Customer, a mapped entity Class located in File/src/pojo/Customer.java, to query the database. Customer is mapped (Mapping) to the AppCustomers Table. Line 9 is a Hibernate DatabaseAccess and more precisely a CRUDOperation (of type Read). The ProgramPath of the read access has a length of 1 and is a MethodCall to findCustomer Method at line 9 (position). The second database access is an HQL Query accessing the AppCustomers Table and has a ProgramPath of length 2: a MethodCall to findAllCustomers Method at line 3 and a second to executeQuery Method at line 6.

12.5.3 Metrics

By exploiting this conceptual schema, we studied and measured some characteristics of the three systems at different levels. For measuring those characteristics, we successively analyzed each selected version in order to observe how the systems evolve over time. We, respectively, selected 242, 164, and 118 versions for *OSCAR*, *OpenMRS*, and *Broadleaf*. We now present the different metrics used to measure the characteristics of each system at the code and database schema levels as well as metrics pertaining to the coevolution of both.

Each of the three considered systems appears to have its own specific database schema growth trend. Figure 12.9 depicts, for each system, the evolution of the number of tables. While the schema of *OSCAR* continuously grows over time, *OpenMRS* and *Broadleaf* seem to have a more *periodic* growth. Table 12.5 shows the number of database changes occurred in the life of each system. There are fewer changes in the *OpenMRS* schema. Its developers rarely remove tables and columns and have a well-prepared extension phase with the addition of 21 tables in November 2011. Except for this period of growth, the schema size

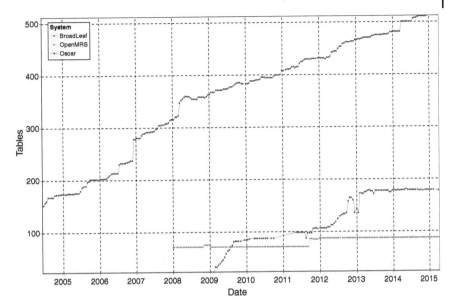

Figure 12.9 Evolution of the number of tables over time.

remains constant. After an initial phase of growth (up to October 2009), the *Broadleaf* schema remained more or less stable until June 2012. From there until February 2013, the schema underwent a strong growth, followed again by a stable phase. Nevertheless, during that stable period, we observe some schema changes with successive additions and removals of tables. A more detailed analysis revealed that those changes correspond to a renaming phase of some tables.

In order to study the coevolution between the source code and the database schema, we focused on three artifacts of our conceptual schema: (1) the tables that are accessed and the way to access them (Figure 12.10); (2) the locations of code and files accessing the database (respectively Figures 12.11 and 12.12); and (3) the distribution of mappings across ORM technologies (Figure 12.13).

Table 12.5 Number of database schema changes in the systems' life.

System	#Added tables	#Added columns	#Deleted tables	#Deleted columns
Oscar	391	12597	32	2442
OpenMRS	27	438	11	100
Broadleaf	240	1425	86	584

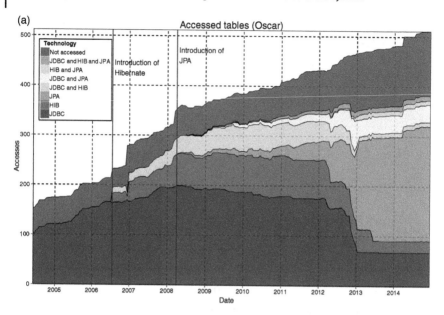

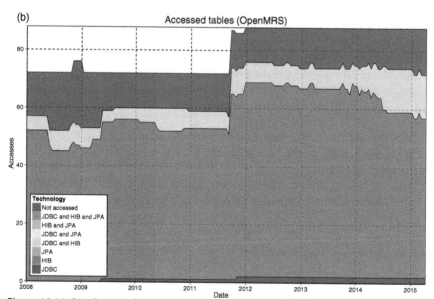

Figure 12.10 Distribution of the accessed tables across the technologies.

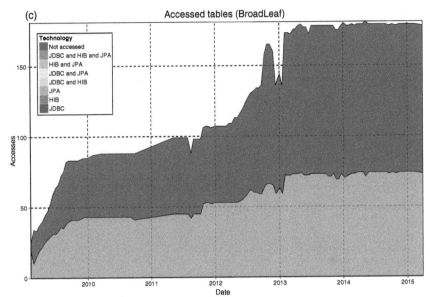

Figure 12.10 (*Continued*)

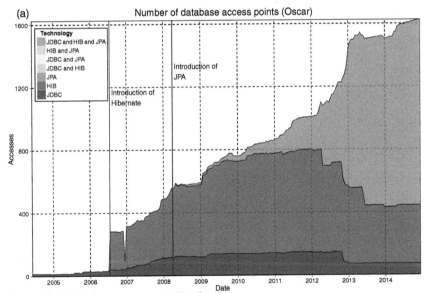

Figure 12.11 Database access point distribution.

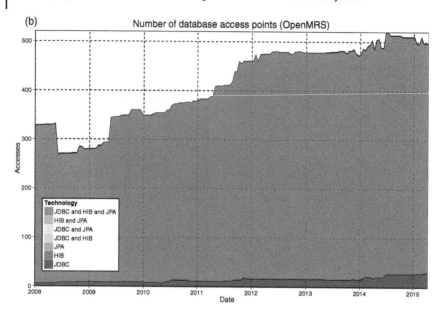

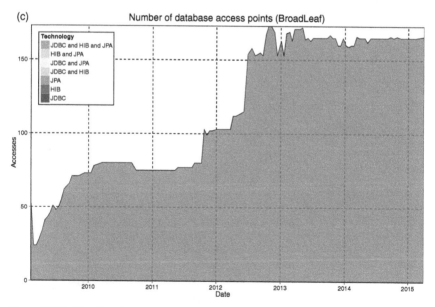

Figure 12.11 (*Continued*)

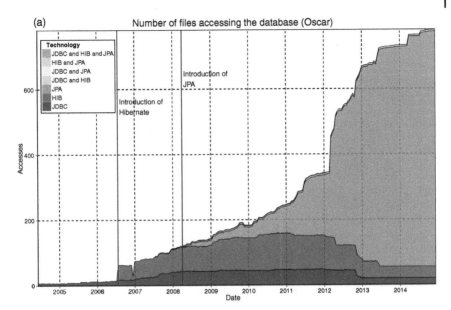

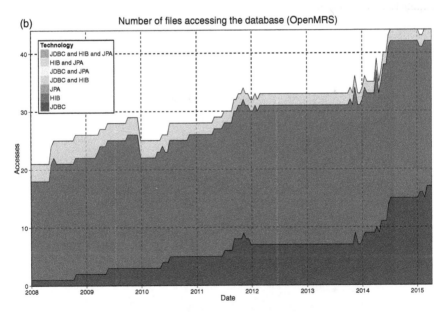

Figure 12.12 The distribution of the files accessing the database.

(c)

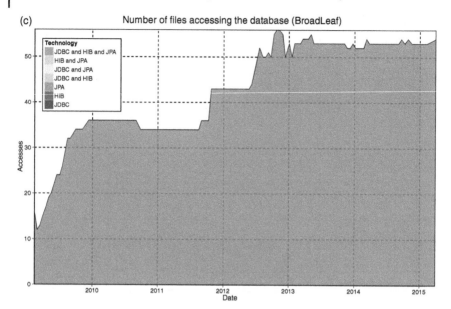

Figure 12.12 (*Continued*)

(a)

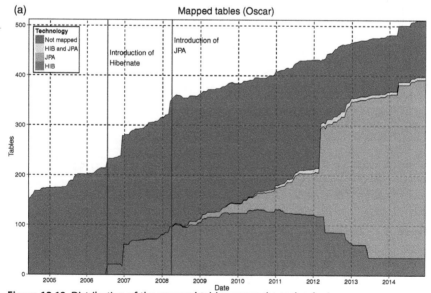

Figure 12.13 Distribution of the mapped tables across the technologies.

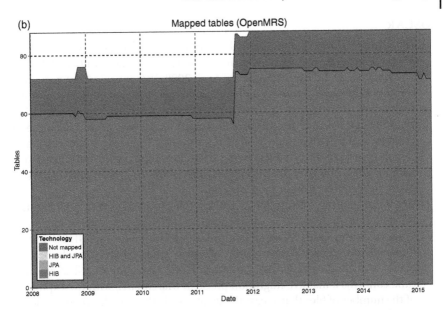

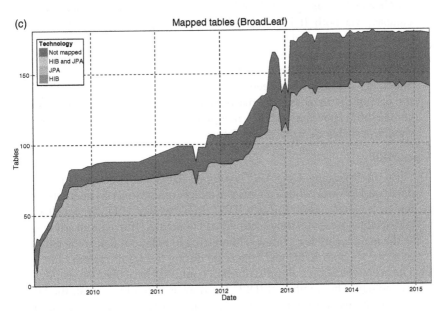

Figure 12.13 (*Continued*)

OSCAR

1) Initially, *OSCAR* only used the JDBC API to access the database. In August 2006, Hibernate was introduced in the system, but the number of JDBC-accessed tables did not decrease. In April 2008, JPA appeared but remained infrequently used up to March 2012. While JDBC was the prevailing technology (in terms of accessed tables) until there, a massive migration phase happened, and JPA became the main technology with a decrease of Hibernate and JDBC usage. Today, the three technologies still coexist, and we observe that many tables in the database are accessed by at least two technologies. This may be considered a sign of bad coding practices, or a still ongoing technology migration process.

2) The database access location distribution follows a different trend. Until the introduction of JPA, there was a majority of Hibernate access locations. Once JPA was introduced, the number of Hibernate and JDBC access locations progressively decreased. We also analyzed the distribution of database technologies across Java files. Here again, the distribution over time confirms a massive migration phase in March 2012 with the explosion of the number of files that access the database via JPA and the decrease of the number of files using JDBC or Hibernate. Some files allow accessing the database via both JDBC and Hibernate and might indicate bad coding practices or nonended migration.

3) The observed migration phase also impacts the ORM mappings defined between the Java classes and the database tables. The majority of the Hibernate mappings has been replaced by JPA mappings. Nevertheless, a big part of the database schema remains *unmapped*. A small set of tables contain both Hibernate and JPA mappings, which is a potential problem that should probably be fixed in the future.

OpenMRS

1) Since the beginning, *OpenMRS* combined JDBC and Hibernate to query its database. However, while a majority of tables are accessed via Hibernate, only a few tables are accessed through JDBC. In November 2011, almost all the 21 added tables are exclusively accessed via Hibernate. Hibernate clearly appears as the main technology, but it is interesting to point out that some tables are accessed via both JDBC and Hibernate during the whole system's life.

2) The access location point distribution confirms that Hibernate is the main technology. The number of JDBC locations is much lower than the Hibernate locations and the number of Hibernate files is the predominant part. What is more surprising is the increasing number of JDBC files in comparison to the limited number of tables accessed via JDBC.

3) Since we observed that Hibernate was the main technology and also the only used ORM, it is not astounding to see that the majority of tables are mapped to Java classes.

Broadleaf

1) *Broadleaf* uses JPA for accessing its database from the programs source code. The number of nonaccessed tables remains very high during the system's life. Moreover, we observe a stabilization of that number from February 2013 (one can see the same pattern regarding the size of the database schema).

2) The access location point distribution also follows this pattern (with a stabilization since February 2013). What is more interesting is that *Broadleaf* looks very well designed and divided from the start of the project with an average of one database-accessing file per table.

3) The ORM mappings are defined on the majority of the database tables and do not evolve anymore since the stabilization period.

12.5.4 Discussion

With our static analysis and the exploitation of our conceptual schema, we studied three data-intensive systems. Through the measurement of database usage characteristics we investigated and understood how the systems evolve over time, how the database and source code coevolve, and how several technologies coexist within the same system. Through our study, we analyzed the history of each system and pointed out that each of them has a specific design and evolution.

OSCAR is a frequently changing system. Code and database schema have continuously evolved. It seems clear that the introduction of a new technology (Hibernate and later JPA) was aimed to replace the previous one; we can clearly identify the decrease in the usage of JDBC (with respect to Hibernate) after the introduction of Hibernate (with respect to JPA). We noticed that those migrations are still ongoing, as can be witnessed by the presence of tables accessed by several technologies, as well as by the presence of several technologies in the same file. A more blatant example is the coexistence of Hibernate and JPA mappings for some tables. Furthermore, the three technologies (JDBC, Hibernate, and JPA) have coexisted for several years and make code and database evolution more complex and time-consuming. *OSCAR* developers even admit it: one "can use a direct connection to the database via a class called DBHandler, use a legacy Hibernate model, or use a generic JPA model. As new and easier database access models became available, they were integrated into OSCAR. The result is that there is now a slightly noisy picture of how OSCAR interacts with data in MySQL." [31]

Compared to *OSCAR*, *OpenMRS* is less prone to changes. Its code has increasingly evolved over time, but there were fewer changes in the database schema, which has remained quite stable over the years. These changes seem to be periodic and better anticipated. Most of those changes are applied to the same versions. Moreover, one can notice that database objects are rarely removed from the schema. Another major difference with *Oscar* is that JDBC and Hibernate co-exist from the beginning of the project and are complementary: No technology aims to substitute the other.

Concerning *Broadleaf*, with further analysis of our measurements, we found that the database objects are rarely removed; almost all the removed tables are actually involved in a renaming process. However, as SQL migration scripts are not provided for *Broadleaf*, identifying table renamings is not an easy and direct process. Among the three systems, *Broadleaf* seems to be the one with the simplest design. Indeed, *Broadleaf* only uses JPA to communicate with the database. Moreover, *Broadleaf* looks well structured and easy to maintain. The detection of database locations in the code requires less effort since the lines of code that access tables are usually regrouped into a single file.

The question of "what is the required effort to maintain/evolve a given data-intensive software system" remains to be studied in our future work.

12.6 Conclusion

Little is known about how, in a data-intensive software system, the software part of the system (i.e., the source code) coevolves with the data part (e.g., the relational database, represented by a database schema). Empirical software engineering research has mainly focused on studying the evolution of the software system, while ignoring its connected data system.

Even less is known about how this coevolution is affected by the different database manipulation technologies used to access the database from the source code. In the case of Java software, for example, a wide variety of technologies are used (including JDBC, Hibernate, Spring, and JPA).

We carried out a coarse-grained empirical study on several thousands of open-source Java software systems to gain insight on how they use database technologies, and how this evolves over time. While low-level technologies like JDBC continue to remain widely used, higher level ORMs and persistence APIs like JPA are becoming increasingly more popular over time. In addition, we observed that close to 40% of database-driven Java systems have used at least two different technologies over their observed lifetime. For most of them, these different technologies were used simultaneously. We also observed that new technologies are introduced faster in (and disappear slower from) large systems than in small ones. Some technologies, like Hibernate, tend to be replaced faster than other technologies.

We complemented the coarse-grained evolutionary analysis by a fine-grained one in which we narrowed down on three data-intensive open-source Java systems. For these systems, we jointly analyzed the changes in the database schema and the related changes in the source code by focusing on the database access locations. We observed, among others, that the very same tables could be accessed by different data manipulation technologies within the programs. We also observed that database schemas may quickly grow over time, most schema changes consisting in adding new tables and columns. Finally, we saw that a significant subset of database tables and columns are not accessed (any longer) by the application programs. The presence of such "dead" schema elements might suggest that the coevolution of schema and programs is not always a trivial process for the developers. The developers seem to refrain to *evolve* a table in the database schema, since this may make related queries invalid in the programs. Instead, they most probably prefer to *add* a new table, by duplicating the data and incrementally updating the programs in order to use the new table instead of the old one. In some cases, the old table version is never deleted even when the programs no longer access it. Further investigations are needed to confirm this hypothesis.

We are convinced that the work presented in this chapter can lead to actionable results. They may serve, for instance, as a sound basis to build recommendation systems. Such systems could suggest which developer(s) to contact and what to do if certain changes should be done in some database schema elements or in some program code accessing the database. They could also help development teams to estimate the effort needed to achieve given (co-)evolution tasks, taking into account the particular technology (or technologies) being used.

12.7 Future Work

This chapter only focused on the technical aspects of how to relate the software and the data parts of a database-driven software system, and how to study their coevolution over time, taking into account the particular database technologies being used. It is, however, equally important to study the *social aspects* of such systems in order to address a wider range of relevant questions. Are separate persons or teams responsible for managing the program code, the database mapping code, the database? How do developers divide their effort across these different activities? If different technologies are being used, are they used by separate groups of developers? How does all of this change over time? We started to address these questions in Ref. [21], but clearly more empirical research is required.

The research results presented here were only focused on Java systems, so similar studies for other programming languages would be needed. Also, the focus was on relational (SQL-based) databases, while many contemporary software systems are relying on NoSQL (i.e., typically nonrelational) database management systems.

The empirical analysis that was carried out could be refined in many ways. By using dynamic program analysis as opposed to static programming analysis, at the expense of requiring more data and processing power. By using external data sources such as mailing lists, bug trackers, and Q&A websites (e.g., Stack Overflow) for measuring other aspects such as software quality (e.g., in terms of reported/ resolved issues in the bug tracker), developer collaboration (through mailing list communication), user satisfaction (using information from bug tracker and mailing list, combined with sentiment analysis). As a first step in this direction, the use of Stack Overflow has been explored in Ref. [32], where it was used to identify error-prone patterns in SQL queries, which is a first step toward a recommendation system supporting developers in writing database-centered code.

Acknowledgments

This research was carried out by the University of Mons and the University of Namur in the context of a joint research project T.0022.13 "Data-Intensive Software System Evolution" as well as a research credit J.0023.16 "Analysis of Software Project Survival" supported by the Fonds de la Recherche Scientifique - FNRS, Belgium.

References

1 A. Cleve, T. Mens, and J.-L. Hainaut (2010) Data-intensive system evolution. *Computer*, **43** (8), 110–112.
2 M. M. Lehman (1996) Laws of software evolution revisited. European Workshop on Software Process Technology (EWSPT), pp. 108–124.
3 C. Ireland, D. Bowers, M. Newton, and K. Waugh (2009) A classification of object-relational impedance mismatch. International Conference on Advances in Databases, Knowledge, and Data Applications (DBKDA), pp. 36–43.
4 E. Rahm and P. A. Bernstein (2006) An online bibliography on schema evolution. *SIGMOD Record*, **35** (4), 30–31.
5 D. Sjøberg (1993) Quantifying schema evolution. *Information and Software Technology*, **35** (1), 35–44.
6 C. Curino, H. J. Moon, L. Tanca, and C. Zaniolo (2008) Schema evolution in wikipedia – toward a web information system benchmark. International Conference on Enterprise Information Systems (ICEIS), pp. 323–332.
7 P. Vassiliadis, A. V. Zarras, and I. Skoulis (2015) How is life for a table in an evolving relational schema? Birth, death and everything in between. International Conference on Conceptual Modeling (ER), pp. 453–466.
8 I. Skoulis, P. Vassiliadis, and A. Zarras (2014) Open-source databases: within, outside, or beyond lehman's laws of software evolution? International Conference on Advanced Information Systems Engineering (CAiSE), pp. 379–393.

9 A. S. Christensen, A. Møller, and M. I. Schwartzbach (2003) Precise analysis of string expressions. International Conference on Static Analysis (SAS), pp. 1–18.

10 G. Wassermann, C. Gould, Z. Su, and P. Devanbu (2007) Static checking of dynamically generated queries in database applications. *ACM Transactions on Software Engineering and Methodology*, **16** (4), 14–27.

11 M. Sonoda, T. Matsuda, D. Koizumi, and S. Hirasawa (2011) On automatic detection of SQL injection attacks by the feature extraction of the single character. International Conference on Security of Information and Networks (SIN), pp. 81–86.

12 S. R. Clark, J. Cobb, G. M. Kapfhammer, J. A. Jones, and M. J. Harrold (2011) Localizing SQL faults in database applications. International Conference on Automated Software Engineering (ASE), pp. 213–222.

13 M. A. Javid and S. M. Embury (2012) Diagnosing faults in embedded queries in database applications. EDBT/ICDT'12 Workshops, pp. 239–244.

14 M. Linares-Vasquez, B. Li, C. Vendome, and D. Poshyvanyk (2015) How do developers document database usages in source code? International Conference on Automated Software Engineering (ASE).

15 A. Maule, W. Emmerich, and D. S. Rosenblum (2008) Impact analysis of database schema changes. International Conference on Software Engineering (ICSE), pp. 451–460.

16 T. Chen, W. Shang, Z. M. Jiang, A. E. Hassan, M. N. Nasser, and P. Flora (2014) Detecting performance anti-patterns for applications developed using object-relational mapping. International Conference on Software Engineering (ICSE), pp. 1001–1012.

17 D. Qiu, B. Li, and Z. Su (2013) An empirical analysis of the co-evolution of schema and code in database applications. Joint European Software Engineering Conference and ACM SIGSOFT International Symposium on Foundations of Software Engineering. ACM.

18 A. Karahasanović (2002) Supporting application consistency in evolving object-oriented systems by impact analysis and visualisation. Ph.D. dissertation, University of Oslo.

19 D.-Y. Lin and I. Neamtiu (2009) Collateral evolution of applications and databases. Joint International and Annual ERCIM Workshops on Principles of Software Evolution (IWPSE) and Software Evolution (Evol) Workshops, pp. 31–40.

20 M. Riaz, E. Tempero, M. Sulayman, and E. Mendes (2013) Maintainability predictors for relational database-driven software applications: extended results from a survey. *International Journal of Software Engineering and Knowledge Engineering (IJSEKE)*, **23** (4), 507–522.

21 M. Goeminne, A. Decan, and T. Mens (2014) Co-evolving code-related and database-related changes in a data-intensive software system. CSMR-WCRE Software Evolution Week, pp. 353–357.

22 A. Cleve, M. Gobert, L. Meurice, J. Maes, and J. Weber (2015) Understanding database schema evolution: a case study. *Science of Computer Programming*, **97**, 113–121.

23 L. Meurice, J. Bermudez, J. Weber, and A. Cleve (2014) Establishing referential integrity in legacy information systems: reality bites! International Conference on Software Maintenance (ICSM). IEEE Computer Society.

24 C. Nagy, L. Meurice, and A. Cleve (2015) Where was this SQL query executed? A static concept location approach. International Conference on Software Analysis, Evolution, and Reengineering (SANER), pp. 580–584.

25 M. Goeminne and T. Mens (2015) Towards a survival analysis of database framework usage in Java projects. International Conference on Software Maintenance and Evolution (ICSME).

26 M. Allamanis and C. Sutton (2013) Mining source code repositories at massive scale using language modeling. International Conference on Mining Software Repositories (MSR). IEEE, pp. 207–216.

27 L. Meurice and A. Cleve (2014) DAHLIA: a visual analyzer of database schema evolution. CSMR-WCRE Software Evolution Week, pp. 464–468.

28 R. Wettel and M. Lanza (2008) CodeCity: 3D visualization of large-scale software. International Conference on Software Engineering (ICSE), pp. 921–922.

29 M. Goeminne and T. Mens (2011) Evidence for the Pareto principle in open source software activity. Workshop on Software Quality and Maintainability (SQM), ser. CEUR Workshop Proceedings, vol. 701. CEUR-WS.org, pp. 74–82.

30 DB-MAIN (2006) The DB-MAIN official website. http://www.db-main.be.

31 J. Ruttan (2008) The Architecture Of Open Source Applications, vol. II, ch. OSCAR.

32 C. Nagy and A. Cleve (2015) Mining Stack Overflow for discovering error patterns in SQL queries. International Conference on Software Maintenance and Evolution (ICSME).

Part IV

Software Product Lines and Variability

13

Dynamic Software Product Lines

Svein Hallsteinsen,[1] Mike Hinchey,[2] Sooyong Park,[3] and Klaus Schmid[4]

[1]*SINTEF ICT, Trondheim, Norway*
[2]*Lero – The Irish Software Research Centre, University of Limerick, Limerick, Ireland*
[3]*Center for Advanced Blockchain Research, Sogang University, Seoul, Republic of Korea*
[4]*Institute of Computer Science, University of Hildesheim, Hildesheim, Germany*

> Any customer can have a car painted any color that he wants so long as it is black.
>
> *Henry Ford,* My Life and Work, *1922*

13.1 Introduction

Henry Ford, founder of the car company that bears his name, is widely regarded as the father of assembly line automation, which he introduced and expanded in his factories producing Model Ts between 1908 and 1913.

What is less known is that Ford achieved this innovation through the use of interchangeable parts, based on earlier work by Honoré Blanc and Eli Whitney. This significantly streamlined the production process over earlier efforts in which parts were often incompatible and one difference in a product meant restarting the entire process.

The result was economies of scale and a line of motor cars that were affordable, built quickly, and of high quality, even if certain choices – paint color, for example – were extremely limited.

13.2 Product Line Engineering

Ford's ideas influenced the development of product line engineering (PLE), which seeks to achieve something conceptually similar to economies of scale:

Software Technology: 10 Years of Innovation in IEEE Computer, First Edition.
Edited by Mike Hinchey.
© 2018 the IEEE Computer Society, Inc. Published 2018 by John Wiley & Sons, Inc.

economies of scope. As Jack Greenfield and colleagues explain in Ref. [1], "Economies of scale arise when multiple identical instances of a single design are produced collectively, rather than individually. Economies of scope arise when multiple similar but distinct designs and prototypes are produced collectively, rather than individually."

Economies of scope imply mass customization, which can be defined as producing goods and services to meet individual customers' needs with near mass production efficiency [2].

PLE provides a means of customizing variants of mass-produced products. Its key aim is to create an underlying architecture for an organization's product platform in which core assets can be reused to engineer new products from the basic family, thereby increasing variability and choice while simultaneously decreasing development cost and lead time.

The software development community has caught on to the usefulness of this approach with the idea of *software product* lines (SPLs).

13.3 Software Product Lines

The Software Engineering Institute (SEI) defines an SPL as "a set of software-intensive systems that share a common, managed set of features satisfying the specific needs of a particular market segment or mission and that are developed from a common set of core assets in a prescribed way" [3].

Developers have successfully applied SPLs in many different domains – including avionics, medical devices, and information systems – in a wide variety of organizations ranging in size from five developers to more than a thousand [4]. Using this approach has consistently achieved improvements in time to market, cost reduction, and quality [5].

A fundamental principle of SPLs is *variability management*, which involves separating the product line into three parts – common components, parts common to some but not all products, and individual products with their own specific requirements – and managing these throughout development.

Using SPLs seeks to maximize reusable variation and eliminate wasteful generic development of components used only once.

As Figure 13.1 shows, SPLs employ a two-life-cycle approach that separates domain and application engineering. *Domain engineering* involves analyzing the product line as a whole and producing any common (and reusable) variable parts. *Application engineering* involves creating product-specific parts and integrating all aspects of individual products. Both life cycles can rely on fundamentally different processes – for example, agile application engineering combined with plan-driven domain engineering.

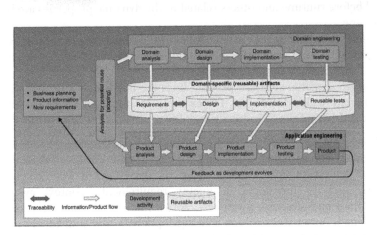

Figure 13.1 Software product lines. SPLs use a two-life-cycle approach that separate domain and application engineering.

13.4 Dynamic SPLs

In emerging domains, such as ubiquitous computing, service robotics, unmanned space and water exploration, and medical and life-support devices, software is becoming increasingly complex with extensive variation in both requirements and resource constraints. Developers face growing pressure to deliver high-quality software with additional functionality, on tight deadlines, and more economically.

In addition, modern computing and network environments demand a higher degree of adaptability from their software systems. Computing environments, user requirements, and interface mechanisms between software and hardware devices, such as sensors, can change dynamically during runtime.

Because it is impossible to foresee all the functionality or variability an SPL requires, there is a need for *dynamic* SPLs that produce software capable of adapting to fluctuations in user needs and evolving resource constraints. DSPLs bind variation points at runtime, initially when software is launched to adapt to the current environment, as well as during operation to adapt to changes in the environment.

Although traditional SPL engineering recognizes that variation points are bound at different stages of development, and possibly also at runtime, it typically binds variation points before delivery of the software. In contrast, DSPL engineers typically are not concerned with preruntime variation points.

However, they recognize that in practice, mixed approaches might be viable, where some variation points related to the environment's static properties are bound before runtime and others related to the dynamic properties are bound at runtime.

In DSPLs, monitoring the current situation and controlling the adaptation are thus central tasks. The user, the application, or generic middleware can perform these tasks manually or automatically.

Although dynamic software product lines are build on the central ideas of SPLs, there are also differences. For example, the focus on understanding the market and letting the SPL drive variability analysis is less relevant to DSPLs,

- whose variation points change during runtime – variation point addition (by extending one variation point) and
- which deals with unexpected changes (in some limited way), changes by users, such as functional or quality requirements, context awareness (optional) and situation awareness, autonomic or self-adaptive properties (optional), automatic decision making (optional), and individual environment/context situation instead of a "market."

Given these characteristics, DSPLs would benefit from research in several related areas. For example, situation monitoring and adaptive decision-making are also characteristics of autonomic computing, and DSPL can be seen as one among several approaches to building self-adapting/managing/healing systems.

In addition, dynamically reconfigurable architectures provide mechanisms to rebind variation points at runtime, while multiagent systems, which focus on the use of agents and communities of agents, are particularly useful for evolving systems such as DSPLs.

Interest in DSPLs is growing as more developers apply the SPL approach to dynamic systems. The first workshop on DSPLs was held at the 11th International Software Product Line Conference in Kyoto in 2007. Several follow-up workshops have been held since.

References

1 J. Greenfield et al. (2004) *Software Factories: Assembling Applications with Patterns, Models, Frameworks, and Tools*, John Wiley & Sons, Inc., New York.
2 M.M. Tseng and J. Jiao (2001) Mass Customization, G. Salvendy (ed.), *Handbook of Industrial Engineering: Technology and Operations Management*, John Wiley & Sons, Inc., New York, pp. 684–709.
3 www.sei.cmu.edu/productlines.
4 www.sei.cmu.edu/productlines/plphof.html.
5 F.J. van der Linden, K. Schmid, and E. Rommes (2007) *Software Product Lines in Action: The Best Industrial Practice in Product Line Engineering*, Springer.

14

Cutting-Edge Topics on Dynamic Software Variability

Rafael Capilla,[1] Jan Bosch,[2] and Mike Hinchey[3]

[1]*Department of Informatics, Rey Juan Carlos University, Madrid, Spain*
[2]*Department of Computer Science and Engineering, Chalmers University of Technology, Goteborg, Sweden*
[3]*Lero – The Irish Software Research Centre, University of Limerick, Limerick, Ireland*

14.1 Introduction

Over the advent of software product lines (SPLs) in the 1990s as a successful approach for building multiple, related products, feature models (FMs) – compact representations of all the features of the products in the SPL – have increased in popularity [1]. Since the past 20 years, a significant body of experience and success of SPL practice in industry has led to a number of successful case stories, summarized in the *Product Line Hall of Fame* book [2], belonging to several industry cases ranging from organizational issues to the more technical aspects. In addition to SPL organizational issues, the goal to maximize reuse across applications and products in order to produce highly configurable software at lower costs are major drivers for product line engineering teams and software companies.

Notwithstanding the popularity of SPL practice in industry, new design and development challenges for complex, pervasive, autonomous, and embedded systems demand new solutions. Today, systems with adaptive and context-aware architectures – including autonomic and ubiquitous computing systems and software ecosystems – require more dynamic capabilities to address runtime needs. Many applications domains and industrial systems require of these runtime capabilities to address self-management, autonomy, reconfiguration, and more flexible configurable options that static variability models cannot handle. This trend requires SPLs to become more adaptable and evolvable, in other words, dynamic. However, these systems must satisfy stringent quality requirements, including safety, reliability, and performance.

Software Technology: 10 Years of Innovation in IEEE Computer, First Edition.
Edited by Mike Hinchey.
© 2018 the IEEE Computer Society, Inc. Published 2018 by John Wiley & Sons, Inc.

Compared to the most traditional practice of software variability [3], allowing for dynamic extension and reconfiguration creates challenges in verifying the behavior of members of an embedded system family, requiring dynamic variability models to manage system behavior predictability while allowing for dynamicity.

In this chapter we summarize previous published work and we delve into the innovative aspects around dynamic variability and its importance for dynamic software product lines (DSPLs). The remainder of this chapter is as follows. Section 14.2 describes the characteristics of software in the post-deployment era. From Section 14.3 onward, we revisit the challenges of runtime variability.

14.2 The Postdeployment Era

For virtually all software, the development process traditionally focuses on understanding customer needs, building a product that meets the company's interpretation of those needs, and then shipping the product [4]. However, an increasingly large community is seeking to upset that model, focusing instead on short development cycles and postdeployment software distribution. The main benefit for customers is that the product continues to improve after they have put it into use.

Although frequent or continuous software deployment has become the norm for Web 2.0 and software as a service (SaaS), organizations are starting to adopt this technology for traditional installed software as well as embedded software-intensive systems. Companies ranging from automotive to telecom companies have adopted continuous deployment and new versions of their software is automatically installed in the products in the field every few weeks or, in some cases, every couple of days.

The challenge that these systems have when deploying new versions is at least threefold. First, the systems deployed in the field can sustain very little downtime, meaning that deploying any new functionality needs dynamic mechanisms to manage variability. Second, many of these systems are deployed in quite diverse ways at customers, meaning that the configuration of the system tends to vary significantly. In order to deal with these variations, the system needs to dynamically configure itself during installation, start-up, and runtime. Finally, the system needs to integrate customer-specific extensions to the functionality. Earlier, with infrequent upgrades, this was performed manually. However, with the adoption of continuous deployment, the integration of customer-specific extensions needs to be performed in an automated fashion. As the evolution frequency of the system software and that of the extensions are not in sync, the system software needs to dynamically adjust its functionality through runtime variability.

One effective mechanism for achieving this is to use dynamic and extensible variation points in the software to manage the most critical and replaceable parts, given that embedded systems demand adaptation capabilities that do not require stopping and restarting the system. Fields such as autonomic computing, domotics, and sensor networks have introduced a niche in which DSPLs can play a key role in supporting runtime changes. Consequently, adapting systems to different contexts may require several reconfigurations that can be satisfied using dynamic variability, and then tackling performance and adaptation challenges that arise.

One interesting development in the continuous deployment of software is that with the increasing frequency of deployment, not all testing activities can be conducted as part of the release cycle. Especially, testing activities that require the system to operate for extended periods of time, such as robustness testing, evaluating memory leakage and reliability assessment, require the system to run for a long time. This means that postdeployment testing is developing into an increasingly relevant activity. This form of testing can, of course, be conducted in the lab, but with dozens, hundreds, or thousands of systems out there with the software deployed already, it makes much more sense to use the live systems for testing purposes as well, as these systems are in operation. Of course, any issues that are found require the system to dynamically adjust its behavior. For instance, the system can deactivate a feature, roll back to an earlier version of a component, change the configuration parameters, and so on in response to identified issues.

Finally, as systems running the same software, but deployed in wildly different contexts perform postdeployment testing, the same mechanisms can be used by each system seeks to optimize its performance. As the company providing the systems has an Internet connection to all these systems for deployment purposes, the systems could exchange information about the results of their optimizations. This would allow for multiple deployments of the same system software to learn from each other and to jointly find the best optimizations much faster than what each system could accomplish on its own.

14.3 Runtime Variability Challenges Revisited

Variability management involves three main challenges. First, industrial reality shows that for successful platforms, the number of variation points, variants, and dependencies between variation points and variants easily reaches staggering levels. The sheer number of variation points often results in having to allocate a rapidly growing percentage of the R&D budget to resolve the complexities resulting from managing such variation. The second challenge pertains particularly to embedded systems, which consist of mechanical, hardware, and software parts. The mechanical and hardware parts also exhibit variation. Such variation differs considerably from software variability in that it tends to primarily involve the system's manufacturing stage and is concerned more with physical dimensioning and assembly than with system functionality. However, the need exists to define dependencies between the mechanical and hardware variations and the software variations [4]. Third, the need for many software systems to handle runtime scenarios, sometimes addressing of critical and real time situations, and where variants must be modified dynamically represent a new challenge for static variability models and conventional SPLs. More and more pervasive, autonomic, and self-adaptive systems required advanced capabilities to address runtime scenarios in unattended mode and hence, manage the variability at postdeployment time.

Dynamic variability[1] can be understood as the ability of a system to address different scenarios at postdeployment time and preferably at runtime, where variants can be activated and deactivated and furthermore added or removed from the variability model once the system is deployed. As software product line engineers and researchers from self-adaptive and autonomic computing areas recognize the need to count with dynamic variability mechanisms able to cope with diversity of runtime scenarios, we highlight a number of design and implementation challenges and benefits using dynamic variability, among them we can cite the following [5]:

Challenge 1

- *Runtime Changes in the Structural Variability*
  Compared to static variability models representing runtime variability, modifying variation points in existing and new software units during system execution, and automating system reconfiguration.
  - *Rationale and Benefits*: Changing the structural variability automatically is challenging but possible in some cases and in a controlled manner. The major benefit in favor of automatic reconfiguration procedures of feature models is for SPL designers, as they can visualize online the changes in the variability model without redrawing it manually. Another expected benefit is the possibility to count with open variability models able to facilitate better the evolution of adding and removing variants with minimal human intervention.

Challenge 2

- *Runtime Validation*
  Automating runtime validation and checking reconfigured feature models to maintain system consistency and stability.

---

1 In this chapter we will use dynamic variability and runtime variability as interchangeable concepts.

– *Rationale and Benefits*: Runtime and online validation is necessary for those systems that need to be reconfigured during execution mode. The major advantage is we avoid stopping the system to check if the new configuration is valid or not.

Challenge 3

- *Runtime Binding*

    Automating the rebinding of system's options is a desired feature for many critical systems supporting variability that have to bind to different alternatives and often motivated by varying context conditions. Hence, support for multiple binding times is a new feature that we expect in dynamic variability approaches.

    – *Rationale and Benefits*: Critical systems that demand to swap between different operational modes (e.g., a power plant with different reconfiguration plants) or systems that need to bind to different alternatives during runtime (e.g., a flight ticket reservation system that needs to rebind to a new service to provide better offers). An expected benefit supporting multiple binding times is that the variability model is not tied to only one binding time, allowing the system to switch between different binding modes after postdeployment time.

Challenge 4

- *Variability Driven by Context*

    Much of the changes that motivated variability at runtime are driven by changing context conditions. Therefore, it seems important for variability model to represent these context features [6] in conventional feature modes and how these context features can be integrated with noncontext ones.

    – *Rationale and Benefits*: Representing context features in variability models help SPL designers to understand better which of the overall set of system's features vary their state more often or predict the appearance of new features (e.g., a new functionality or new device) and where they should be placed in the feature model. Solutions for this challenge will ease the way to understand and manage context information using software variability techniques.

Challenge 5

- *Feature Interactions and Collaborative Features*

    This challenge refers to the interactions between features [7]. Many systems exchange information at real time and conventional feature models do not reflect such interactions, as these are only represented by "requires" and "excludes" constraints. This challenge can be understood as a federated problem of information exchange in systems of systems and complex software-intensive systems.

– *Rationale and Benefits*: Operational dependencies in a given system [8] or between different systems need a more powerful representation mechanism to let the SPL designer know which context and noncontext information two subsystems are exchanging. A step beyond the representation of operational dependencies is the representation of those feature that collaborate exchanging information or if a feature is able to activate and deactivate other features [9]. The expected benefits are clear for SPL designers as they have a more accurate knowledge about which features interact or change during runtime, and avoiding the rigidity of static feature models.

Challenge 6

- *Reconfiguration and Redeployment*
  It is understood as the ability of software artifacts and systems to change its current configuration, which in some cases, a redeployment at runtime is needed.

  – *Rationale and Benefits*: Many systems need to be deployed several times and having automatic deployment procedures, quite useful in some application domains (e.g., telecommunication systems), will reduce the burden of software engineer to reconfigure the redeployed system. This challenge is not strictly a property or capability of dynamic variability mechanisms, but it can be perceived as an ability or consequence of changes in the structural variability, changes in the configuration of software product, or a modification in the binding time of variants when system changes between different operational modes (Figure 14.1).

The tension between open and closed variability models and the increasing need of systems for self-adaption and its ability to be configured at "any time" are the major drivers for the six challenges described in this section. However, not all the systems demanding runtime capabilities have to address all these challenges as not all demand or pose the same characteristics or desired runtime properties. For example, some context-aware systems may only need to activate/deactivate certain features dependant of context conditions (e.g., switch lights on/off) while others like a complex airport management system (AMS) may need a new device or capability (e.g., a fog detector) that must be plugged and reconfigured dynamically. Consequently, dynamic variability solutions are not for all systems and not all these challenges must be addressed as a whole.

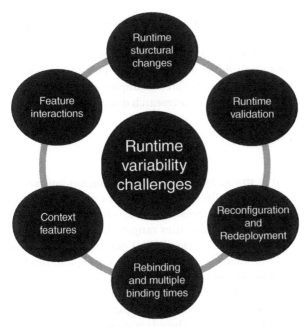

Figure 14.1 Runtime variability challenges as ongoing research topics to be explored in dynamic software product line approaches and systems demanding dynamic variability solutions for self and nonself adaptation goals.

14.4 What Industry Needs from Variability at Any Time?

Nowadays, robots, self-adaptive systems, and ubiquitous systems among others use a combination of context information with some kind of runtime manager to adapt their behavior dynamically. These systems basically activate and deactivate system features according to varying environmental conditions or provide some kind of smart response at runtime and with minimal human intervention. More sophisticated critical systems (e.g., military weapons) can adapt their response or navigation plan at real time but often based on preplanned alternatives. However, the challenge to, for instance, add new devices or features at runtime and not initially planned, or provide smarter reactive capabilities that can reconfigure and redeploy systems dynamically is still challenging for many application domains. In this light, industrial systems that exhibit different grades of smart capabilities can benefit from dynamic variability and COP languages able to incorporate more complex but flexible mechanisms to select between different alternatives in unattended mode.

At present, only few in lab systems and industry have experience with dynamic variability mechanisms, as an open and extensible feature model that can evolve against varying circumstance and unforeseen requirements. As dynamic variability solutions are still immature, they cannot be proven in real systems a complete solution and only partial experiences have been tested so far. In addition to some promising domains described in Refs [3,10], where dynamic variability can be used, we present three examples we believe interesting enough for the reader to understand new research directions for dynamic variability models.

Example 1: Internet of Things

In the Internet of Things (IoT) space, dynamic and emerging configuration of devices is required as some of the IoT-enabled devices are mobile and expect to dynamically interact with devices that they encounter in their environment. As different research communities ranging from cyber-physical systems (CPS) to wireless sensor networks (WSN) and mobile-wearable devices use sensors for providing smart sensing and actuating capabilities for different purposes, there is a qualitative change on how these systems can offer more sophisticated responses to end users and system operators. Smart buildings, smart cities, and smart transportation are typical examples where dynamic variability mechanism can increase the adaptability of such systems to changing environments. The increasing spectrum and proliferation of IoT devices and the interaction between human and things (human-in-the-loop) [11], create a number of complex scenarios where human intervention can be minimized on behalf of dynamic variability solutions able to manage more automatically the interaction sensors, devices, and capabilities that are added and removed and swap dynamically between different system configurations.

Example 2: Casual Gaming

In the space of casual gaming, the dynamic variability is driven by analysis of the continuous data stream generated by thousands of players. The system will identify when players get stuck in or bored with a game and respond to it by offering freebies to overcome a difficult level or by recommending other games. However, the strategies used for responding to the behavior by the players are evolving constantly and require different variations to be added to the system at runtime and even new variability points if the R&D has identified that certain new strategies are required to improve player engagement.

Example 3: Intelligent Vehicle Systems

Smart vehicles are a kind of CPS using a plethora of sensors to provide a smart reaction at real time, where more and more intelligent cars or self-driving vehicles like Google's car offer advanced capabilities for drivers. Among these new capabilities we can find Connected Infotainment Systems, Mobileye Forward Collision Warning (FCW), and automotive night vision systems. Large companies like Bosch (Robert Bosch Car Multimedia GmbH) are experiencing the IoT in the car on infotainment services, where users demand for driver assistance and information and entertainment with smartphone integration and intelligent security. The integration of sensors, head units between ECUs and data, and services between vehicle and the cloud is used to provide advanced driver assistance systems. In this light, dynamic variability solutions can be used to aggregate or add dynamic data or functions and provide smart responses using the vehicle sensors. A huge quantity of variances for different languages, views, and transitions can be managed more efficiently using dynamic variability models, configuring the variants and updating vehicle's system configuration dynamically using the vehicle connectivity subsystem. In the case of collision prevention systems like the FCW, the car can stop automatically when mobile vision detects an obstacle in the route (e.g., a preceding vehicle) and dynamic variability can switch dynamically between different configurations to detect different types of obstacles.

14.5 Approaches and Techniques for Dynamic Variability Adoption

Dynamic variability is not a matured concept yet, and there is still an ongoing but promising research on which techniques are suitable to support the dynamic aspects of software variability and address the challenges discussed in Section 14.2. From our experience and observations from research and industry we review and report some alternatives described in a previous work [10] and other research initiatives.

Technique 1: Changes in the Structural Variability

Changing the structural variability at runtime is a major challenge beyond the simple activation and deactivation of system's features. The possibility to change features dynamically can benefit many systems that attempt to predict in a controlled manner unforeseen situations. To date, few proposals address this challenge. The solution we adopted in Ref. [4] and refined in Ref. [10] suggest the notion of supertypes as classifiers if related features and we use these supertypes in the case a new feature is added or changed into a feature model. An algorithm (not yet implemented) will perform the automatic inclusion of such new feature in the feature model.

First, the DSPL designer should define beforehand the list of supertypes and compatible supertypes (i.e., two or more equivalent supertypes) and each feature or variant should have a predefined supertype. Systems variants can be anchored in the feature model if the supertype of the new feature is the same or equivalent to the supertypes of the parent and sibling features, according to certain criteria. Moving variants to a different location is complex but part of this problem can be automated using, for instance, the proposed supertypes. Nevertheless, some problems may arise if the new feature can be placed in more than one location in the feature model. In that case, we need to discriminate and establish a preference to include the new feature in the most convenient place. Second, removing a variant means dropping it from the feature tree and removing any logical formula using this variant. Software variability management mechanisms must check the feature's dependencies on other variants when removing it. Finally, moving variants can be seen as a removal followed by an inclusion operation.

Figure 14.2 exemplifies the case using a similar figure to that described in Ref. [4] to show in a very straightforward manner the inclusion of a new feature, automatically in the variability model. The scenario we use belongs to a smart home system (SHS) that remotely controls a smart building's security, ambient living, and multimedia features. The left-hand side of Figure 14.2 shows a subset of the home's sample feature model, which consists of three variation points for different functional system features: security, ambient living, and multimedia. The table in the figure defines the supertypes and basic types. For example, the ambient living variation point's supertype is "ambient," but the basic variant types are integer (a range of numerical values for the heating system) or Boolean (e.g., lights can be switched on or off). We can manage the SHS software

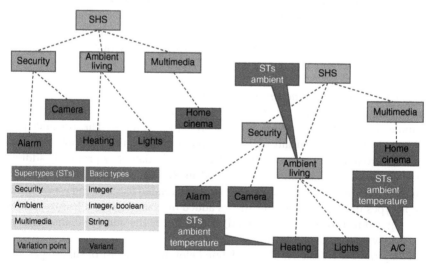

Figure 14.2 Subset of a smart home system' feature model altered dynamically when a new variant is added.

manually or automatically, and some options can be controlled remotely using a Web application or mobile phone.

The system can also adapt to the ambient living conditions. At runtime, it can detect if a new module or device has been added and then reconfigure itself to incorporate the new functionality. The feature tree automatically includes the new A/C feature because it has the same supertype as its new parent (ambient living) and the heating system variant. The right-hand side of Figure 14.2 shows the result of this operation. There are many incompatibility scenarios in which variants cannot be added. For example, in Figure 14.1, the security subsystem does not share compatible supertypes with the multimedia subsystem, and a new feature for controlling the home's locks cannot be included under the multimedia subsystem.

Other ongoing research efforts are testing an algorithm using supertypes with the OSGi platform to add and remove features but they did not test yet the case where a new feature can be placed in two different locations. In a similar vein to Refs [4,12,13], the authors in Ref. [14] describe a framework called Famiware used to reconfigure ambient intelligence systems' plans in heterogeneous WSN devices. The approach supports the evolution of Famiware configurations at runtime and clone devices represented as features to include different configurations. However, altering features using the cloning technique of Famiware allows adding and removing features from the same type, but not from different types like in Ref. [4], but it remains a bit unclear where the new cloned features are added in the feature model. Our last and recent approach describes the challenge of the dynamic evolution of the structural variability, and Baresi et al. [15] propose an architecture to manage the dynamic evolution of DSPLs and synchronization issues. This approach uses cardinality-based feature models like in Ref. [14] but it also does not provide clues where to plug new features in the variability model.

Technique 2: Runtime and Online Validation

Feature models use "require" and "exclude" constraints to limit the scope of the product line products. Traditionally, the hundreds of constraints used to delimit the number of allowed products are checked automatically but in "off-line" mode by specific tools (i.e., SAT solvers) [16]. Nevertheless, the need of open variability models that demand adding and removing features at runtime demand also check the existing or new constraints at runtime. Hence, checking feature constraints "at any time" and preferably in "online" mode turns to be a new capability necessary to support runtime variability[2]. Features added, removed, or changed dynamically require checking old or new constraints at runtime [10] but the time constraints are changed and

---

2 Optimization and reparation of constraints, when these change dynamically, is out of the scope of this chapter.

checked and will also depend on how critical the system is. Therefore, the problem for checking feature constraints at runtime relies on the following two issues: (i) A mechanism or algorithm to add and remove constraints automatically when a features change and (ii) the time (i.e., from design time to runtime) when we need to check the "satisfiability" of the modified constraint model.

Technique 3: Runtime Binding and Multiple Binding Modes

The notion of *binding time* is a property of variability models that describe the moment in which the variability is realized, that is, the time where variants are bounded to concrete values. In conventional SPLs, only one binding time (from design time to runtime) is often selected to realize the variability during product instantiation. In other cases, part of the variability is realized at "design/ compilation/build/assembly" time while other subset of the variants bind to concrete values during configuration time or after postdeployment time. However, in most of the approaches for binding variants there is no possible transition from one binding time to another or, in other words, supports multiple binding times concurrently.

Not many approaches in the literature describe the role of binding time during variability realization. Some classifications about binding time and the possibility to bind group of related features in a single unit have been proposed. These and other approaches are discussed in Chapter 4 [3]. Nowadays, the promise and challenge of runtime variability in support of open variability models where variants and binding time modes can be modified at runtime, offer new possibilities to change product's variants dynamically [17] and more flexibly than before. Moreover, some systems (many of them are critical) demand to change between different operational modes. This might be the case of a power plant that cannot stop its normal operational mode but some parts of the system must be configured at runtime (i.e., some variants map to different values) and the new configuration must be applied and the system is reconfigured dynamically (sometimes in unattended mode and in some other case with minimal human intervention). As stated in Ref. [3], "features may cross from one binding time to another, but depending on how separate the two binding times are."

We summarize in Table 14.1 a subset of our single and multiple binding times approach described in Ref. [4] but we focus on the most dynamic part where the transition between binding times is more obvious.

We use the term "pure runtime" to distinguish runtime bindings that occur during the first or every startup from those that occur only when the system is already running. The transition column describes the possible outcomes when multiple bindings occur. For a predominant binding time (for example, pure runtime), we define which binding times are supported simultaneously and which systems or software applications can bind to a different operational mode. To

Table 14.1 Single and multiple binding times and the transitions between them.

Binding time	Static/ dynamic binding	Configurability level	Binding on the developer/ Customer side	Transition between binding times
Configuration (Cf)	S/D	Medium/high	D/C	Cf → Dpl Cf → RT
Deploy (Dpl) Redeploy (Rdpl)	S/D	Medium/high	D/C	Dpl → Rdpl Rdpl → Cf
Runtime (RT) start-up	D	High	C	Dpl → RT Rdpl → RT RT → Rdpl RT → Cf
Pure Runtime (PRT) (operational mode)	D	Very high	C	RT → PRT PRT → Cf Cf → PRT PRT → PRT

illustrate the transition between different binding times, Figure 14.3 describes in the nodes possible operational modes of a system that use variability at runtime and the edges represent these transitions where variants can be bound at different times as feature cross through different binding modes.

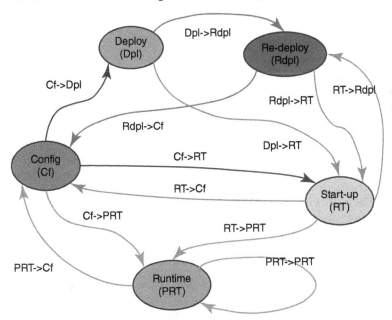

Figure 14.3 Transition between multiple binding times according to Table 14.1.

For instance, once variants are configured a system can be deployed and some other variants need additional configuration according to the server where the software will run (e.g., different IP addresses). In other cases once the software is configured it can run for its first time (RT) or normally (PRT). Systems that are deployed can enter into a first start-up mode (RT) to configure additional parameters of the environment (e.g., using dynamic libraries) or in some special cases the need to be redeployed (Rdpl) again before the start-up (e.g., a case a server fails and a new machine is added using the same configuration and the variants need to bind to the old values, but not new configuration process is performed). Systems running for it first time may go through a configuration process or they can be redeployed several times (Rdpl). In this case where it might be necessary to configure (Cf) the system again or some parameters can be configured at redeployment time without stopping all system functions. Finally, systems that configure parameters during RT should go to the pure runtime mode (PRT) where values of the variants can change dynamically or go to a configuration mode if the system has to be stopped.

Finally, for a given binding mode, there are some experiences rebinding at runtime. This is, for instance, the case of variability implemented in web services where different services are selected dynamically (e.g., different flight providers) or industrial systems that change, for instance, a navigation plan dynamically. It is not our aim to describe in this chapter all these experiences but the reader should be aware of the existence of experiences where system's variants can be mapped to different values in a controlled manner dynamically.

Technique 4: Context Variability

More and more context aware plays an important role for systems and devices that exploit context information. Awareness is a property of systems that is perceived as a combination of knowledge and monitoring [18] aimed to: (i) gather information from the context, (ii) perform some kind of reaction and/or modify the behavior of a system, and (iii) aware users or other devices about changes in the environment. From consumer electronics to industrial systems, a plethora of devices and systems exploit context data. New devices such as wearable technology and smart appliances use context information in the consumer electronics domain. In other practice areas, intelligence vehicles can share data about the traffic to notify urban traffic control centers and also receive information from the context at real time. Moreover, unmanaged vehicles like robots need to adapt their behavior according to varying context conditions, while in more complex scenarios, dynamic variability using context data can be used to modify the behavior of swarm systems. Therefore, managing the variety of scenarios of systems using context knowledge is a green field for dynamic variability approaches that offer paths to model complementary aspects in variability models not addressed before.

Context analysis is increasingly perceived as a complementary technique of domain analysis aimed to identify and represent context properties. Likewise, domain analysis is a major complex human task used to identify objects and operations relevant in an application domain. Context analysis is a complementary activity used to identify and model a system's context properties and the possible transitions between its operational modes. The approach described in Ref. [6] suggests the strategies to model these context properties as context features using variability models, as these highlight better the role of dynamic variability models where runtime reconfiguration is the goal for many adaptive and smart systems using context knowledge. The first strategy uses a different branch to model context features apart from noncontext features. This case is preferred by some implementations and in principle the easiest way to model context properties, as using a separated branch in the feature model makes it more reusable if we need to replace one context by another. However, this approach may induce additional dependencies between context and noncontext features. The second strategy requires more upfront modeling effort as it combines in the same feature model both context and noncontext properties. This strategy might be less reusable but it reduces the number of dependencies between features. However, the designer must define if a feature must be labeled as context feature.

In addition, the appearance of some programming languages using context information (i.e., context-oriented programming languages – COP) can be used to describe and implement context changes using specific programming techniques. ContextL and JCOP [19,20] are examples of these languages able to support the variations of context features at runtime. These languages often use the notion of layer to enclose context-related behavior and the activation and deactivation of these layers according to changes in the context. The work presented in Ref. [21] describes interesting aspects about the identification and management of context information and requirements variability and states the importance of the dependencies between context and behavior.

From the dynamic software product line perspective, context analysis should encompass the following tasks: (i) *identify system physical properties,* (ii) *identify features that modify the structural variability dynamically,* (iii) *define operational rules for the activation of context features* and for those that change in the feature model, and (iv) *define multiple binding modes* enabling the transition between system's operational modes accordingly to the context information sensed. Context variability extends the traditional perspective of feature modeling for systems that exploit context properties dynamically. The combination of context features and dynamic variability techniques are an excellent way to supply automatic reconfiguration mechanisms for critical context-aware systems. As usual, the approaches and maturity of approaches using context feature modeling with special focus in DSPLs are summarized in Table 14.2.

Table 14.2 Runtime variability challenges and ongoing potential solutions.

Challenge	Solutions	Maturity
Runtime changes in the structural variability	Supertypes to classify features automatically [4]	Algorithm defined but not yet fully implemented and tested. Only some trial adding features have been done but is still missing the cases where features can be placed in different locations
	Adding and removing features automatically using supertypes and the OSGi platform	Partially implemented and ongoing work but not published yet
	Dynamic variability for reconfiguring WSNs and feature models [12,13] using supertypes	Partially implemented as prototype
	The Famiware framework is used to reconfigure WSNs runtime [14]. It can add/remove features dynamically using clones and from the same type. Famiware can add constraints and groups of features at runtime too	Implemented as prototype
	Architecture to support the dynamic evolution of DSPLs and synchronization of models during runtime evolution. Rebinding issues are addressed [17]	Published but seems not been implemented yet
Runtime constraint checking	Automated analysis of feature models in off-line mode [16]	Tools like FaMa and other SAT solvers are available
	Adding and checking constraints at runtime	No solution available and not published yet to the best of our knowledge at the time this chapter was written
Automatic rebinding and multiple binding modes	Taxonomy of binding times [22]	Published
	Feature binding time (FBU) units [23]	Published and some experiences with a Virtual Office Printer (VOF)
	Multiple binding times and transitions among them [4]	Published
	Rebinding approaches are several in the literature where variants match to different values several times during reconfiguration operations	Several approaches and experiences published in various application domains like dynamic binding of web services

Table 14.2 (*Continued*)

Challenge	Solutions	Maturity
Context variability	Classifiers to group features in different contexts [24]	Published
	Two different approaches for modeling context variability [6]	Published
	Context variability analysis as an extension of domain analysis is suggested as an activity for DSPLs [10]	Published
	Context features described in the Famiware middleware [14]. This approach follows implicitly strategy A for modeling context variability as described in Ref. [6]	Implemented
	Context ontology for smart home systems (SHS) under a DSPL approach [25]	Implemented
	CANDEL (Context As dyNamic proDuct Line) is a generic framework that uses OWL for representing context information as a collection of context primitives under a DSPL approach [26]	Published
	Context-oriented programming languages (COP). There are several approaches in addition to Refs [19,20]	Available
Feature interactions	Basis on feature interactions using software variability techniques [7]	Published
	Collaborative context features [9]	Published
Reconfiguration and redeployment	Several works in different application domains. Some of them have been discussed or cited in the chapter	Published and tested

Technique 5: Collaborative Features

As stated in Ref. [8], feature interactions are playing more and more important role for variability mechanisms during system execution. A feature interaction happens when the behavior of one feature is affected by the presence of another feature or when new features can be added or removed dynamically to the system. Because in many critical systems features are not isolated, the ability to activate and deactivate features dynamically demands a careful check of runtime constraints by runtime managers (e.g., the typical scenario of an elevator that cannot move if the number of persons exceeds the allowed weight or the case where the elevator stops according to the activation of an emergency condition). Therefore, as systems need stringent real-time requirements, feature interactions at runtime mode introduce an extra level of complexity for dynamic variability approaches that have to deal with changes in the behavior at execution mode.

In this light, telecommunications systems are the most visible examples of feature interactions, such as the seminal work describe in Ref. [27]. Today, self-adaptive systems, service-based systems, and cloud models among others [28,29] impose new runtime constraints for feature interactions in various application domains (e.g., intelligent transportation, smart cities). From our perspective as a future research agenda, feature interactions can occur at the following levels or application scenarios:

- *Feature Composition*: Features can be composed to provide a bigger functionality or provide a federated collaborative model where different entities participate to dynamically provide additional services. The Internet of Things, smart cities, or smart transportation are good candidates where feature composition can offer more complex services to the citizen.
- *Real-Time Communication*: In many critical systems, feature exchange information at real time to let users be aware of certain situations (e.g., emergency) and also to interconnect subsystems more efficiently.
- *New Functionality and Behavior*: Sometimes it is desired to reconfigure a system with a new functionality avoiding stopping the normal system's operational mode, and adding features dynamically may impact on the existing behavior supported by a concrete product configuration. Therefore, adding and removing features using a dynamic variability mechanism provoke a set of interactions that must be checked, in particular, when new constraints are added at "any time."
- *Predicting Confliction Options*: Because of the critical nature of many systems, when the behavior of the system is modified due to changes in the environment, a feature or system's functionality fails, or a new feature impacts on other existing features, it is important for many existing systems (e.g., self-tolerant systems) to anticipate a wrong system functioning and the impact a feature has on the rest of the subsystems. This is an important security concern worthy to explore for many of the today's critical systems.
- *Smart Collaborative*: Some systems are smarter than others and they can also benefit from collaborative capabilities. This is the case of swarm technology where a substantial body of interactions between features at runtime make swarm systems smarter than others.

These and other research challenges based on the collaborative nature of many modern systems that can be engineered using dynamic variability

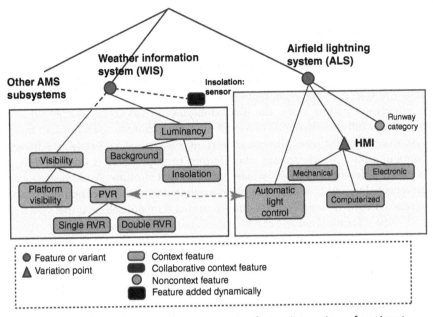

Figure 14.4 Collaborative context feature managing feature interactions of an airport management system (AMS).

techniques bring new opportunities and solutions to investigate feature interactions and how these features can be modeled and represented in current variability models. Just as an example, in critical complex systems of systems like the case of airport management systems (AMS) described in Ref. [9], feature interactions occur at two different levels: (i) features that exchange information at real time and (ii) new features that can be added into two-level critical systems in an AMS. In this approach, we modeled the context features in the feature model but we also annotated those collaborative ones to highlight the presence of feature interactions in a complex system like the AMS, formed by at least 15 different subsystems. Figure 14.4 shows an example on how feature interactions are represented, as we called these *collaborative context features*.

Figure 14.4 describes both context and noncontext features following the first strategy defined in Technique 4, but it also model which of these context feature pose collaborative capabilities supporting feature interactions between both AMS subsystems. In addition, we can see that a new "insolation sensor" feature for the WIS subsystem has been added dynamically using mechanisms like those described in Technique 1. Feature interactions are playing an increasing role in complex systems where different functional parts or subsystems interact at runtime, and the combination of dynamic variability techniques, context-awareness, and runtime constraint checking mechanisms are crucial for the success to implement collaborative features that can be managed dynamically using software variability approaches.

Technique 6: Reconfiguration and Redeployment

Runtime reconfiguration and automatic or semiautomatic deployment is an ability of systems to be reconfigured at runtime or exhibit self-reconfiguration capabilities. In some cases, the new configuration has to be redeployed and partially or fully automated to reduce the burden of human operations. In many systems, variability can play an important role to select between different configurations. In other cases, the binding time property is used to switch between different operational modes, preferably at runtime. As there are many systems belonging to different application domains (e.g., smart home systems, wireless sensor networks, telecommunications domain, self-adaptive systems) that can be reconfigured and maybe redeployed dynamically, we will not explain or describe the details of each particular reconfiguration, but rather we want to highlight that software variability and more specifically dynamic variability mechanisms are important to offer good solutions for those systems that need to be reconfigured dynamically. Examples given in Refs [11–13,17,25] show that reconfiguring systems variants at runtime in combination with SAT solvers and redeployment issues at runtime, like in Ref. [30], is still challenging and the activation/deactivation of system variants, understood as a new configuration, require of specific runtime managers and automated control loops to address the diversity of different system's configurations. Nevertheless, checking and validating at runtime the satisfiability of any new configuration before deployment require mechanisms to check changes in the constraint model dynamically. In other cases, the capabilities of new nodes where the reconfigured software will be redeployed must ensure the quality requirements when the deployment units are deployed on runtime servers that can be added or detached.

Table 14.2 summarizes the challenges and the potential solutions dynamic variability can offer to DSPL approaches and for those systems demanding runtime reconfiguration and enhanced adaptation capabilities.

14.6 Summary

In this chapter we have sketched and summarized the legs of runtime variability mechanisms based on the progress made since 2009. The increasing number of self-adaptive, autonomous, context-aware, and smart systems needs more and more combination of context knowledge with smart behavior and adaptation capabilities in order to address with the diversity of varying scenarios. Consequently, runtime variability mechanisms are perceived a suitable solution to cater the dynamic variations of systems. Moreover, the collaborative aspects of systems of systems induce a new capability in current variability approaches, as a critical and smart systems need to exchange information at runtime before the activation and deactivation of system's features.

Another important area worthy to explore is the role of multiple and dynamic binding times, in particular, for those systems that must switch between different operational modes and force variants to bind their values at different times is another advantage of dynamic variability models, as this can offer a transition between two or more binding times with minimal or no human intervention. As a consequence, variability management is becoming more complex when system needs to address with runtime concerns but more efficient from the perspective of managing the variants once the system has been deployed. The reader can find a broader discussion of many of these challenges in Ref. [31], which covers other aspects and trends of today's software variability research.

Context-oriented programming (COP) languages are another alternative useful to be used by dynamic variability implementations as they can offer mechanisms to activate and deactivate context features, but the integration of these languages with more popular solutions and middleware is an important concern developers need to address. Finally, recent technologies like drones demand collaborative capabilities to perform individual but coordinated missions. Hence, collaborative features become important for this kind of system. In those cases where the collaborative aspects demand a smarter behavior, swarm technology is interesting to be explored to combine the capabilities and aim of swarm systems with dynamic variability mechanisms. Other application domains like intelligent transportation systems require a smart behavior and adaptation to different runtime scenarios (e.g., smart on-board obstacle detection) and also how smart vehicles exchange traffic information at real time. All in all, we can find in many of the today's systems a large variety of scenarios where adaptive behavior is required and where dynamic variability mechanism can be used as a green field to improve the adaptation capabilities of modern software systems and ecosystems.

14.7 Conclusions

Much has been said and researched on software variability over the past 20 years, but the emerging paradigm is of dynamic software product lines and more specifically, the increasing interest on dynamic variability. The progress made in the past few years show an increasing trend and interest by researchers and companies on what dynamic variability solutions can offer. In this chapter, we tried to provide an updated and compendium of existing runtime variability technology and mechanisms and suggest important application domains where this solution can be applied. As we still need more powerful dynamic variability implementations that can be offered under an integrated view from the perspective of variability management, we expect more research efforts over the next years and also, into how these solutions can be tested in different kind of systems where adaptation and smart behavior is a must.

References

1 K. Pohl, G. Böckle, and F. Van der Linden (2005) *Software Product Line Engineering: Foundations, Principles and Techniques*, Springer.

2 F. van der Linden, F. J. Schmid, and E. Rommes (2007) *Software Product Lines in Action*, Springer.

3 R. Capilla, J. Bosch, and K. C. Kang (2013) *Systems and Software Variability Management, Concepts, Tools and Experiences*, Springer.

4 J. Bosch and R. Capilla (2012) Dynamic variability in software-intensive embedded system families. *IEEE Computer*, **45** (10), 28–35.

5 J. Bosch and R. Capilla (2011) The promise and challenge of runtime variability. *IEEE Computer*, **44** (12), 93–95.

6 R. Capilla, O. Ortiz, and M. Hinchey (2014) Context variability for context-aware systems. *IEEE Computer*, **47** (2), 85–87.

7 S. Apel, J.M. Atlee, L. Baressi, and P. Zave (2014) Feature interactions: the next generation. Report from Dagstuhl Seminar 14281.

8 K. Lee and K.C. Kang (2004) *Feature Dependency Analysis for Product Line Component Design*, ICSR Springer, pp. 69–85.

9 R. Capilla, M. Hinchey, and F.J. Díaz (2015) Collaborative context features for critical systems. VaMoS 43.

10 R. Capilla, J. Bosch, P. Trinidad, A. Ruiz-Cortés, and M. Hinchey (2014) An overview of Dynamic Software Product Line architectures and techniques: observations from research and industry. *Journal of Systems and Software*, **91** (5), 3–23.

11 J.A. Stankovic (2014) Research directions for the Internet of Things. *IEEE Internet of Things Journal*, **1** (1), 3–9.

12 O. Ortiz, A. B. García, R. Capilla, J. Bosch, and M. Hinchey (2012) Runtime variability for dynamic reconfiguration in wireless sensor network product lines. Proceedings of the 16th International Software Product Line Conference, SPLC, vol. 2, pp. 143–150.

13 M.L. Mouronte, O. Ortiz, A.B. García, and R. Capilla (2013) Using dynamic software variability to manage wireless sensor and actuator networks. 2013 IFIP/IEEE International Symposium on Integrated Network Management (IM 2013), pp. 1171–1174.

14 N. Gámez and L. Fuentes (2013) Architectural evolution of FamiWare using cardinality-based feature models. *Information & Software Technology*, **55** (3), 563–580.

15 L. Baresi and C. Quinton (2015) Dynamically evolving the structural variability of dynamic software product lines. 10th International Symposium on Software Engineering for Adaptive and Self-Managing Systems.

16 D. Benavides, S., Segura, and A. Ruiz Cortés (2010) Automated analysis of feature models 20 years later: a literature review. *Information Systems* **35** (6), 615–636.

17 A. Helleboogh et al. (2009) Adding variants on-the-fly: modeling meta-variability in dynamic software product lines. Proceeding of the 3rd International Workshop on Dynamic Software Product Lines, Carnegie Mellon University.

18 E. Vassev and M. Hinchey (2012) Awareness in software-intensive systems. *Computer*, **45** (12), 84–87.

19 P. Costanza and R. Hirschfeld (2005) Language constructs for context-oriented programming: an overview of ContextL DLS'05 Proceedings of the 2005 symposium on Dynamic languages, pp. 1–10.

20 M. Appeltauer, R. Hirschfeld, and J. Lincke (2013) Declarative layer composition with the JCop programming language. *Journal of Object Technology*, **12** (2), 1–37.

21 T. Kamina, T. Aotani, H. Masuhara, and T. Kamai (2014) Context-oriented software engineering: a modularity vision. MODULARITY Proceedings of the 13th International Conference on Modularity, pp. 85–98.

22 C. Fritsch, A. Lehn, T. Strohm, and R. Bosch (2002) Evaluating variability implementation mechanisms. Proceedings of International Workshop on Product Line Engineering (PLEES), 59–64.

23 J. Lee and D. Muthig (2008) Feature-oriented analysis and specification of dynamic product reconfiguration. *ICSR 2008. LNCS*, 5030, Springer, Heidelberg, pp. 154–165.

24 H. Hartmann and T. Trew (2008) Using feature diagrams with context variability to model multiple product lines for software supply chains. Proceedings of the 12th International Software Product Line Conference (SPLC 08), IEEE CS, pp. 12–21.

25 C. Cetina, P. Giner, J. Fons, and V. Pelechano (2013) Prototyping Dynamic Software Product Lines to evaluate run-time reconfigurations. *Science of Computer Programming*, **78** (12), 2399–2413.

26 Z. Jaroucheh, X. Liu, and S. Smith (2010) CANDEL: product line based dynamic context management for pervasive applications. Proceedings of the IEEE Complex, Intelligent and Software Intensive Systems (CICIS 10), pp. 209–216.

27 M. Calder, M. Kolberg, E. Magill, and S. Reiff-Marganiec (2003) Feature interaction: a critical review and considered forecast. *Computer Networks*, **41** (1), 115–141.

28 B. Cheng, R. de Lemos, H. Giese, P. Inverardi, J. Magee, et al. (2009) Software engineering for self-adaptive systems: a research roadmap. *Software Engineering for Self-Adaptive Systems*, LNCS 5525, Springer, pp. 1–26.

29 L. Baresi, S. Guinea and L. Pasquale (2012) Service-oriented dynamic software product lines. *IEEE Computer*, **45** (10), 42–48.

30 F. Cuadrado, J.C. Dueñas, and R. García-Carmona (2012) An autonomous engine for services configuration and deployment. *IEEE Transactions on Software Engineering*, **38** (3), 520–536.

31 J. Bosch, R. Capilla, and R. Hilliard (2015) Trends in systems and software variability. *IEEE Software*, **32** (3), 44–51.

Part V

Formal Methods

15

The Quest for Formal Methods in Software Product Line Engineering

Reiner Hähnle[1] and Ina Schaefer[2]

[1]*Department of Computer Science, Software Engineering, Technische Universität Darmstadt, Darmstadt, Germany*
[2]*Institute of Software Engineering and Vehicle Informatics, Technische Universität Braunschweig, Braunschweig, Germany*

Formal methods could overcome the limitations of current SPLE practice, ensuring high product quality while decreasing time to market.

15.1 Introduction

Diversity poses a central challenge in modern software system development. Typically, engineers create system variants simultaneously to address a wide range of application contexts or customer requirements. For example, modern premium-class cars have up to 10^{20} possible configuration variants for the same model. Apart from the interior and exterior designs, customers can select from numerous extras, such as driver-assistance systems and safety or entertainment packages. Car manufacturers assert that such variability is necessary to meet consumers' expectations and constitutes a key success factor. Likewise, there is a vast array of modern medical devices to support diagnosis and intervention, such as X-ray, ultrasound, computer tomography, and magnetic resonance imaging machines, to meet diverse customer requirements. More generally, application software on desktop computers is becoming increasingly configurable to meet users' needs. Word processing and spreadsheet applications, for example, offer many options to customize their look and feel. This trend toward high software configurability extends to the operating system level: A recent study reveals that the Linux kernel distinguishes from among some 5000 features, of which 4800 are user-configurable [1].

Software Technology: 10 Years of Innovation in IEEE Computer, First Edition.
Edited by Mike Hinchey.
© 2018 the IEEE Computer Society, Inc. Published 2018 by John Wiley & Sons, Inc.

15.2 SPLE: Benefits and Limitations

Diversity adds to complexity because developers must anticipate variability in the requirements analysis, design, implementation, and validation stages and then realize it in the completed artifacts. Software product line engineering (SPLE) [2] aims to alleviate this complexity by providing a set of systems with well-defined commonalities and variabilities. When developing these product lines, software engineers create customized, reusable assets and assemble them into actual products during application development.

SPLE offers a commercially successful approach that can improve both time to market and quality. For example, after introducing product line engineering, medical systems provider Phillips Healthcare reported a 50% reduction in both time to market and product defect density, and a two- to fourfold overall reduction in development effort (www.splc.net/fame.html).

However, current SPLE practice faces several obstacles. First, further reducing time to market without sacrificing product quality is difficult. This is especially true for applications with high safety and security requirements, such as those in the medical or automotive domains, which mandate product certification and verification. Quality assurance emerges as an even more pressing problem, given that software systems tend to become long-lived and evolve over time to adapt to changing requirements. And maintaining a product line is more difficult and expensive than single-system maintenance. After each change cycle, the product line architecture degrades and sizable investments must be made for rearchitecting, recertification, and reverification.

A major limiting factor of quality assurance in existing SPLE practice is the heterogeneity of modeling formalisms in different development phases. During requirements analysis, designers frequently use feature description languages to define a product line's scope, while in family design they typically apply architecture description languages to represent components common to all products. Software developers, however, deploy various behavioral description formalisms, such as state charts or message sequence diagrams, to model system behavior at early design stages, while during the implementation phase #ifdef's or component composition is used. As a consequence, when the code base evolves, very often the connection to the variability model is lost.

The lack of a uniform semantic and methodological foundation makes it difficult to ensure consistency of the different views when developing a product line. Furthermore, the only way to provide executable artifacts for prototyping or visual animation in early development stages is to create a concrete product in an implementation language, such as C or Java. This language choice, however, forces premature design decisions that should be addressed only in later stages of the development process.

15.3 Applying Formal Methods to SPLE

15.3.1 Formal Methods

have the potential to overcome the limitations of current SPLE practice, ensuring high product quality while decreasing time to market. Based on notations that have a semantics defined with mathematical rigor, formal methods allow for modeling a system and its assumed properties precisely and unambiguously. Formal system models provide the input of tools for various kinds of dynamic and static analyses, automated test case generation, model checking, and functional verification. During the past decade, formal methods and their accompanying tools have moved from the academic to the commercial realm. Java Path Finder, KeY, KIV, Frama-C, PEX, SLAM, Specware, Spec#, Terminator, and Vcc are among the many tools that incorporate the formal semantics of industrial programming languages, such as C, C#, C++, and Java, and developers have applied them to production code in various contexts.

15.3.2 Uniform Formal Modeling Framework

Researchers have recently proposed several formal approaches to SPLE. Most of these approaches focus on feature or architecture description languages with formal semantics. Furthermore, some researchers have used behavioral models based on generalized temporal logic to provide generic frameworks.

We argue that SPLE should be cast as a model-centric development process relying on a uniform formal modeling framework. Such a framework and its underlying modeling language have to satisfy the following requirements.

15.3.3 Formal Semantics

The modeling language should be capable of expressing all relevant system aspects and their variability based on a common formal semantics. Aspects specific to a particular deployment platform or programming language (scheduling, for example) can be left partially unspecified in early development phases.

15.3.4 Refinement

In later development stages, models should be refined to incorporate additional design decisions. During refinement, tools can check the preservation of consistency or functional properties. In this way, model refinement facilitates all phases of model-centric development.

15.3.5 Compatibility

The framework should be compatible with traditional models of system diversity to ease the transition to a formal, model-centric approach. It must be possible to apply feature modeling to capture a product line's scope or to use architecture description techniques for standard component-based software development.

15.3.6 Behavioral Specification

The modeling framework should contain rich behavioral specification mechanisms in addition to structural description techniques that allow for modeling and reasoning about system behavior. Projections of the overall model provide specific views on the product line for specific purposes, for example, to focus on the component structure. A uniform semantic foundation ensures consistency of the different views. Specifically, the relation between feature models, architectural models, and behavioral component descriptions can be formally established with tool support.

15.3.7 Variability, Evolution, and Reuse

Variability modeling to represent system diversity is integral to a uniform modeling framework. Variability should be captured as a first-class entity to facilitate visualization and analysis. In addition to the anticipated variability of initially planned products, modeling concepts should be flexible and expressive enough to handle unanticipated changes to support product line evolution. The language should provide primitives for reusing artifacts between different system variants. Integrating reuse mechanisms necessitate specifying and analyzing common product components only once.

15.3.8 Modularization

The modeling language should contain structuring mechanisms to express products and their variability modularly and hierarchically. Modularization allows splitting the product line model into manageable parts to alleviate design complexity. Hierarchical decomposition facilitates distributed development and fosters separation of concerns. Modularity and hierarchical decomposition, in connection with the explicit representation of variability, provide the foundation of efficient model analysis and validation by incremental and compositional reasoning.

15.3.9 Executability

Models should be executable at different levels of abstraction to allow simulation, visualization, and symbolic execution. Analysis of executable product models reveals errors in system behavior in the early design stages. For ease of use, simulation and visualization tools should be integrated into the development environment.

15.3.10 Verification

Test case generation and a range of static analysis techniques, including resource analysis and formal verification, should be integrated in the development environment to rigorously ensure structural or behavioral constraints on both the family and product-model levels.

15.3.11 Code Generation

When models are refined to contain sufficiently many details, code generation techniques make it possible to implement products directly from the specified system models. Code generation should be automatic. It should not require manual intervention, decrease time to market, and enable reverse engineering.

15.4 The Abstract Behavioral Specification Language

One specific uniform modeling framework that attempts to address the requirements already stated has been proposed in the form of the modeling language ABS (Abstract Behavioral Specification) [3], which is being developed since 2009. The core of ABS is an *executable*, concurrent OO language with a fully *formal semantics*. See Figure 15.1 for an overview of the conceptual layers of ABS.

Data modeling in ABS can be performed on the basis of parametric abstract data types (ADTs). These can in subsequent stages be *refined* into classes with method implementations. On top of ADTs is a pure functional programming layer with pattern matching akin to a light, first-order version of the programming language Haskell. ADTs and functions can occur inside imperative programs that in turn can be used to declare method implementations as part of a lightweight OO framework that uses Java-like syntax. The latter enforces programming to interfaces (classes have no type but only serve as implementations) and strong encapsulation (all fields are strictly private and can only be accessed via method calls from other objects).

ABS is an asynchronous concurrent language with a cooperative scheduling approach and futures. This means that all synchronization points are made explicit by the modeler and preemptive scheduling is disallowed. As a consequence, no races on shared data can occur. Objects may be active (they start to execute on their own after initialization) and distributed among several processors. The latter permits actor-like programming in ABS.

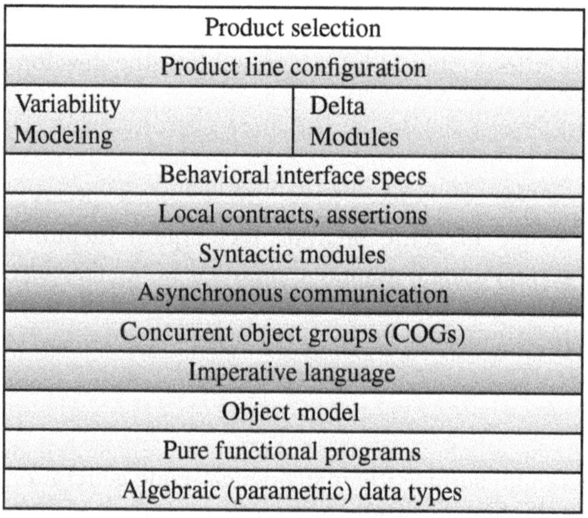

Product selection	
Product line configuration	
Variability Modeling	Delta Modules
Behavioral interface specs	
Local contracts, assertions	
Syntactic modules	
Asynchronous communication	
Concurrent object groups (COGs)	
Imperative language	
Object model	
Pure functional programs	
Algebraic (parametric) data types	

Figure 15.1 Modeling layers of the ABS.

The ABS language has been designed to be easily accessible; anyone with basic knowledge in functional, OO, and distributed programming can master it within a few days. The syntax is *compatible* with widely used notational conventions. In addition, there is a *module system* with explicit exports and imports that allows structuring effectively the name space of large projects.

It is possible to *formally specify* the behavior of ABS models with contracts at the granularity of methods as well as behavioral invariants for a whole system. ABS has been carefully designed to permit *scalable* dynamic and static analyses of different sorts. For example, there is a test case generator (for *concurrent* ABS), a deadlock analysis, a resource analysis, and even a compositional program logic for functional *verification* [4].

The tools based on all but the last are *fully automatic*. As ABS is executable, it is also possible to generate code from ABS models. Currently, there are *code generators* for Java 8, Java ProActive, Haskell, and Erlang.

But the aspect where ABS really deviates from other notations is its tight integration with a *variability modeling* layer that enables model-centric SPL development. Before we detail this more, we briefly explain how the connection is realized: ABS implements *delta-oriented programming* [5,6], a meta programming concept that was designed for *reuse* in OO programming languages: Assume we want to modify a given program P such that it realizes a new feature F, resulting in a program P_F. Then we describe the necessary changes to P in terms of a "delta" Δ_F that describes in a constructive manner how to get from P to P_F. Concretely, the changes are represented in terms of modifications, deletions, and additions of methods, classes, and interfaces, where it is allowed to modify and thereby reuse the original version of any method in P. A suitable compiler can then generate P_F from P when Δ_F is provided.

Now, given a feature diagram that characterizes the variability inherent in a product line by means of its configuration options, it is natural to associate with each of its features F a corresponding realization in terms of a delta module Δ_F or a suitable combination of delta modules. To this end, ABS includes a product line configuration language that defines potential products by associating features with one or more delta modules. Finally, to obtain a concrete product, one merely needs to select it from the configuration file and instantiate the feature attribute values in the implementation artifacts.

15.5 Model-Centric SPL Development with ABS

Integrating feature-oriented modeling of SPLs with implementation-oriented, executable descriptions in one single formalism on the basis of a common formal semantics has numerous advantages. It lets developers analyze the consistency of various modeling concerns, such as feature modeling, architectural descriptions, and behavioral component specifications. Language concepts for artifact reuse help ensure consistency and correctness through formal analysis techniques. Executable models of the product line, as well as of individual products, support the use of simulation and visualization techniques during all phases of family and application engineering. This helps developers discover and correct defects early, and permits rapid prototyping of products for communication with stakeholders.

Formal models allow automatic generation of test cases at both the family and product levels, which is essential for reusability and maintainability. At the product level, test cases can be reused for different products that share common components, enabling formal verification of critical system requirements during early development stages. Derived products are immediately certifiable. The product line model's modular and hierarchical structure supports efficient validation and verification based on incremental and compositional reasoning. Code generation from formal models strives to decrease time to market without sacrificing quality. Certified code generators preserve critical requirements established at the modeling level for generated products. Model-centric development supports product line maintenance and evolution. Changes can be performed at a high level of abstraction and propagated consistently. The code for *evolved* products can be automatically regenerated. To deal with legacy applications or evolution at the code level, developers can use model mining techniques to derive a formal model of the system from existing code. Several of these opportunities have been explored and validated within the ABS framework based on industrial case studies [7,8].

15.6 Remaining Challenges

Languages such as ABS are a step in the right direction, but we must point out a number of challenges that remain on the path to a systematic, model-centric approach to SPLE that can take advantage of formal methods.

15.6.1 Scaling to Family-Based Analysis

To take full advantage of SPL-based development it is important to perform expensive activities as much as possible on the level of a product family rather than for each separate product. But to do so, techniques and trade-offs for many kinds of static analyses at the family level are not yet well enough understood. This holds specifically for complex activities such as deadlock analysis, resource analysis, test case generation, or formal verification.

15.6.2 Integration into Existing Workflows

The ABS modeling framework is implemented as an Eclipse extension and integrates a wide range of productivity tools. But this is at best a starting point for integration into industrial SPLE workflows. In particular, a connection with industrial scale variability modeling tools for the feature modeling level will boost industrial adoption of those techniques.

15.6.3 Legacy Systems

Closely related to the previous issue is the problem of how to take advantage of the techniques sketched in this chapter for legacy systems. Very few software are developed completely from scratch. How can one systematically (and perhaps semiautomatically) re-engineer existing code into ABS or other modeling frameworks? For extraction of variability from an existing set of existing legacy variants, family mining approaches [9] are already applied to industrial scale software, but an approach for refactoring on the modeling or implementation level is still missing.

15.6.4 Maintenance

ABS improves on the development of a set of variable software systems at one point in time. However, evolution of this set of variable systems is not considered yet. In particular, modeling concepts to explicitly capture evolution over time on the feature modeling level and on the structural and behavioral level need to be considered. As a starting point, hyper feature models [10] can be integrated into the ABS that explicitly comprise a notion of feature versioning, while delta modules of the ABS can be extended also to capture temporal change caused by evolution.

15.7 Conclusion

Software product line engineering aims at developing a set of variant-rich systems by systematic reuse. The integration of formal methods into this development process is a promising approach to at the same time ensure high quality of the developed product variants. The Abstract Behavioral Specification language (ABS) is an integrated modeling language comprising variability modeling with structural and behavioral system modeling based on a formal semantics targeting this goal. However, open challenges for formal methods in SPLE still remain, such as the integration into existing development workflows and tools as well as the maintenance and evolution of existing legacy systems.

References

1 S. She et al. (2010) The Variability Model of the Linux Kernel. Proceedings of the 4th International Workshop on Variability Modeling of Software-Intensive Systems, ICB, pp. 48–51.

2 K. Pohl, G. Böckle, and F. J. van der Linden (2005) *Software Product Line Engineering: Foundations, Principles and Techniques*. Springer, New York.

3 E.B. Johnsen, R. Hähnle, J. Schäfer, R. Schlatte, and M. Steffen (2010) ABS: A Core Language for Abstract Behavioral Specification. *Formal Methods for Components and Objects*, Springer, 142–164.

4 D. Clarke, N. Diakov, R. Hähnle, E.B. Johnsen, I. Schaefer, J. Schäfer, R. Schlatte, and P.Y.H. Wong (2011) Modeling Spatial and Temporal Variability with the HATS Abstract Behavioral Modeling Language. *Formal Methods for Eternal Networked Software Systems*, SFM, 417–457.

5 R. Bubel, A. Flores-Montoya, and R. Hähnle (2014) Analysis of Executable Software Models. *Formal Methods for Executable Software Models*, SFM, 1–25.

6 I. Schaefer, L. Bettini, V. Bono, F. Damiani, and N. Tanzarella (2010) Delta-Oriented Programming of Software Product Lines. *Software Product Line: Going Beyond*, Springer, pp. 77–91.

7 K. Villela, T. Arif, and D. Zanardini (2012) Towards product configuration taking into account quality concerns. Software Product Line Engineering Conference, ACM Press, vol. 2.

8 E. Albert, F. S. de Boer, R. Hähnle, E. B. Johnsen, R. Schlatte, S. L. Tapia Tarifa, and P. Y. H. Wong (2014) Formal modeling and analysis of resource management for cloud architectures: an industrial case study using Real-Time ABS. *Service Oriented Computing and Applications*, 8 (4), 323–339.

9 D. Wille, S. Holthusen, S. Schulze, and I. Schaefer Interface variability in family model mining. SPLC Workshops 2013, pp. 44–51.

10 C. Seidl and U. Aßmann (2013) Towards modeling and analyzing variability in evolving software ecosystems. *VaMoS*, Article No. 3, (1–3), p. 8.

16

Formality, Agility, Security, and Evolution in Software Engineering

Jonathan P. Bowen,[1] Mike Hinchey,[2] Helge Janicke,[3] Martin Ward,[3] and Hussein Zedan[4]

[1]School of Engineering, London South Bank University, Borough Road, London, UK
[2]Lero – The Irish Software Research Centre, University of Limerick, Limerick, Ireland
[3]Software Technology Research Laboratory, De Montfort University, Leicester, UK
[4]Department of Computer Science, Applied Science University, Al Eker, Bahrain

16.1 Introduction

"A complex system that works is invariably found to have evolved from a simple system that worked. The inverse proposition also appears to be true: A complex system designed from scratch never works and cannot be made to work. You have to start over, beginning with a working simple system."

– Gall's Law (Gall, 1986, page 71)

Complex systems have always been problematic with respect to software development. Simplicity is desirable, but inevitably the reality of dealing with a customer means that requirements are likely to change, with a corresponding loss of elegance in the solution. A good software engineer will design with the knowledge that the system is likely to evolve over time, even if the exact nature of the changes is unknown. Such expertise only comes with experience and an innate aptitude, especially in the understanding and use of abstraction (Kramer, 2007), whether formally or informally, or both. Software engineering approaches, such as object orientation and modularization in general (e.g., the Z notation schema construct), can help in minimizing the problems of change if used carefully, following standard patterns of use (Hinchey et al., 2008).

Formal methods have been advocated for improving the correctness of software systems (Bowen and Hinchey, 2012), and agile software development

Software Technology: 10 Years of Innovation in IEEE Computer, First Edition.
Edited by Mike Hinchey.
© 2018 the IEEE Computer Society, Inc. Published 2018 by John Wiley & Sons, Inc.

has been promoted to enable adaptive development in the face of changing requirements, typically introducing additional complexity in the process. This chapter provides a brief overview of these approaches, concentrating on their use in combination. Two specific aspects are considered in more detail, namely security applications, where correctness (e.g., through the use of formality) is especially important, and software evolution, where an agile approach can be particularly beneficial.

16.2 Formality

"It is a miracle that curiosity survives formal education."
– Albert Einstein (1879–1955)

Formal methods (Boca et al., 2010; Hinchey et al., 2010) have traditionally been a slow and cumbersome way to develop a software system, providing the benefit of lower error rates using a mathematical approach from the requirements specification onward (Bowen et al., 2010). They provide an important software engineering technique in systems where integrity is important (Hinchey et al., 2008), for example, in the case where safety or security is central aspects of the system to be designed. While a formal approach can be used to undertake proofs, potentially at great cost, a formal specification also provides a framework for undertaking rigorous testing, potentially with a cost saving since the specification can be used to direct the tests that are needed (Hierons et al., 2009). Without a formal specification, testing is a much more haphazard affair. This is in addition to using the formal specification to guide the implementation itself by programmers.

An issue of using formal methods in industry can be a misunderstanding of the term, as the quotation at the start of this section demonstrates (Bowen and Hinchey, 2014). If a formal approach is to be used, its relevance must be understood by all involved in the team, from the management downward (Coram and Bohner, 2005), even if formality is not actually used by everyone. In fact, it is much easier to teach software engineers to *read* formal specification than to *write* them. The ability to read and understand the specification is normally needed by most people involved on a software development team (e.g., programmers and testers), whereas writing the specification requires the involvement of a much smaller number of more highly trained people.

16.3 Agility

"There's nothing to winning, really. That is, if you happen to be blessed with a keen eye, an agile mind, and no scruples whatsoever."
– Alfred Hitchcock (1899–1980)

Agile software development provides an iterative increment approach where the requirements and the associated solution evolve through the collaboration of team members. Rapid response to change is encouraged. This contrasts with the traditional view of formal methods, but modern tools can enable a much more agile approach even within formal development. As an example, the RODIN tool (http://rodin.cs.ncl.ac.uk) minimizes the amount of reproof that is needed if the system is changed. Tools like the Alloy Analyzer (http://alloy.mit.edu) are relatively quick to learn for a capable software engineer and are also fast to use in an agile manner (Black et al., 2009).

The concept of agile formal methods first appeared in the literature in the mid-2000s (Eleftherakis and Cowling, 2004; Hall, 2005; Paige and Brooke, 2005), with events such as the FM + AM (Formal Methods and Agile Methods) Workshop now explicitly addressing the issue (Larsen et al., 2010). In 2009, a position paper on formal methods and agile software development was published in *IEEE Computer* to highlight the debate (Black et al., 2009).

While we do not really hold the view that agility may be used by "unscrupulous" developers in general, as could be implied by the quotation above, we do believe that agile developers could benefit from some formal methods training, at least in reading formal specifications, even if they do not apply the approach completely rigorously.

In the following two sections, we consider two important software engineering issues with respect to agility and formality, namely system security and software evolution.

16.4 Security

Can agile methods produce secure software, perhaps where the security properties have been formalized? Opinions regarding this question remain split. Whilst agile methodologies such as Scrum (Schwaber and Beedle, 2001) and XP (Beck, 2000) continue their advance into mainstream software development, with sometimes impressive results, there are still reservations in areas where security is a paramount concern to stakeholders. Until relatively recently there was little focus on how to integrate best security practices into agile development, although these shortcomings have been pointed out several years ago (Beznosov and Kruchten, 2004).

One of the key issues in addressing this problem is to make security requirements explicit and to include security concerns in the product backlog with adequate priority, so that they continue to be addressed by the development team during the iterations (Alnatheer et al., 2010). Agile methods are customer-driven and strive to satisfy the customer. This frequently leads to a focus on developing functionality that produces the primary business value. Security on the other hand is concerned with risk and the prevention of misuse of the developed functionality that is (unfortunately) often not valued as highly and therefore not addressed in early sprints. Consequently, it is necessary to integrate security activities in the agile development process (Keramati and Mirian-Hosseinabadi, 2008) and its practices (Baca and Carlsson, 2011; Musa et al., 2011).

One approach of addressing security early in an agile development context is the use of "evil stories." This is an agile adoption of misuse cases (Sindre and Opdahl, 2001) to describe the functionality that an attacker would be able to exploit. The development then takes on two dimensions: (i) to implement user stories and (ii) to avoid implementing evil stories. Another practice that integrates security principles in agile development is the use of a technique called *protection poker* (Williams et al., 2010), in which security risks are quantified by the agile team. The game proceeds similarly to the widely known agile technique *planning poker* that is used to establish effort estimates for user-stories.

That security is a major concern for companies employing agile methodologies is evident in the recent adaption of Microsoft's Secure Development Lifecycle (SDL) (Howard and Lipner, 2006) to integrate with agile projects (Sullivan, 2010). The key problem that is addressed here is how activities from the SDL can be integrated effectively into the short release cycles that characterize agile development projects. The approach divides SDL activities in three categories: (i) every sprint, such as running automated security-analysis tools and updating the threat model; (ii) bucket requirements, consisting of verification tasks, design review activities and response planning; and (iii) one-time requirements, which include, for example, the development of a baseline threat model.

So, whilst efforts are well underway to integrate security practices in agile methodologies, there is a risk that many actual development efforts will ignore these or that development teams in the short-term lack the knowledge and training to actually produce secure products. However, agile principles such as communication and practices such as pair-programming may help in disseminating the knowledge throughout the development team. Certification remains a potential issue as it requires detailed, at the highest security levels formal, documentation. Sullivan's (Sullivan, 2010) approach can help here by mandating activities that need to be included in every sprint and requiring a (scope-reduced) final security review at the end of each sprint.

16.5 Evolution

Real software systems are continually evolving. Their evolution is often in response to the evolution of their environments: new functionalities are added and/or existing ones are removed – due to the need to address changes in business requirements and/or economic forces – new platforms are developed and/or new technologies are introduced. The coevolution between software systems and their environment continue to present a major challenge as the nature and the rate of evolution of both entities are highly unpredictable.

This necessitates a new paradigm shift in the way software systems are and will be developed. What is required is *agility* in the development without sacrificing *trustworthiness*. It is important that the emergent behaviors of coevolution, for example, adding/removing functionalities, should not be chaotic, perhaps through the use of formality.

Software migration is an important type of evolution, in particular, assembler migration (Ward et al., 2004a). The majority (over 70%) of all business-critical software currently runs on mainframes and over 10% of all code currently in operation is implemented in assembler. The total sum of 140–220 billion lines of assembler code are still in operation (capers), much of which is running business-critical and safety-critical systems. The percentage varies in different countries. For example, in Germany, it is estimated that about half of all data processing organizations use information systems written in assembler. There is also a large amount of IBM 370 assembler currently in operation.

However, the pool of experienced assembler programmers is decreasing rapidly. As a result, there is increasing pressure to move away from assembler, including pressure to move less critical systems away from the mainframe platform, so the legacy assembler problem is likely to become increasingly severe.

Analyzing assembler code is significantly more difficult than analyzing high-level language code. With a typical well-written, high-level language program, it is fairly easy to see the top-level structure of a section of code at a glance: conditional statements and loops are clearly indicated, and the conditions are visible. A programmer can glance at a line of code and see at once that it is, say, within a double-nested loop in the ELSE clause of a conditional statement or easily identify an iteration structure. The situation in assembler code is different and more complex. In assembler code, there will be simply a list of instructions with labels and conditional or unconditional branches. A branch to a label does not indicate whether it is a forwards or backwards branch, and a backwards branch does not necessarily imply a loop.

If a large body of assembler code can be replaced by a smaller amount of high-level language code, preserving its correctness without seriously affecting performance, then the potential savings (in the form of software and hardware maintenance costs) are very large. If the case for code migration is made adequately, then the process of migration should be highly agile to further increase benefit.

Another major example for coevolution and the need for rigorous agile processes can be seen within the embedded systems domain, the majority of which are used within critical applications. Many embedded systems were developed for processors with limited memory and processing capability, and were therefore implemented in tightly coded hand-written assembler. Modern processors are now available at a lower cost, which have much more processing and memory capacity and with efficient compilers for high-level languages such as C. To make use of these new processors the embedded system needs to be reimplemented in a high-level language in order to reduce maintenance costs and enable implementation of major enhancements. There are many challenges with some assemblers that are particularly relevant to embedded systems processors (such as 16-bit addresses and 8- or 16-bit registers). Rigorous formalized agile development becomes important in this situation.

A sound agile approach to software evolution has been developed, based on transformation theory, and is associated with an industrial-strength program transformation system (see Ward et al., 2008; Ward and Zedan, 2010b; Yang and Ward, 2002). The approach to agility and evolution via migration involves four stages (Ward et al., 2008):

1) translate the assembler to wide-spectrum language (WSL),
2) translate and restructure data declarations,
3) apply generic semantics-preserving WSL to WSL transformations, and
4) apply task-specific operations as follows:
   a) *For Migration* translate the high-level WSL to the target language.
   b) *For Analysis* apply slicing or abstraction operations to the WSL to raise the abstraction level even further.

Wide-spectrum language, the transformation theory, and how program slicing can be defined as a transformation within the theory are fully explained and analyzed in Ward and Zedan (2002, 2007, 2010a, 2010b, 2011a) and Ward et al. (2004b). Further, the mathematical approach to program slicing lends itself naturally to several generalizations, the most important and general of which is conditioned semantic slicing (Ward and Zedan, 2010a).

In practice, the usual automated migration of assembler to C takes the following steps:

1) Translate the assembler listing to "rawWSL." This translation aims to capture the full semantics of the assembler program without concern for efficiency or redundancy. Typically, each assembler instruction is translated to a block of WSL code that captures all the effects of the instruction.
2) The data layout of the assembler program is analyzed and converted to the equivalent structured data using records, fields, and possibly unions if necessary. (Note that the data layout is not changed.)
3) The rawWSL is restructured and simplified by applying a large number of correctness preserving WSL transformations. These restructure the control flow to generate structured IF statements, WHILE loops, and so on. They also remove redundant code and use dataflow analysis to remove register

usage where possible. The most difficult part of analyzing assembler code is tracking return addresses through subroutines to determine subroutine boundaries.

4) Finally, the restructured WSL is translated to the target language. This is a fairly simple transliteration process, since the code is already structured and simplified.

This approach enables a formal agile methodology to be applied to real software, aiding the software evolution process.

The transformational programming method of algorithm derivation (Ward and Zedan, 2013) starts with a formal specification of the result to be achieved, together with some informal ideas as to what techniques will be used in the implementation. The formal specification is then transformed into an implementation, by means of correctness-preserving refinement and transformation steps, guided by the informal ideas (see Figure 16.1). The transformation process will typically include the following stages:

1) Formal specification.
2) Elaboration of the specification.
3) Divide and conquer to handle the general case.
4) Recursion introduction.
5) Recursion removal, if an iterative solution is desired.
6) Optimization, if required.

At any stage in the process, subspecifications can be extracted and transformed separately. The main difference between this approach and the invariant-based programming approach (and similar stepwise refinement methods) is that loops can be introduced and manipulated while maintaining program correctness and with no need to derive loop invariants. Another difference is

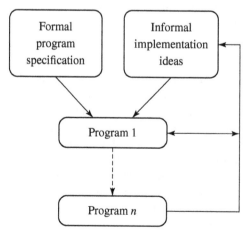

Figure 16.1 Transformational programming method of algorithm derivation.

that at every stage in the process we are working with a correct program: there is never any need for a separate "verification" step. These factors help to ensure that the method is capable of scaling up to the development of large and complex software systems.

The method has been applied to the derivation of a complex linked list algorithm: the "Polynomial Addition" problem in Donald Knuth's book *Fundamental Algorithms*, which uses four-way linked lists. The derived source code turned out to be over twice as fast as the code written by Knuth to solve the same problem.

This method was also used to derive a polynomial multiplication algorithm using the same data structures: this started with a trivial change to the formal specification (replace "+" by "*") and the transformational derivation was guided by the same informal ideas as the addition algorithm. The result was an efficient implementation of polynomial multiplication that worked first time. Another paper (Ward and Zedan, 2013) uses this method to derive an implementation of program slicing from the formal definition of slicing, defined as a program transformation.

16.6 Conclusion

In conclusion, the authors assert that the combination of formal and agile approaches is a worthwhile goal in the application of software engineering methodologies to real computer-based systems. Of course, a note of caution is in order (Larsen et al., 2010). Using heavyweight formal methods with full program proving are likely to be difficult and not worthwhile in a typical agile setting. On the other hand, this is a rare approach within industry in any case, largely due to the problems of scaling and the difficulty of using the available tools. Much more typical when formal methods are applied in practice is a lighter touch with just the use of formal specification to improve early understanding, to guide the programmer, and perhaps to aid proper testing. In this context, combined use with agile development is more reasonable and likely to succeed, if applied judiciously with experienced engineering judgment.

There are additional issues to consider in specialist areas such as safety- or security-related systems, but even in these cases, the combination of formal and agile techniques has potential. An agile approach is especially applicable in response to evolving systems, for example, where the software may need to be completely upgraded to a new language. By adding a formal foundation, agile evolution can be applied in a sound manner to large real software systems, with suitable formalized transformation rules. Automated verification of incrementally changing systems has potential where tractable (Bianculli et al., 2015). For the future, further experience of the combination of formal and agile approaches is needed in a realistic industrial setting.

Acknowledgments

This is an expanded version of a previous article (Bowen et al., 2014). Jonathan Bowen thanks Museophile Limited for financial support.

References

A. Alnatheer, A.M. Gravell, and D. Argles (2010) Agile security issues: an empirical study. In: *Proceedings of the 2010 ACM-IEEE International Symposium on Empirical Software Engineering and Measurement (ESEM'10)*, ACM, pp. 58:1–58:1.

D. Baca and B. Carlsson (2011) Agile development with security engineering activities. In: *Proceedings of the 2011 International Conference on Software and Systems Process (ICSSP'11)*, ACM, pp 149–158.

K. Beck (2000) *Extreme Programming Explained: Embrace Change*. The XP series. Addison-Wesley.

K. Beznosov and P. Kruchten (2004) Towards agile security assurance. In: *Proceedings of the 2004 Workshop on New Security Paradigms (NSPW'04)*, ACM, pp. 47–54.

D. Bianculli, A. Filieri, C. Ghezzi, and D. Mandrioli (2015) Syntactic-semantic incrementality for agile verification. *Science of Computer Programming*, **97**, 47–54.

S. Black, P.P. Boca, J.P. Bowen, J. Gorman, and M.G. Hinchey (2009) Formal versus agile: survival of the fittest. *IEEE Computer*, **42** (9), 37–45.

P.P. Boca, J.P. Bowen, and J. Siddiqi (eds.) (2010) *Formal Methods: State of the Art and New Directions*. Springer-Verlag.

J.P. Bowen and M.G. Hinchey (2012) Ten commandments of formal methods . . . ten years on. In: *Conquering Complexity*, M.G. Hinchey and L. Coyle (eds.), Springer-Verlag, Part 3, pp. 237–251.

J.P. Bowen and M.G. Hinchey (2014) Formal methods. In: *Computing Handbook*, T.F. Gonzalez, J. Diaz-Herrera, and A.B. Tucker (eds.), 3rd edition, Vol. 1, Computer Science and Software Engineering, Part 8, Programming Languages, Chapter 71, CRC Press, pp. 1–25.

J.P. Bowen, M.G. Hinchey, H. Janicke, M. Ward, and H. Zedan (2014) Formality, agility, security, and evolution in software development. *IEEE Computer*, **47** (10), 86–89.

J.P. Bowen, M.G. Hinchey, and E. Vassev (2010) Formal requirements specification. In: *Encyclopedia of Software Engineering*, P.A. Laplante (ed.), Taylor & Francis, pp. 321–332.

M. Coram and S. Bohner (2005) The impact of agile methods on software project management. In: *Proceedings of the 12th IEEE International Conference and Workshops on the Engineering of Computer-Based Systems (ECBS'05)*, IEEE Computer Society. DOI: 10.1109/ECBS.2005.68.

G. Eleftherakis and A.J. Cowling (2004) An agile formal development methodology. In: *Proceedings of the 1st South-East European Workshop on Formal Methods: Agile Formal Methods: Practical, Rigorous Methods for a Changing World (SEEFM03)*, D. Dranidis and K. Tigka (eds.), South-East European Research Centre (SEERC), pp. 36–47.

J. Gall (1986) *Systemantics: The Underground Text of Systems Lore. How Systems Really Work and How They Fail*, 2nd edition, General Systemantics Press.

J.A. Hall (2005) Realising the benefits of formal methods. In: *Proceedings of ICFEM 2005: Formal Methods and Software Engineering, Lecture Notes in Computer Science*, K.-K. Lau and R. Banach (eds.), Vol. 3785, Springer-Verlag, pp. 1–4.

R.M. Hierons, K. Bogdanov, J.P. Bowen, R. Cleaveland, J. Derrick, J. Dick, M. Gheorghe, M. Harman, K. Kapoor, P. Krause, G. Luettgen, A.J. H. Simons, S.A. Vilkomir, M.R. Woodward, and H. Zedan (2009) Using formal specifications to support testing. *ACM Computing Surveys*, **41** (2), 1–76.

M.G. Hinchey, J.P. Bowen, and E. Vassev (2010) Formal methods. In: *Encyclopedia of Software Engineering*, P.A. Laplante (ed.), Taylor & Francis, pp. 308–330.

M.G. Hinchey, M. Jackson, P. Cousot, B. Cook, J.P. Bowen, and T. Margaria (2008) Software engineering and formal methods. *Communications of the ACM*, **51** (9), 54–59.

M. Howard and S. Lipner (2006) *The Security Development Lifecycle: A Process for Developing Demonstrably More Secure Software*. Microsoft Press Series. Microsoft Press.

H. Keramati and S.-H. Mirian-Hosseinabadi (2008) Integrating software development security activities with agile methodologies. In: AICCSA 2008: IEEE/ACS International Conference on Computer Systems and Applications, pp. 749–754.

J. Kramer (2007) Is abstraction the key to computing? *Communications of the ACM*, **50** (4), 36–42.

P.G. Larsen, J. Fitzgerald, and S. Wolff (2010) Are formal methods ready for agility? A reality check. In: *Proceedings of the 2nd International Workshop on Formal Methods and Agile Methods (FM+AM 2010), Lecture Notes in Informatics*, S. Gruner and B. Rumpe (eds.), Vol. 179, Gesellschaft für Informatik E.V.

S.B. Musa, N.M. Norwawi, M.H. Selamat, and K.Y. Sharif (2011) Improved extreme programming methodology with inbuilt security. In: ISCI 2011: IEEE Symposium on Computers Informatics, pp. 674–679.

R.F. Paige and Brooke P.J. (2005) Agile formal engineering. In *Proceedings of IFM 2005: Integrated Formal Methods, Lecture Notes in Computer Science*, J. Romijn, G. Smith, and J. van de Pol (eds.), Vol. 3771, Springer-Verlag, pp. 109–128.

K. Schwaber and M. Beedle (2001) *Agile Software Development with Scrum*. Prentice Hall PTR.

G. Sindre and A.L. Opdahl (2001) Templates for misuse case description. In: Proceedings of the 7th International Workshop on Requirements Engineering, Foundation for Software Quality (REFSQ 2001), pp. 4–5.

B. Sullivan (2010) Security development lifecycle for agile development. In: Proceedings of Blackhat DC, www.blackhat.com/presentations/bh-dc-10/Sullivan_Bryan/BlackHat-DC-2010-Sullivan-SDL-Agile-wp.pdf.

M. Ward and H. Zedan (2002) Program slicing via FermaT transformations. Proceedings of the 26th Annual IEEE COMPSAC.

M. Ward and H. Zedan (2007) Slicing as a program transformation. *ACM Transaction on Programming Languages and Systems (TOPLAS)*, **29** (2), 1–53.

M. Ward and H. Zedan (2010a) Combining dynamic and static slicing for analysing assembler. *Science of Computer Programming*, **75** (3), 134–175.

M. Ward and H. Zedan (2010b) Transformational programming and the derivation of algorithms. In: *Proceeding of 25th International Symposium on Computer and Information Science*, The Royal Society.

M. Ward and H. Zedan (2011a) The Formal Semantics of Program Slicing for Non-Terminating Computations. Submitted to *Theory of Computing*, 2011.

M. Ward and H. Zedan (2011b) Deriving a slicing algorithm via FermaT transformations. *IEEE Transactions on Software Engineering*, **37** (1), 24–47, 2011.

M. Ward and H. Zedan (2013) Provably correct derivation of algorithms using FermaT. *Formal Aspects of Computing*, **26** (5), 993–1031.

M. Ward, H. Zedan, and T. Hardcastle (2004a) Legacy assembler reengineering and migration. In: Proceedings of the IEEE International Conference on Software Maintenance (ICSM).

M. Ward, H. Zedan, and T. Hardcastle (2004b) Conditioned semantic slicing via abstraction and refinement in FermaT. Proceedings of the IEEE International Working Conference on Source Code Analysis and Manipulation (SCAM).

M. Ward, H. Zedan, M. Ladkau, and S. Nateberg (2008) Conditioned semantic slicing for abstraction; industrial experiment. *Software Practice and Experience*, **38** (12), 1273–1304.

L. Williams, A. Meneely, and G. Shipley (2010) Protection poker: the new software security "game." *IEEE Security Privacy*, **8** (3), 14–20.

H. Yang and M. Ward (2002) *Successful Evolution of Software Systems*, Artech House.

Part VI

Cloud Computing

17

Cloud Computing: An Exploration of Factors Impacting Adoption

Lorraine Morgan[1] and Kieran Conboy[2]

[1]*Lero – The Irish Software Research Centre, Maynooth University, Maynooth, Ireland*
[2]*Lero – The Irish Software Research Centre, NUI Galway, Galway, Ireland*

17.1 Introduction

The rapid emergence, prevalence, and potential impact of cloud computing has sparked a significant amount of interest among IS and IT industry and research. It has "the potential to transform a large part of the IT industry" (Armbrust et al., 2010) and be a "catalyst for innovation" as cloud computing becomes "cheaper and ubiquitous" (Brynjolfsson et al., 2010). A recent survey of 527 large and midsize organizations revealed that three in every four are using cloud adoption to gain competitive advantage either through agility, increased innovation, reduced costs or scalability, or indeed through a combination of these (HBR and Verizon, 2014).

There are, however, a number of limitations of the current cloud computing body of knowledge. For example, research efforts have been largely dedicated to addressing technical problems (Khajeh-Hosseini et al., 2010; Leimeister et al., 2010). Moreover, the perceived benefits and challenges of cloud computing lack strong empirical validation, as despite a small amount of research (e.g. Iyer and Henderson, 2010), the body of knowledge is comprised of position papers (e.g. Armbrust et al., 2009, 2010) and relies heavily on anecdotal evidence found mainly in white papers, web articles, technical reports, and practitioner papers (Morgan and Conboy, 2013). A key issue not being addressed in current research is that many cloud adopters are still experiencing substantial difficulties in their attempts to effectively leverage the transformational business capabilities afforded by cloud computing (Linthicum, 2012; Da Silva et al., 2013). We argue that this lack of success is due to a failure to address the true nature of cloud technology adoption. Hence, this study begins to address the need to examine our theory of innovation adoption by investigating the factors that impact cloud adoption, using the technology–organization–environment framework (Tornatzky and Fleischer, 1990) as a lens. To achieve the objective, the following three research questions were formulated:

1) What technological factors impact the adoption of cloud computing?
2) What organizational factors impact the adoption of cloud computing?
3) What environmental factors impact the adoption of cloud computing?

We begin by describing the theoretical background to the study (Section 17.2). This is followed by a discussion of the research design (Section 17.3) and the findings (Section 17.4). Finally, we conclude by discussing the implications of our work (Section 17.5).

17.2 Theoretical Background

17.2.1 Defining Cloud Computing

The concept of cloud computing is generally regarded as the evolution or at least a culmination of previous theories such as grid computing, utility computing, and cluster computing (Vouk, 2008; Iyer and Henderson, 2010; Yang and Tate, 2009; Foster et al., 2008). However, there is currently no single, universally accepted definition of the term "cloud computing" (Foster et al., 2008; Vouk 2008; Yang and Tate 2009; Iyer and Henderson 2010; Weinhardt et al. 2009). From a review of the literature, it is clear that many definitions exist (e.g. Armbrust et al., 2009; Motahari-Nezhad et al., 2009; Mell and Grance, 2009), however, the term is vague, polymorphous, and multidimensional, and is often interpreted and applied inconsistently in the literature (Leimeister et al., 2010). The US National Institute of Standards and Technology (NIST) has published a working definition (Mell and Grance, 2009) that is often cited and viewed as one of the more articulate, clear yet comprehensive classifications of cloud computing, and as Sriram and Khajeh-Hosseini (2010) state, has "captured the commonly agreed aspects of cloud computing." This definition, which will be the one adopted in this study, describes cloud computing as containing the following:

i) Five characteristics – on-demand self-service, broad network access, resource pooling, rapid elasticity, and measured service.
ii) Four deployment models – private clouds, community clouds, public clouds, and hybrid clouds.
iii) Three service models – Software as a Service (SaaS), Platform as a Service (PaaS), and Infrastructure as a Service (IaaS).

17.2.2 Conceptual Model

The theory of innovation, and in particular information systems innovation, suggests that adoption of an innovation is often far from simple. For example, the use of classical diffusion theory (Rogers, 2003) to study organizations has been criticized for focusing primarily on simpler innovations being adopted autonomously by individuals and being less applicable to complex technologies and to technologies adopted by organizations (Fichman, 1999). In addition, there are weaknesses in innovation adoption research in its failure to take adequate consideration of the business context and its integration with the overall environment (Swanson, 1994). Moreover, there has been an excessive focus on adoption at the individual level and not enough at the organizational level (Eveland and Tornatzy, 1990). It is, therefore, evident that the theoretical foundation for our study needs to take into consideration specific factors such as the technological, organizational, and environmental circumstances of the organization. Thus, we draw on the works of Tornatzky and Fleischer (1990), in particular their technology–organization–environment (TOE) framework. This framework consists of three elements that influence the process by which innovations are adopted – the technology, organization, and environment. Given its reliable theoretical basis, empirical support and the potential to apply it to IS innovation domains (Kirkbesoglu and Ogutcu, 2012; Oliveira and Martins, 2011), we believe the TOE framework is useful in studying the adoption of cloud computing. Moreover, this framework has been elaborated on in relation to IS adoption studies carried out by Morgan and Finnegan (2010), Dedrick and West (2003), Zhu et al. (2006), and Chau and Tam (1997).

The technological context relates to the technologies available to an organization. Its focus is on how technology factors influence the adoption process (Tornatzky and Fleischer, 1990). According to Rogers (2003), five technology characteristics influence the likelihood of adoption – relative advantage, compatibility, complexity, trialability, and observability. Relative advantage refers to the level to which an advantage is perceived as better than the idea it supersedes. Compatibility is the degree to which an innovation is perceived as being consistent with the existing values, past experiences, and needs of potential adopters. Complexity relates to the perceived difficulty of understanding and using the innovation while trialability refers to the degree to which the innovation can be tried and tested in small chunks over time. Finally, observability refers to the level to which the results of an innovation are visible to the technology adopter (Rogers, 2003). The organizational context looks at the structure and processes of an organization that constrain or facilitate the adoption and implementation of innovations (Tornatzky and Fleischer, 1990). Additionally, Tornatzky and Fleischer (1990) propose that the external environmental context, that is, the industry, competitors, regulations, and relationships with governments, in which an organization conducts its business, presents constraints and opportunities for technological innovations.

17.3 Research Method

The objective of this study is to examine the factors impacting cloud adoption. The study was categorized as exploratory due to the scarcity of empirical work in the area of cloud computing adoption. Thus, Marshall and Rossman (1989) suggest that either a case study or field study research methodology can be used. This helps to uncover the complexity of the organizational processes relevant to the context studied (Kaplan and Duchon, 1988). The advantages of the field study include the ability to collect large amounts of information quickly and it also enables the researcher to gain greater insights as regard causes of the processes behind the phenomenon under study (Galliers, 1992). Field studies are deemed appropriate if the researcher enters the field with a good idea of the research questions to be addressed and the manner in which the data will be collected and analyzed (Buckley et al., 1976). Thus, the researchers decided that a field study would be appropriate, as it would facilitate the collection of data from a larger number of informants, which is useful in gaining a broad understanding of benefits and challenges in the context of cloud adoption.

17.3.1 Selection of Participants

For this study, we decided to draw on the perspectives of two different groups – (i) service providers who we believed could provide a better understanding of benefits and challenges of adopting cloud computing, based on their own interaction with, and feedback from clients, and (ii) organizations that have adopted cloud computing solutions who could provide us with information regarding benefits of adoption as well as potential challenges. As such, access to a diverse range of firms operating in different industry contexts was considered ideal to serve this purpose. The cloud initiatives in each company differ in terms of amount, type, and use of cloud technology adopted. A description of the cloud initiatives in each firm is outlined in Table 17.1.

17.3.2 Data Collection and Analysis

Data gathering took place between October 2012 and February 2014 with 10 companies (see Table 17.2) and was primarily personal face-to-face interviews, a technique well suited to exploratory research such as this because it allows expansive discussions to illuminate factors of importance (Oppenheim, 1992; Yin, 2003). Interviewees were senior decision-makers with experience of assessing cloud computing adoption. Each interview was based on a structured protocol around three issues, with the interviewers asking probing questions based on responses. These three issues were (i) the level of adoption, (ii) perceived benefits of cloud computing, and (iii) perceptions of technological, organizational, and environmental challenges to adoption. The interviews lasted between 50 and

Table 17.1 Description of cloud initiatives in each firm.

Organization[a]	Description	Industry	Co. size	Cloud initiative	Interviewees
		Service providers			
Miral	Management consultancy firm advising SMEs on implementation of proven international best practice quality environmental health and safety and information security management systems	Consulting (SaaS offering)	12	MiralLive suite of management system online tools include continuous improvement, training, asset management and documentation control, delivered via SaaS	Managing Director (2 interviews) Developer (1 interview)
BoltIT	Network and IT infrastructure provider; consulting on IT managed services, networking, and communication solutions	IT and Networking Solutions (IaaS offering)	5500	BoltIT's Cloud Infrastructure Service provides businesses with a modular IT infrastructure provided on a subscription basis, covering networking; network traffic and security; storage; a systems and software catalogue; backup service and self-service portal	Chief Technology Officer (1 interview)
SourcePro	SourcePro.com was established in 2009 and provides tools to evaluate new suppliers, cope with tender responses, and implement best practice procurement processes	Procurement software (SaaS offering)	21	The company's cloud-based e-sourcing service (called SourcePro.com) allows users to find and evaluate new suppliers with an easy-to-use approach to quotations, tenders, and other aspects of the procurement process	Chief Executive Officer (2 interviews) Executive Director (2 interviews)
Wind Technologies Ltd.	An Irish-owned and operated business technology consultancy company	Business Technology Consultants (SaaS offering)	30	Expansive range of business solutions to offer clients whether on-premise or in the cloud. The company also design cloud technology strategies and aid clients in the successful delivery of projects	Practice Director (1 interview) CTO (1 Interview)

(continued)

Table 17.1 (Continued)

Organziation[a]	Description	Industry	Co. size	Cloud initiative	Interviewees
Santos, Ireland	Santos is a technology company that operates in more than 170 countries around the world. They provide infrastructure and business offerings that span from handheld devices to supercomputer installations	Information Technology (SaaS, IaaS, PaaS)	4000	Provides full range of cloud offerings, SaaS, IaaS and PaaS to enterprises, service providers, governments, and developers	CTO Manager (1 interview)
		Customers			
ABC Consulting	A European-based business unit of a larger multinational organization	Consulting	112 in business unit	Cloud software used for project management and reporting/ communication across all 17 projects within business unit	Partner (2 interviews) 4 Project Managers 3 Developers
APM	APM, also a client of SourcePro, is a public sector body, headquartered in Dublin, with overseas offices in Amsterdam, Germany, UK, France, Russia, USA, China, and Sweden	Public Sector Body (Food and Drink)	200	The company has adopted SourcePro. com e-sourcing system in their procurement environment	Procurement Officer (1 interview)
IBTB	IBTB is another public sector client of SourcePro. The company offers a number of clinical and diagnostic services to hospitals throughout the country	Public Sector Body (Health)	630	The company has adopted SourcePro. com e-sourcing system in their procurement environment	Purchasing Manager (1 interview)

Traxel	Electronics	16	Traxel, a customer of Miral, specializes in the delivery of customized and integrated GPS vehicle tracking systems and fleet management solutions for leading businesses in over 30 countries worldwide	The company use the MiraLive continuous improvement tools to manage their ISO systems	IT Manager (1 interview)
InfoMos	Global Securities Processing	250	This company, also one of BoltIT's customers, is a global leader in providing modern, high-volume software applications for middle office, back office, and corporate actions automation within the global financial markets industry	The company's ASP operations are hosted within Clearstream's Outsourced Computing Centre. Internally, they leverage BoltIT's Cloud Infrastructure service in their development environment	Product Management (2 interviews) IT Manager (2 interviews) Developer (1 interview)

a) Pseudonyms used to protect anonymity.

Table 17.2 Factors impacting cloud adoption.

Factor	Description[a]
	Technological
Relative advantage	+ Cost savings + Time savings + Scalability
Compatibility	+ ability to streamline and improve internal processes − Integrating with existing systems − Bandwidth and connectivity
Complexity	− Resistance and uncertainty among staff
Trialability	+ Can engage in pilot projects/trials
	Organizational
Improved collaboration	+ More collaboration along the supply chain + More team engagement − Cloud systems need to be more intuitive to user needs
Traceability and auditability	+ Traceable and transparent audit trail
IT Manager resistance	+ Opportunities for IT Managers if they adjust their skills to suit cloud landscape − IT Managers' jobs may become obsolete
	Environmental
Regulatory and legal environment	+ Locked down processes on data confidentiality and secure data centers − Need for cloud standards that address compliance/data protection concerns − Perception of the term "cloud"
Real-world examples	+ Safety-net factor for managers wishing to adopt cloud technologies − People need to be educated on how best to manage/govern cloud adoption

a) + positive effects, − concerns.

120 min. The questions were largely open-ended, allowing respondents freedom to convey their experiences and views, and expression of the socially complex contexts that underpin cloud technology adoption (Oppenheim, 1992; Yin, 2003). The interviews were conducted in a responsive (Wengraf, 2001; Rubin & Rubin, 2005) or reflexive (Trauth & O'Connor, 1991) manner, allowing the researcher to follow up on insights uncovered midinterview, and adjust the content and schedule of the interview accordingly.

In order to aid analysis of the data after the interviews, all were recorded with each interviewee's consent, and were subsequently transcribed, proofread, and annotated by the researcher, and then coded using nVivo. Also, venting was used, whereby results and interpretations are discussed with professional colleagues to avoid the problem of what Kaplan and Duchon (1988) call multiple realities. Findings were continuously presented and discussed with colleagues and practitioners informally. In any cases of ambiguity, clarification was sought from the corresponding interviewee, either via telephone or e-mail. Supplementary documentation relating to the cloud technologies and their use were also collected. These included a comprehensive review of publicly available documents, including websites of firms, company brochures, white papers, and so on. Data analysis used Strauss and Corbin's (1998) open coding and axial coding techniques. This approach encourages researchers to be flexible and creative (Sarker et al., 2000) while imposing systematic coding procedures (Strauss and Corbin, 1990). This form of analysis facilitates the development of substantive theory without prior hypotheses, and can be utilized in the absence of, or in conjunction with, existing theory (Strauss and Corbin, 1990; Urquhart, 1997). Open coding is "the process of breaking down, examining, comparing, conceptualizing, and categorizing data" (Strauss and Corbin, 1998). In the initial phase, "open coding" was used to determine the main ideas in each transcript. These ideas were then grouped by significant headings (technology context, organizational context, and the environmental) to reveal categories and subcategories. The next phase involved "axial coding" that is the process of relating categories to their subcategories. As a list of codes began to emerge, the analysis moved to a higher level of abstraction, looking for a relationship between the codes. Once a relationship had been determined, the focus returned to the data to question the validity of these relationships. Additional follow-up interviews were arranged with all of the original interviewees to elicit further, richer, more focused information. This was done to confirm, extend, and sharpen the evolving list of categories.

17.4 Findings and Analysis

17.4.1 Technological Factors Impacting Adoption

Four technological characteristics were evident in this study as influencing the adoption decision: relative advantage, compatibility, complexity, and trialability. Given that the extent of cloud adoption among customers was only moderate or at pilot phase, observability was not seen as relevant.

17.4.1.1 Relative Advantage
The *relative advantage* was seen in terms of savings on software and hardware costs. The lower costs associated with cloud computing has been cited as a key benefit in the existing literature (see Farrell, 2010; Goodburn and Hill, 2010;

Geelan, 2009). The fact that users can pay-as-they-go, for what they need, rather than paying on an ongoing basis for excess capacity was something that was viewed as extremely beneficial by the majority of study participants. Additionally, the move away from perpetual capital expenditure to operational expenditure was also cited as a cost benefit. For example, study participants in InfoMos explained how they were able to significantly reduce hardware costs. This company relies heavily on virtualization to leverage the most out of their hardware. However, by adopting a cloud service, they found they were able to save money on servers, which cost in the region of €12,000–13,000.

Scalability, a cited benefit of cloud computing (see Forbes, 2011; Armbrust et al., 2009; Iyer and Henderson, 2010), was viewed by most study participants as being extremely valuable with the adoption of cloud solutions and had a positive impact on relative advantage. For example, the managers at InfoMos explained that they had gone through a large growth pattern in the last year and were continually outgrowing resources available to them in-house. Moreover, relative advantage was also seen in terms of time savings. Faster implementation time is viewed as a benefit of cloud computing (Forbes, 2011; Goodburn and Hill, 2010), something that was also evident in this study. Both study participants in IBTB and APM that adopted the SourcePro.com e-sourcing system explained that the turnaround time in terms of implementing the system was viewed as extremely effective. These two companies were up and running on the system in 24 h, which is beneficial when one considers that traditional IT systems implementation can typically take a lot longer. Similarly, both managers in InfoMos explained that actual implementation time is vastly reduced with cloud technologies. As one manager in this company elaborated, "older style deployments could take anything from six to eighteen months. Cloud technologies are an out of the box solution that we could turn around in a matter of weeks" (Product Manager, InfoMos).

17.4.1.2 Compatibility

The *compatibility* of cloud technologies was found to be consistent with the technologies, skills, and tasks of various adopters in the study. For example, the majority of the customers in the study revealed that there is much value in the ability to streamline and improve internal processes as a result of cloud adoption. The IT manager at InfoMos explained that with cloud adoption, they can instantly deploy new versions of applications and templates for test functions, development functions, and support functions "in a matter of minutes" compared to "three to four days" prior to cloud adoption. Similarly, the Executive Director at SourcePro explained that they build cloud-based templates for common spend areas, which their customers in general find very valuable. Alternatively, their customers can choose to design their own templates if they wish, which again is viewed as something beneficial. Nonetheless, this same service provider (i.e., SourcePro) revealed that integrating cloud systems with existing organizational IT systems, for example, ERP systems, could pose a challenge to long-term adoption and acceptance of cloud computing. As cloud computing adoption becomes more popular, integration may become more complex, and so SourcePro are working on ways to improve integration.

In terms of compatibility, issues around bandwidth and connectivity are concerns for adopters. From a business point of view, organizations have to rely on connectivity to the network or data centers. For example, the study participants in InfoMos explained that bandwidth and connectivity to the cloud is as much of a concern as the actual performance and the facilities that are on offer from the cloud provider. Nonetheless, the adoption of cloud computing in InfoMos is very much at pilot phase in their development environment. Production applications like payroll, source controls, are not hosted in the cloud but this is something the company is presently considering. The IT manager further pointed out that when moving forward to this next phase of adoption in their production activities, they are going to need decent bandwidth, which has a cost attributed to it.

17.4.1.3 Complexity

For service providers in the study, complexity does not constrain cloud adoption because they believed cloud systems are easy to use. However, for customers in the study, complexity manifested in the form of staff who resist or are uncertain as to how to use the cloud system. In persuading employees to use cloud systems, study participants in SourcePro and Miral believed that it is important to build a system that is intuitive to peoples needs. The Procurements Officer at APM explained that for somebody working in procurement, it is very straightforward for them using the SourcePro system but for the nonprocurement people, it can be quite challenging. Presently, APM have nine procurement staff using the system but eventually want to increase usage to 30 employees in the Dublin offices and also staff based in their overseas offices. Similarly, there are seven people in IBTB using the system, but again they are investigating how best to roll it out across the organization. The Procurements Officer at APM pointed out that "some training and handholding" is necessary at the start while the Purchasing Manager at IBTB argued that "give it six months or a year, it definitely is going to show true value to employees in what it's costing us and what it will deliver".

17.4.1.4 Trialability

The analysis showed that *trialability* is also an important factor impacting cloud adoption. All of the adopters in the study have carried out various trials and experimentations with their respective cloud systems. For example, the Product Manager at InfoMos described how they have successfully gone through a proof-of-concept phase whereby they have proved that everything they want to do can be done in the cloud and can be done with the performance that the company requires. Both managers in IPTB and APM also explained that it is necessary to create an environment or structure whereby public sector bodies could engage in pilot projects around cloud in a risk free environment. There would still have to be audit trails and essentially a case of value for money. The Procurements Officer at APM explained that they carried out some trials with the SourcePro system and came up with an action plan of 20 improvements to the system. This manager further elaborated, "some of these changes were not so small. I mean with some of them I was very surprised at how quickly they [SourcePro] turned them around. So they are eager to keep the clients that they have now very happy." Prior to adoption, all of the customers in the study participated in various feasibility studies around cloud adoption. Personnel were involved in investigating how the cloud system would work and how it would be secured on the cloud.

17.4.2 Organizational Factors Impacting Adoption

17.4.2.1 Improved Collaboration

The analysis revealed that one organizational factor impacting customer adoption was the desire to *improve collaboration* and promote openness both inside and outside organizations. All of the customers in the study explained that the adoption of cloud has resulted in more collaboration along their supply chain, improved team engagement and communication inside firms, and more learning and information sharing. In terms of more team engagement and collaboration, the Purchasing Manager at IBTB explained that

> "we can all go in and just see what's going on. Whereas before I might be doing something and I might not think to tell people. But they could literally go in now and see for themselves. When people feel that they are engaged with things and they know what's going on . . . like from a work point of view . . . you know, they feel they are part of something".

From the perspective of the service providers in this study, the CTO at Miral described how it was crucial to actively engage with partners and customers in various cloud efforts while the managers at SourcePro explained how they welcomed feedback from customers, as well as new ideas on how to improve their system. Similarly, the CEO at Miral explained that while he was very happy with the MiralLive system and believed it promoted collaboration in client organizations, it is "still a database to me, not a collaborative tool." However, going forward, this company wants to make the system more intuitive to user needs so that it will become an "internal facebook" of sorts.

17.4.2.2 Traceability and Auditability

Another organizational factor impacting adoption included *increased traceability and auditability*. According to researchers, such as Armbrust et al. (2009) and

Iyer and Henderson (2010), cloud capabilities such as traceability enables the usage of every information service within an organization to be tracked. The ability to trace the history, location, or application of an item through recorded documentation is vital for ensuring that companies conform with internal and external constraints. Internally, compliance rules may require companies to audit the use of their data from other parts of the world (Iyer and Henderson, 2010). All of the customers in the study need to show an audit trail of where data is stored for regulatory and legal purposes. Thus, the ability of service providers to provide a traceable and transparent audit trail demonstrates compliance and data integrity. As the Executive Director at SourcePro pointed out "transparency and integrity are very important with public and private sector bodies . . . for both sectors we need to demonstrate that we are doing things properly."

17.4.2.3 IT Manager Resistance

Adopting cloud systems represents a shift in organizational norms and culture. One organizational challenge that impacts cloud adoption is IT Manager resistance – those that fear "losing control of their IT environment." For example, the project manager at Traxel explained that IS/IT managers like to be in control of data and services, thus there is a perception among them that "if it ain't broke, don't fix it" in terms of cloud adoption. This manager further elaborated that you can observe quantifiable benefits with cloud adoption like increasing efficiency and lowering costs but you fall into that unquantifiable "but what if it breaks? Where are we left then?" situation. Thus, IT managers not only feel a threat to their positions but also to their responsibilities, which is to ensure that services are available to the organization at all times. In ABC Consulting, some of the managers refused to adopt the technologies available in any form, and even refused to participate in a pilot phase. This also caused issues in terms of widespread adoption, in that, while over 90% of the 112 members of ABC Consulting routinely used the cloud features as planned, "it was inevitably the senior managers that did not" (ABC Developer). Also, there were inconsistencies and duplication in effort across the projects, caused by the fact that some mangers instructed their staff to use certain cloud-based tools and others did not. Similarly, the Practice Director at Wind explained that "there's an element of 'turkeys voting for Christmas' in relation to this, in that the IT departments, especially the guys who are actually in charge of the physical boxes- they don't like this idea of cloud."

According to several study participants, the massive transition to cloud may result in many IT managers' jobs becoming obsolete in a few years. Nonetheless, service providers in this study believed that there are still tremendous opportunities for IS/IT managers, if they adjust their skills and capabilities to suit the cloud landscape. The Practice Director at Wind further explained that the way they try to sell cloud computing to IT managers is to be as inclusive as possible. He further elaborated, "so we sell to them by saying, you know instead of administering the kit that's physically within your four walls, you are just now being the administrator of something that exists somewhere else. But you are still an important part of the picture. You still need to be an administrator on the system, just not locally."

17.4.3   Environmental Factors Impacting Adoption

17.4.3.1   Regulatory and Legal Environment

Our analysis revealed that the *regulatory and legal environment* was the main environmental factor impacting cloud adoption. For example, adopters such as IBTB, APM, TRAXEL, and InfoMos referred to issues around data jurisdictions, data confidentiality, and security risks. Both managers in InfoMos explained that with the BoltIT offering they feel safe in the knowledge that they are aware of where their data centers are actually hosted, as well as the legislation around the jurisdiction in which they are hosted. The Product Manager in this company further revealed that "certain datacentres are scattered across the world and sometimes you can specify which data-centre you are going into. But with regard to disaster recovery they have to fail over to other data centres around the world and that may mean that some very pertinent information or data will end up in a jurisdiction where it shouldn't be for legal purposes." The analysis also revealed that there is huge risk averseness in the public sector and this presents many challenges for widespread adoption of cloud. For example, the Purchasing Manager at IBTB explained that there is a loss of control once data is put in the cloud and, "if we go out on a limb to try something innovative and it doesn't work, what will happen is you end up in the newspapers. And nobody wants this corporate image of inefficiency." In adopting the e-procurement system, both managers in IBTB and APM added that there were a lot of hurdles to jump through in terms of getting approval and support from senior management. The Purchasing Manager at IBTB further elaborated that there is no problem with cloud adoption once it is done in a controlled and risk-free environment because "there are issues for cloud computing in the public sector. Who owns the information? Where is it stored? These types of things."

The majority of study participants also stressed that there is a need for new cloud standards that address issues between cloud vendors and customers regarding data protection, compliance concerns, security, and so on. The presence of such standards is a comforting factor in adopting cloud computing because as one manager revealed, "if a hosting company takes my business, I would expect to see that they have addressed certain business continuity and data protection standards. A company's data can be its 'baby'" (Project Manager, Traxel). Thus, regular meetings take place prior to cloud adoption with service providers to ensure that proper data protection or governance procedures are in place and that systems are implemented in a risk free environment. Service providers also need to be transparent about where data is stored if cloud adoption is to continue to grow. To overcome security and privacy concerns with cloud adoption, two of the service providers (i.e., BoltIT and SourcePro), explained that they have "locked-down processes" on data confidentiality and information repositories are outsourced to secure data centers.

Interestingly, several of the study participants in the study referred to people's perception of the word "cloud" as being a potential barrier to cloud adoption. For example, the CEO at Miral, the Procurements Manager at APM, and the CTO at BoltIT mentioned that while people are comfortable "banking online, passing around hard drives and USB keys, or leaving laptops on trains," once the word "cloud" is mentioned, this evokes a negative reaction. As one study participant pointed out, "you know sometimes you would wonder if the word "cloud" hadn't been around, would we be better off?" (CEO, Miral) while one customer in the study admitted that "the word cloud scares some people" (Project Manager, Traxel).

The Practice Director at Wind Technologies Ltd. also pointed out that security is and will continue to be a concern to widespread cloud adoption "you know if you build a bigger safe, there is always going to be somebody who wants to crack that safe. Clients need to examine exactly what they are doing now to see if it is any more secure that what vendors are proposing in relation to cloud technologies. I guarantee it is not." Additionally, both managers in Traxel and Wind Tech advised that for those firms thinking about implementing a cloud system, but not entirely sure of it, should start with a lightweight application or something that is nonmission critical, "so in other words if it did actually crash for a week, would your business crumble? And if the answer is no, then listen, why don't we just see? Let's put that on the cloud, we will show you the benefits of it. We will show you what it's all about. And if that goes well, then we do a second one. And then all of a sudden you know the issues just go away" (Practice Director, Wind Technologies).

17.4.3.2 Real World Examples

The study found that customers would like to see more real-world examples of successful cloud adoption. However, the Practice Director at Wind Technologies pointed out that there are some nice case studies available on cloud adoption and that people are beginning to see "that there is nothing to be scared of" and most importantly the business benefits of cloud adoption. The Purchasing Manager in IBTB noted that senior managers in the public service would like to see more real-world examples of successful community clouds. This acts as a safety net for managers, because as the Purchasing Manager at APM pointed out, "it's the fear of loss of control and the risk of it . . . do you want to be first one to do it?" However, it was found that once people are educated on how best to govern and manage the process, public sector cloud computing would be more rapidly adopted.

17.5 Discussion and Conclusion

As discussed earlier, while some existing research has examined the benefits of cloud adoption, the research is largely based on anecdotal evidence and is generally focused on technical issues regarding adoption (Morgan and Conboy, 2013). This study revealed the various factors that impact cloud adoption and lends support to some of these findings. For example, technological factors included relative advantage in terms of time savings (i.e., fast turnaround in terms of implementation), cost savings (i.e., reduced capital expenditure), and increased scalability (i.e., provision of ad hoc services on a scale that is needed). In terms of compatibility, customers in the study referred to the need for better bandwidth and connectivity for more widespread adoption in their respective organizations while service providers pointed out the need for better integration. Technological complexity was also a factor in persuading employees to use cloud systems, as was the ability to carry out trials and pilot phases in risk free environments. Interestingly, one of the organizational factors that emerged was the desire to improve collaboration. It was evident from the study that the cloud introduces a shift in the way companies interact with external sources and even in the way employees interact with each other inside the organization. This has the potential to leverage more innovation and facilitate engagement and collaboration along a company's supply chain. Nonetheless, issues surround security and legal issues highlight the need for educational awareness of security and regulations in various jurisdictions in which datacenters are hosted.

There are a number of themes crossing these challenges, which emerged during the analysis of the findings and warrant further research. First, previous research highlighted the need for studies of more user-related challenges as opposed to technical issues (Iyer and Henderson, 2010). Given that cloud computing has the potential to streamline internal processes and hence productivity, the role of IT managers in the future is likely to along with their skill sets. Obviously, this may not bode well with IT managers who view cloud technologies as something that will eventually kill their profession. Similarly, another challenge to widespread adoption of cloud computing is the uncertainty and resistance that may exist among employees. It is widely known that introducing a new innovation can result in employee resistance, particularly if there is a lack of understanding of the change or indeed a lack of knowledge on how it will affect their work, for example, may be fear of eventual downsizing. Thus, senior decision-makers in organizations need to prepare employees for this new learning curve by providing training and communication in advance of cloud implementation. Additionally, there has to be an awareness of what is actually being introduced and people need to know what the benefits are. The study provides empirical support for theories associated with traditional adoption of innovation (i.e., Rogers, 2003; Tornatzky and Fleischer, 1990) in better explaining the adoption of cloud computing. Additionally, the results of the study are useful in providing a better understanding of how certain challenges impact adoption that may in turn lead to more informed managerial decision-making processes regarding adoption of cloud systems.

17.5.1 Limitations and Future Research

In terms of limitations of the study, while a key contribution of the paper lies in its description of cloud adoption, it is difficult to assess whether the levels of adoption in each case are superior to the use of traditional noncloud technologies. Second, it should be noted that while Tornatzky and Fleisher's framework is suitable for addressing the research questions at hand, there are many other lens that could be used to study cloud adoption. There is a need to consider the adoption of cloud technology within a wider portfolio of research that examines return on investment, strategic integration and knowledge exchange, and transfer, for example. Finally, the study is limited by the bias and nongeneralizability of this type of qualitative research. However, as discussed in Section 17.3, the researchers took all appropriate steps to minimize and account for these limitations.

Further research should consider the role of the IT manager and changing skill sets in the future cloud landscape. The inclusion of service providers in our sample helped provide a more complete picture of the overall challenges to cloud computing adoption. However, the majority of the customers in the study have only partially adopted cloud computing. Thus, future research should consider those customers that have significant adoption of cloud to help provide an insight into any remaining challenges of cloud adoption that were not uncovered in this study. To conclude, our research design was exploratory, and further research can now explore each factor or take a more explanatory approach using this study as a foundation. Alternative theoretical lenses to technological, environmental, and organizational factors could be considered, so that a more integrated perspective on the complexities surrounding the adoption of cloud computing may be achieved. Furthermore, identifying correlating best practices to resolve these challenges would be beneficial.

References

Armbrust M. et al. (2009) Above the clouds: a Berkeley view of cloud computing, EECS Department, University of California, Berkeley. Available at http://www.eecs.berkeley.edu/Pubs/TechRpts/2009/EECS-2009-28.html

Armbrust, M., Fox, A., Griffith, R., Joseph, A.D., Katz, R., Konwinski, A., and Zaharia, M. (2010) A view of cloud computing. *Communications of the ACM,* 53(4), 50–58.

Brynjolfsson, E., Hofmann, P., and Jordan, J. (2010) Cloud computing and electricity: beyond the utility model. *Communications of the ACM,* 53(5), 32–34.

Buckley, J., Buckley, M., and Hung-Fu, C. (1976) *Research Methodology and Business Decisions,* National Association for Accountants, New York.

Chau P.Y.K. and Tam K.Y. (1997) Factors affecting the adoption of open systems: an exploratory study. *MIS Quarterly,* 21 (1), pp. 1–24.

DaSilva, C.M., Trkman, P., Desouza, K., and Lindic, J. (2013) Disruptive technologies: a business model perspective on cloud computing. *Technology Analysis and Strategic Management.* doi: 10.1080/09537325.2013.843661.

Dedrick J. and West J. (2003) Why firms adopt open source platforms: a grounded theory of innovation and standards adoption. Proceedings on the Workshop on Standard Making: A Critical Research Frontier for Information Systems, Seattle, Washington, pp. 236–257.

Eveland, J. and Tornatzky, L. (1990) The deployment of technology. In *The Processes of Technological Innovation,* Tornatzky, L. and Fleisher, M. (Eds.), Lexington Books.

Farrell R. (2010) Securing the cloud: governance, risk and compliance issues reign supreme. *Information Security Journal: A Global Perspective,* 19, 310–319.

Fichman R.G. (1999) The diffusion and assimilation of information technology innovations. In *Framing the Domains of IT Management: Projecting the Future. Through the Past,* Zmud R.W. (Ed.), Pinnaflex Educational Resources, Inc., Cincinnati, OH.

Forbes (2011) The Economic Benefit of Cloud Computing. Available at http://www.forbes.com/sites/kevinjackson/2011/09/17/the-economic-benefit-of-cloud-computing/.

Foster I. et al. (2008) Cloud computing and grid computing 360-degree compared. Grid Computing Environments Workshop. IEEE, pp. 1–10. Available at http://dx.doi.org/10.1109/GCE.2008.4738445.

Galliers, R. (1992) *Information Systems Research: Issues, Methods and Practical Guidelines,* Blackwell Scientific Publications, Oxford.

Geelan, J. (2009) *The top 150 players in cloud computing: SYS-CON's cloud computing journal expands again its list of most active players in the cloud ecosystem.* Available at soacloud.utilizer.com

Goodburn M.A. and Hill S. (2010) The Cloud Transforms Businesses. Financial Executive, December.

HBR and Verizon (2014) *Business agility in the cloud,* HBR Analytic Services, July 2014. Available at verizonenterprise.com/resources/insights/hbr.

Iyer B. and Henderson J.C. (2010) Preparing for the future: understanding the seven capabilities of cloud computing. *MIS Quarterly Executive,* 9 (2), 117–131.

Kaplan, B. and Duchon, D. (1988) Combining qualitative and quantitative methods information systems research: a case study. *Management Information Systems Quarterly,* **12**(4), 571–586.

Khajeh-Hosseini A., Sommerville I., and Sriram I. (2010) Research challenges for enterprise cloud computing. 1st ACM Symposium on Cloud Computing, SOCC 2010.

Kirkbesoglu E. and Ogutcu G. (2012) Impact of inter organisational networks on adoption process of information technology. *International Journal of Business and Social Research,* **2** (3). doi: http://dx.doi.org/10.18533/ijbsr.v2i3.174.

Leimeister S., Riedl K., and Krcmar H. (2010) The Business Perspectives of Cloud Computing: Actors, Roles and Value Networks. Proceedings of the 18th European Conference on Information Systems (ECIS), Pretoria, South Africa.

Linthicum, D. (2012) *Buyers say the cloud is already tired out.* Available at http://www.infoworld.com/d/cloud-computing/buyers-say-the-cloud-already-tired-out-203760

Marshall C. and Rossman G. (1989) *Designing Qualitative Research,* Sage Publications, California.

Mell P. and Grance T. (2009) *The NIST Definition of Cloud Computing,* National Institute of Standards and Technology.

Motahari-Nezhad H.R., Stephenson B., and Singhal S. (2009) Outsourcing business to cloud computing services: opportunities and challenges. Technical report HPL-2009-23, January.

Morgan L. and Conboy P. (2013) Key factors impacting cloud computing adoption. *IEEE Computer,* **46**, 97–99.

Morgan L. and Finnegan P. (2010) Open innovation in secondary software firms: an exploration of managers' perceptions of open source software. *The DATA BASE for Advances in Information Systems,* **41** (1), 76–95.

Oliveira T. and Martins M.F. (2011) Literature review of information technology adoption models at firm level. *The Electronic Journal Information Systems Evaluation,* **14** (1), 110–121.

Oppenheim, A. (1992) *Questionnaire Design, Interviewing and Attitude Measurement,* Continuum, New York.

Rogers E. (2003) *Diffusion of Innovations,* 5th Edition, Free Press, New York.

Rubin H. and Rubin I. (2005) *Qualitative Interviewing: The Art of Hearing Data,* Sage, Thousand Oaks, CA.

Sarker, S., Lau, F. and Sahay, S. (2000) Building an inductive theory of collaboration in virtual teams: an adapted grounded theory approach. *Proceedings of the 33rd Hawaii International Conference on System Sciences.*

Sriram I. and Khajeh-Hosseini A. (2010) Research agenda in cloud technologies. Proceeding of IEEE CLOUD 2010, Miami, FL, USA.

Strauss A. and Corbin J. (1990) *Basics of Qualitative Research: Grounded Theory Procedure and Techniques,* Sage Publications, Newbury Park, CA.

Strauss, A. and Corbin, J. (1998) *Basics of Qualitative Research: Techniques and Procedures for Developing Grounded Theory*, 2nd ed., Sage, Thousand Oaks, CA.

Swanson, B. (1994) Information Systems Innovation among Organizations. *Management Science*, **40**(9), 1069–1092.

Tornatzky L.G. and Fleischer M. (1990) *The Processes of Technological Innovation*, Lexington Books, Massachusetts.

Trauth E. and O'Connor B. (1991) A study of the interaction between information, technology and society. In *Information Systems Research: Contemporary Approaches and Emergent Traditions*, Nissen H., Klein H., and Hirchheim R. (Eds.), Elsevier, The Netherlands, pp. 131–144.

Urquhart, C. (1997) Exploring analyst–client communication: using grounded theory techniques to investigate interaction in informal requirements gathering, in Information Systems and Qualitative Research, Lee, A.S., Liebenau, J., and Degross, J.I. (Eds.), Chapman and Hall, London.

Vouk, M. (2008) Cloud computing issues, research and implementations. *Journal of Computing and Information Technology*, **16**(4), 235–246.

Weinhardt, C., Anandasivam, A., Blau, B., Borissov, N., Meinl, T., Michalk, W., and Stosser, J. (2009) Cloud computing: a classification, business models, and research directions. *Business & Information Systems Engineering*, **1**(5), 391–399.

Wengraf T. (2001) *Qualitative Research Interviewing*, Sage, London, UK.

Yang, H. and Tate, M. (2009) Where are we at with cloud computing?: A descriptive literature review. *ACIS 2009 Proceedings: 20th Australasian Conference on Information Systems*.

Yin, R. (2003) *Case Study Research: Design and Methods*, London, Sage.

Zhu K., Kraemer K.L., and Xu S. (2006) The process of innovation assimilation by firms in different countries: a technology diffusion perspective on e-business. *Management Science*, **52** (10), 1557–1576.

18

A Model-Centric Approach to the Design of Resource-Aware Cloud Applications

Reiner Hähnle[1] and Einar Broch Johnsen[2]

[1]*Department of Computer Science, Software Engineering, Technische Universität Darmstadt, Darmstadt, Germany*
[2]*University of Oslo, Norway*

18.1 Capitalizing on the Cloud

The planet's data storage and processing are moving into the clouds. This has the potential to revolutionize how we interact with computers in the future. A cloud consists of virtual computers that can only be accessed remotely. It is not a physical computer, and you do not necessarily know where it is, but you can use it to store and process your data and can access it at any time from your regular computer. If you still have an old-fashioned computer, that is. You might as well access your data or applications through your mobile device, for example while sitting on the bus.

Cloud-based data processing, or cloud computing, is more than just a convenient solution for individuals on the move. Even though privacy of data is still an issue, the cloud is already an economically attractive model for a startup, a small to medium enterprise (SME), or simply for a student who develops an app as a side project, due to an undeniable added value and compelling business drivers [1]. One such driver is *elasticity*: businesses pay for computing resources when these are needed, and avoid major upfront investments for resource provisioning. Additional resources such as processing power or memory can be added to a virtual computer on the fly, or an additional virtual computer can be provided to the client application. Going beyond shared storage, the main potential in cloud computing lies in its scalable virtualized framework for data processing, which becomes a shared computing facility for multiple devices. If a service uses cloud-based processing, its capacity can be adjusted automatically when new users arrive. Another driver is *agility*: new services can be quickly and flexibly deployed on the market at limited cost, without initial investments in hardware.

Software Technology: 10 Years of Innovation in IEEE Computer, First Edition.
Edited by Mike Hinchey.
© 2018 the IEEE Computer Society, Inc. Published 2018 by John Wiley & Sons, Inc.

Currently, more than 3.9 million jobs are associated with cloud computing in the United States, and more than 18 million jobs worldwide.[1] The European Union (EU) believes[2] that cloud-based data processing will create another 2.5 million jobs and an annual value of €160 billion in Europe by 2020. However, reliability and control of resources constitute significant barriers to the industrial adoption of cloud computing. To overcome these barriers and execute control over virtualized resources on the cloud, client services need to become resource aware.

18.2 Challenges

Cloud computing is not merely a new technology for convenient and flexible data storage and implementation of services. Making full usage of the potential of virtualized computation requires nothing less than to rethink the way in which we design and develop software.

18.2.1 Empowering the Designer

The elasticity of software executed in the cloud means that designers have far-reaching control over the resource parameters of the execution environment: the number and kind of processors and the amount of memory, storage capacity, and bandwidth. These parameters can even be changed dynamically, at runtime. This means that the client of a cloud service cannot merely deploy and run software but can also fully control the trade-offs between the incurred cost of running the software and the delivered quality of service.

To realize these new possibilities, software in the cloud must be *designed for scalability*. Nowadays, software is often designed based on specific assumptions about deployment, including the size of data structures, the amount of random access memory (RAM), and the number of processors. Rescaling may require extensive design changes, if scalability has not been taken into account from the start.

18.2.2 Deployment Aspects at Design Time

The impact of cloud computing on software design goes beyond scalability issues: traditionally, deployment is considered a late activity during software development. In the realm of cloud computing, this can be fatal. Consider the well-known cost increase for fixing defects during successive development phases [2]. IBM Systems Sciences Institute estimated that a defect that costs 1

---

1 Forbes, December 2014, http://www.forbes.com/sites/louiscolumbus/2014/12/12/where-cloud-computing-jobs-will-be-in-2015.
2 Digital Agenda for Europe, http://ec.europa.eu/digital-agenda/en/european-cloud-computing-strategy.

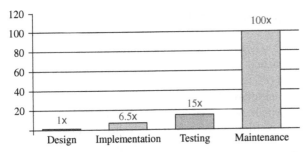

Figure 18.1 Relative costs to fix software defects for static infrastructure (source: IBM Systems Sciences Institute). The columns indicate the phase of the software development at which the defect is found and fixed.

unit to fix in design costs 15 units to fix in testing (system/acceptance) and 100 units or more to fix in production (see Figure 18.1). This estimation does not even consider the *impact cost* due to, for example, delayed time to market, lost revenue, lost customers, and bad public relations.

Now, these ratios are for *static* deployment. Considering the high additional complexity of resource management in virtualized environments, it is reasonable to expect even more significant differences. Figure 18.2 conservatively suggests ratios for virtualized software in an *elastic* environment. This consideration makes it clear that it is essential to detect and fix deployment errors, for example, failure to meet a service-level agreement (SLA), already *in the design phase*.

To make full usage of the opportunities of cloud computing, software development for the cloud demands a design methodology that (i) takes into account deployment modeling at *early* design stages and (ii) permits the detection of *deployment errors* early and efficiently, helped by software tools such as simulators, test generators, and static analyzers.

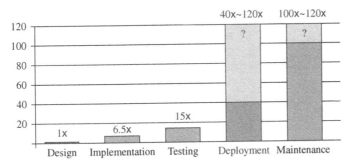

Figure 18.2 Estimate of relative costs to fix software defects for virtualized systems with elasticity, from [3].

18.3 Controlling Deployment in the Design Phase

Our analysis exhibits a *software engineering challenge*: how can the validation of deployment decisions be pushed up to the modeling phase of the software development chain without convoluting the design with deployment details?

When a service is developed today, the developers first design its functionality, then they determine which resources are needed for the service, and ultimately the provisioning of these resources is controlled through an SLA (see Figure 18.3). The functionality is represented in the *client layer*. The *provisioning layer* makes resources available to the client layer and determines available memory, processing power, and bandwidth. The SLA is a legal document that clarifies what resources the provisioning layer should make available to the client service, what they cost, and states penalties for breach of agreement. A typical SLA covers two aspects: (i) a *legal contract* stating the mutual obligations and the consequences in case of a breach and (ii) the technical parameters and cost figures of the offered services, which we call the *service contract*.

Today the different parts of a deployed cloud service live in separate worlds, but we need to connect them. In a first step, the provisioning layer is made available to the client, so that the client can observe and modify resource parameters. We call this the *Cloud API*. This is *not* the same as the APIs that cloud environments currently provide to their clients: our ultimate goal is to move deployment decisions into the *design phase*. We advocate that client behavior is represented by an *abstract behavioral model* of the client application.

How can the vision just sketched possibly be realized? In the remaining chapter, we will try to give one answer. We report on an effort toward a model-centric approach to the design of resource-aware cloud applications that we undertook as part of a European project (www.envisage-project.eu). It is based on a modeling language called Abstract Behavioral Specification (ABS).

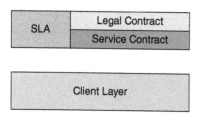

Figure 18.3 Conceptual parts of a deployed cloud service.

18.4 ABS: Modeling Support for Designing Resource-Aware Applications

The modeling language ABS is a concurrent, executable modeling language [4] with a formal semantics. It has been designed for being easy to learn and to use: ABS comprises data type, functional, imperative, and OO abstractions in an orthogonal, modular manner and with popular notational conventions (Java-ish syntax).

Before we sketch the main characteristics of ABS, let us explain why it is particularly well-suited as a basis for model-centric design of resource-aware cloud applications [5]. From Figure 18.4, three main requirements emerge:

1) The need for an abstract interface (the "Cloud API") to the provisioning layer.
2) The need to connect SLAs to the client layer, where the key point is to formulate service contract aspects of SLAs relative to a semantics expressed as a formal specification.
3) Finally, the modeling framework must admit various static and dynamic analyses.

ABS fits this bill perfectly: it features a reflection layer that allows to describe timed resources of various kinds in an abstract manner. ABS has a formal semantics and comes with a correctness notion relative to formal behavioral specifications; most importantly, ABS was designed for being formally analyzable and comes with a wide range of scalable, interprocedural "early" as well as "late" analyses [6], including resource consumption, deadlock detection, test case generation, runtime monitoring, and even functional verification.

The concurrency model of ABS is asynchronous and based on cooperative scheduling with futures: to call a method m with parameter p on an object o asynchronously, we use the syntax "o!m(p)". This creates a new task in o's processor to be scheduled at some future time point while the caller simply continues to execute and no preemption takes place. This approach to

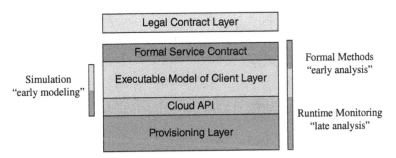

Figure 18.4 Making services resource-aware.

concurrency excludes one of the most problematic aspects of parallel code: data races. However, one must address two issues: first, how to synchronize with the caller upon m's termination and return its result; second, how to enable multitasking. In ABS it is possible to assign the result of asynchronous method calls to variables that have a future type. These provide a handle to retrieve the result once it is ready. Futures are in ABS are closely related to scheduling: await is a statement with one argument that releases control over the processor and enables rescheduling as soon as its argument evaluates to true. If the argument has the form f?, where f has a future type, this amounts to giving up control until the task associated with f is ready. Afterward, its result can be safely retrieved with the expression f.get.

18.5 Resource Modeling with ABS

ABS supports the modeling of deployment decisions and resource aware-ness [7]. Let us illustrate the modeling of resource-aware systems in ABS by considering a virtualized service in which user requests trigger computational tasks whose *resource cost* varies with the size of input data. The system consists of a service endpoint, worker objects, a database, a load balancer, and a resource manager that controls scaling of the pool of worker objects (see Figure 18.5). The service endpoint can be modeled in ABS by a class that implements a service endpoint interface SE with the method invokeService(Rat cost), where cost is an abstraction over the input data.

When the service endpoint receives a request to invoke the service, it obtains a Worker object from a LoadBalancer and asks that Worker to process the request.

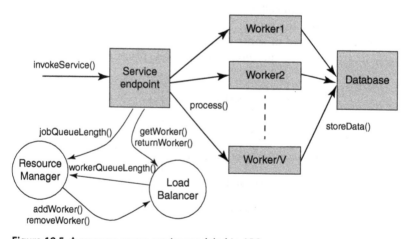

Figure 18.5 A resource-aware service modeled in ABS.

```
class ServiceEndpoint(Duration responseTime, ResourceManager rm,
                Database db, LoadBalancer lb) implements SE {
    Int lengthOfQueue = 0;

    Fut<Bool> invokeService(Rat cost){ Fut<Bool> success;
    lengthOfQueue = lengthOfQueue + 1;
    Worker w = await lb!getWorker();
    [Deadline: responseTime] success = w!process(cost);
    lengthOfQueue = lengthOfQueue - 1;
    await success?;
      Bool s = success.get;
    return success;
    }
    Unit run(){
    await duration(1,1);
      rm!jobQueueLength(lengthOfQueue);
    this!run();
    }
}
```

Here, the return type of invokeService is a future that will eventually
contain the value True if the service invocation was processed within the
specified response time and False if that deadline was violated. The annotation [Deadline: responseTime] is used to specify a local deadline to the
method activation of process in class ServiceEndpoint. That class has
responseTime as a parameter for processing service requests. The method
run makes objects of an ABS class active; that is, this method is automatically
activated when the objects are created. Here, the run method suspends
execution for a given time interval, reports on the size of its queue length
(stored in the variable lengthOfQueue) to a ResourceManager, and then
calls recursively itself.

Let the class WorkerObject implement the Worker interface with a
method process.

```
class WorkerObject(Database db) implements Worker {

    Bool process(Rat taskCost) {
    [Cost: taskCost] skip;
    [Deadline: deadline()] Fut<Bool> f = db!accessData();
    f.get;
      return (deadline() > 0);
    }
```

```
    DC getDC(){ return thisDC();}
}
```

We see how the nonfunctional specification of the computation is integrated into the ABS model: The resource cost of the local computation is modeled by a **skip** with an annotation [Cost: taskCost], where taskCost represents the cost of processing the input data. The executing method passes on the remainder of its own deadline to the method call to the database db with the annotation [Deadline: deadline()].

The Worker objects are deployed on *deployment components*. This is a modeling concept in ABS for locations where execution takes place (e.g., virtual machines or containers). An object in ABS can find its own location by the expression thisDC().

The service endpoint interacts with a LoadBalancer to acquire a Worker by the method getWorker and to return a Worker by the corresponding method releaseWorker. A LoadBalancer can, for example, be implemented by a round-robin load balancer, as shown below. Similar to the run method of ServiceEndpoint, the run method here reports on the total number of deployed Worker objects to the ResourceManager before calling itself.

```
class RoundRobinLoadBalancer(ResourceManager rm, CloudProvider
cloud, Int nResources, Database db) implements LoadBalancer {
    List<Worker< available = Nil;
    Int numberOfMachines = 0;

    Unit run(){ ... }
    Worker getWorker(){ ... }

    Unit releaseWorker(Worker w){
    available = appendright(available,w);
    }
    Unit addWorker(){
    DC machine = await cloud!launchInstance(
        {CPU:nResources, PaymentInterval:1, CostPerInterval:1});
    [DC: machine] Worker w = new WorkerObject(db);
    available = appendright(available,w);
    numberOfMachines = numberOfMachines + 1;
    }
    Unit removeWorker(){
    if (available != Nil) {
    Worker w;
```

```
            w = head(available);
            available = tail(available);
         DC machine = await w!getDC();
            cloud!releaseInstance(machine); }
     }
}
```

Two methods control the usage of resources by the service: `addWorker` interacts with the `CloudProvider` to deploy a new `Worker` on a deployment component with CPU processing capacity `nResources` and with billing for each time interval at cost 1; similarly, `removeWorker` removes a `Worker` and releases the deployment component of that `Worker`.

Observe that the processing time of a task depends on its cost and on the processing capacity of the deployment component where it is deployed. The overall cost of running an ABS model of a service depends on the cost of the billing period and on the number of deployment components that have been actively deployed per billing period. The `CloudProvider` interface is part of the ABS library and provides a highly configurable API for launching, acquiring, and releasing deployment components modeling virtual resources. It also provides cost accounting; for example, method `getAccumulatedCost` returns the accumulated cost at any time during execution. Hence it realizes the *Cloud API* stipulated above.

The class RM implements the `ResourceManager` interface, which defines a policy for scaling the service. In our model, this is done at regular intervals by comparing the ratio between the lengths of the job and worker queues to the thresholds `upper` and `lower`. More advanced policies could, for example, consider the number of deadline violations in a sliding window (such as the last 24 hours) or other aspects of an SLA.

```
class RM(Rat lower, Rat upper) implements ResourceManager {
    Int jobQueue = 0; Int workerQueue = 0; LBManager lb;

    Unit run(){
    await duration(1,1);
    // check conditions for scaling up
        if ((jobQueue / workerQueue) > upper) { lb!addWorker(); }
    // check conditions for scaling down
    if ((jobQueue / workerQueue) < lower) { lb!removeWorker(); }
    this!run();
    }

    Unit register(LBManager r){lb = r;}
    Unit jobQueueLength(Int n){jobQueue=n;}
```

```
        Unit workerQueueLength(Int n){workerQueue=workerQueue+1;}
}
```

In this example, we have specified the cost directly as an argument to the `process` method. For a detailed ABS model that models the actual execution of the method, automated tools help the modeler to analyze the model and to extract cost annotations.

18.6 Opportunities

Making deployment decisions at design-time moves control from the provisioning layer to the client layer. The client service becomes resource-aware. This provides a number of attractive opportunities.

18.6.1 Fine-Grained Provisioning

Business models for resource provisioning on the cloud are becoming more and more fine-grained, similar to those we know from other metered industry sectors such as telephony or electricity. It is an increasingly complex decision to select the best model for your software. So far this complexity is to the advantage of *resource providers*. Design-time analysis and comparison of deployment decisions allow an application to be deployed according to the optimal payment model for the *end-users*. Cloud customers can take advantage of fine-grained provisioning schemas such as spot price.

18.6.2 Tighter Provisioning

Better profiles of the resource needs of the client layer help cloud providers to avoid over-provisioning to meet their SLAs. Better usage of the resources means that more clients can be served with the same amount of hardware in the data center, without violating SLAs and incurring penalties.

18.6.3 Application-Specific Resource Control

Design-time analysis of scalability enables the client layer to make better use of the elasticity offered by the cloud, to know beforehand at which load thresholds it is necessary to scale up the deployment to avoid breaking SLAs and disappointing the expectations of the end-users.

18.6.4 Application-Controlled Elasticity

We envisage autonomous, resource-aware services that run their own resource management strategy. Such a service will monitor the load on its virtual machine instances as well as the end-user traffic, and make its own decisions about the trade-offs between the delivered quality of service and the incurred cost. The service interacts with the provisioning layer through an API to dynamically scale up or down. The service may even request or bid for virtual machine instances with given profiles on the virtual resource market place of the future.

18.7 Summary

We argued that the efficiency and performance of cloud-based services can be boosted by moving deployment decisions up the development chain. Resource-aware services give the client better control of resource usage, to meet SLAs at lower cost. We identify formal methods, executable models, and deployment modeling as the ingredients that can make this vision happen. A realization of our ideas has been implemented on the basis of the modeling language ABS. We illustrated our ideas with a concrete case study around a representative service provider scenario that consists of fully executable ABS code.

Acknowledgments

This work has been partially supported by EU project FP7-610582 Envisage: Engineering Virtualized Services.

References

1 R. Buyya, C.S. Yeo, S. Venugopal, J. Broberg, and I. Brandic (2009) Cloud computing and emerging IT platforms: Vision, hype, and reality for delivering computing as the 5th utility. *Future Generation Comp. Sys.*, **25** (6), 599–616.

2 B.W. Boehm and P.N. Papaccio (1988) Understanding and controlling software costs. *IEEE Trans. SW Eng.*, **14** (10), 1462–1477.

3 E. Albert, F. de Boer, R. Hähnle, E.B. Johnsen, and C. Laneve (2013) Engineering virtualized services. In *2nd Nordic Symp. Cloud Computing & Internet Technologies*, M.A. Babar and M. Dumas (eds.), ACM, pp. 59–63.

4 E.B. Johnsen, R. Hähnle, J. Schäfer, R. Schlatte, and M. Steffen (2011) ABS: A core language for abstract behavioral specification. In *Proc. 9th Intl. Symp. on Formal Methods for Components and Objects*, B. Aichernig, F. de Boer, and M.M. Bonsangue (eds.), Springer, vol. 6957 of LNCS, pp. 142–164.

5 E. Albert, F. de Boer, R. Hähnle, E.B. Johnsen, R. Schlatte, S.L. Tapia Tarifa, and P.Y.H. Wong (2014) Formal modeling of resource management for cloud architectures: An industrial case study using Real-Time ABS. *J. of Service-Oriented Computing and Applications*, **8** (4), 323–339.

6 R. Bubel, A. Flores-Montoya, and R. Hähnle (2014) Analysis of Executable Software Models. Formal Methods for Executable Software Models. 14th Intl.

School on Formal Methods for the Design of Computer, Communication, and Software Systems, SFM, Advanced Lectures. LNCS 8483, pp. 1–25, Springer.

7 E.B. Johnsen, R. Schlatte, and S.L. Tapia Tarifa (2015) Integrating Deployment Architecture and Resource Consumption in Timed Object-Oriented Models. *Journal of Logical and Algebraic Methods in Programming*, **84** (1), 67–91.

Index

Software Technology: 10 Years of Innovation in IEEE Computer, First Edition.
Edited by Mike Hinchey.
© 2018 the IEEE Computer Society, Inc. Published 2018 by John Wiley & Sons, Inc.

exponential organizations 17
Extensible Markup Language (XML) 123, 213
extensions and add-ons 38
external factors (EF) 52
eXtreme Model-Driven Design (XMDD) 144
eXtreme Programming (XP) 142

f

Facebook 18
failed test 203
fault diagnosis 210
fault tolerance 26
feature models (FMs) 247
Firefox web browser 38
flow analysis 245
 complete mixed reactors, tracer analysis of 245–247
flow and quality equalization 253–256
 average loading rate equation 256
 diurnal variation of flow rate 255
 graphical solution for equalization volume 256
 time-varying wastewater flow rate 254
 variable flow rate 254
flow irregularities 248
focus on application logic 147
formality 283
formalization 161
formal methods and agile methods (FM+AM) 283, 284
formulation of requirements 163
Forward Collision Warning (FCW) 255
Frama-C 275
function 158
 anthropology 158
 biology 158
 chemistry 158
 engineering 158
 feature 159
 mathematics 158
 medicine 158
 operational context 159
 organization 158

requirement 159, 160
"functional" and "nonfunctional" requirements 155
fundamentals
 innovation in the memcomputer 8
 principle of SPLs 244
 project management practices 67
 on requirements and system models 162–163

g

Gall's Law 282
GAR model 117
Gdal tool 25
generative programming 25
generic autonomy requirements (GAR) 107
GitHub 48, 50, 51
 packages 51
global communication infrastructure 18
global software engineering (GSE) 60
 challenges and recounted problems in areas 62–63
 IEEEXplore search 61
 practitioners not read GSE domain-specific articles 63
GME 26
GNU/Linux operating system 43
GNU R language 23, 24
goal achievement 110
goal identification 110
goal-oriented requirements engineering (GORE) 107, 117
goal-related constraints 110
goals models 110
GORE. *see* goal-oriented requirements engineering (GORE)
Gottlieb Daimler 18
GPS navigation devices 19
graphical user interface (GUI) 18
graphics 37
grDevices 37
grid computing 296
GUI. *see* graphical user interface (GUI)